Impact
of
TELEVISION
On Political Awareness
Of
Rural Masses

Impact of TELEVISION On Political Awareness Of Rural Masses

P.V. Sharada

GYAN PUBLISHING HOUSE
New Delhi - 110002

Impact Of
TELEVISION
On Political Awareness Of Rural Masses

ISBN : 9788121204170

Published in 2014 in India by
Gyan Publishing House
23, Ansari Road, Daryaganj,
New Delhi - 110002
Phones : 23261060, 23282060 Fax : 23285914
e-mail : books@gyanbooks.com
website : gyanbooks.com

Laser Typesetting at : Vinayak Printers, Delhi
Printed at : Salasar Imaging System, Delhi

LIST OF TABLES

CHAPTER ONE

Television as an Instrument of Social Change

The antennas on the roof tops are increasing day by day all over the world. Today there is scarcely a country which is not utilising television with a view to achieving its cultural, social, political and economic development. TV gives information by transmitting programmes through space satellites to and from people all over the world. Media men often view TV as an electronic magic carpet, the 20th Century's creation of the technological revolution, the great instrument of persuasion, and the most powerful weapon for social change. Things which were considered as luxuries in the past have become sheer necessities today. TV is treated as their constant companion by people in advanced countries. This indicates the tremendous mark it has made on world civilization.

A unique combination of commercial, political, academic and cultural programmes is the main characteristic feature of TV. The scope of TV programmes can be broadly visualised from three angles, i.e. information, education and entertainment. With communication satellites the task of realising its basic functions has become much easier and the purpose more effective.

Men of many lands contributed to the development of TV. TV was made possible by electronic discoveries in the late 19th Century and early 20th Century. In 1884 Paul Nipkow, a German, patented a scanning disc for transmitting pictures by wireless. Charles F. Jenkins a German again began his study of the subject around 1880. The English physicist, E.E. Fournier d'Albe conducted experiments in the 1900s. In 1915, Marconi predicted "visible telephone". In 1923 physicist Vladimir Zworykin, a Russian-born American, applied for a patent on the iconoscope camera tube. In the years that followed, there were more experiments by E.F.W. Alexanderson and Philo T. Farnsworth of Russia and by John L. Baird in England. An experimental TV programme was sent by wire between New York and Washington by the Bell Telephone Laboratories in 1927. The next year Bell experimentally televised outdoor programmes. The Federal radio Commission reported that "a few" broadcast stations were experimenting with video in 1928. In the same year WGY Schenectady, N.Y., broadcast the first TV drama. A large screen TV was demonstrated by Radio corporation of America, at a New York theater in the year 1930. Radio Corporation of America (RCA) tested outdoor TV pickup at Camden, N.J., in 1936. By 1937 there were 17 experimental TV stations operating.[1]

Many advanced countries in the world have tried to fully utilise the potentialities of TV for their political and socio-economic development. Extensive research has been conducted to assess the impact of TV on the minds of the people. In the light of these studies, many developing countries have realised the need for a sophisticated technology like TV which could bring revolutionary changes especially among illiterate masses. Presently, many countries are utilising the satellite facility for live telecasts.

Satellite communication system is effectively binding the World with its threads of sight and sound. Today, one can sit at home and simultaneously watch the events that are taking place even in very remote corners of the world. Applying space technology in the communication system is one of the world's recent developments. It strengthens the social, political and economic fabric of the world.

Mere invention of technology will not accomplish the task of effective communication. Its value is decided on the way it utilised. Inspite of technological development, a major portion of the population in underdeveloped countries is not fully aware of the events that are taking place, and are also deprived of effective enjoyment of their right to information. For example, a poor Indian peasant knows little or nothing about his counterpart in a foreign country. Unless this gap is bridged, development of any sort is not possible. These facts have lead to the idea of using satellites for the purpose of broadcasting. Mass communication technology accelerates the interaction among various cultures of the world. Especially in countries with high population the majority of which being illiterates, this technology can bring about certain radical and imperative changes.

Population, illiteracy and poverty are the three major problems faced by a developing country today. Television, which has shown a tremendous result in advanced countries, can be used as a major instrument in solving these problems and bring about changes in the long run. Considering these possibilities, a worldwide satellite Television experiment called SITE (Satellite Instructional Television Experiment) was initiated for the upliftment of the rural masses.

In September 1969, a memorandum of understanding was signed between ISRO (Indian Space Research Organisation) and the NASA (National Aeronautical and Space Authority) of the United States of America. This memorandum lead to the development of the satellite instructional TV experiment (SITE). It is an agreement between the two countries to co-operate in undertaking an experiment in instructional Television via satellite. The USA had the responsibility of providing an application technology satellite (ATS) and placing it in orbit in such a way that it would be available to

India for a whole year. India had the responsibility of production of earth stations, receiving stations, microwave transmitters and receiving sets, of programmes for education, instruction and entertainment.[2]

The social benefit of satellite television was expected to break all barriers between nations and also to help promote an understanding among them. There is a relationship between the economic development and social change in a country. Communication plays an important role in bringing social change. Hence a country which needs to develop itself requires the assistance of communication system.

India is a developing country. Therefore, the significance of mass media in this country needs no exaggeration. It can have great impact. Government of India has been taking several steps in educating the masses and bringing awareness through modern media. A majority of our population is living in rural areas. According to the provisional totals of 1981 census, 23.31 percent of the 685 million people live in urban areas and the remaining 76.68 percent in rural areas. While the urban population is concentrated in 4029 towns, the rural population is spread over 6.05 lakh villages (including 48,087 uninhabitated villages).[3]

Inspite of tremendous strides in urbanization, industrialization and mechanization India is still for behind in many aspects. If it has to compete with other countries of the world in economic development and overall progress, India has to start from the village level in its nation building programme. The backwardness of our rural folk chiefly lies in their poverty, innocence, ignorance, illiteracy and inhibitions. The planners desire to give them higher aspirations, with the intention of individual self development that ultimately leads to national development. The existing formal education system is not able to cater to the needs of the present situation. Hence a medium like television should be made thoroughly extensive in its use for mass educational programmes.

Here it may be questioned why TV when there are more formal institutions and other media? The major problem here is that the rural folk is too poor to engage their grown up children in long years of schooling which in their opinion fetches nothing in the end. Being ignorant of the advantages of the small family system, the poor have many children and undergo several hardships to even feed them. This may be due to the feeling that daily labour gives them daily bread and is by far the best solution to their problem.

Coming to the print media, it appeals to people who can read and understand and as such it is popular only among a limited sections of the people. Next, the radio is more popular even among illiterates including women and children. Though Radio is still very popular among the villagers, the TV with its additional quality of colour vision is attracting the masses. Here it can be said that the audio and visual combination of TV is a capable medium if the programmes of rural mass education are to be meaningful.

The broadcast media provides an opportunity for rural participation in their programmes. The kind of individual participation which brings the media to the masses may be more interesting way of presentation than the monotony of listening to routine talks and lectures.

Then, if the broadcast media, especially the TV, is so powerful as to give our poor village rural folk individual self recognition, then why not exploit it more fully for their own benefit ?

The invention of communication satellites has given us a chance to experiment on this basis. Utilization of TV for socially purposive programmes is not limited to India alone. It was experimented even in some advanced countries also. The ATS-6 satellite in USA and Anik Satellite in Canada are used to provide programmes for isolated communities and for tribal people. The Communist countries score in promoting the widest access to media like Radio and TV.[4] The most extensive test of TV as a vehicle of literacy teaching has been made in Italy.[5]

Illiteracy is a major obstacle for the fast growth and development of a nation. Countries like Japan and Russia have promptly recognised this as a serious problem and have taken it as a challenge to completely eradicate illiteracy in order to build up a new society. In Japan within less than 40 years of Meiji restoration the transformation of an illiterate mass into literate and enlightened people was achieved. Similarly, the Soviet Union after the Socialist revolution mobilized all the instruments of state and society for eradication of illiteracy in the shortest period of time.[6]

In the light of the experience of other countries and in view of the dangers ahead by naglecting the issue, the Government of India has recognised the magnitude of the problem and accordingly formulated various schemes to educate the masses. A comparative study with other nations reveals that our efforts are not enough for the magnitude of the problem. Use of sophisticated technology like TV has already been introduced in different fields like agriculture, education etc., but we are still far behind.

The development of a country sometimes depends on the type or system of the government it adopts. The requirements of a democratic country may differ from a communist country or a totalitarian state. Public opinion is the basis for the democratic form of government. When people are involved in the formation of the government and its policy making, an awareness of the rights and responsibilities and duties of citizens becomes the first and foremost necessity. The role of political parties and their leaders is as important as the role of citizens for the effective functioning of a democratic society. Formal and non-formal political education that is being imparted by institutions must be supplemented by political leaders from time to time. In a democracy it is upto the elected leaders to provide an environment which makes every common man feel that he is an important citizen.

A basic knowledge about politics becomes imperative when it comes to the people choosing a leader. The right understanding of the body politic helps to choose good and efficient leaders without any pressure or influence. Political education teaches what is democracy, the difference between democracy and totalitarianism, the rights and principles of democratic citizens and also the purpose of national policies.

Communication researchers observed TV as a potent medium in forming public opinion and illuminating the political fabric of a nation. Describing how politicians can effectively reach the unknown voters through this channel, they say that when a particular medium is popular among the public there is little chance of their accepting a political leader who is not well acquainted to them through that media. A politician can impress a majority of people with a TV speech than going round the corner of every village and explaining his policies.

The power of the mass media in familiarising and enhancing the personal charisma of a leader is another aspect to be considered. As Wilbur Schramm argues, in a developing country where the media are relatively scarce and the stream of the names in the news is smaller, this power of the media may be even greater than it is in economically developed countries and may provide a way to build leadership[7].

Development of TV has facilitated many political leaders to reach millions of voters without moving from their place. It is evident from the history that they have gained access to the public through televised political campaigns. President Kennedy used live televised conferences and debates in American presidential elections. Many political observers believe that his performance in the campaign debates on TV with Richard Nixon was the decisive fator in his election to the Presidency. Subsequently, Carter and Reagan also concentrated on their TV programmes to impress the public.[8]

Considering the role of TV in political affairs, especially in a developing country where the rural population is more, the present study attempts to know the influence of TV on villagers with reference to their levels of political awareness. To convert the ignorant village folk into intelligent thinking citizens the first step should be to provide them an atmosphere of social and political awareness. Especially in a democracy where the policies of the government are the needs of the people, a basic knowledge of this system becomes necessary. To educate the mass of population in this area must naturally start with political education. This is already being done by formal institutions as well as by mass-media. In view of the effectiveness of TV when compared to other media in shaping public opinion it was intended to study the impact of television on the rural masses and the role it plays in creating political conciousness among them. Ten villages in Andhra Pradesh have been selected as the sample and the political programmes telecast over Hyderabad TV were taken to study the impact. Before proceeding to the details of the study a brief account of TV in the world as well in India and a few aspects pertaining to TV may need to be mentioned here.

Television in the World

At present many countries in the world are trying to project their profile through TV. In doing this, they are not only having a common medium but are also having common objectives and definite goals. Nations like Sri Lanka that have hesitated to introduce TV in the beginning are now utilizing the services of TV. However, there are countries like Tanzania which did not go for TV since it has other priorities like health and universal literacy.[9] In 1975 UNESCO reported that 30 countries of Africa and Asia had no TV. During the past decade there was a rapid expansion of TV in the world.[10]

An examination of the broadcasting systems in a global perspective reveals the following features.

Except in a few countries all advanced countries enjoy autonomy in broadcasting. But even while full autonomy exists, commissions and special committees restrict superfluous expression and misuse of the media. In developed countries, while a few channels are continuously engaged in educating the public, a few others orient them on matters of home and foreign policies. Regarding entertainment, a twenty four hour up-to-date multiform service is being made available by private broadcasting corporations. In developing countries due to lack of funds and a limited channel system there is comparatively less effective transmission; non-availability of multiple channel system has over burdened the programme planners with much to do under severe limitation.[11]

As AED (Academy for Educational Development) reports, the programmes in these countries are largely imported, much of it from the United States. The report notices a trend towards the emergence of National TV production centres such as in Egypt and Mexico which produce programmes of increasing appeal to neighbouring countries. It further states that few nations can invest the money required to produce entertaining TV programming. The appetite of TV system for new programming requires a market of many millions to finance production. Therefore, for most countries TV will continue to be an international medium with a high degree of foreign cultural influence.[12]

The revenue for this medium comes in three ways, the licence fee, the commercial revenue and the government aid. The form of revenue varies from one country to another. Commercial advertising brings in the bulk of the income in most of the countries, except where advertizing is limited or totally banned.[13] For example, Indonesia had discontinued commercials on its Television in 1981 after finding that they were having a destablizing effect on Indonesian society by promoting wants in the form of luxury goods and services which the common people have no means to acquire.[14]

It is observed that TV has dominated the other media in some of the countries. The circulation of news papers, Radio listening and movie going have been heavily affected due to TV in advanced countries includiug Japan. The results of a comparative study done between India and Japan in 1970 are prese-

Comparative Study of Growth of Different Media In India & Japan

Sl.	*Newspaper Circulation*		*Film Audience*		*Number of Radios*		*Number of Television Sets*	
No.	*India*	*Japan*	*India*	*Japan*	*India*	*Japan*	*India*	*Japan*
1.	21.7 crores (1965)	4.4 crores (1965)	310 crores (1971)	73 crores (1946)	15.59 lakhs (1958)	57 lakhs (1945)	6.2 thousand (1962)	9 1 lakh (1958)
2.	29.3 crores (1970)	5.3 crores (1970)	372 crores (1975)	112.7 crores (1958)	53.99 lakhs (1965)	91.6 lakhs (1950)	37 thousand (1971)	68.6 lakhs- (1961)
3.	37.4 crores (1977)	5.86 crores (1975)	420 crores (1979)	86 crores (1961)	64.84 lakhs (1966)	1.46 crores (1958)	6.77 lakhs (1977)	2.28 crores (1971)
4.				21.6 crores (1970)	2.06 crores (1979)	22 lakhs (1967)		

Note—Figures in respect of Radio subscribers of Japan are not available after 1971.

Source—*Mass media in India 1980-81,* Published by Ministry of Information and Broadcasting, New Delhi, 1982, p 78-

ted in the following table.[15] In Colombo a drastic drop in movie house attendance for locally produced films has been reported by the presidential committee of inquiry. According to the report the decline which began in 1980 has registered a loss of 20 million seats for Simhala films[16]. This trend shows that TV may supercede all the other media when it becomes available to each and every person. However, the high cost of TV set may be an obstacle in this direction. Considering the fact that TV is a costly medium, it is doubtful in the first place, that the common man, a poor villager can afford to purchase himself a set and feel the desired impact of TV. With growing demand for entertainment among urban viewers, there is a possibility of programmes following a commercial pattern. It is also observed that the present day programmes are in keeping with this trend.

Then why should the developing countries invest crores of rupees on this luxury entertainment when there are other immediate problems of urgent priority to be tackled ? Similar doubt was expressed when Radio programmes were started in India.[17] But now, the Radio has reached even the remotest areas of our country. This is largely due to the transistor revolution. But the cost of TV is not comparable to the transistor Radio. Due to the above facts providing TV sets to rural areas has been undertaken by the governments as a part of development of TV. For example, China could achieve progress in supplying TV sets in its programme of rural mass education.[18]

It is evident from the above discussion that the organization of TV medium is not an easy task especially in developing countries. However, with all the difficulties TV continues to grow in all these countries including India.

History of Television in India

TV transmission started in India (1959) long before SITE was even thought of. The major aim and objective in introducing TV in India was rural development. In view of its backwardness it was intended to utilize TV for the upliftment of rural masses by creating social awareness among them.[19] For doing this India faced, and is still facing, a unique obstacle. The uniqueness of our country's problem lies in the multilingual nature of its people. We do not have enough financial strength to counteract this problem. Though the hardware technology was readily available in the market, introduction of TV in India was not possible because of lack of trained personnel and knowledge in the software aspects and also due to the huge financial implications.

In 1959, with the help of UNESCO's grant, a study was conducted in India to test the use of TV, as a medium of education, rural uplift, and community development. The result of the study conducted after an year's transmission of special educational programmes proving positive and encouraging, the next stage of educational programmes for Delhi schools was taken up in 1961. Six years later i.e. in 1967 came the pilot project of agricultural communication initiated by late Dr. Vikram Sarabhai which was primarily aimed at demonstrating the effectiveness of TV as a medium for propagating improved farming practices. With the introduction of agricultural programmes a number of telecasts were organized in rural areas. Earlier from 15th August 1965 onwards, a daily one hour transmission was introduced in the evening. The second TV centre in the country was commissioned in Bombay in 1972. The Srinagar and Amritsar centres were inaugurated in 1973 while Calcutta, Madras and Lucknow found place on the TV map two years later, making it a network of seven centres including the relay station at Pune. In the meanwhile, at international forums on space communication, suggestions were being made for pilot project for assessing the practical uses of space communication technology. India was selected for the experiment. SITE transmissions were inaugurated on August 15, 1975 reaching 2,400 villages in the backward areas in Andhra Pradesh, Bihar, Karnataka, M.P., Orissa and Rajasthan representing a wide range of linguistic, cultural, climatic and agricultural regions of the country.[20]

The growth of TV in India was slow in the beginning. Since the necessary technology was at the stretch of the hand and due to the experience gained during SITE, the development of Indian TV was rapid after SITE.

The significant events that took place in the history of TV in India and the other information such as number of TV transmitters etc. is as below.[21]

Introduction of commercials in TV	.. 1sth January 1976
TV separated from All India Radio	.. 1sth April 1976
Operationalization of INSAT 1A and inauguration of National programmes and colour telecast	.. 1sth August 1982
INSAT 1A abandoned	.. 8th September 1982
Launching of INSAT 1B	.. 30 August 1983
Operationalization of INSAT 1B	.. 15th October 1983
Inauguration of 2nd Channel in Delhi	.. 17th September 1984
Morning transmission inaugurated	.. 23rd February 1987
News bulletins for hearing impaired	.. 15th October 1987

Number of TV Transmitters

Total TV transmitters	.. 221
Main centres	.. 12
Relay centres	.. 8
INSAT centres	.. 6
HPTs/LPTs linked with Delhi	.. 153
HPTs/LPTs linked with Bombay	.. 25
HPTs/LPTs linked with Hyderabad	.. 17

Coverage

Total population in lakhs	.. 4843 (72%)
Total area (in '000 sq. kms)	.. 1519 (48%)

TV Sets

The first indigenous black and white TV receiver was produced in India in 1969. From a production level of a few thousand sets in 1970, the industry had grown to produce 3 million sets in 1986. Of this, 21,50,000 were black and white and 8,50,000 colour sets. This is expected to go upto 29.2 million by 1990 and 45.6 million by 1992.[22]

Policy Guidelines

The Television medium is based on psychological principles. According to the mass communication theories, people take the assistance of mass-media to confirm their ideas, beliefs and convictions. The psychological effects may be positive or negative depending on the individuality of the viewer. Hence the Ministry of Information and Broadcasting has formulated certain policy guidelines for the proper functioning of radio and TV.

Coverage to government's programmes, publicity to developmental programmes, importance to rural population programmes to eradicate social evils, balanced coverage of news and other features and coordination between different media units are some of the important guidelines.[23] While giving free hand in its programming the policy guidelines imposed certain restrictions and also make it clear that the broadcast media has to operate very cautiously. The AIR Code, which also applies to Doordarshan, was adopted in 1968 and revised in 1970 states that Broadcasts on All India Radio by individuals will not permit :

1. Criticism of friendly countries;
2. Attack on religion or communities;
3. Anything obscene; or defamatory;
4. Incitement to violence or anything against maintenance of law and order;
5. Anything amounting to contempt of court;
6. Aspersions against the integrity of the President, Governors and Judiciary;

7. Attack on political party by name;
8. Hostile criticism of any state or the centre; or
9. Anything showing disrespect to the Constitution or advocating change in the Constitution by violence; but advocating changes in a constitutional way should not be debarred.[24]

Committees—Recommendations

The media under government's control is certain to face a lot of problems and complications. The discharge of functions may not be so efficient with limited resources and multiple restrictions. Keeping in view the possibility of probable difficulties in the functioning, the government has constituted different advisory committees under the chairmanship of eminent people and experts in the field of broadcast media. Accordingly, in 1964 the government appointed a committee on information and broadcasting under the chairmanship of Sri Ashok K. Chanda. This was the first enquiry committee appointed at the initiative of Late Smt. Indira Gandhi the then minister for Information and Broadcasting who felt that Broadcasting needed a fresh look. The Chanda Committee made three major recommendations in its report which was published in 1966. It suggested that AIR be converted into a corporation run by a Board of Governors on the BBC model: that television be separated from Radio and given a twenty-year development plan; and that the Vividh Bharathi channel be commercialised and its profits ploughed back into radio for the improvement of programmes. After four years, the government rejected the first recommendation on the ground that the time was not ripe for AIR to be converted into a corporation. While Government did not prepare a long-range plan for the development of TV, it did agree that the country needed TV and that it should be expanded within the available resources. Separation was affected only a decade later. The Chanda Committee's proposal to commercialise the Vividh Bharathi channel was accepted and brought into effect in 1967, though here also it took nearly ten years before the profits were actually made available to AIR[25].

In 1978 the Verghese Committee submitted its report on autonomy. The recommendations of the above committee will be discussed under 'AUTONOMY'.

With the increase in the number of transmitters all over the country, the necessity for the software development of Doordarshan has grown. So the government appointed a committee under the Chairmanship of Dr. P.C. Joshi to give recommendations on the software aspects of our television. In a report submitted in 1985 the Committee expressed doubt about the rural orientation of the present TV programming. Criticizing the commercial attitude adopted by TV, the committee advised the restructuring of its programme pattern[26]. As observedby P.C. Chatterji, the three enquiry committee reports are comprehensive documents which have made on an average two hundred and thirty recommendations each covering almost every aspect of broadcasting. They are spaced over a period of nearly twenty years and it is remarkable that they agree on several of their recommendations[27].

Advisory Committees

Doordarshan gets guidance from various advisory committees consisting of eminent non-officials and experts in the field. There are eight Advisory Committees functioning for the benefit of Doordarshan which includes the Media Advisory Committee at the Centre, the Central Advisory Committee for the utilisation of INSAT, Programme Advisory Committees at the Doordarshan Kendras, Advisory Committees on various categories of programmes such as family welfare programmes, science programme and the like. Special attention is paid to maintaining contact with agricultural universities, and in certain cases programmes are produced jointly by stations and universities. Though Doordarshan maintain contact with a large number of non-official bodies such as academic institutions, social welfare groups etc., such contacts are informal and no official procedure has been laid down for maintaining them[28].

Autonomy

Invention of modern technology has changed our life pattern to a great extent. The impact of modern technology on our lives has been seriously viewed by the futurologists. Along with the research and development in scientific areas, man has to follow some ethics and code of conduct for his own welfare. The full use of modern technology had to become restricted for the sake of peaceful living. This may be applicable to comunication system also where the usage of modern technology is increasing day by day.

History says that from the beginning the political systems have invented communication structure to meet their needs such as getting support to their policies etc. Starting from smoke signals, drummers and runners to present day television, the communication system is being utilized to get backing to the purposes and policies of the government. The exploitation of media is also observed from the beginning such as giving selected information to the people.

The United Nations commission on human rights has called information as one of the basic rights. One cannot deny the right to information. Knowledge has to be communicated from one person to another. But at the same time the media cannot be used without considering the evil effects.

To quote Nehru "Freedom from ignorance is as essential as freedom from hunger. The mass-media which are very useful have an element of danger in them in that they may be distorted for private gain. The rich group or the rich nation can flood the country and the world through the mass-media with its own view of things which may or may not be the correct one."[29]

The electronic media are highly powerful. Autonomy to electronic media has been under debate since broadcasting started in India. The issue has been viewed from different angles. According to the Indian Constitution Broadcasting together with posts and Telegraphs, Telephones, Wireless and other like forms of communication are in the union list and, therefore, are the exclusive responsibility of the Union or Central Government.[30] According to K S. Duggal :

> "When Radio was introduced in India in the late thirties the then rulers tried as far as possible to keep the radio free from political controversy. The media advisors Lionel Fielden and Ahmed Shah Bokhari have convinced their masters that once Radio loses its credibility with the listeners it would cease to have any meaning.
>
> "When India became independent, Nehru seriously considered according of autonomy to AIR on the lines of BBC. However, he could take no concrete steps towards relaxing the control over the media. Mrs. Gandhi when she came into power as Information and Broadcasting Minister and later as Prime Minister announced than the old practice would continue. She said "It is important that the channels should not be subject to political and economic control which could constrain the flow of information".
>
> The Chanda Committee recommended among other things the setting up of two autonomous corporations for Radio and Television. This, however, was not acceptable to the government. It was argued that as the press and films were in the private sector, Radio and TV must remain with the government to build its image."[31]

Submitting it's report on autonomy, the Verghese Committee recommended a single National Broadcast Trust instead of autonomous regional corporations or even a federation of state government corporations. There will be a large measure of power delegated to the regional and local levels, so that the organisation enjoys the advantages of quick decision making, sensitivity to local problems, familiarity with local customs and taste, and close linkages with various governments and institutions.[32]

As K.S. Duggal further observes :

> "The Verghese Committee recommended that the freedom of the Press and Broadcasting is derived from article 19(1) (a) of the constitution which guarantees freedom of speech and expression to every citizen. Accordingly the National Broadcasting Trust has proposed it to be a national trustee of the collective right of the Indian people to freedom of speech and expression through the broadcast media. To this end it suggested that the proposed corporation be defined as 'a corporate citizen of India' so that it might exercise and enjoy all the fundemental rights and obligations given to individual citizens.
>
> The Prasara Bharathi bill that was introduced in Parliament by the Janata Government diluted the recommendations made by the group, while rejecting the proposed constitutional amendment altogether. With the collapse of the Janata Government, even this bill lapsed.
>
> When the Congress (I) came into power again, one of the earliest announcements it made was that Radio and TV would continue to function as departments of government. They would however, have functional autonomy."[33]

But many political thinkers and media experts view government's control as monopoly over the media. In this connection Ashok Mitra says that the constitution gives the centre the right to control, but not the right to monopoly over the media. In a country of India's diversion and complexities. Television and Radio offer the quickest and widest reach. The monopoly of the media is the most precious weapon which the ruling party possesses in the battle for winning the people's mind.[34] Explaining the unsatisfactory performance of our TV and the problems it has under government's control, Ramesh Thaper states that "The tasks of transformation, of building the alternative vision, are too complex for bureaucratic communication. The freeing of the electronic media will free the mind of India."[35]

Autonomy for broadcasting is a critical issue. In countries where illiteracy is not a problem, people can receive information through the media with objectivity. But in our country the condition is quite contrary, especially in the rural areas, which are backward in all aspects. It is easy to influence the rudimentary thoughts of the people with a powerful medium and this is the kind of exploitation that is taking place today in the fields of free press and movies. Political and business motives have dominated our free press and films giving room to perversion, Hence it is unthinkable to leave the electronic media in the hands of a vested few – in the name of autonomy. At the same time free flow of correct information cannot be arrested in the name of control. A judicious method has to be identified and adopted while using this sophisticated technology. Eventhough full autonomy was given to broadcast media in some advanced countries, there is a constant check on their functioning from time to time. For example, the BBC which is considered as impartial and independent broadcasting authority is also under fire from its government. Thatcher herself has in the past publicly criticized the BBC for corrupting the morals of the young by broadcasting too much sex and violence.[36]

Keeping the above arguments and practical implications in mind the government must formulate a policy where both the programmes of the government as also the public views are given a due place.

Economics of Television

Financing for Broadcasting is wholly made from the consolidated fund of India. The budget for AIR and Doordarshan is presented as part of the expenditure of the Ministry of Information and Broadcasting.

A major portion of the revenue for television comes from the commercials. The Revenue from commercials continues to increase over the years. There is substantial increase in revenue from 77 lakhs during 1976-77 to 74 crores during 1987-88 (i.e.

upto October 87 only). The yearly licence fee has been abolished since March 85. Now only one time excise duty of Rs. 100/- per TV set is levied at the time of purchase.

The growth of television is very high during Sixth Five Year Plan period. The expansion was so rapid that from July 84 onwards till the end of the year almost every day one transmitter was commissioned in some corner or other of the country. This shows that the expenditure was more on hardware side than on software. This fact has been recognised in the seventh five year plan and the policy makers have therefore placed greater emphasis on the development of software facilities.[37]

Seventh Plan Schemes

An outlay of Rs. 700/- crores has been approved in the seventh plan for the developmental schemes of Television in the country. The plan includes replacement of all black and white equipment which has completed its useful life, establishment of regular studio centres at 12 places and programme, generation facilities at 12 more places. Coupled with the proposed extension of microwave network, Doordarshan will be able to provide primary service in each state in the local language. The total number of production facilities would be 47 and the coverage would extend to 80 per cent of the population.

The long term objective of television is that the largest number of people in the country should have access to three TV programmes.

1. The primary service in the language of the state and originating within the state.

2. The national service available on domestic recievers to all viewers in addition to the primary service.

3. The educational service which again has to be available on all domestic receivers and ultimately provide educatio nal programmes on various subjects at primary, secon dary and university levels at times convenient to the target

audience and in the language in which education is being imparted in that area.

Besides the above it is also desirable that programmes for special audiences be made available but these need not be on domestic receivers nor necessarily in the language of the state.[38]

Programme Pattern

Education, information and entertainment are the three major aims of TV programming. Sometimes entertainment is mixed with information i.e. humour is used wherever possible to drive home a point. Dialogues, discussions, playlets and other folk forms like Burra Katha are use to present the programmes which involves the participation of the villagers. Music is a part and parcel of every programme. Sometimes a small beat of the drum or a flick of a string may convey much more than words. Scripts for the programmes are prepared by experts in the particular fields and presented by trained artists. As far as possible visual aspect is given importance in the programmes. Sometimes suitable pictures with commentry are substituted whenever films are not available. Though the format of the programmes on Television is fixed, it varies depending upon the occasional, seasonal and other special programmes. For example major sports events, political conventions etc.

At present the following three types of programmes are available on TV.

(i) **Regional Programme.** This is transmitted in local languages from the respective programme production centres generally between 6.00 PM and 8.40 PM. These include programmes of information, education inbuilt with entertainment addressed to general and specific audiences including farmers, women, children, youth, industrial workers and others.

(ii) **National Programme.** A common national programme for a duration of 155 minutes between 8.40 PM and 11.15 PM on all days of the week except Saturdays when it goes upto midnight is telecast from Delhi which is carried by all the transmitters in the country. The national programme is relayed after the rigional telecast. However, Madras receives the National from 9.00 PM. This programme aims at fostering social, economic and cultural awareness, promoting the spirit of national integration and projecting the progress made by the country in various fields. Besides, two news bulletins—one in Hindi and another in English—are also telecast. Other items in the national programme include art, music, dance and programme based on literary work in various Indian languages and important features/discussions on Current Events. Programmes of entertainment sponsored privately and produced by eminent producers are also telecast.

In addition to National programme, Network programme is also being organised on Saturday afternoons and Sunday-full day. Saturday afternoon service is mainly meant for the housewives and children. The service is on the air from 1.45 PM. On Sundays from 9.00 AM. to 12.15 PM. a number of sponsored serials and Doordarshan's own programmes are telecast for the entertainment of viewers. From 1.15 PM. to 4.00 PM a feature film in regional language is telecast. In its Sunday network, Doordarshan has recently introduced a 15 minutes news bulletin in sign language with narration in English under the title News for the Hearing Impaired.

Morning Transmission is also being aired on the entire network for a duration of 45 minutes, starting from 7.30 AM. Besides, two news bulletins—one each in Hindi and English—the programme includes visual presentation of 'Vande Mataram' followed by items of physical excercise and entertainment. The transmission also includes programmes like 'Money matters' providing information on the latest trends in economy. Important personalities are also interviewed.

(iii) **Area specific and development oriented programmes** for the INSAT clusters are telecast for a duration of 35 to 40 minutes. Programmes on National Integration and Communal

Harmony are telecast both in National Network as well as by the various programme producing Kendras in the local languages. These programmes are telecast in various entertaining formats, including mushairas, quawalis, documentaries, sponsored programmes, plays and quiz programmes.[39]

INSAT based Doordarshan Kendras make programmes in a different way. For programmes intended for rural people via satellite it conducts research in the beginning known as **formative research**. The plan of the programme is first given to the viewers. Opinions are called for and then the programmes are prepared. Sometimes the programmes are prepared in advance keeping in view the requirements of the viewers and the feed back is analysed.

Objectives of the Programmes

Agriculture : Programmes on agriculture, animal husbandry, forestry irrigation, cottage and small scale industries, health, hygiene and sanitation etc. of varying duration hard core items pertaining to these aspects are telecast supported by suitable visuals of film in order to promote greater agricultural production. In respect of these programmes special chunks are assigned taking into account the viewing habits of the rural audience. The entertainment aspect is not neglected. For making these programmes more palatable folk songs, folk dances, playlets and special features on festive occassions are also in the day to day programmes.

Family welfare has been one of the important themes where the thrust has been for limiting the size of the family and bringing about qualitative changes in the standard of life the people. These programmes received promotional publicity in various forms and formats Doordarshan utilized the funds provided by the Ministry of Health and family welfare for the production of documentaries on the advantages of FP of varying durations and in different languages to make an impact on the people.

Special audience Programmes. Children, adolescents, youth, women, industrial workers, intellectuals, elderly persons, and the general citizens at large – A large number of programmes keeping in view the varied interests and need of these audience groups are produced with their involvement and participation.

Music and Dance. To reflect cultural heritage, tradition and to enterain people a substantial percentage of transmission is devoted to music programmes. These include vocal and instrumental music (classical, folk and modern).

The dances of India also find a place of pride in the Doordarshan's programmes. Folk and modern dance are also encouraged and their votaries invited to perform.

Drama. Produce and telecast drama on various social themes almost every week.

Feature Films. A number of good feature films in Hindi and other regional languages are telecast. Since TV is a family medium the suitability of fims for family viewing is taken into consideration for selection of films.

Sports. Cultivation of interest in and promotion of sports has been one of the major objectives of Doordarshan.

News and Current Affairs. The aim and objective of the news and current affairs programmes telecast from Doordarshan are to widen the awareness of the people about the major events and developments within and outside the country and to deepen their understanding of current social, economic and political events and issues.[40]

Audience Research

Doordarshan in it's approach for progressive planning relies heavily on the feedback received from the people by way of letters, views individual or collective expressed in meetings or critical reviews made in the press. In addition, through the scientific system of surveys, audiences reactions are analysed by the Audience Research Units which are in-built in the Doordarshan organizational setup.

The Audience Research Unit of All India Radio conducts over 120 field surveys and nearly 1,000 panel surveys during the course of a year. In the field surveys some 44,000 radio and TV households are contacted to assess the quantum of listening/viewing and to determine demographic and other characteristics.

Doordarshan has fourteen units attached to its main Kendras and post-SITE centres. They attempt to monitor the quantitative viewing of programmes through field surveys, panel surveys, analysis of viewers' letters and the like. Some studies conducted by them have been on subjects such as the impact of TV on children, surveys on Family serials etc.

The Indian Institute of Mass Communication (IIMC) functions in New Delhi as an autonomous body under the Ministry of Information and Broadcasting. Among other things it conducts studies on the impact of media on audiences. Some studies have concerned themselves with AIR/Doordarshan programmes. The two departments co-operate with the IIMC and take note of its findings. Research work has also been conducted by private organisations such as the Operations Research Group (Baroda), the Public Opinion Quarterly and some university departments of communication.[41]

Commercial Service

Commercial service of Doordarshan was started in January 1976 from seven Kendras and later extended through more Kendras. The scheme of sponsored programmes was introduced in 1983 enabling various organizations, business houses etc. to sponsor either programmes produced by them or imported programmes or programmes produced by Doordarshan[42].

The advertisements are telecast as per the provisions of the code for commercial advertizing. The code prohibits advertising of tobacco, liquor and gambling, including betting on horse-racing and other sports.[43] The booking of commercials, static or film spots and the sponsored programmes is done through the advertizing agencies and in some cases directly by the advertizers. As a matter of policy upto 10% of the total transmission duration can be utilised for commercial advertizements.[44]

The revenues from commercials increased to Rs. 74 crores (upto October 87) from a meagre Rs. 77 lakhs in 1976-77. The steady increase in the revenues is evident from the following.[45]

Year	*Revenue earnings in Crores*
1976-77	Rs. 0.77
1977-78	Rs. 2.20
1978-79	Rs. 4.97
1979-80	Rs. 6.16
1980-81	Rs, 8.09
1981-82	Rs. 11.60
1982-83	Rs. 15.89
1983-84	Rs. 19.79
1984-85	Rs. 31.43
1985-86	Rs. 60.20
1986-87	Rs. 98.31
1987-88 (Upto Oct. 87)	Rs. 74·49

International Relations

In accordance with the policy of the Government of India cultural agreements have been signed with some 20 countries which include Yugoslavia, France, USSR, Hungary and Czechoslovakia. These agreements include a section which deals with broadcasting. Exchange of programmes, co-operation in the field of technology, assistance to visiting news correspondents of other countries, and training and exchange of personnel are included in the agreements. Programme exchange has been largely confined to music but AIR and Doordarshan have also supplied scripts of plays (in English translation) to foreign organisations. There is programme exchange and co-operation in different fields, though no cultural agreement has been signed with USA. In the area of training AIR and Doordarshan have both benefitted from and made considerable contributions to the Asian Institute of Broadcast Development (AIBD) in Kualalumpur.[46]

Training

In service training for Television staff is provided at the Film and Television Institute of India at Pune, The Institute was set up initially for films in 1960 and a television section was added in 1974. Courses at the FTII have varied between six and four months depending on the pressure to open new TV centres.[47]

Annual Awards For TV Programmes

Awards for TV programmes are given annually for the best programmes produced and telecast by Doordarshan during each calender year. The aim of these awards is to promote the art of TV as a medium of communication and means of self-expression and to raise the standards of Doordarshan production. The awards are of two types : best production Awards and individual excellence Awards[48].

Television being a central government organisation its distribution system and functioning is uniform throughout the country. Doordarshan, Hyderabad (the sample district selected is located around the city of Hyderabad) which is part and parcel of central TV net work is also functioning on the similar lines as discussed earlier. However, some specific aspects about Hyderabad TV needs to be mentioned here since the same was choosen for the present study.

History of Television in Andhra Pradesh

In Andhra Pradesh, Television transmission commenced from the Capital city of Hyderabad in 1977. Earlier in 1975-76, Andhra Pradesh was one of the states which benefitted by the SITE experiment. The role played by Hyderabad TV as a part of the experiment is worth mentioning. Since the software aspects and other arrangements have to be looked after by India, every state here was fully prepared for the experiment.

The SITE programme was so organized that it would be received simultaneously by 24,000 villages located in six different states in India each wlth its own regional language. These states were selected partly for technological reasons based upon satellite location and partly for reasons of relative economic backwardness. Approximately 400 villages were selected for SITE in each state. Rangareddy, Medak and Mahaboobnagar districts in Telangana area and Kurnool district in Rayalaseema area of Andhra Pradesh are covered under the above scheme[49].

A total of five hundred and fifty five community TV sets (VHF sets) have been installed under Hyderabad Transmitter Range out of which 407 sets are installed by the Government of India and the remaining by Andhra Pradesh Government. Under INSAT direct receiption scheme in Mahaboobnagar aud Kurnool districts the government of India installed 375 community TV sets. Audience (men, women and children) on a daily average are in the range of 200-400 per community TV set. It is understood that this figure usually more than doubles on feature film days.[50]

The SITE is a historical event. For the first time a satellite has been used for transmitting TV programmes at international level. The findings of the research done after the experiment says that the rural masses of A.P. have responded with enthusiasm and motivation and in some areas people showed more interest compared to other states.

The regional programmes for the evening broadcast were

produced mainly at the base production centres located in 4 cites of Hyderabad, Cuttack, Ahmedabad and Delhi which took responsibility for 4 days in a week. The research and development work for hardware was done primarily at ISRO at Ahmedabad and the ECIL at Hyderabad. Three years were spent on planning by ISRO. The satellite was lifted into the space in May 74.[51] A few findings given in UNESCO report about Andhra Pradesh during SITE experience are worth looking before proceeding to know the structure of TV in the state.

Audience Size

A comparison of the audience size in the six clusters shows that except in the states of Andhra Pradesh and Orissa, in all other states the audience tended to decrease as the programme proceeded. However, in the states of Andhra and Madhya Pradesh the programme continued to draw a steady number of viewers.

The Hyderabad programmes were broadcast in two states. Andhra Pradesh and Karnataka. With regard to presentation and comprehension the most frequently occuring comment was that the programme presentation was interesting and good.

Regularity In Attendance

Between adults and children the latter were found to be more regular in attendance in Andhra Pradesh and in Madhya Pradesh.

The response was highest in AP with 71% return of cards and, he lowest in Bihar with only 28 :. The response from the other states was around 60%.[52]

The above information speaks that the television impact on the villagers of Andhra Pradesh is satisfactory. With the provision of TV service all over the state recently, people of Andhra Pradesh both urban and rural are enjoying the programmes.

Area and Population

The area of A.P. is 2, 75,068 sp.kms. The population of the state as per the 1981 census provisional figures is 5.35,49,673. The state has a rural population of 410.62 lakhs and urban of 124.87 lakhs. Andhra Pradesh is the fiifth largest state in the country both in area and population. There are 23 districts in the state. A.P. is primarily an agricultural state.

Capital	Hyderabad
Principal languages	Telugu and Urdu
Literacy	29.94
Number of News papers	1071 (dailies 62
Circulation of Newspapers	18.03 lakhs
Radio Stations	Hyderabad, Vijayawada, Vishakha-patnam Cuddapah and Adilabad.[53]

Hyderabad Television (Upagraha Doordarshan Kendra, Hyderabad) is primarily a rural centre catering to community TV villages in the surrounding districts. It has been doing so since 1975 when the SITE programmes commenced. It was in October 77 that Hyderabad transmitters became operational. Andhra Pradesh is the second state where in all the relay centres were linked with the regional Kendra via INSAT B. Maharashtra being the first one. Since the SITE covered only Telangana and Rayala-Seema areas the Andhra area was totally deprived of the enjoyment of TV for a long time. With the installation of transmitters and Sattellite relays this deficiency was covered to some extent from 14th January 86. The progammes that are telecast from Hyderabad are now feeded throughout A.P. The total area covered by Hyderabad Doordarshan Kendra is approximately 95,000 sq. kms. The total population covered is 254.63 lakhs, out of which 95.29 lakhs is urban population and 159.34 lakhs is rural.

Andhra Pradesh like many other states is noted for diversities in culture. In addition to Telugu which is the main language, Urdu is also widely spoken especially in Telangana areas. This calls for special attention on the part of the programme makers to satisfy the needs of the prorgramme viewers.

It is very difficult to satisfy the different tastes of people at one and the sametime. The massiveness of the medium poses a challenge to the broadcasters. Before trying to teach a concept through projection the programme makers attempt to create an interest for learning in the minds of the viewers. The medium has to maintain a balance betweem urban demand and the rural needs. Hence the task is not an easy one in practical terms with limited technical resources, inadequate training in software aspects and financial drawbacks.

An overall view of the TV was discussed hitherto with a sociological perspective. TV, like a tree, has various branches related to different subjects, Each branch needs detailed study. Political broadcasting which is concerned with the present study is one among them. This area has some background which requires special attention. The next chapter has been devoted for the main focus of the study i.e. political broadcasting and the research work done in the field of political communication.

REFERENCES

1. Charles S. Steinberg, Ep., *Mass Media and Communication.* (Hastings House Publishers : New York, 1972), pp 262-263.
2. *The SITE Experience*, Reports and papers on mass communication, No. 91 (UNESCO: Paris, 1983). p 7.
3. Primary Census Abstract, General Population, Part II B(i) Series-1, *Census of India*, 1981.
4. *An Indian Personality for Television*, Vol.I., report of the working group on software for Doordarshan (Publication Division, Ministry of Information and Broadcasting, New Delhi, 198?). p 34

5. Wilbur Schramm, *Mass Media and National Development*, (Stanford University Press : Stanford, California, 1964), p 162.
6. *An Indian Personality for Television*, op. cit., p 90.
7. Schramm, op. cit., p. 135.
8. Edwin Emery, Phillip H. Ault and Warren K. Agee, *Introduction to Mass Communications*, Vakils, Feffer and Simons Pvt. Ltd. : Bombay, 1969)- p 18.
9. *An Indian Personality for Television*, op. cit., p 35.
10. *The United states and Debate on the World Information Order*, a report by Academy for Educational Development, Inc. (From the collections of American Library, New Delhi), p 87.
11. *Akash Bharathi National Broadcast Trust*, Report of the working group on Autonomy for Akashvani and Doordarshan, Voll. II (New Delhi, 1978).
12. The US and debate on the world information order, op. cit., p. 88.
13. *Akash Bharathi*, op. cit.
14. *An Indian Personality for Television*, op. cit., p 35.
15. R. Thiagarajan, "Electronic Media in the Eighties" in *Mass Media in India 1980-81*, edited by Research and Reference Division, Ministry for Information and Broadcasting, (Publication Division, I & B Ministry, New Delhi, 1982), p 74.
16. Bede Perera, TV cuts audience for Cinema (Sri Lanka), *World Broadcast News*, Nov. 1985 (Publishers of Broadcast, Management/Engineering : New York.
17. V. Patanjali, "Television : Towards meeting the challenge for change" in *Mass Media in India 1981-83*, compiled by Research and Reference Division, Ministry of Information and Broadcasting (Publication Division, Ministry of I & B, New Delhi, 1984), p 148.
18. *An Indian Personality for Television*, op. cit., p 23.
19. V. Pathanjali, op. cit., p 148.
20. Pathanjali, op. cit., p 149-150.
21. *Television India 1987*, A report by the Audience Research Unit, Doordarshan New Delhi, 1987, p 15, 52.
22. *Manorama Year Book* 1988, (Kottayam, India), p 553.
23. *U.L. Baruah, This is All India Radio* (Publication Division, Ministry of Information And Broadcasting, New Delhi 1983), pp 80-82.
24. P.C. Chatterji, *Broadcasting in India* (SAGE : New Delhi, 1987). p 105.
25. Ibid., pp 165-166.

26. *An Indian Personality for Television*, Report of the working group on software for Doordarshan (Publication Division, Ministry of I & B, New Delhi, 1985).

27. Chatterji, op. cit., p. 178.

28. Chatterji, op. cit., p. 94.

29. *An Indian Personality for Television*, op. cit., p 3.

30. P.C. Chatterji, *Broadcasting in India,* (SAGE : New Delhi, 1987), p 58.

31. K.S. Duggal, *Indian Broadcast Media Year Book 1982,* (Marwah Publications : New Delhi. 1983), pp. 103-104.

32. *Akash Bharathi,* National Broadcast Trust, Vol. I, Report of the working group on Autonomy for Akashvani and Doordarshan (Ministry of Information and Broadcasting, New Delhi 1978), pp 224-225.

33. K.S. Duggal, op. cit., p. 105.

34. Ashok Mitra, "States' rights over the Media", in *News Times,* 30 July 1986, Hyderabad, p 6.

35. Ramesh Thapar, "Decontrolling the air waves", *Illustrated Weekly of India,* April (6-12) 1986, (Bombay).

36. *Indian express* (Hyderabad), September 20th, 1986.

37. *Television India 1987,* A report by the Audience Research Unit, Doordarshan, New Delhi, pp 43-44.

38. "Development of Television Broadcasting in India", in *Indian Television today and tomorrow*—A note prepared at Regional Seminars and National Colloquium organised by NAMEDIA. New Delhi, 1986, from the collections of Mass Communication Centre, Jamia Milia Islamia University, New Delhi).

39. *Television India,* op. cit., p. 9.

40. K.S. Duggal, op. cit., pp 45-51.

41. P.C. Chattereji, *Broadcasting in India* (SAGE : New Delhi, 1987), pp 86-87.

42. *Manorama Year Book, 1986,* (Kottayam, India), p 570.

43. Chatterji, op.cit., p 147.

44. Duggal, op. cit., p 54.

45. Duggal, op. cit., p. 54 (Figures upto 1982).
Manorama Year Book, 1988, op. cit., p 553.

46. Chatterji, op. cit., pp 95-96.

47. Chatterji, op. cit., p 90.

48. *Television India 1987,* op. cit., p 7.

49. *The SITE Experience* Reports and papers on mass communication No. 91 (UNESCO : Paris, 1983). p. 8.

50. *The Advent of Colour*, Hyderabad Doordarshan in 1986. A report by Research and Evaluation Cell, Doordarshan Kendra, Hyderabad p 6.

51. *The SITE Experience*, op. cit., p. 9.

52. *The SITE Experience*, op.cit., 12, 25, 28, 51.

53. *Andhra Pradesh Book Year 1986*. (A DNF Publication, Hyderabad), pp (iv), 227.

CHAPTER TWO

Political Broadcasting—A Review

The broadcast media became popular during wars and other major political events. Interpersonal relations between people behind and in front of the tiny screen became a force to reckon with. "The whole world is watching" was the chant of the demonstrators who were clubbed by police outside democratic convention in Chicago in 1968.[1] As described by David M. Abshire, Radio was put to extensive political use during the period between the two world wars. This was evident at the time of the outbreak of the world War II in 1939. With this, international broadcasting and the importance of public opinion grew and became popular. When war ended the western government continued their war time communication media at the same level. Radio Moscow has been highly active during the war from 1945 to 1951 the BBC was the principal voice of the west.[2] After the war. As said by Wilson P. Dizard party leaders in all communist countries even today express high hopes for TV as the chief instrument for the propagation of Marxist and Leninst schools of thought.[3] This is the trend in communist countries, whereas public opinion is the basis for a democratic form of government. Public opinion is important for the effective functioning of democracy and mass-media has an important role to play in the creation and crystalisation of public opinion.

Public opinion is not readymade. It is created. According to Sachdeva, it is created mainly because it is concerned with a matter of public importance and not one particular group of people. Public opinion is meant for social welfare at Large, It is arrived at after careful thought because it is a deliberate adjustment of public to a situation. He says that there are three stages in the formation of public opinion. First, the emergence of an issue; secondly, discussions on pros and cons with proposed solutions, and thirdly, arrival at a consensus.[4]

The chief agencies of public are, the press, literature, Radio, TV and movies. These agencies shape public opinion both individually and together. A minimum political education is found to be necessary for the formation of public opinion. The media influences the public opinion and is, in turn influenced by it.

Political Communication

Communication begins at home. The child's mind forms certain irrevocable impressions through communication received from its parents and other family members. These impressions act as a basis for all other opinions formed later. Home is followed by school, creches, environment, and the society of which the individual is a member. The impressions thus formed in an individual's mind right from his childhood ultimately define his opinion about the social, economic, cultural, religious and political conditions in his environment. Thus an individual's opinion is formulated through a process of continuous education by communication. Thus, communication makes him aware of the various issues confronting the society. If an individual has to be a good citizen, he has to have an insight into the working of his government. This starts with political communication, or in other words, public political education. Read H. Blake and Edwin O. Haroldsen define political communication as the communication that has actual or potential effects on the functioning of a political state or other political entity. According to them several important institutions are used for the purpose of political communication.

Organizations. Parties, union, public bureaucracies and other mass organizations capable of linking the elite-sub elite and broad sections of citizenry. These are relatively national in scope and relatively permanent.

Groups. Groups are less permanent, less institutionalized and often less pervasive, tentative collections.

Mass-Media. Helps both in enabling the elite to talk with another and in linking the elite to other chains such as inter-personal networks, organizations etc.

Specialized Channels. Demonstrations and special events used for the aggregation and articulation of interests under special circumstances.[5]

Political communication was verbal before press, radio and TV came into existance. Today these form an integrated part of communication system. In democratic countries, the need for rapid and precise communication has grown and the necessity to use mass media to cater to this need.

Communication in a democracy is a complicated task inherent with several limitations and restrictions. The mass-media are under constant pressure from the ruling party on one side and opposition on the other. If there is only one political party, it may do justice even with limited facilities, whereas in a democratic country with the ruling party and several other opposition groups, the mass media faces an insurmountable task in doing full justice to varied interests.

Inspite of the above limitations, many democratic countries are providing a wide range of information to the public. This enables people to form their individual opinion and nourish their own point of view. Keeping in view the necessity to politically educating each and every citizen at individual, national and international levels, the broadcast media, that is, the radio and the TV are covering a wide variety of programmes. The following are some of the concepts that are relevant to the broadcast media.

International Political Communication

The vein of international political communication is basically diplomatic. It has become an important nucleus around which centre several national matters. As Frank L. Kaplan observes the media is engaged in a continuous stream of ceaseless and clever bombardment of massages at the international level. Much of the international media aims at reinforcing friendly images held in other nations of the country engaged in the propoganda effort. Foreign news is a significant item in every-day news bulletins. Interest in the foreign affairs is especially pronounced among the educated. However, the general public is also now showing keen interest in view of the potential impact the foreign events have on the domestic scene. Business, commerce, finance, trade, and industry are the main foci of attention in international communication.[6] An awareness of domestic conditions and an understanding of international affairs is required for political awareness. The international communication system should be committed to the principle that it is the responsibility of the press, radio and TV not only to inform but also to educate the public about foreign events, so that the population as a whole is better prepared to evaluate and judge the effectiveness and propriety of its government's foreign policies and actions.

As Kaplan says, every independent nation in the world has become interdependent. Therefore, what happens in Nicaragua, the people's Republic of China, India or even Upper Volta or Mali, may, at some point in the future, if not immediately affect some other nation directly or indirectly.[7]

Describing the importance of international communication in Democracies, W. Philips Davison says,

> "A democratic form of government implies freedom of the two way international communication as well as

domestic freedom of information. Many of the groups that contend and interact in a democracy require ideas and information from abroad if they are to form and function, and individuals no less frequently seek information from other countries to satisfy personal needs. Any person who wishes to take an intelligent interest in the foreign policy of his own nation must have access to foreign news and opinions. If the democratic process is to function, the right of individuals to incoming information must be assured. If all democracies restricted the 'outflow' of information, this would mean that for each the range of incoming information would be greately narrowed, a situation that might be expected to lead to the gradual undermining of democracy everywhere. Communications from abroad, if they are to have an effect, must find users among the population of the receiving country. Furthermore, if these ideas are to be politically influential, the users ordinarily must be organised in some way in political parties, industrial enterprises, or groups sharing public opinion."[8]

Bias in Political Communication

Political bias shows itself in the form of curtailment of information. In political communication, editing and censoring news item are not uncommon. At times emphasis is placed on what editors believe people want to know rather than on what people ought to know. In the Indian scene for example, criticism by the non-ruling parties of the ruling party's prejudice in imparting news is an everyday affair. But it must be understood that this is only natural where power rests with ruling party. In India diversity is a striking feature. Hence a single picture is interpreted in diverse way, and thus does not satisfy one and all. A part of the audience feel that there is a prejudice —a colouring of the actual picture, where political news is concerned. On the other hand, the ruling party might feel the bias on the part of the public is of its own making and hence is not the fault of the party of government.

Bias in the print media is suspected to be wide-spread, whereas Radio reporting comes under lesser suspicion. TV may be reliable to some extent when compared to the above two because a visual happening is shown as it actually happened, although the voice reporting the incident might hide a fact or two. Sincerity on the part of the reporters and journalists can help to a large extent in winning the confidence of thc public.

Frank L. Kaplan opines that this bias is more pronouneed in the international scene. The industrialised countries which are dominating the world's power and economy are also dominating the flow of information. It is a notable feature that the foreign wire-services give priority to news items like poverty, disasters and conflicts while giving news about developing countries. The developing countries are not able to counter these and defend themselves. This led to the birth of organisations like 'The Third World News Pool' in 1976 for the purpose of collecting and disseminating news from developing countries throughout the world. He also says that the editors and news directors may not be as familiar with the public's news interests as they claim to be. To this end he quotes a Harris Survey conducted in 1978 and reported widely in the press, which compared the attitudes of reporters, editors and news directors with those of media consumers on the question of what people look for in their newspapers. The survey indicated that media personnel underestimate the public interest in international news. For, while 41% of the public surveyed expressed great interest in foreign news only 5 percent of the sample of media practitioners believed media consumers to be concerned with this news category. Kaplan further observes that continuous projection of a single personality especially on TV is one more form of significantly open bias. Besides insulting the Viewer's intelligence, such projections do nothing to improve universal understanding. Also the sight on television screen or in a news photo of a single foreign face out of a large crowd during an isolated repugnant incident may create a false impression as something typical of the entire population or ethic group which the singled-out individual may represent.[9] There is also the point of how much relevance a news item is to the audience especially the foreign news. Too much irrelevance results in disinterest and apathy among viewers.

Bias in political communication may be allowed if it aims at the welfare and safety of the society. For example, reporting on racial or communal riots and other forms of violence, which mostly turn out to be politically motivated. Studies have proved that reporting of violence triggers further violence. As Rechard Clutterbuck observes, especially among children and teenagers the aggressive instincts are aroused by what they see on TV. If cheaply obtained unwanted and irrelevant information is televised, it may tend to create uncalled for tendencies in the minds of children and adolescents. This is especially true where crime, sex and violence are projected without any reservation.[10]

Broadcasting from Parliament

Report on parliamentary proceedings are something everyone is familiar with today. Everyday newspapers carry pictures and commentaries regarding what goes on at the top levels. Radio gives news several times during a day and brings us upto-date on parliamentary affairs. The TV news bulletins colourfully present the faces of our leaders cutting a ribbon, laying a foundation stone, laying a wreath or receiving officials. In the background, a well trained voice reads out the occasions marking the ceremonies. This kind of presentation is a very ancient practice which is still continuing inspite of several strides made in live telecasting. Special events like a dignitary's visit, a celebration like that of the Republic day, a convention or a summit like the SAARC, or a sports event are all important in their own way.

This being so, there is also the some degree of interest among the public to watch simultaneously the parliamentary sessions and their elected leaders. The public are deeply interested in actually seeing for themselves the steps involved in the ultimate decision-making which affects them.

According to Norman Swallow when the subject of direct televising of parliamentary affairs was taken up in countries like UK, some critics felt that there are some politicians who feel that to have the paraphernalia of TV inside the national debating chamber would be an inconvenient intrusion. To some persons there is something degrading and cheap about the very idea that members of parliament, conducting their business in a place of privilege should be seen doing so in the very homes of those who put them there.

He also says that the deep fear of the possible consequences of TV's invasion into such a precious place is not confined to Britain or to the members of parliament at Westminister, but other have also expressed doubts of a more reasonable sort which are still widely held on both sides of the Atlantic. To this end he quotes Governor Brad Ford.

> "It has been frequently suggested that it would be a help to the voters if the deliberations of the legislative proceedings were televised as a public service. It would be that it would be just the opposite. The business of legislative assemblies for a great majority of the sessions is necessarily dull, drawn out and unexciting. No attempt by an honest TV camera recording the scene could make it otherwise, and the casual viewer would come to the conclusion that the Legislature was a do-nothing-body. In this kind of TV, sight could be lost of the fact that to be successful it needs either action, drama, historical significance or the intimacy of personalities in scence."

Explaining further the author states that it would be impossible to televise constantly the whole of parliamentary proceedings. Therefore, some process of selection is necessary. But the editing procedure by itself would be unfair to parliament as an institution i.e., if it confined itself to the moments of drama. If it did not, it might be a very dull programme. There are no doubt some dramatic instances in parliament for example, a budget debate, an inter-party clash on foreign policy, or vote of no-confidence in the government etc. But these moments of drama are infrequent. Much of the parliamentary affairs are dry and tedius to a layman and yet highly significant to any one who cares about its broader duties. What is dramatic will usually be important, but what is important is not always dramatic. However, we cannot say that there should not be a live coverage at all, because there is a possibility of incorrect and biased reporting by the press and other media regarding certain aspects that serve democratic purposes such as near parochial points made by Members on behalf of their own constiuents, protests of all kinds, and the airing, in non-party debate.[11]

In the light of the above discussion it would be desirable to have at least major events of daily proceedings (video recordings) late in the evening with the help of a commentator who must be trained to describe the proceedings as they happened without adding his own interpretation.

Installation of TV cameras in parliament has occured sometimes in Britain. In certain other countries also parliamentary debates have from time to time been televised. But that was all. According to available information, live telecast of parliamentary proceedings has not yet begun any where in the world. But there is a chance of this happening early in countries where full autonomy of broadcasting exists. In some advanced countries discussions are going on, which might yield a positive result at a future date. As said by Norman Swallow, the truth is surely that parliament which represents the people cannot for ever cut itself off from the people. If the parliament's activities are reported daily in the newspapers how can they in logic be excluded from the nation's Sitting rooms ?[12] But in a country like India where broadcasting is owned by the government, there is still no thought of parliamentary discussions being telecast live. Reports and reviews are still the order of the day.

Budget Broadcasts

The concept of budgeting has a household importance. Budget is important for conducting the day-today expenditure in a sensible way. This applies not only to the housewife and the businessman, but also to the nation at large. It is imperative that the income and expenditures are judiciously balanced if any progress is to be made in the economic life of a nation. Household budgeting is a private matter. Privacy and its attendant secrecy are, however, not applicable at the national level. The yearly budget is a much awaited document for members belonging to all strata of society. The housewife is concerned with the household expenses, health and schooling matters of her children, her husband and herself. She waits for the annual budget as it tells her how the prices of commodities she requires in her day-to-day routine are likely to change in the coming year. The tax issue catches the interest of every earning person. Export and import of goods interest the businessman. The prices of petrol and other fuels are of concern to every vehicle owner and commuter. Thus the yearly budget which the government announces is highly relevant and important to the public.

Budget broadcasting is popular programme on Radio and TV, and is eagerly awaited. Even people who are not regular followers of the media will tune in their sets on that particular day to listen and learn about the budget. The Radio and TV give out the news regarding the budget even before the press can print and distribute their newspapers. In addition to the verbatim presentation of the budget, commentaries and discussions by financial experts and opposition leaders are also a regular feature. There is a social awareness clearly visible on the street corners, homes and workplaces. Though it comes once in a year there is no other broadcast which has such universal appeal.

Ministerial Broadcasts

Even though occassions are frequent for the Prime Minister and President of India to voice their opinions, decisions, and strategies, the media gives equal importance to other ministers when occassions calling for their explanation arise and in matters of their respective departments. For instance, this is true of broadcasting at the state level also.

There is also a definite need for such broadcasts which may be termed as important because it is also the duty of the ministers to inform the public of decisions taken at the administrative level. For example, the finance minister is called in for an interview or discussion (like Janvani programme on TV) where a certain tax is concerned. The Minister of Railways finds an occasion to face the public at times of hike in railway fares or a serious lapse that caused an accident. Similarly, the education minister feels the need to explain a new policy on education (as declared by the prime Minister).

One additional advantage of such broadcasts is that the public become familiar with the persons at the top level. Frequent appearances create an intimacy between the viewers and the viewed.

Political Advertising : Election Campaigns

Advertising used by political parties before elections is called political advertising. The election campaigns mainly use banners, posters, pamphlets, hoardings, wall writings, badges, etc. This kind of political advertising furthers the party's popularity among the people. The election campaigns help in reinforcing and mobilising the opinions of the electorate. An important feature in an election campaign is what politicians or campaigners say, how they say it, and how effectively they say it. The main aspects of an election campaign are the use of media campaign material and face to face platform speeches. Political leaders generally start their campaign with heavily printed highly meaningful "motto" of their party. They exhibit this in banners and posters with a specific symbol in every nook and corner of the state. With the same "motto" in mind the partymen use imagination and select slogans, captions and cartoons and exhibit them in vantage public places. The ultimate gain of such effort is psychological. This kind of visual pictures get imprinted in the minds of the people, especially among those people who have an open mind. While these conventional modes of electioneering are very expensive, audio and video cassettes which are specially prepared are able to reach more houses. Highly dramatic, poetic literature with music in the background have immediate impact on the minds of the people. But even this is a costly affair. A poorman cannot afford the luxury of a cassette player.

Likewise public meetings which necessiate a political leader to reach places in person is, though common, a difficult task. The personal charishma is indeed a plus point in this regard. But this is also expensive. The party to move with its leader, workers, their transport and other paraphernalia is wholly strenuous, difficult and uneconomical.

Today election campaigns are carried on through the mass media of communications, especially the Press, Radio and TV. These election campaigns are carried on in a mass scale by the newspapers. Just before elections, Radio and TV allow election campaining under a special programme called the "party political broadcasts". Except this, the broadcast media in our country does not allow any further election campaigning.

In other countries especially in the United States election campaigning is most intensive on TV. Considering TV's mass appeal and mass reach, Care is taken to make these campaigns interesting and effective. Regardless of the cost involved the partymen continuously project the image of the party and the leader.

Edwin Diamond and Stephen Bates opine that, political advertizing on TV represents a form of persuasion. According to them this is thirty years old. They say

> "A new venture in this type of advertising is the thirty second or sixty second commercial spot over the broadcast media. These spots are called Polispots. This has developed both distinct, rhetorical modes and distinct visual styles. The Polispot has also grown to dominate political campaigns in US especially in the large states

and in presidential elections. For example, of the 29 million in federally allotted campaign funds that Ronald Regan and Jimmy Carter each spent in 1980 almost half went in to political advertizing mainly on TV".

Political campaigning before elections is improving each day especially with the support of mass-media. In India in the recent years, the electronic media like films, audio and vedio casettes have been playing an active role.

Party Political Broadcasts

As said earlier, political advertising or party advertisement is most intensively done before election time. Party advertisements are carried on in a number of ways. TV medium is one among them. Party political broadcasting involves interaction with the state. The mass media should extend fullest cooperation to these parties in reaching the people. This is one form of political eduaction. Atleast in the election year, the different parties come to the people either in person or through the media and inform the people of their policies and programmes.

In United kingdom, political broadcasting began to be seriously developed in 1928 when the BBC was given freedom to broadcast on controvercial issues. The importance of broadcasting as a medium for spreading political ideas and knowledge among a widening public was soon recognised by the parties.[13]

As U.L. Baruah describes in the "United States, the Federal communication has laid down a doctrine of equal opportunities to all candidates. In Australia, facilities are given to only those political parties to broadcast on the eve of elections which are contesting atleast five percent of the seats, and have polled in the previous elections five percent of the total votes cast or had a member elected to parliament. Such broadcasts are in addition to those which the broadcasting authorities might arrange on their own at the time of election or on a regular basis for political education of its listeners or viewers." The objective is furtherence of party interest by projecting its policy and programmes. The oppostion parties put a great deal of stress on these broadcasts. In India, party political broadcasting is of a recent origin. Our TV and Radio are providing the different political parties to broadcast on the eve of elections. "The proposals made by the Chief Election Commission in 1962 gave each national party fifteen minutes each with an additional 15 minutes for the ruling congress party. This was not acceptable to the communist party of India and the Jansangh. The Election Commission made similar efforts in 1967 and 1971 but failed. The Janata party government decided in May 1977 that facilities for broadcasting should be provided equally to National and Regional parties on the eve of State Assembly elections in June 1977. Each political party recognized by the Election Commission and given an election symbol under Election symbols (reservation and allottment) Act 1968, was given equal opportunity to broadcast from the broadcasting stations in the states concerned for the first time when elections to state assemblies were held in ten states and two union territories in June 1977. Broadcast facilities were given to all the national and regional parties contesting the elections, from all the Radio and TV stations located in the state. There were two rounds of broadcast of a duration of fifteen minutes each by each political party on Radio and one on TV. The schedule of broadcasts was drawn up by lots by station Directors located at state capitals in the presence of the Chief Electoral Officer and the representatives of political parties. The language of the broadcasts and names of the speakers were decided by the respective political parties. Independent candidates challenged these broadcasts as discriminatory. However, the courts did not uphold these. Broadcasts were prerecorded usually at the state capitals and copies of tapes were sent to all stations in the state in order to ensure an uninterrupted broadcast.[14]

Public Opinion Polls

Opinion poll is an important aspect in any field work. This is especially significant when it comes to politicians, during or before their campaigning to gauge the opinion of the public in matters of their needs or requirements, their aspirations etc.

Policy making also becomes need oriented if made on the basis of opinion polls. Any aspect of society which concerns the common man can be improved only if the public are encouraged to participate. In advanced countries some research organisations continuously provide information in various fields. For example attendance at Sunday mass, drop outs among the blacks from schools or number of fans for a movie star etc. The relevance of these researches becomes important in so far as they determine vital turning points in the organization of the society. For example, surveys conducted by the broadcast media seek feedback from the various strata of the society. They learn the public's view points in this kind of feed back. In the United States Roper organization has conducted a famous opinion poll on the subject of "news" and came up with the result that TV news had the most wide spread appeal. Another such organization is the "Harris Poll" also in the United States.[15]

In India also, the broadcast media have conducted widespread opinion polls in order to get some feedback from the public. Many surveys have been conducted by the research units of Radio and TV in the area of political broadcasting also. These serve as a guideline for the programme makers in planning and presenting of future programmes.

Election Bulletins

Hitherto election results were announced to the public on blackboards displayed at the counting centres and over the Radio through special election news bulletins. This was good enough but was uot within everybody's reach. People had to take the trouble of going to the display centres in order to learn the trend about how various parties are faring. This was the plight of even the candidate himself who is contesting. The radio on the other hand was more convenient although one had to wait till the special broadcast was on air.

Recently, TV has taken upon itself the task of announcing election results. Further, this is being done in a very sophisticated manner. It is not only conveying the information in a very short time (almost simultaneously with the counting) but also doing this in an analytical manner with the assistance of computers. This analysis is presented to the viewers in a discussion form. There is a panel of members who discuss and analyse the voting trend. This is a novelmethod of presenting the election results. This highly sophisticated type of comparison, conclusion and prediction is attracting more and more audience.

The Impact of Mass Media In Political Communication

Communication is a basic necessity in society. Mass-communication has become the order of the day. Experts in the field are gravely concerned about the effects of mass-communication on the minds of the people in so far as it concerns social change.

Knowledge is possible only through communication. Communications of this kind is called education. In the task of nation building, it is imperative that each inch individual in society is moulded into a maturet intelligent and responsible citizen. Education thus must be aimed at this. As a good citizen, each individual must in his turn contribute his mite to the task of nation building. This he can do only with full possession of facts about his government, leaders, body politic, the economic policy of the nation, its foreign policy etc. Here the role played by mass media is important in the sense that it reaches the masses in a conveniently short time. Mass-media is being fully exploited by the media experts for the purpose of mass education.

In our country, especially in rural India, stress is on educating the masses in the small family men, women and child welfare, nutrition, agriculture, importance of literacy etc. Our main concern here is to learn the impact of mass media in political communication.

The Radio and TV from the time of their inception have been presenting to their audience information regarding the national and domestic scene under their programme called 'THE NEWS'. But how much do our people especially the poor rural folk receive the news as it should be received ? How many realize the importance of their own participation in the national scene ? How many of them have basic political knowledge about the government ? How many are aware of the political system which democracy requires ? How many have even the bare minimum political desire to cast their vote ? Their and many other such questions have to be answered if one wants to gain an insight into the impact of the mass media communication.

Political scientists in the past believed that people did not change merely by reading a paper or listening to the Radio. There had always been suspicion among the people. They always sought support from other media and also their own interpersonal relations in their community. These interpersonal relationship was with a definite person in society called opinion leader. The opinion leaders inform themselves with the help of mass media. These opinion leaders were the link between mass media and the audience. This two-step flow of information was assumed by the political thinkers to be the significant feature of the impact of mass media in political communication. This was in the past. With the advent of communication through television, older beliefs began to fade away. The belief that political communication may (to atleast some extent) directly influence the viewers' mind began to take shape.

In any country, political mass communication is most intensive during the time of elections. For this reason some researchers felt the election time was the right time for their studies and surveys. The following are some of the theories based on which studies were conducted.

Michale Gurevitch and Jay G. Blumler who have contributed much to the field of political communication especially through Television opine that "assumptions about the political impact of the mass-media have played a formative past in guiding the direction of mass communication research, ever since its inception. In so far as the pioneer investigators accepted popular impressions of the media as omnipotent and capable of being employed for manipulative purposes, it was natural, that much research attention should have been paid to communication influence on people's political opinions and attitudes.

It is equally obvious why such a preoccupation with persuasive effects should have resulted in an imbalance of activity favouring studies of the audience at the expense of other elements in the communication process. Dramatic examples of seemingly successful uses of mass-media to propagate political beliefs and ideology in World War I and 1930's, plus the growth of political science interest in empirical analysis of voting behaviour, gave rise to and reinforced the conviction that the prime target for research should be process of opinion and attitude change among individual receivers of mass communication messages."[16]

Political Communication Research in India

In India political mass communication is fast gaining popularity, but research studies to the effect have been few. A specific nature of mental preparedness is yet to be created among the public in order that a survey on political awareness or one on voting inclination can be done meaningfully. Research work has however not been totally nill. The Press, Radio and TV have each independently conducted some studies. But these have been limited to social or educational impact. Surveys on how much effect the mass media has in influencing political attitudes are yet to gain ground in India.

Research work done in this field so far has been mainly in the form of a few intensive surveys done at the time of elections. Studies on the impact of political communication have not been extensive enough to judge the growth of political consciousness among the people. As we will see now research work has been on related aspects in political awareness.

The following are some of the works recorded in India with special reference to the role of TV.

Research work and surveys were conducted as part of follow-up of SITE done in the 1970s. After a thorough examination of the feedback, experts in the field are of the opinion that "the role of TV in the developmental support of communication as well as for mass-education has been well established. Our experience of SITE in 75-76 has indicated that acceptance of community TV was quite high in rural areas. Collective interest, common goal of TV viewing and continuous exposure to TV have emerged as important factors in breaking community barriers between different castes and groups. It could therefore be safely concluded that multiplication of community TV in village would generate an unprecedented force paving the way for a desired social change.[17]

Uma Narula presents the results of a research study done by IIMC on the trends of the recent elections in India which reveals the existence of a variety variables and complexities that guided voting decisions and behaviour of masses. In examining the role of communication channels the agenda setting role and interpersonal communication channels play a significant role in election process. Though the Indian press has played a negligible role in the education and participatory involvement of the masses in political communication it has always played a significant role in directing the public thinking to poll considerations. These considerations include caste, creed, regional biases, hero, worship, particular sympathy waves and familialties.[18]

J.S. Yadava's study is based on analysis of data collected in a nationwide study of the election campaign during the eighth parliamentary elections held in December, 1984. The main focus of the study was on media coverage campaign material and the audience reactions. The theoretical consideration here was that the election campaign helps in reinforcing and mobilizing the opinions of the electorate and not so much converting them. He says that during a period of 18 to 24 months preceding the elections the mass media serve to place the current issues of politics on the agenda of citizens discussion. Through the interplay of mass-media and interpersonal communication, the essence of major political issues gets disseminated widely among the electorate even among illiterates and those living in remote areas. As a result they form their impressions and opinions about leaders and parties. During the election campaign the contending parties and candidates try to consolidate such impressions and opinions about selected political issues in the form of their major election themes and appeals so as to convert them into actual voting in their favour as opposed to their opponents. The campaign heightens the interest of the voters in public affairs. But the voters selectively expose themselves to election information and appeals. They invariably read more news about their respective favourite political parties and leaders. They will pay greater attention to the arguments supporting their already favourite leaders, whether they are in the press, posters, public meetings or advertisements. The result is largely reinforcement and mobilisation and not much change in inclinations and opinions as such.

To this end Dr. Yadava closely observed the so called political advertising and campaign procedures adopted by each party before the elections. Dr. Yadava made an indepth observation of how much publicity material like print, electronic media, especially audio and visual cassettes were used to gain the attention of the electorate. A notable observation in the study is the consideration of prevailing mental and emotional atmosphere in the country during that period. He noted that campaigns were carried on by some parties, without any cost considerations whereas someother parties which could not compete due to lack of funds were able to make only limited use of the available modern techniques of persuasion. In his conclusion Dr. Yadava implies that effective campaigning although does not get totally accepted by the voters, it certainly helps in reinforcing the impressions and opinions that already exist in the minds of the voters.[19]

As part of the SITE an effort was made to measure the gain in political information empathy, national integration and views regarding administrative efficacy and over all political socialization. It was found that there was a statistically significant difference in the gains of the TV viewers over the control group. On the question of empathy, the hypothesis was that with exposure to television, people would be able to empathize with the different roles and it was found that the hypothesis was supported. Both male and female viewers gained significantly over the control group in empathy. On national integration, it was found that there was a significant gain here also when one takes the political socialization area as a whole inclusive of all the various subareas. One finds that only the frequent viewers had changed in a positive direction in large measure compared to the control group. The relatively lower gain of illiterate female frequent viewers perhaps indicated that rural Indian women were perhaps by and large not interested in politics. The greater gain in political socialization among illiterate males suggests that television and audiovisual media can be effective despite lack of formal education.[20]

Audience research unit of Delhi Door Darshan has conducted a survey to study the impact of political broadcasts on TV. It covered both urban and rural areas. A three phase model was used. A fixed sample of respondents were interviewed before and after telecast as well as during the telecast period. The survey was conducted at the time of 1980 Lok Sabha elections.

The report of the study says that a good majority of the respondents found the telecasts to be useful. A majority of the viewers marked the utility of such telecasts in terms of clarification of parties' programmes and policies. To some, such telecasts provided political education. Listening to these broadcasts was considerable in both the rural and urban areas. The response regarding the practical utility of these broadcasts were as follows.

— helped to identify programme and policies of various political parties.
— enabled to listen to the voices of the leaders.
— reached the illiterate masses.
— created political consciousness among the people.
— saved time and money for both the voters and the politicians.[21]

An intensive study of the communication process at village level was undertaken during the lok sabha elections in 1971 with the following objectives in view.

(1) To document all the communication events that take place during the election period in and around a village.

(2) To study the total inflow of information about the election into the village. and

(3) To investigate the channels and mechanism of spread of information within the villages.

Mandothi a village in Haryana, formed the focus of the study.

The sample study in the village revealed that the majority of the respondents first came to know the news about the forthcoming elections mainly through public meetings, party propaganda, and their kinsmen and friends in the village. Mass-media, Radio and Newspapers were of lesser significance in this regard. However, comparatively speaking, the persons belonging to the upper castes and having education, first received the news more often through the Radio than the lower castes and the Harijans and, illiterate respondents came to know about it mainly through party propaganda, kinsmen and friends.

Further it was found that the respondents were exposed to the election propaganda mainly through the public meetings. The majority (75.5%) of the respondents attended atleast one public meeting. Moreover, exposure to public meetings seemed to have induced the respondents to attend other sources of election information also.

The respondents by and large gained their knowledge and information base as a result of the election campaign. However, they were still not clear about the ideological issues involved in the elections or the programmes of the contesting parties.[22]

Operation research group is the first one in the country to undertake research on TV, starting with the first study of community television in Srinagar valley in 1974 for Information and Broadcasting Ministry and followed by a major national study on SITE for the Planning Commission in 1976. Since then, it has been conducting several studies both for TV stations as well as for advertizers. Most of them limited to Metro cities.

The third round of this national index study was carried out in 40 towns across the country, between 10th and 15th May 1986. A national quota sample of 1150 youths in the age group 18-25 years with a minimum education level of

SSC were interviewed for their views on certain current issues of national importance. Of the 1150 youth interviewed 52 percent were males.

Media Choice for News

Newspapers score over TV in all the zones except north zone as far as dependence for news is concerned. Only 13% of youth reported that they depended more on Radio for news.

Nearly 40% of the youth reported that they believe in TV news more. An equal proportion expressed that they believed more in press news.

Youth in the north and west zones believed more in the news on TV where as youth in east and south zones believed more in the news published in newspapers.

Among Radio, TV and Newspapers the dependence for news is as follows.[23]

Media Depended on for News

Zone	*Percentage depended on*			*Total*
	Radio	T V	News papers	
North	11.4	46.5	42	297
East	17.3	29.0	53.7	110
West	9.8	42.5	42.7	325
South	16.2	26.6	57.2	421
All	13.3	36.4	50.3	1153

The belief in news from Radio, TV and Newspapers is as follows.

Zone	*Percentage believing more on*			*Total*
	Radio	*T V*	*Newspapers*	
North	13.5	49.5	47.5	297
East	29.1	28.2	42.7	110
West	10.1	46.2	43.7	325
South	23.5	36.8	39.7	421
All	17.7	41.9	40.4	1153

J.S. Yadava and Zahoorul Haq in a study of coverage and treatment of the news in different media state that "Government control the media, Radio and TV and give more of the official news than the privately owned press. By official news we mean news about or relating to government. But the closer scrutiny shows that there was not much of a difference between the government owned media and the press."[24]

Audience research unit of Doordarshan Kendra, Bombay made a sample study on viewing to newscasts by citizens of Bombay. The study revealed that

(1) 100% TV viewers of Bombay view newscasts either regularly or frequently;

(2) Almost equal number of respondents (67% each) were of the opinion that coverage of political events in all the three bulletines was alright however, a little over 1/4 (26%) found it exclusive;

(3) The present frequency of current affairs was found adequate.

This study revealed that about 55% were of the view that the news and current affairs coverage was impartial and balanced.[25]

B.N. Mukherjee made an empirical study in five developing countries (India, East Pakistan, Nigeria, Chile and Israel) on the subject of mass-media and political modernity. The purpose was to analyze in detail the effects of mass media exposure on factory workers level of general information and subjective efficacy. The analysis is based on data collected from rank and file factory workers interviewed in 1963-64 under the auspices of the Harward University project on socio-cultural aspects of development. The specific objectives of the study were to determine whether. (1) There exists a direct relationship between mass-media exposure and level of general information, rather than a relationship interposed by the level of education attained by the respondent, (2) Exposure to news papers and radio function more as independent determinants of general information than as intervening variables. The analysis shows that contact of sociological studies with mass media such as Radio and newspapers has been conceptualized both as independent and as intervening variables.[26]

Dr. Yadava's assumption was that there is a noticeable association between backwardness or underprevileged condition and deprivation of communication resources. Dr. Yadava felt that the underprevileged needed (i) Information resources, (ii) Information processing capacity and (iii) The risk taking capacity.

He collected data from a few rural areas regarding exposure levels of respondent to the medium of Radio and compared this with his data on income levels of a few urban groups not exposed to mass media. He concluded his study in the following words.

"Despite many limitations, there is no alternative to the use of mass media communication if we want to reach the vast number of the underprevileged and tackle some of their immediate and pressing problems. To achieve this the media should shed their class-character and truly become media of mass education"[27].

A study was conducted by Indian Institute of Mass Communication in Mahendergarh district of Haryana with the objective to understand the utilization of mass media and interpersonal sources of communication in the rural areas.

The sample was spread over all the nine development blocks, Three villages in each of the nine blocks were selected for the study and 50-60 respondents were selected randomly from each of the selected village. In all 1374 respondents were interviewed with the help of an interview schedule.

The analysis revealed that no single media enjoyed the preference of majority of the people and a rational media mix is the most desired for reaching the masses for developmental information and messages. Training programmes seem to be gaining acceptance for imparting developmental information and education to the people[28].

Resource Utilization for Development Information Needs

Objectives. The main objective of this study is to see the patterns of information source utilization for development. Effort is made to identify the communication channels utilized for dissemination of development information to the rural masses by the government. The specific objectives are;

—The type of development information disseminated and received through these channels.

—To identify the type of additional development information that the rural masses need and the preferred channels for such information.

The analysis of the data implies that both rural and urban masses have high exposure to mass media, interpersonal and folk media channels. But utilization of these communication channels for development information is low. Masses get bulk of information which is more general in nature. A negligible percentage receive miscellaneous categories of information such as sports, international news, science, business etc. Even people demand more of general and miscellaneous type of information from mass media channels. They do not demand more of development information from mass media channels. Whatever development information they get or want the masses would prefer media channels to interpersonal channels, though in reality they only get opportunity to contact interpersonal sources to get development information. Even among interpersonal sources all the channels are not adequately utilized by the government to disseminate development information.[29]

As can be seen from the above mentioned research done in

India much has been talked about on mass-media impact at the time of elections. There are some advantages and disadvantges in relying heavily upon the evidence drawn from election campaigns alone. Ithiel-de sola pool (1963) observes that elections are among other things a laboratory. He meant by this that we usually know when an election will be held enabling researchers to prepare their field work thoroughly in advance. The form, the outcome will take the casting of votes for alternative candidates or parties—is not only known as well, but is typically exact, measurable and readily related to measures of other variables. Since that form does not change with the passage of time, findings of a succession of campaign studies can be conveniently compared with each other. And finally, since the election campaign is an occassion for the launching of intensive attempts at persuasion the researches can observe not only how voters react to the various political offerings but they can also put their theories about such processes to a stringent empirical test. But many analysts do not suppose that voting as such is the only political act worthy of study from a communication stand point. The limitations of this focus are it directs attention to short term effects (over the campaign period) at the expense of the more gradual cumulation over a large span of time of media influences on peoples political beliefs. Another is that it deals only with manifestly political messages and ignores the more diffuse but possibly more pervasive ideological implications of other forms of media content such as soapoperas, family comedies, adventure serials, advertizements etc. However, attempts were made by the researchers in the past to counteract these limitations.[30]

Although in India various aspects have been covered by a few studies, they do not give an adequate clue to a general understanding of the impact of mass media in influencing political thinking of society. A number of studies were carried out after SITE, the result of which pertained to educational, social and political aspects. It is now almost 10 years since this was done. At present some more studies are being done both in the universities and other research organisations. The results of these are not yet available.

In the light of the above, there is a need for a study dealing exclusively with political impact of TV. Towards this end, a research design has been drawn to assess the impact of TV on rural masses with special reference to their political awareness. The details of the design of the study and other related aspects are discussed in the next chapter.

REFERENCES

1. *Television and behaviour*, Ten years of scientific progress and Implications for the eighties, Vol. I, summary report by National Institute of Mental Health (From the collection of American Library, New Delhi).
2. David M. Abshire, "International Broadcasting a new dimension of Western Diplomacy", *The Washington papers No. 35*, (SAGE Publications; London, 1976), p. 18.
3. Wilson P. Dizard, *Television a world's view*, (Syracuse Press, Syracuse, 1966), p. 201.
4. Sachdeva D.R. and Vidya Bhushan, *An Introduction to sociology*, (Kitab Mahal, Allahabad, 1967), p. 592.
5. Reed H. Blake and Edwin O. Haroldsen, *A Taxanomy of concepts in Communication*,) Hastings House Publishers, New York, 1979), pp. 44-45.
6. Frank L. Kaplan, "The plight of foreign news in the United States Mass Media, An Assessment", *Gazette-XXV No. 4, 1979* from the collections of AIR Library, New Delhi, p. 30.
7. Ibid., p. 31.
8. W. Phillips Davison, "The role of communication in democracy" in *International and Intercultual Communication*, ed. Heinz-Dietrich, Fischer and John C. Merill. (Hastings House Publishers, New York, 1970), pp. 34-35.
9. Kaplan, op,, cit., pp. 30-31.
10. Richard Clutter Buck, *The Media and Political Violence*, (The Macmillan : London, 1983), p xxiv.

10. Norman Swallcw, *Factual Television*, (Focal Press: London, 1966), pp. 123-125.

11. Ibid, p. 126.

12. *BBC Hand Book, 1979*, (Published by BBC: London), p. 185.

14. U.L. Baruah, *This is All India Radio*, (Publication Division, Ministry of Information and Broadcasting: New Delhi, 1983), pp. 170-172.

15. *Wall Street Journal*, Vol. XCV No. 75.

16. Michale Gurevitch and Jay G. Blumler, *Linkage between the Mass-media and Politics*, (A model for the analysis of political communication system) (University of Leeds Press; Leeds, 1978).

17. *INSAT 1B basic information*, (Audience Research Unit: Doordarshan, New Delhi, 1984).

18. Uma Narula, "Electorate choice—a process of communication", *Communicator*, Jan. 85, (Quarterly Journal of the Indian Institute of Mass-Communications, Vol. XX No. 1), New Delhi), pp 24-25.

19. J.S. Yadava, "Campaign and voters choice: 1984 Parliamentary elections, (*Communicator*, Jan. 85, Indian Institute of Mass Communications, New Delhi), pp. 18-23.

20. *The SITE Experience*, Reports and papers on mass-communication, No. 91 (UNESCO: Paris, 1983), pp 36.

21. U.L. Baruah, *This is All India Radio* (Publication division, Ministry of I & B: New Delhi, 1983), p 179.

22. J.S. Yadava, *Communication and Parliamentary Elections (1971)*, A study in a Haryana village (Department of Research, Indian Institute of Mass Communication, New Delhi).

23. *National Television Ratings*, A study by the Operations research group, (a Private Organisation, New Delhi, 1986).

24. J.S. Yadava and Zahoorul Haq, *Coverage and Treatment of News in Different Media*, A Report by the Department of Communication Research, Indian Institute of Mass Communication, New Delhi.

25. Audience research unit, Doordarshan Kendra, Bombay (A Study on viewing to newscasts).

26. B.N. Mukharjee, *Mass Media and Political Modernity*, an empirical study of five developing countries (National Psychological Corporation: Agra, 1979).

27. J.S. Yadava, "Mass media should tackle immediate problems of the under-privileged", *Communicator, Vol. XX No. 1, April-July 1985*. (Indian Institute of Mass Communications, New Delhi).

28. Nawal Singh, *Communication and development information needs*, a study of Mahindergarh District (Haryana), (Indian Institute of Mass Communications, New Delhi, 1984).

29. Uma Narula and B.K. Kuthiala, *Resource Utilisation for Development Information needs*, (Indian Institute of Mass Communications, New Delhi, 1984).

30. Jay G. Blumler, *The political effects of mass communication*, The Audience Unit 8, The Open University—Social Sciences a third level course, (Walton Hall, Milton Keyness).

CHAPTER THREE

Methodology

This chapter is devoted for a discussion of methodology adopted in the study. In the first chapter, an historical account of the evolution of TV as an educational and cultural agency in different countries and its social significance with reference to rural areas is presented and discussed. An attempt is made in the second chapter to scan the relevant literature which includes both empirical and theoretical contributions in the area of TV and national development.

The present chapter is an attempt to develop a frame of reference for the study. There are three important components involved in the present study. They are :

1. The impact of Television
2. The political awareness
3. The rural masses

The Impact of Television

The term television is referred here as "Broadcast media" for the purpose of convenience. Only the functional use of TV has been stressed and the technical details have been excluded.

TV is commonly understood as an audio-visual medium of communication. Though TV is a piece of hardware, when combined with the extensive paraphernalia of software serves its basic function of communication. Although Radio broadcasting is older, TV with its additional advantage of visual communication has become an important component of broadcasting. For this reason even this study is concerned solely with "Broadcasting through TV" to the exclusion of Radio. Though technically the usage may be different (telecasting) the term broadcasting is used here to give one an understanding of the social usage of TV. The use of the word broadcast stems from early United States Naval reference to "broadcast" of orders to the fleet. Now it is used to describe Radio service to the Public[1].

Broadcasting is presenting information or a message to a widespread audience. The nature of broadcasting lies in its ability to cover vast areas and huge masses at one and the same time. Another important feature of the broadcasting system is its uniformity. It is somewhat official and thoroughly purpose oriented. As Hilda Matheson states Broadcasting is not a machine, though it makes use of an apparatus. But fundamentally it is a harnessing of elementary forces, a capturing of sound and voices all over the world to which hitherto we have been deaf. On one hand, broadcasting enlarges the frontiers of human interest and on the other it shrinks the earth's surface. It is a milestone in the development of communications and marks a new stage in civilization. The author further states that Broadcasting might have evolved as an answer to some need in the developing world. With the evolution of society from simple to complex, there arose an urgent need to devise an organization capable of expressing its human and economic unity. The need for rapid interchange of news and views for familiarizing each country with the ideas and habits of all other countries and above all the need for an education which may fit men and women, literates and illiterates for the complicated world of tomorrow—all these needs should find in broadcasting an instrument fitted to serve them. Like in any other invention, Broadcasting also has good and bad features. It is stimulating, constructive and valuable in so far as it can stiffen individuality and inoculate those who listen with some capacity to think, feel and understand.[2]

The technical apparatus of boardcasting here are the "Broadcasting media" namely the audio medium of Radio and the audiovisual medium of Television, though as mentioned earlier, this study deals solely with TV to the exclusion of Radio.

Coming to the impact of TV, the word Impact also needs an explanation here. In this study, the word Impact may be taken to mean "effect" or "influence". Here the concern is the effect that TV has on the society in general and on the rural masses in the particular. It is observed that the concept of studying social impact and making an assessment of it is a recent one. A reference to the systematic study of the social impact assessment (SIA) by Kurt Finsterbusch may be relevant here since it explains the importance given to this concept and the need to study the same. "As an area of applied science SIA was born with the National Environment Policy Act (NEPA) in 1969. This act requires an environmental impact statement (EIS) which evaluates impacts on the environment for all actions funded or conducted by the Federal government which significantly affect the environment. The social environment is included in the acts concept of the environment. Therefore, SIA is included in the EIS. The original purpose of NEPA was to protect the environment as much as possible from irreparable damage from public construction projects and from environmental policies. The inclusion of SIAs in EISs expand their purpose to include the protection of social units, that is individuals, households, organizations, neighbourhood and communities from adverse consequences of public actions. Social impact assessments are evaluations of policy alternatives, in terms of their estimated consequences. In the process some new alternatives and some modifications of the proposed alternatives may suggest themselves"[3].

Any action programme produced or done for the benefit of sociey must thus have a social impact. This principle may be applied in the field of communications through broadcasting also. In broadcasting the communicator is interested in ascertaining the effect he achieves on an audience with his message. The concern here is to study the effect of the message broadcast over TV, and how these messages affect the formation and functioning of the human personal and social organization. As Martin D. Carter says especially since the second world war there has been a great deal of anxiety over the effect that the mass-media may have on the community and the individual they exist to serve and entertain. The media and especially TV have become the focus of attention.[4]

The effects of Broadcasting can be many and different. The impact of any message that is given by the communicator may require to be measured through the questions like whether people paid any attention to the message and understood it, whether it has changed their opinions, whether they felt it useful, whether they have reacted as a result of it etc.

Since human behaviour is very complicated and unpredictable, measurement or scaling is a difficult task faced by the researcher. Here no amount of imagination or intution is acceptable however shrewed one may be. Various tools have been developed by experts in the field of communication research to measure the impact of programmes broadcast by TV.

The effects of broadcasting may be of two types. Some are short term and other long depending on the goals or aims of the programmes. The same rule applies to the field of political awareness. For example, news bullettins on election results serve a short term purpose, whereas a programme on adult education is a long term scheme to remove illiteracy.

Political Awareness

According to Peter H. Merkl, politics is a process at work everywhere and continuously in the smallest groups as well as among great powers on the international level. He says that the origin of the word 'politics' and 'political' began with the emergence of the 'polis' i.e., the "city-state", community of ancient Greece. Thinkers like Plato and Aristotle and many of their Greek contemporaries felt that the affairs of the polis as worth being framed into a scientific subject. They observed that the participation of the individual in the life of the polis and felt it a necessary condition for human self realization. The politics of other communities outside the city, state of ancient Greece were looked down upon as being too barbarian even for consideration. In line with this, there was little distinction between public and private affairs of the individuals community life. All behaviour of the citizens had a political cannotation. After the rise of multinational empires such as those of Alexander the Great, the words politics and political came nearer in scope and meaning to their current usage. Public and private life was clearly distinguished. A cosmopolitan attitude replaced narrow communal feelings. Political activities were markedly different from educational, religious or military activities. The political body or state became just one more of the several communities in which an individual might be a member.

According to him, several schools of thought contribute to the meaning of politics and also take from it. Thus there is a historical origin of politic and a geographical explanation for its emergence. There is a grain of truth in such claims but it is a fallacy to claim that all politics is due to a single cause alone. There are a few implicit things in politics and they are the existence of freewill, the essential freedom of choice and the freedom to change things.[5]

Describing politics as the first comprehensive study of the political system Alwin J. Rubinstein and Garold W. Thumm say that the state or the political institute is an association with a pre-determined goal. The Statesmen or politikos who handle the affairs of the state are not the same as the monarch of a kingdom. They are trustees of state's political system.[6]

Analyzing the texts on British politics, Colin Leys says that British thinkers discussed politics in the light of institutions through which a particular segment of political life where Parliamentary party competetion, and the conduct of Government are carried on.[7]

Eric Rowe observes the political system as a part of the social system which forms one branch of the social institution. Thus political activity can be found in all aspects of social life. There may be links to economic, religious, educational patterns in the society. But the political system may be isolated from economic and other systems for the purpose of definitions and analysis.[8]

Roy V. Peel and Joseph S. Rousek say that politics is usually defined as the science and art of government and as such covers the entire field of political life and behaviour.[9] The 'Chambers Every day Dictionary's' meaning of the word politics as the science of government also supports the above definition.[10]

Peel vividly describes the practical nature of politics "As distinguished from government, politics is the art of the pratical and the science of actual things. Government is defined as a society of men and women who have accepted a set of rules governing their status and relationships. It is ofcourse also the apparatus of governance. The buildings, the personnel, the materials, the supplies, the regulations and the routines whereby the whole system functions. The portion of it which is confined to the applications of Laws we call administration but since we have learned that no administration exists which may be divorced from politics, politics includes administration within the scope of its interest."[11]

In our context, an awareness of or even a bare minimum consciousness of politics can be called "political awareness". We often hear phrases like "I do not believe politics", "he is above politics" and "we keep out of politics". These phrases denote a distaste for the subject. But they do definitely indicate an awareness of what the subject implies, thereby indicating a political awareness among the very people who dislike it. Hence to attend to the "arrangements" of political institutions means firstly to learn the type of activity. Politics makes a call upon individual knowledge. This in turn necessiates education and political education.

An individual begins his learning at home. The process is

called socialization. Here socialization may be understood, to be the art of the making a man fit in this society. When learning has a social relevance it becomes socialization. Barrie Stacey explains political socialization as a process by which the values, beliefs and emotions of a political culture are passed on to succeeding generations. The process starts at an early age and continues through out life. The institutions of family, school, church, work groups, political parties and so on being its agencies.[12] In this context Mukhopdhayaya says that the process by which political culture is shaped at the individual level and at the community level is passed on from generation to generation is called political socialization. Political socialization shapes and transmits a nation's political cultrue.[13]

Grace Jones defines political socialization as a process of initiation into the traditions and dominant values of the political system. She also argues that political socialization experiences are not irrevocable and they do not necessarily pre-determine specific political choices by the adult throughout his life. The individual continues to undergo new experiences and is capable of change."[14]

It is generally believed that unless a person has the knowledge of the programmes that are being implemented he will not develop the required attitude in order to adopt them. Therefore, gaining knowledge is one of the prerequisite for the subsequent process of development. In view of this, the information giving process must be thorough in order to make the target people understand the nature and scope of whatever programmes that are implemented for their benefit. Knowledge of the programmes is generally disseminated either through the extension system in developmental block or through mass-media like Radio. Newspapers, and recently Television.

Mukhopadhyaya says that the importance of Mass-media as an agent of political socialization depends on which type of social setting it operates. The social setting may be rural or urban and the particular type of people is a factor which determinent of the way in which a person would interpret and react to the performance by the mass-media.[15]

In this study the main concern is to assess as to what degree a person has become "politically concious" through the Television medium.

Rural Masses

Although it is hard to define the word 'rural', a general understanding is possible with respect to what may be termed a rural community. M.C. Whitby et. al. say that "rural areas might be defined simply as those in which agriculture and forestry are the predominant form of productive economic activity". In today's understanding what is not urban is understood to be rural. Thus it is easier to conceive a rural area in comparison with the urban area.[16] It is observed that what is urban in one country may not appear to be convincingly so in another. In United States for example communities of less than 2,500 persons are usually classed as rural.[17] Describing the demographic features of rural India, S. Bala Krishna says that a place with 200 inhabitants or more is declared as a town in Green Land, Sweedon and Faeroe Islands (besides other indicators in the latter two cases) where as the minimum population required for a place to be declared as a town in Japan (apart from other indicators) is as high as 30,000. All the same certain broad criteria are followed by various countries of the world for the purpose of defining an urban area. These are administrative, local government, ecological economic and urban characteristics. Following the non-uniform definitions of a rural area it is found that 61% of the world's population lives in rural areas (1975). The corresponding percentages for more developed and less developed countries are 31 and 73 respectively. It will be seen that the developed countries are highly urbanized whereas the developing countries are mostly rural based. At present (1981) 76.69% of the population in India live in rural areas. This percentage was 89 at the turn of the century and the decline has been relatively more rapid since independence.[18]

In addition to population, as a main feature of distinction between rural and urban, certain observable differences in behaviour also enable us to make some valid distinctions. For example, the pattern of interaction appears to be an important criterion to distinguish a rural from an urban community. According to Alwin L. Bertrand, powerful kinship relations mark a rural community.[19] This context Alan W. Childs and Gary B. Melton say that as a psyhcological construct, ruralness might of course be defined on the basis of the attitudes and values typically held by people living in rural communities. As they are differentiated from urban dwellers rural people are said to be (relative to urban people) conservative, religious, work-oriented, intolerant of diverse ideas, familistic, individualistic, fatalistic and so forth. There is some evidence to support the contention that there are real differences in these values between urban and rural populations. For example, there is evidence that dissemination of new knowledge tends to occur relatively slowly in rural cultures.[20]

The discussion can be concluded with an observation made by Whitby et al. that the behavioural characteristics which distinguish rural and urban residents are no longer to be observed. Increased personal mobility, larger income and exposure to the universal communications media, press, radio and TV have tended to result in the two groups having similar if not identical social view points and habits. It is thus becoming increasingly difficult to exactly separate a rural and urban community. It has to be understood only in the context in which it has been used[21].

Coming to masses the word 'masses' denotes large number of people. Analysts, regard the word 'mass' as a somewhat emotional term. According to them there are in fact no masses. Mass denotes collectivity i.e., "a collection of individuals not identical but related".

Masses are not an impersonal mob. Their personalities are not submerged in a crowd. A very large group is called a mass. Individual counting per head is generally difficult. In this context broadcasting is meant for the masses. Here masses can be understood as all people put together. Masses is a vast ocean of people who serve as the target audience for broadcasting. Masses, compared to groups are strong and powerful. Mass that originates from the rural background may be known as rural masses.

Hypotheses

Based on the above discussions the study broadly attempts to know certain relationships that may be present between different variables. The following hypotheses have been formulated to test these relationships and their nature.

1. Television can have greater impact on rural masses as compared to other media of mass communications.
2. There is a positive relationship between the degree of exposure to Television programmes and the political awareness of rural masses.
3. The subvariables namely Caste, Sex, Occupation, Education, Social participation and Age have a significant influence on the levels of political awareness of rural masses.

Keeping the above formulated hypotheses in view the study has been designed.

Discussion of the Variables and other Sub-variables in this Study

In this study two types of variables namely independent and dependent are clearly distinguishable. The TV programmes are taken to be independent variables where as their impact on the rural masses especially in their political awareness is a dependent variable. The said impact again may vary according to the age, sex, caste, education, occupation and social participation of the individuals which act as independent sub-variables. These variables influence changes observed in the political awareness of the rural masses. Hence political awareness becomes the dependent variable.

While discussing sub-variables, even the most general observation would be that in any society there exists a definite stratification. These strata help to identify the variables, that influence a person's beliefs, attitudes or awareness towards a particular issue. So also political awareness is influenced by certain factors, such as age, sex, education, occupation and social participation. These factors, take on a more significant role in a rural background. Here, other factors also such as caste, religion, economic status play an important part in influencing a person's political awareness. The expected influence of each subvariable independently may be analyzed as follows :

Age. The first thing here is that with age comes experience and maturity. This is probably why a minimum age is fixed for all citizens for all purposes including voting. For example, a person who is 40 years of age would have seen the rise and fall of several governments. He may attribute his own reason for such happenings but what matters here is the experience and maturity, that is gained thereafter which guides a person's opinion. With this frame of mind he exposes himself to political programmes and messages given by the different media.

Although age gives one a very special mature kind of thinking it limits one's participation. For example, we normally see youth participating actively in all the fields, particularly in politics.

Sex. In this aspect there is a general opinion among analysts that politics is a male concern. It is generally observed that women show less interest in politics compared to the other sex. This may be on account of the fact that males are more exposed to outside world where as women confine themselves to the household activities in our society. Though media of mass communication like Press, Radio and TV are bringing the world into the home, it is everybody's observation that women are less advanced in political matters with few exceptions. Hence it can be said that these differences may have an influence in receiving political messages.

Education. One might think education makes one politically aware and improves his understanding and involvement. Education helps in the understanding of political messages that are given over the different media. If we observe the present day politics, it is not only the educated but also others who are participating equally in politics. We also often hear about the apathy among educated towards politics.

Therefore, keeping the above in view, it may be expected that education as a variable may influence political awareness eitherway.

Caste. Caste and community structure is very pronounced in rural areas as compared to urban. Generally, caste makes itself obvious in all activities of people. Where the media are concerned, the broadcast media gives information or political messages which do no touch upon the caste.

The studies conducted on rural masses after Sattellite Instructional Television Experiment (SITE) have explained the role of caste in rural environment[22]. J.S. Yadava's "Communication and Parliamentary Election (1971)" study also examined caste as an influencing factor in rural communities.[23] It is generally noticed that even in the present day politics, the influence of caste has its own impact. Since the present study is on rural masses it may be presumed that caste may influence the political awareness of the sample.

Occupation. A person's occupation may also have a marked influence on his/her political knowledge. For example, a business man is in close contact with his political contemporaries to know about changes in his everyday dealings. The educationists and professionals are aware of political situations with the help of the education at hand. The factory workers and labour leaders are in constant touch with politics through their unions. Likewise, there are also certain occupations where there is little scope for the promotion of political awareness. Thus it can be assumed that occupation is an important factor in affecting political communication.

Economic or Financial Status. This simply means that a person with more money has more amenities, for example, a TV to spend his evenings or learn about the Worlds around him. A man with resources can venture into schemes for educating himself, his children and family. He has money to better his farm methods or improve his techniques in Industry. Financial status gives a person the confidence to meet people and know things. He has the scope to improve his knowledge day-to-day regarding political events, situations, opportunities in education, markets in business or trade etc.

Social Participation. This is highly dependent on one's personality. How much he can push himself in society with membership in social organisations etc., matters a lot in judging what that person becomes. Even a friendly chat with a neighbour, a regular game of chess in the club in the evenings or a membership in the co-operative credit society, all come under' 'exposure' to the world. Exposure gives knowledge about the world. This is what is required also for political awareness.

Methodology

This study has been conducted primarily with the help of the interview schedule. An interview schedule has been selected because the sample chosen constitutes the rural population, who are illiterates or semi-educated and hence unable to read a questionnaire or answer it in the written form on their own. (The Interview Schedule is included in the thesis as Appendix).

Firstly, a pilot study was conducted and the type or response from this sample called for a four-point scale. Thus a four point scale was decided upon as total, major, minor and nil—these being the scale for the measurement of the different levels of political awareness. The entire study therefter has been done in the interview schedule pattern. Questions were asked orally and the respondent's answers were noted.

The interview schedule has been divided into five sections.

Section-I. Pertains to details regarding the respondent's socio-economic status, and this was related to the level of political awareness.

Section II. Pertains to the degree of exposure to the different media whether the respondent has a TV set, his programme preferences, amount of time spent in being exposed to the media etc. Questions pertaining to the categorisation of programmes—educational, recreational and political—the category of programme for which the degree of exposure is greatest or maximum were also included in this section.

Section III. Pertains to questions on exposure to News, language problems faced if any, which news is preferred etc. This section tries to assess the political awareness gained from News.

Section IV. Pertains to question on current affairs. Certain topical programmes were mentioned to see the degree of interest or asses the awareness.

Section V. Deals with some miscellaneous questions on programmes over TV. Questions were framed to know the choice of media as a source of information and also suggestions from their end were invited.

Identification of Programmes

News and current affairs have been identified as the two major programmes on political education. News is a regular programme while current affairs is a programme concerned with topical and sea sonal issues.

News. News in Telugu comes on Hyderabad TV evryday or ten minutes at 7.30 PM. In addition, Hyderabad TV relays two news bulletins one in Hindi and one in English each of twenty minutes duration. Relay of morning news bulletins in both Hindi and English with ten minutes duration of each has begun with effect from 23.2.1987.

An analysis of the content of regional news and othe political programmes is given below.[24]

The ten minute regular bulletin gives National and International news (40%) and Regional News (60%). This percentage allotment was the reverse hitherto and changed only recently.

National news covers central news and news about major developments in other states.

National News — 35%

International News	—	5%

In the 5% International news, the coverage is on major developments that have bearing on International peace, India's relations with other countries and human rights.

Regional News Covers :

Economic (developmental) News	—	10%
Political News	—	20%
Sports News	—	15%
Cultural and Religious News	—	10%
Miscellaneous	—	5%

This percentage margin is flexible depending on the season, i.e., current events and issues are alloted more time in the bulletin. For example, election results during elections, sports during important national and international competition, Parliament/Assembly coverage during the sessions.

Coverage. The activities of the President, Prime Minister, Governor and Chief Minister are given primary importance in the regional news followed by the major activities of the other Cabinet members of the state.

Coverage in the news bulletin also reflects the opinion of different political parties on major political issues, their policy statements, and public demonstrations on various issues.

News coverage on riots and violence is generally not given prominence in a bulletin in the belief that such news triggers off more violence. Only the most important and necessary bits are presented. Reporting of major political events is a common thing, for example, the President's tour or the Prime Minister's tour, the, 'Mahanadu' etc.

News Presentation. A script is prepared based on the contents in the news and then presented. Film coverages are given whereever possible and if this is not available, stills, paper cuttings, graphics or hand-written slides are shown.

Where indepth coverage is not possible in the short time of news, documentaries are prepared and presented in detail (a film with background voice reporting or describing the activity).

Current Affairs

Assembly News. This is given during the season. 30 to 35% news is on the questions and answers discussed, bills, other incidents including controversies and walk-outs. TV news correspondent covers and reports in detail these sessions. Other news agencies also contribute such news if required.

Party Political Broadcasts. This is common during election time all over the country.

Special Election Bulletin. This is also common all over the country at the time of election. No election analysis is given at the state level.

Budget Broadcasts. At the central level, this is given in Hindi and English. Only highlights are given in the regional news bulletins. A cross-section of people are taken for interview to know the public opinion about the budget. At the state level, regional news gives in detail the statement of accounts, allocation of funds for projects, etc.

Voting. This is another programme that gives political education on the voting system. During election time, people are educated with regard to the value of their vote etc.

Measuring Awareness

A person's awareness or knowledge about a given thing is abstract, that is it does not easily come to a scale of measurement like the length and breadth or weight of given thing, or even the IQ levels in Intelligence tests. A person's awareness of a given thing is revealed only after seeing his response to certain objective questions. In fact, some deviation from the objective, towards related facts or ideas is also required in order to learn about the person's awareness. Measuring awareness directly then is a difficult task. Awareness cannot to judged or measured just by asking a question or two. All people do not have one and the same degree of awareness about a certain thing. There is difference in levels of awareness. This is why four levels of awareness have been fixed in the interview schedule—total, major, minor and nil. This is the four point scale fixed for the study, to measure awareness.

The concern here is to see what or how much TV contributes to this awareness. The TV is also an institution which has the objective of educating the public. The difference is that it also imparts non-formal education. The teacher in a classroom prepares lesson plan and goes about with specific objectives, while the students take down notes and build up their knowledge step by step. Such formal education is not done by the TV. Here it is the non-formal education with far-sighted and broad objectives. The ultimate goal however is to impart knowledge and increase the general awareness among the public.

Although TV does not follow the step by step pattern of formal education, it does follow the main levels in education —i.e., cognitive, connative and affective. These three domains are covered in the levels of awareness taken in our scale. Here it may be asked why the domains themselves were not fixed for the scale. The reason is that domain testing of awareness is possible only if the different programmes of TV are categorised accordingly. The education given by TV is on a mass scale with very broad objective. Also, this varies with the changing seasons. Although the education given is planned only with the domains in view, it is received by the masses each at their own level of understanding, for example. International News given by TV. The four levels taken are

(a) We will be knowing the trade relations between our country and the other countries (4)

(b) The overall global scene can be known (3)

(c) Foreign personalities are now familiar to me (2)

(d) not useful (1)

The respondent's answer was identified in one of the scales. If there was also a different kind of answer it was also taken in an open end form. Hence the scaling is also flexible, to accommodate other opinions.

Information about the Sample Selected for the Study

The Ranga Reddy district of Andhra Pradesh in the Telangana region has been selected for the study. The reason being that people in this region are sufficiently exposed to TV programmes for a long time and also the government has installed several TV sets in this region.

In 1976 SITE was conducted in India and Andhra Pradesh (Telangana region) was one of the main centres selected for the experiment. Soon after this experiment, which was in fact a study for a period of one year, India introduced TV nationwide. Thus the rural masses of Telangana had the benefit of continuity immediately after their exposure to TV through SITE. Although one of two transmitters were installed in other places of Andhra Pradesh, the people were not receiving Telugu programmes.

Now it is not even a year since transmitters were introduced all over Andhra Pradesh. These transmitters are relaying Telugu programmes but the reception is limited to a small area around these transmitters. The government has not specifically provided any TV sets in the villages after the recent installation of transmitters.

The INSAT scheme covers Mahaboobnagar, Medak and Ranga Reddy districts of Telangana region. The Government as a part of the scheme provided TV sets in these villages. The programmes in this scheme are limited to 45 minutes in the morning and 35 minutes in the evening. These programmes are totally rural-based.

Our concern is regarding programmes that give political awareness to the people. These programmes are news and current affairs. Only the rural areas of the Ranga Reddy District of the Telangana region of Andhra Pradesh have been receiving Telugu News since five years. All villages in the Ranga Reddy District are provided with TV sets in the INSAT scheme. The Mahaboobnagar and Medak districts did not have the same degree of exposure to News as the Ranga Reddy district had.

The Ranga Reddy district has the benefit of long time exposure to political programmes as well as all other programmes since the year of SITE. This induced the villagers to buy private sets, and TV viewing became a regular feature among these people. This is mainly the reason for selecting these people as the sample for this study. If we had to depend only on the community TV sets, the study would have posed problems, because if there was a breakdown due to repair or failure these sets do not function at all. At such times, the meagre few who owned a private set entertain some of the other villagers who depended on the community sets. To such people, TV viewing became irregular and their exposure limited.

It may be questioned here that the villages chosen for the sample are too near to the city of Hyderabad and the people may have urban influence, thus becoming a biased sample. But the aforesaid limitations are more severe, i.e., the long time exposure to TV especially political awareness oriented programmes and individual TV sets are a must for this study. If these are not available, the study have been a futile excercise.

Secondly, for technical reasons the installation of transmitters is done only in cities and towns. The transmission reaches the limited areas around these transmitters. Such areas would also have city or town influence. Hence, even these districts would have been a biased sample. For this reason the "urban influence" part had to be met with either way.

To overcome the urban influence the study has been done in progressively interior villages leaving out those immediately near to the city. Also some villages have been left out for the reason that already political life and participation is great there.

Again, the villages of Ranga Reddy District are agriculture-based. The people here are mainly agricultural labourers or land tillers. This is a chief factor which makes a people 'rural'.

The villages selected were Pedda Amberpet, Injapur, Torrur, Turaka Yamjal, Koheda, Kompalli, Chevella, Muhammedabad, Gandeed and Reddi palli.

As said earlier, distance was taken as a measure to limit the urban influence. In Ranga Reddy district the number of private Television sets has gradually decreased as the distance from the Hyderabad city increased. This is due to the poor reception in distant areas.

In Muhammedabad there are only 5 to 6 TV sets, where as in Gandeed and Reddi palli the number of TV sets are 1 and 2 respectively. In other villages there exist TV sets ranging between 10 and 20. The Government TV sets in almost all sample villages seldom work and are under repairs.

Respondents of 21 and above age only were selected for sample since this age limit is a pre-requisite for a person to cast his vote. The harm of a voter casting his vote without political awareness is more severe as compared to a non-voter.

Attempt was made to take men and women in equal ratio, but unfortunately only seventy (out of a total of 200) women have come forward after a great persuasion. Twenty from each village could be drawn with great difficulty for reasons such as less number of TV sets, hesitation to express and other reasons.

As far as possible, one person from one house was choosen to represent different socio-economic background. Though different cross section of people were tried, the sample for Scheduled Tribe was nil, and as regards scheduled Castes very few were available. This is because the Scheduled castes do not own any TV sets and other caste people generally do not encourage them to watch their TVs and also because the government TV sets are generally out of order.

The data as regards to the population, area, literacy etc. of each village is shown in the following table.

As compared to the other regions of the state, Telangana

can be regarded as a backward area since this region was under the regime of Nizam, where the people were deprived of educational facilities for a considerably long period. Since the medium of instruction as also the official language was Urdu only six out of a hundred were literates at that time[25]. However, many political movements took place in the area in the past. Mass media especially Poetry, Folklore and recently newspapers have played a significant role in these political movements. Television is a new medium and its impact is yet to be assessed.

The study has been conducted in the above mentioned villages covering different corners of the Ranga Reddy district. The date collected was tabulated and put to statistical tests. The analysis of the obtained values according to different categories of programmes and other observations during the study are presented in the following chapter.

Area and Population Particulars of the Sample Villages**

Village	*Area in Sq.KM.*	*Population*					*Literates**	
		Men	*Women*	*Total*	*SC*	*ST*	*Men*	*Women*
1. Amberpet	16.14	1503	1334	3837	632	6	620	239
2. Koheda	36.98	2717	2512	5227	892	16	870	300
2. Turaka Yamjal	20.52	1902	1788	3690	712	50	560	218
4. Torrur	9.74	1757	1746	3503	528	Nil	560	151
5. Injapur	4.39	1002	951	1953	613	5	439	115
6. Chevella	12.05	1634	1042	3036	618	13	725	251
7. Kompally	10.77	1617	1525	3142	595	134	515	220
8. Gandeed	9.04	1158	1116	2274	564	14	376	92
9. Mohammadabad	46.98	4200	4168	8368	903	673	1572	629
10. Reddipalli	5.26	668	694	1362	—	130	177	67

Villages from Sl. No. 1 to 5 comes under Hayatnagar mandal.

Village at Sl. No. 6 is under Chevella mandal.
Village at Sl. No. 7 is under Kutbullapur mandal.

The remaining villages i.e. from Sl. no. 8 to 10 falls under Gandeed mandal.

*Literate : A person who can both read and write with understanding in any language is to be taken as literate. A person who can merely read but cannot write is not literate. It is not necessary that a person who is literate should have received any formal Education or should have passed any minimum Educational standard (*Census of India 1981* Series-I India Part II A (I), p 97).

***Mandala Gananka Darshani*, Ranga Reddy District, A.P. State, August 1985.

REFERENCES

1. Charles S. Steinberg, Ed., *Mass Media and Communication*, (Hastings House Publishers : New York, 1972), p 243.
2. Hilda Matheson, *Broadcasting* (Thornton Butterworth Ltd; London 1933), pp 14 and 16.
3. Kurt Finsterbusch, *Understanding Social Impacts—Assessing the Effects of Public Projects*, Vol. 110, (SAGE: London, 1980), pp 13-14.
4. Martin D. Carter, *An Introduction to Mass-Communication and Problems in Press and Broadcasting* (Macmillan: London, 1971).
5. Peter, H. Merkl, *Political Continuity and Change*, (Allied Publishers: New Delhi, 1975), pp 7-9.
6. Alwin J. Rubinstein and Garold W. Thumm, *The Challenge of politics, ideas and issues*, (Prentice Hall: New Jersey, 1963), pp 5-6.
7. Colin Leys, *Politics in Britain* (Verso: London 1986).
8. Eric Rowe, *Modern Politics, An introduction to behaviour and institutions*, (Humanities Press: London 1969).
9. *Introduction to Politics*, ed, Roy V. Peel and Joseph S. Roucek (Thomas Y. Crowell Company 1941) pp 108-109.
10. *Chambers Everyday Dictionary* (Arnold Heinemann Publishers, New Delhi, 1975), p 557.

11. *Introduction to Politics*, op. cit., pp 108-109.
12. Barrie Stacey, *Political Socialization in Western Society—An analysis from a life span perspective* (Arnold Heinemann (India), New Delhi, 1978, p 2.
13. Mukhopadhyay, Amal Kumar, *Political Sociology*, (K.P. Bagchi & Co: Calcutta, 1977) p 103.
14. Grace Jones, *The political structure*, (Longman: London, 1976).
15. Mukhopadhyay, op. cit., p 117.
16. M.C. Whitby et al., *Rural resource development, an economic approach*, (Methuen and Co.: London, 1978), pp 7-8.
17. Alwin L. Bertrand, *Basic Sociology*, (Appleton-Century-Crofts: New York, 1973), pp 423-424.
18. S. Bala Krishna, "Some Demographic Features of Rural India", *Rural Development in India Some Facets* (National Institute of Rural Development : Hyderabad, 1981), pp 55-56.
19. Alwin L. Bertrand, op. cit., pp 423-424.
20. *Rural Psychology*—Ed. Alan W. Childs and Gary B. Melton, (Plenum Press: New York, 1983), p 5.
21. M.C. Whitby et al., *Rural resource development*, (an economic approach), (Methuen and Co. Ltd., London, 1978.
22. *The SITE experience*, Reports and papers on mass communication No. 91 (UNESCO: Paris, 1983), p 26.
23. J.S. Yadava, *Communication and Parliamentary Election (1971)*. A study in a Haryana village (Indian Institute of Mass Communications, New Delhi), p 74.
24. News Unit, Doordarshan, Hyderabad (From an interview with the staff).
25. Varavara Rao, *Telangana Vimochanodyamam—Telugu Navala Samaja Sahitya Sambandhalu.*

CHAPTER FOUR

Analysis and Interpretation

Television is now not entirely a new experience to many of us. We are very much familiar with its day to day political programmes. Television has given extensive visual coverage to the recent political events. All national and International political figures are now more familiar to us and we watch them almost in blood and flesh. As said by Tom Wicker people who once had been too isolated to know much of what was happening in the great world had become engaged with public affairs; people who had found the news an irrelevant bore saw it transformed by the power of television in to fascinating visual terms. In the sixties and seventies every survey showed that most Americans got the news first from television and automobile radio. The broadcast media, therefore had taken over the front page function of newspapers (except for "exclusive" stories they independently developed, which were not available to broadcasters)[1].

Though television ranks high in its potential to present political material in an impressive way than other media, we hear a lot of criticism about it among urban viewers and intellectuals. Many criticize Indian Television for its over emphasis on the Government's programmes and ruling party's activities. and thus doubt its efficacy in representing and therefore shaping public opinion. People with individual political thinking use the broadcast media only to get on hand information rather than as a reliable source.

With all its merits and demerits, Television continues to project its political programmes and people are viewing them regularly. Hence, taking considerable note of these criticisms, an attempt has been made in this study to know how far the political programmes on our Television are reaching the masses, their reception of political content, impressions, opinions and assess its potency and utility as a means of educational or recreational medium for the rural folk.

The study was conducted during the period between the village Mandal elections and Cooperative Society elections i.e. between 1986 and 1987, But no impact of such atmosphere was observed among the respondents. It was noticed that they did not link their local issues to Television's political coverage. Some respondents, however, suggested that the facility of pre-election party broadcasts should also be extended to Mandal elections.

The data have been analyzed and presented in the form of tables in this chapter. Different aspects of political broadcasting have been separately analyzed. An attempt has been made to locate in which area Television's role was more effective and in which area the effect was limited. The possible reasons for the differences have been discussed. For the sake of convenience the analysis and interpretation has been divided into five parts. The first part deals with the general impact of Television i.e. degree of exposure to Television, programme preference, time spent and other media habits. The second part relates to Television and political programming. The third part seeks to investigate whether the sub-variables such as age, sex, caste, education, occupation and social participation etc. have any influence on the political awareness of the sample. The fourth part reflects the mean score analysis and relationship between political awareness and certain selected aspects. The final part envisages the correlation and regression coefficients of awareness.

PART-I

Ownership of Television set etc.

Being a costly item, owning a Television set is considered a luxury, especially in villages. The problems related to providing Television sets in the rural areas by the Government have been discussed in the first chapter. In the sample study, 60% of the respondents have their own Television sets (Table-1). Inspite of the fact that the villagers are nearer to the urban areas and have been receiving Television programmes for more than a decade, a good percentage of them (40%) do not have sets of their own.

All the respondents of the study are regular viewers of Television programmes (Table-2).

60.5% view television in their own houses whereas 28% watch Television in the neighbouring houses (Table-3). People who watch TV in community centres constitute 11.5% only. The respondents who watch TV in others' houses are forward caste and backward caste people. It would appear that the scheduled caste people are generally not allowed to watch TV in others' houses, and so it is these people who come to community centres (where the Government provides TV sets) to watch television programmes.

However, since the Television sets in community centres may be going out of order quite often, the exposure of the scheduled caste groups regularly to various programmes may be limited. Some of the scheduled caste people however, had continuous exposure and access to TV viewing as they were themselves the employees in the community centres.

For the last one decade, the weaker sections have become habituated to view Television sets provided by the Government. Some of the respondents have even given an impression that it is the responsibility of the government to provide a community Television set, and also to see that it is kept in working condition. The villagers also complained about the undue delay in repairing the Television sets when they go out of order.

TABLE 1

Distribution of the Respondents According to Ownership of Television

		Yes	*No*	*Total*
Male	Fre	64	66	130
	%	49.23	50.77	
Female	Fre	56	14	70
	%	80.00	20.00	
Total	Fre	120	80	200
	%	60.00	40.00	

Fre. : Frequency—% : Percentage

TABLE 2

Distribution of the Respondents According to Exposure to TV (Whether they see TV or not)

		Yes	*No*	*Total*
Male	Fre	130	—	130
	%	100.00	—	
Female	Fre	70	—	70
	%	100.00	—	
Total	Fre	200	—	200
	%	100.00	—	

Fre. : Frequency – % : Percentage

TABLE 3

Distribution of the Respondents According to Place of Viewing

		At home	*At community centre*	*At others' places*	*Total*
Male	Fre	65	20	45	130
	%	50.00	15.38	34.62	
Female	Fre	56	3	11	70
	%	80.00	4.29	15.71	
Total	Fre	121	23	56	200
	%	60.5	11.5	28.00	

Fre. : Frequency—% : Percentage

Further, some villagers expressed the opinion that although some of the scheduled caste people could afford a Televsion set, they would not like to show off their status and position before other communities by owning a luxury item like Television which may deprive them in claiming various government benefits that are available for the poor section in the villages.

Time spent before TV

The amount of time spent daily before Television is an important aspect to be considered in assessing the influence of the medium. The respondents could not definitely say the actual time they spend before the television. However, six time intervals have been framed depending on the information obtained (Table-4). More than half i.e. 56.5% watch TV daily for one hour. Those who watch TV for two hours constitute 9.5%. 23% of the sample spend 2 to 3 hours before TV. The

TABLE 4

Distribution of the Respondents According to Time-Spent Before Television

		1 hr	2 hrs	2 to 3 hrs	3 to 4 hrs	4 and above	depends on programme	Total
Male	Fre	73	7	36	5	4	5	130
	%	56.15	5.38	27.69	3.85	3.08	3.85	
Female	Fre	40	12	10	1	5	2	70
	%	57.14	17.14	14.29	1.43	7.14	2.86	
Total	Fre	113	19	46	6	9	7	200
	%	56.5	9.5	23.00	3.00	4.5	3.5	

Fre. : Frequency — % : Percentage

percentage under the other three time intervals is negligible i.e. below 5%. All the villagers tune the sets from the beginning of the transmission. This may not mean that they watch the whole transmission. According to them, the actual watching depends on their convenience and programme preferences. Men sit before TV during regional news time and watch programmes around that time. Women prefer entertainment programmes, including features spread over as serials, features films, film songs and other cultural programmes.

As seen from the responses, more than half of the people covered by the sample, view television for one hour a day. Here it may be noticed that there is a wide difference between second and third range. The persons in the 2 to 3 hours range are those who keep their TV sets tuned from 7 to 10 pm and watch items of their choice. The sample also include people who watch television for limited periods like 15 minutes, 20 minutes or even 30 minutes. These people have been categorized in the last range.

Impact of TV on other Audio-Visual Media :

It is understood that when compared to other media of mass communication TV is more attractive. In order to know whether TV has affected Radio listening and movie going certain questions have been asked. All the villagers (including the scheduled castes) interviewed have Radio sets. It is observed that the respondents who do not have their own TV sets are mostly dependent on the Radio for various programmes though they go out to watch television for a short period.

67% of the sample switchover to Radio either when Television transmission is not available or when they tune off the TV (Table-5). Usually they listen to radio during morning and afternoon. Thus 33% listen to Radio during television transmission also. Most of these respondents are those who do not possess their own TV sets. A mere 4 to 5 respondents who have TV sets said that they would tune to Radio for certain programmes (like Tuesday Drama) even when Television transmission is on.

Though Radio also presents varied programmes, most of the villagers preferred TV to Radio during evenings. In addition to the visual impact the other reason for preferring television is that they are habituated to use this particular medium every evening. Instead of switching over to Radio in the middle they prefer to continue viewing television for all sorts of programmes including NEWS. Another limitation that was pointed out was that "they could not pay attention to both the media simultaneously".

TABLE 5

Distribution of the Respondents According to Influence of TV on Radio Listening

		Yes	*No*	*Total*
Male	Fre	58	72	130
	%	44.62	55.38	
Female	Fre	8	62	70
	%	11.43	88.57	
Total	Fre	66	134	200
	%	33.00	67.00	

Fre. : Frequency—% : Percentage

Out of a total of ten villages only two have cinema theatres. People in other villages have to necessarily come to the city to see the movies. It is generally said that the TV has reduced the movie house attendance by giving atleast three feature films in a week. Few questions were put to know to what extent this was true (Table-6). 89% of the respondents are in the

TABLE 6

Distribution of the Respondents According to Influence of TV on Movie Going Habit

		a		b					
		Yes	*No*	*Yes*	*No*	*To a large extent*	*To some extent*	*Nill*	*Total*
Male	Fre	113	17	58	55	25	33	55	130
	%	86.92	13.08	44.61	42.31	22.13	29.20	48.67	
Female	Fre	65	5	57	8	37	20	8	70
	%	92.86	7.14	81.43	11.43	56.92	30.77	12.31	
Total	Fre	178	22	115	63	62	53	63	200
	%	89.00	11.00	57.5	31.5	31.00	26.5	31.5	

Fre. : Frequency — % : Percentage

habit of seeing the movies in cinema theatres, where as the remaining sample do not see movies at all.

In respect of 57.5% of the respondents there was a change in movie going habit after the introduction of movies on Television, whereas 31.5% felt no difference in this regard. The latter percentage constitutes mostly youth and women. Change to a great extent was found in case of 31% and to some extent in case of 26.5%.

Suitability of Timings

According to 89% of the respondents the timings of telecasting of different programmes is suitable for their viewing (Table-7). But, for the remaining respondents i.e. 11%, timings are not suitable. This part constitutes mostly agricultural labourers. These people have suggested substitute timings which are convenient to them. Some women felt that it would

TABLE 7

Distribution of the Respondents According to Suitability of Timings

		Yes	*No*	*Total*
Male	Fre	114	16	130
	%	87.69	12.31	
Female	Fre	64	6	70
	%	91.43	8.57	
Total	Fre	178	22	200
	%	89.00	11.00	

Fre. : Frequency—% : Percentage

be good if the telecast commenced still earlier and that the introduction of afternoon programmes would be convenient for their viewing. Since the suggestion came from a very small fraction of the sample, it may be understood that a large majority are satisfied with the present timings. It may be recalled that the programme timings have been designed keeping the rural atmosphere in view. This is the main reason for such highest percentage of suitability.

Influence of TV on daily activities

It is understood that in the beginning when Television was introduced in some countries tremendous change was observed in the living habits and values of the people where televison acted as a cultural force. This was noticed even in advanced countries like U.S.A.

To see whether the same change is taking place in India also the villagers were asked whether they adjust their routine according to the television programme schedule. For this, majority of the respondents (74%) said that they complete their work and make themselves free for Television (Table-8). It is observed that a highest percentage i.e. 91.43% of women adjust their household chores to watch TV programmes. It shows that even women who do not have TV sets also arrange their routine in order to be present before the TV sets in their neighbours' houses.

It is noticed that for 26% of the sample, their own work is more important compared to TV engagements. A higher percentage of men fall under this category. Even among men a higher percentage (64.62%) try to adjust their routine to watch TV programmes. Though there were no TV luncheons or TV dinners, it is observed that as a visual home entertainment medium TV is influencing the life styles of the rural masses.

Discussion during transmission

Many observers feel that experience of one way communication of Television may promote passiveness among viewers if they sit for long hours before TV. To explore whether the viewers are watching programmes as mere spectators or some

TABLE 8

Distribution of the Respondents According to Influence of TV on Daily Activities

		Yes	*No*	*Total*
Male	Fre	84	86	130
	%	64.62	35.38	
Female	Fre	64	6	70
	%	91.43	8.57	
Total	Fre	148	52	200
	%	74.00	26.00	

Fre. : Frequency—% : Percentage

mental activity is involved in it, the sample were enquired. Here it is very interesting to note that majority of the respondents (89%) discuss about the programmes with family members, neighbours, friends etc. (Table-9). Again here, womens' share is a little more than men, though they limit their discussion with family members since most of them are housewives.

In both these areas i,e. adjusting the routine engagements and discussing about the TV programmes the reply was immediate as if these were quite natural.

Programmes Preferred

Television presents a large variety of programmes catering to the needs of audience with different tastes. The total schedule of programmes was mainly classified as Educational and Recreational. Though the political programmes fall under the category 'Educational', the main focus of the study is on political programmes. So these programmes have been separately categorised in the present study.

TABLE 9

Distribution of the Respondents According to Discussion During Transmission

		Yes	*No*	*Total*
Male	Fre	111	19	130
	%	85.38	14.62	
Female	Fre	67	3	70
	%	95.7	4.29	
Total	Fre	178	22	200
	%	89.00	11.00	

Fre. : Frequency—% : Percentage

It is gathered from the interviews that villagers watch all kinds of programmes every day on TV i.e. Educational, recreational and political. Keeping aside the general pattern of viewing of the programmes, they were asked to name their first choice of preference in order to identify which category of programmes was more appealing to them.

A higher percentage (62.5%) have preferred entertainment (Recreational) programmes as their first choice followed by political (23%) and other Educational programmes (14.5%) (Table-10). Here the political programmes were again divided as NEWS and CURRENT AFFAIRS. While the former is a regular feature the latter is occasional. The response to cuerent affairs was practically NIL. The above figures indicate that majority have preferred entertainment programmes to other programmes. However, a wide range of difference is noticed between men and women in this regard. In respect of women the preference for recreation is very high i.e. 87.14%. A small percentage (8.57%) opted for political and a negligible 4.29% preferred other educational programmes.

In case of men, the difference between these three categories is not sharp as may be seen in the Table-4. (Educational 20%, recreational 49.23%, political 30.77%). These differences between men and women also reveal that TV is not a mere entertainment tool but may equally and effectively serve its fundamental purpose of educating the masses.

TABLE 10

Distribution of the Respondents According to Programmes Preferred

		Educational	*Recreational*	*Political*		*Tolal*
				News	*Current Affairs*	
Male	Fre	26	64	40	—	130
	%	20.00	49.23	30.77	—	
Female	Fre	3	61	6	—	70
	%	4.29	87.14	8.57	—	
Total	Fre	29	125	46	—	200
	%	14.5	62.5	23.00	—	

Fre. : Frequency— %: Percentage

A general observation reveals that feature films, film songs and cricket in the recreational programmes, agriculture in the educational programmes and News in the political category are the most popular programmes mentioned by them.

Criticism

A lot of criticism has been received from the respondents regarding TV programmes. Though popular, too much of cricket on TV is often criticised especially by some of the aged people. Some elderly villagers expressed deep concern, as students spend more time before television and neglect their academic studies. Though it is good to note that the agricultural programmes are regularly watched, relevance of such programmes was also questioned.

One landlord in Kompally village claimed that he is more advanced is various agricultural techniques than those shown on television. It is surprising that a young woman in injapur village heavily criticized the dairy programmes on TV for their non applicability in day-to-day life. In Pedda Amberpet again, a landlord questioned the relevance of agricultural programmes when there was severe water problem prevailing in the land. On the while the agricultural programmes, according to many of the respondents are not applicable in the actual field. One may have to carefully examine whether this criticism is widely prevalent through out the state or is confined to this sample only, which however, has a more non-agricultural flavour.

Criticism about NEWS will be disscussed in detail separately in the category 'political'.

Choice of the media as a source of Information

Newspapers and other magazines are also circulated in rural areas though not as large as in urban areas. It is commonly said that while accepting a new knowledge the rural masses have more faith and belief in the words of their friends and neighbours and family members than than the mass media. Of course it is an established fact that the Radio has been the most popular media of mass communication in rural areas. To assess the credibility of TV amongst all the above information sources, a question has been asked at the end of the interview.

A higher percentage (51%) of the sample quoted TV as their major source of information followed by Newspapers (24%) and Radio (22%) (Table-11). As far as men are concerned the difference of percentage between these three sources is very little, There is also a change in the order of their preference, since 30% mentioned Radio as compared to Newspapers (28.46%).

TABLE 11

Distribution of the Respondents According to Choice of the Media as a Source of Information

		T.V.	*Radio*	*News Papers*	*Friends, Family Members & Neighbours*	*Others*	*Total*
Male	Fre	50	39	37	3	1	130
	%	38.46	30.00	28.46	2.31	0.77	
Female	Fre	52	5	11	2	0	70
	%	74.29	7.14	15.71	2.86	—	
Total	Fre	102	44	48	5	1	200
	%	51.00	22.00	24.00	2.5	0.5	

Fre. : Frequency—% : Percentage

However, in case of women, for a majority (74.29%) of them, TV happens to be the major source of information. Here it is surprising to note that 15.71% read newspapers for information. This is rather unbelievable point in respect of rural women, who are mainly housewives, but the proximity of these villages to the city and also a considerably good percentage of educated women (about 30% studied 10th class or more) may also explain the interest of the women in newspapers. A few of them may even have claimed as a matter of vanity. Radio occupies third place with a low percentage of 7.14%.

The main reasons mentioned by the sample to feel a particular medium as their major source of information are as below.

Television

Understanding is more due to visual effect and they could retain the information in their minds for a considerably long period.

Radio

Though TV's effect is more, the duration of the programme is very short as compared to Radio. Since Radio gives information through out the day, some of the sample mentioned Radio as their major source of information. Some of the agricultural labourers and business people said that by the time they reach home the Telugu programmes in TV will be almost at an end. Therefore, they listen to Radio at the place of work for information. People who do not own TV sets also fall under this category.

Newspapers

TV and radio broadcast programmes according to a fixed schedule. This requires people to adjust their timings in order to receive information, whereas one can go through all kinds of news if one sits half-an-hour or so with a newspaper, and that too when one feels convenient to do so. This is however, applicable to literates only.

Language preferred for NEWS

When analyzed according so the languages (Table–12), Telugu News, as one would expect, is watched by a vast majority of the respondents (196/200) followed by Hindi

(106/200). The latter is on account of the influence of Urdu on the Telangana people. The respondents who watch English news consists of 66 persons (66/200). In respect of English news through the understanding is difficult still many watch the news. This is because the news timings are more convenient where men find time to sit before TV very leisurely. Another reason mentioned by the respondents for watching the news other than Telugu is that visuals are used more in these news bulletins whereas the visuals in regional news bulletins are very less and sometimes even none.

As per the data, English appears to be difficult to understand for more number of respondents (135). However, people who expressed difficulty in respect of Hindi are not negligible i.e. 99. While coming to the level of difficulty in understanding the situation most of them experienced the problem to a large extent whereas for the other two levels i.e. 'to some extent' and 'not much' the number is almost one and the same. However, women outnumbered men in experiencing difficulty to a large extent (Table-13).

Type of news preferred

As far as the variety of news items is concerned, the respondents are not very particular about the types (items) of news (69.5%). The reason expressed is that it is necessary to know all types of news whether international, national or regional (Table-14).

News content preferred

When asked which kind of news i.e. political or economic or cultural appeals to them more, here also, many villagers preferred all kinds of news (Table-15). However, a significant percentage (39%), mainly consisting of men are interested more in political news. Political news is followed by economic news (7.5%).

Suggestions and response to TV programmes

At the end of the interview two more questions were asked

TABLE 12

Distribution of the Respondents According to Language Preferred for News

		Telugu	*Hindi*	*English*	*Telugu & Hindi*	*Hindi & English*	*English & Telgue*	*Telgu Hindi & English*	*Total*
Male	Fre	41	1	1	36	1	8	42	130
	%	31.54	0.77	0.77	27.69	0.77	6.15	32.31	
Female	Fre	42	1	0	13	0	2	12	70
	%	60.00	1.43	—	18.57	—	2.86	17.14	
Total	Fre	83	2	1	49	1	10	54	200
	%	41.5	1.00	0.5	24.5	0.5	5.00	27.00	

Fre. : Frequency—% : Percentage

TABLE 13

Distribution of the Respondents According to Language Problem in Following News

		English			Hindi			Englisn and Hindi			Total
		To a large extent	*To some extent*	*Not much*	*To a large extent*	*To some extent*	*Not much*	*To a large extent*	*To some extent*	*Not much*	
Male	Fre	9	12	10	3	2	6	24	15	7	130
	%	6.92	9.23	7.69	2.31	1.54	4.61	18.46	11.54	5.38	
Female	Fre	18	0	0	1	1	0	37	1	2	70
	%	25.71	—	—	1.43	1.43	—	52.86	1.43	2.86	
Total	Fre	27	12	10	4	3	6	61	16	9	200
	%	13.5	6.00	5.00	2.00	1.5	3.00	30.5	8.00	4.5	

Fre. : Frequency—% : Percentage

to invite suggestions regarding some programmes on TV, through which the political awareness among the rural masses can be promoted, and secondly whether at any time they have responded to TV programmes by writing letters to Doordarshan. No suggestions were forthcoming spontaneously. However, after a lot of persuation 43 percent of the respondents have given a few suggestions which are divided into four categories as below (Table-16).

(a) Increasing the duration

(b) More visual coverage

(c) More programmes in regional language and

(d) Others

TABLE 14

Distribution of the Respondents According to the Type of News Preferred

		Regional	*National*	*Global*	*All*	*Total*
Male	Fre	31	11	3	85	130
	%	23.85	8.46	2.31	65.38	
Female	Fre	15	1	0	54	70
	%	21.43	1.43	–	77.14	
Total	Fre	46	12	3	139	200
	%	23.00	6.00	1.5	69.51	

Fre. : Frequency—% : Percentage

TABLE 15

Distribution of the Respondents According to the Content of News Preferred

		Poltical	*Economic*	*Cultural*	*All*	*Total*
Male	Fre	68	10	2	50	130
	%	52.31	7.69	1.54	38.46	
Female	Fre	10	5	0	55	70
	%	14.29	7.14	—	78.57	
Total	Fre	78	15	2	105	200
	%	39.00	7.5	1.00	52.5	

Fre. : Frequency—% : Percentage

TABLE 16

Distribution of the Respondents According to Suggestions for Improvement of Political Programmes on TV

		Suggestions				
		Increasing Duration	*Increasing Visuals*	*Preference for local language and local coverage*	*Others*	*Total*
Male	Fre	8	0	7	26	130
	%	6.15	—	5.38	20.00	
Female	Fre	9	5	10	21	70
	%	12.86	7.14	14.28	30.00	
Total	Fre	17	5	17	47	200
	%	8.5	2.5	8.5	23.5	

Fre. : Frequency—% : Percentage

Though these suggestions were not new and extraordinary, they reinforce the need to implement such measures.

As regards to the second question the response is very negligible (7 respondents) (Table-17). Among them five reacted to recreational programmes followed by educational (2). The political programmes have no response at all.

TABLE 17

Distribution of the Respondents According to the Reaction to TV Programmes (Letters)

		Educational	*Recreational*	*Political*	*Total*
Male	Fre	1	5	0	130
	%	0.77	3.84	—	
Female	Fre	1	0	0	70
	%	1.43	—	—	
Total	Fre	2	5	0	200
	%	1.00	2.5	—	

Fre. : Frequency—% : Percentage

PART II

Degree of Exposure to Political Programmes

Coming to the main focus of the study, this part deals with questions relating to the actual political awareness of the rural people. Knowledge of the names of the Prime Minister, President, Governor, and Chief Minister of the state can be considered as a bare minimum political awareness for any citizen. A question has been framed to known whether the respondents have this minimum knowledge.

Studies have revealed that TV plays greater role in familiarizing national leaders to the masses. An attempt was also made to see how far our TV is performing this role with regard to the above four personalities.

Of the 200 respondents interviewed an average of 91% could name the above four personalities (Table-18). It is

TABLE 18

Distribution of the Respondents According to Knowledge About the National Leaders

		President	*Prime Minister*	*Chief Minister*	*Governor*	*Total*
Male	Fre	124	114	129	118	130
	%	95.38	87.70	99.23	90.77	
Female	Fre	62	62	63	59	70
	%	88.57	88.57	90.00	84.29	
Total	Fre	196	176	192	177	200
	%	93	88	96	88.5	

Fre. : Frequency—% : Percentage

perhaps rather sad to note that 9 persons out of a hundred do not even know the names of, or recognise the President, Prime Minister or the Chief Minister. Here it may be mentioned that the formal terminology of the portfolios was beyond the comprehension of some illiterates particularly among the scheduled castes. However, the way in which they identified these personalities is interesting. Some identified Mr. Zail Singh as 'the biggest man of the country', Mr. Rajiv Gandhi as the 'Son of late Mrs. Indira Gandhi', Mr. N.T. Rama Rao as the 'King of the State', and Smt. Kumudben Joshi as simply 'Lady with short hair style'. Though these people have only a vague idea about the rank or the work of these personalities, a typical rural characteristic of identifying the people mainly by sex, appearance, mannerisms, sentiments etc. was observed here.

Among the above four, the Chief Minister ranked first in the identification (96%) followed by the President (93%), Governor (88.5%) and Prime Minister (88%). The difference in these percentages is not much and therefore need not be taken as an indication of greater familiarity. The earlier acquintance as a Matinee 'Idol' and the Rs 2/- kg rice scheme in respect of Mr. N.T. Rama Rao seems to be reasons for his greater familiarity, whereas personal appearance combined with TV coverage in respect of Mr. Zail Singh and Mrs. Kumudben Joshi seems to be the reasons for their familiarity. In respect of Mr. Rajiv Gandhi though the TV coverage was more, he was not familiar with the masses to an equal degree and he was identified more as the son of the Late Prime Minister Mrs. Indira Gandhi.

It is everybody's knowledge that TV gives coverage to all these four important leaders in its news bulletins. A question as to whether the respondents have seen the leaders on the TV or outside was put and the response received strongly supports the above observation. The response shows that 61.5% of the sample have seen these leaders only on TV, while 29.5% have watched them only at other places. However, 9% have seen them both on TV as well as at other places (Table 19). The familiarity of these leaders through TV among women folk compared to men is very high i.e. 94.28%. This figure shows the capacity of TV in influencing the women, in other political matters also especially in a society where rural women are mostly illiterates and confined to kitchens. Even among the men the people who got familiarity with these leaders through TV is quite significant (43.85).

Places other than TV where these leaders are watched are factories, inaugural functions, developmental programmes and party political meetings etc.

As explained earlier keeping the objectives of the programmes and the expected responses from the viewers a four point scale has been designed to assess the levels of awareness. The following political programmes are discussed accordingly (Table 20).

Economic News

Response to these news items was quite within their expected levels of understanding. In this area, the respondents

TABLE 19

Distribution of the Respondents According to their Source of Information for the Knowledge About the National Leaders

		Television	*Other Places*	*Both*	*Total*
Male	Fre	57	57	16	130
	%	43.85	43.85	12.30	
Female	Fre	66	2	2	70
	%	94.28	2.86	2.86	
Total	Fre	123	59	18	200
	%	61.5	29.5	9.00	

Fre. : Frequency—% : Percentage

TABLE 20

Distribution of Levels of Awareness Among the Respondents According to Political Programmes Viewed

Programme	*Sex*		*Levels of Awareness* 4	3	2	1	*Total*
Economic News	Male	Fre	12	47	21	50	
		%	9.23	36.16	16.15	38.46	130
	Female	Fre	0	8	12	50	
		%	—	11.43	17.14	71.43	70
	Total	Fre	12	55	33	100	
		%	6.00	27.50	16.5	50.0	200
International News	Male	Fre	20	65	10	35	
		%	15.39	50.00	7.69	26.92	130
	Female	Fre	1	37	19	13	
		%	1.43	52.86	27.14	18.57	70
	Total	Fre	21	102	29	48	
		%	10.5	51.00	14.5	24.0	200
News about Political Parties	Male	Fre	26	50	17	37	
		%	20.00	38.46	13.08	28.46	130
	Female	Fre	3	12	3	52	
		%	4.29	17.14	4.29	74.28	70
	Total	Fre	29	62	20	89	
		%	14.50	31.00	10.00	44.50	200
Ministerial Broadcasts	Male	Fre	33	45	26	26	
		%	25.38	34.62	20.00	20.00	130
	Female	Fre	6	16	30	18	
		%	8.57	22.86	42.86	25.71	70
	Total	Fre	39	61	56	44	
		%	19.50	30.50	28.00	22.00	200

Contd.

News about riots and violence	Male	Fre	13	57	34	26	
		%	10.00	43.85	26.15	20.00	130
	Female	Fre	6	15	41	8	
		%	8.57	21.43	58.57	11.43	70
	Total	Fre	19	72	75	34	
		%	9.50	36.00	37.50	17.00	200
Assembly Broadcasts	Male	Fre	10	38	52	30	
		%	7.70	29.23	40.00	23.07	130
	Female	Fre	1	4	8	57	
		%	1.43	5.71	11.43	81.43	70
	Total	Fre	11	42	60	87	
		%	5.50	21.00	30.00	43.50	200
Pre-party Election Broadcasts	Male	Fre	38	31	29	32	
		%	29.23	23.85	22.31	24.61	130
	Female	Fre	4	4	5	57	
		%	5.71	5.71	7.15	81.43	70
	Total	Fre	42	35	34	89	
		%	21.00	17.50	17.00	44.50	200
Programmes on vote casting	Male	Fre	5	34	25	66	
		%	3.85	26.15	19.23	50.77	130
	Female	Fre	4	4	19	43	
		%	5.71	5.71	27·15	61.43	70
	Total	Fre	9	38	44	109	
		%	4.50	19.00	22.00	54.50	200
Election News	Male	Fre	32	74	13	11	
		%	24.62	56.92	10.00	8.46	130
	Female	Fre	14	24	22	10	
		%	20.00	34.28	31.43	14.29	70
	Total	Fre	46	98	35	21	
		%	23.00	49.00	17.50	10.50	200

Budget Broadcasts	Male	Fre	41	42	12	35	
		%	31.54	32.31	9.23	26.92	130
	Female	Fre	15	3	1	51	
		%	21.43	4.28	1.43	72.86	70
	Total	Fre	56	45	13	86	
		%	28.00	22.50	6.50	43.00	200
Messages by National Leaders	Male	Fre	31	51	28	20	
		%	23.85	39.23	21.54	15.38	130
	Female	Fre	4	25	27	14	
		%	5.71	35.71	38.58	20.00	70
	Total	Fre	35	76	55	34	
		%	17.50	38.00	27.50	17.00	200
Janavani	Male	Fre	29	11	5	85	
		%	22.31	8.46	3.85	65.38	130
	Female	Fre	1	2	1	66	
		%	1.43	2.86	1.43	94.28	70
	Total	Fre	30	13	6	151	
		%	15.00	6.50	3.00	75.50	200
Recall of Political Events	Male	Fre	0	4	12	23	
		%	—	10.26	30.77	58.97	39
	Female	Fre	0	0	0	4	
		%	—	—	—	100.00	4
	Total	Fre	0	4	12	27	
		%	—	9.30	27.90	62.79	43

frequently mentioned about hearing such news on the Radio too. When an attempt was made to know the nature of reaction this particular news was having, most of them expressed a feeling of helplessness (50%) about the price situation. 16.5%

of them felt that they were receiving atleast somekind of this news through TV. Their general opinion is that the increase in prices is inevitable. The fact whether or not TV educates one in this regard does not matter much for them. However, the information about the price situation seems to be received with greater interest than as indicated. As many as 27.5% of them are able to analyze the price situation, compared to mere receivers. Only 6% have stressed the importance of the consumer movement to resist such situation.

The interviews brought out the general dissatisfaction among the rural masses that the support price for their products is very less but they are bound to purchase the same consumer items at a higher rate later : this they attribute to Government's policies. None of the sample expressed the way in which the TV has to present this particular news except desiring everyday market prices to be included. One more prominent observation is that the news is received by both sexes with equal interest and enthusiasm.

International Political News

The response to International news was also in good degree. It was seen that 76% are now familiar with the international personalities through television. Out of this, 10.5% emphasized the need for trade relations beetween the countries. Another 51% stated that they could now recognize international figures. For this segment of the sample, there appears to be no other use. Non-viewers and others who donot understand (or express) the matter consists of the remaining 24%.

Out of all political programmes, the main source for this particular knowledge is the English news bulletin and to some extent the Hindi bulletin, but definitely not the Telugu news. They suggested that Telugu news must also carry enough visuals and films related to international affairs instead of general clippings. The sample made no other specific criticism.

It emerges from the study that on the whole, the understanding of international news among villagers is improving with their axposure to TV. They are now atleast able to say who is who. The commonly recognised foreign personalities are Ronald Reagan. Gorbachev and Margaret Thatcher.

News about Political Parties

Indian TV's role in this area is always a topic for debate. Critics often talk of bias in reporting about political parties vis-a-vis the ruling party. The respondents' views support this opinion of bias. Most of the respondents expressed about too much publicity for the ruling party programmes.

Out of 55.5% of the sample who are exposed to this news 31% are receiving information about the policies and programmes of different political parties on various issues. 10% could identify the political parties which are functioning actively. 14.5% stressed the need for such information which gives an idea to the public on whether the political parties are working together for national development. A significant percentage (44.5%) stated that they are not in receipt of any news of such type. Women viewers are more in this category.

Respondents suggested that TV should educate as to the importance of the political parties in a democracy. They insisted equal visual coverage to all potitical leaders.

Ministerial Broadcasts

Ministerial broadcasts is another area where the sample expressed dissatisfaction over the large coverage given to the ministers especially to the Prime Minister. The sample appears to have not appreciated the basic intention behind these broadcasts. This may be one of the reasons for such criticism. The ministers have the privilege to appear on TV by virtue of their position only to publicize the governments' policies and programmes as a whole.

78% of the sample are regular viewers of ministerial broadcasts. This indicates the popularity of the programme. The sample received the news with interest to understand whether their activities are aimed at national development (19.5%). 30.5% could know the day-to-day activities of the ministers. 28% of the respondents could recognise both central and state ministers. Here the often mentioned ministers are Sri P.V. Narasimha Rao, Shri J. Vengal Rao, Late Sri T. Anjaiah, Sri P. Indra Reddy, Sri M.S.S. Koteshwara Rao. This is of course apart from Prime Minister, the President, the Chief Minister and Governor.

An interesting observation is that the central ministers who are popular in the local area ore recognised more often as compared to ministers of other regions though the former are not given any extra coverage over TV. For example, Sri J. Vengala Rao, Sri P.V. Narasimha Rao and Late Sri T. Anjaiah were such since they had held Chief Ministers' post earlier.

The main source for information about central ministers is Hindi and English news bulletins and for the local ministers the regional news in Telugu.

News about Riots and Violence

In the recent past, the media coverage on riots and violence, particularly those in Sri Lanka and Punjab, and those during by elections was more. When asked the need for such news on TV, most of the sample deeply felt the necessity. The villagers' response to such news especially women folk was emotional. 36% felt that this news helps in taking precautionary measures in such dangerous situations. 37.5% could assess the situation prevailing in the present society.

Only 9.5% of the sample could understand how these riots and violence disturb peace in society and only this meagre few could conceive of a riot-free, ideal, social atmosphere for their everyday living. Such news was not useful to 17%. This obviously includes non-viewers and others who felt the news as unwarranted. The information was unreliable to a very small part of the sample.

Almost all expressed deep sympathy for the people of Punjab and Sri Lanka. They were so deeply touched by the visual coverage that some of them were actually in tears.

Assembly Broadcasts

The programmes discussed above are presented regularly through news. Assembly/parliament broadcasts are not a regular feature. Whenever the Assembly or Parliament is in session the proceedings are covered. Therefore, the response to these occasional features was comparatively less. The table also reflects the same. In addition to Hindi and English news coverage, resume of the Parliament's day's proceedings in presented at around 11 p.m. on TV everyday during the Parliament session. But this programme is not popular among the villagers.

The regional TV Kendra does not present any special programme on Assembly proceedings except a short coverage is the regular news. 56.5% of the sample are exposed to it, which is definitely an encouraging sign in this direction. The remaining 43.5% consists of non-viewers and women, who though watch the programme find it beyond their comprehension.

A good percentage (30%) of the villagers exposed to the programme could know how the elected representatives discuss the issues in the Assembly. For 21% it gave a basic understanding as to how the official assembly proceedings are conducted. A meagre 5.5% (which mainly includes village Sarpanches and other political workers) are of the opinion that this particular news helps to enable them to judge the capacity of their elected representatives and to take decision to solve the problems on their own.

Most of the villagers expressed happiness over these broadcasts as they felt they could never attend either Assembly or Parliament in person.

However, the Radio is a major source of information to the villagers in this aspect since it broadcasts special features on

Assembly proceedings. The behaviour of the elected representatives in the Assembly was vehemently criticized by some of the villagers. A very low percentage suggested live telecast of Assembly and Parliament proceedings.

Party Election Broadcasts

These broadcasts were held three years ago. Each recognised party was allotted fifteen minutes time during Parliament elections in 1984 and Assembly elections in 1985. Since the time gap is wide, most of the villagers (44.5%) could not recall these programmes vividly. This is very less in respect of women sample. But the remaining 55.5% could recall these programmes because of their interest in party politics and due to visual impact. 17% got familiarity with the party leaders. The sample which could understand the philosophy of different political parties consists of 17.5%.

It is quite interesting to note that around 21% opined that such broadcasts provide an opportunity for the voters to assess the capabilities of different party leaders/candidates and take a decision. Another observation is that the final decision of the voter is not entirely based on these broadcasts. When asked why they watch such broadcast, they said that they simply wanted to hear what was being said.

Programmes on Casting a Vote

This is an educative programme but of an occassional nature. At the time of major elections, TV through disscussions, snippets and slogans educates the voters as to the value of the vote and how to cast it. Almost all the sample watched these telecasts with interest. 45.5% have been directly benefited from these programmes. Though 54.5% of the villagers have the knowledge of such information, they strongly opined the need and importance of such educative programmes for those who are unaware of it. Among the rest of 45.5% sample, 4.5% have literally started exercizing their franchise only after watching these telecasts. The value of the vote was realised by atleast 19%. A major part of the sample (22%) have learnt to cast their vote at the polling booth. None of the villagers have mentioned about the interviews with the election Commissioner and election officers on TV.

Thus, it is revealed from the study that the small snippets and dialogues with the support of graphics and other visuals have attracted the masses more than the official interviews with the election officers. When asked whether they started casting their vote only after watching the TV, some of them said with a smile that they are doing it for a long time where as the introduction of TV is only recent.

Election News

Television is performing a good job in this area. Especially during the recent general elections to Parliament (1984) and Andhra Pradesh Assembly elections (1985) it excelled in presenting information of election results in an attractive way. A major portion of the sample (89.5%) tune to TV for election news including special election news bulletins. The reasons mentioned for such interest are :

(1) They need not search for alternative source for information (17.5%),

(2) It serves as a first hand information of election results (49%).

(3) It presents a clear picture of pre and post election scene (23%),

The remaining 10.5% consists of non-viewers but not critics. The computer election analysis on TV was not mentioned by any one. This may be attributed to language problem or to an innate diffidence to the use of computers and the sophistication in the analysis.

Prior to TV. Radio was giving special election bulletins round the clock and used to be the only source for first hand election information. But our results indicate that 89.5% of the villagers are tuning to TV for first hand election news. This may due to two reasons.

(1) The particular sample's regular exposure to only TV during that certain period and

(2) The visual entertainment (feature films) in between the news bulletins round the clock.

Another interesting observation is that : when the researcher asked some of the women why they preferred TV for election information to neighbours and family members, the rcasons put forward were :

(a) TV gives reliable information and
(b) Others may tease them by giving wrong information.

Budget Broadcastes

Budget information is related to economic news as both deal with the economic matters of the country. Economic news is a regular feature whereas the budget news is broadcast once in year i.e. at the time of presentation of budget in Parliament/Assembly. Therefore, here the budget broadcasts are dealt with separately.

The special budget bulletins (Central) are in English and Hindi only but not in the regional languages. In regional news only highlights of the budget are covered. On account of this limitation, as expected, the response to such bulletins is lesser (57%). The remaining 43% consists of people,

(a) Who missed the bulletins
(b) Who are not interested
(c) Who could not follow etc.

Most of the respondents referred to central budget only as compared to state budget. This may be because

(1) The state budget does not directly affect them

(2) Most of the essential commodities are under Central List.

Out of the 57% a significant part (28%) have received information from the budget broadcasts as regards to the benefits conferred on them and additional taxes imposed. As regards to the first hand information only 22.5% preferred TV.

While for election news 49% of the respondents preferred TV as first hand source of information, the percentage in respect of budget news, such preference has significantly come down. The reasons assumed for this are :

(1) Because of less exposure to TV on account of language problem and

(2) Less excitement as compared to electrons' results.

Only 6.5% have referred to the programmes of interviews with different cross sections of the society on this subject.

The study was conducted during the months of April and May. Though the budget was presented just before the study, the response was less as stated above (57%). Thus, it can be said that there exists a relationship between regular exposure to media and level of awareness of people irrespective of importance of the programmes.

Messages by National Leaders

On national days like Republic Day and Independence Day and Festivals etc. messages by national leaders on the importance of such occasions as also the prevailing political atmosphere in the country are broadcast over TV.

The higher percentage (83%) of exposure to these items is an indication that such infrequent broadcasts are attracting the masses. The festive atmosphere of the occasion may be one of the reasons for viewing the programme (27.5%). It was felt that these broadcasts are very important and also necessary since the celebration of the festivals has a traditional value (38%).

17.5% of the respondents could understand the depth of these leaders and their approach to national issues through these speeches. For some of them among the above, such telecasts are very educative since they give an account of events that took place before and after independence in a chrononological order. The remaining 17% are the combination of non-viewers, apathetic group and a fraction who could not express their reactions.

The study brought to light some of the following observations in this area.

(1) The sample could not recall the President's message given on the eve of Independence day and Republic day.

(2) Likewise, the Chief Minister's message on such occasions as Religious festivals were also not recalled by the villagers though such ones are in the regional language.

It is clear from their response that any programme presented in a lengthy and leisurely manner with special touches of colour and gaiety attract viewers and these occassions remain in their memory for a long time.

Janvani

Janvani (though now discontinued) came over TV on experimental basis. This is an interview with one Central Minister by a selected audience. The purpose was chiefly to bring to light the Ministry's plans, objectives, and functioning. It also served as an occassion for people to clarify their doubts and problems. This programme which was scheduled after 9.00 p.m. was in Hindi with occassional questions asked in English.

This programme though not in the regional language and has been discontinued since long, has been included in the interview for the following reasons.

The main responsibility of the media in political affairs is to create a platform for interaction between the government and the people. In our country the free press is extending more opportunities to people's voice on various issues/problems to be projected through newspapers as compared to broadcast media. Under these conditions, the programme Janvani was broadcast for a limited period on experimental basis over TV.

In order to assess the impact of this particular programme on rural masses the same was included in the interview schedule,

Due to aforesaid reason, as foreseen earlier non-viewers formed a majority of the respondents (75.5%). A notable feature in this area is that among the 24.5% viewers more than half (15%) of the sample showed highest level of awareness as per the scale. People satisfied with the Government's initiative in knowing their problems consist of 6.5%. Through this programme a negligible part (3%) could clear some of their doubts. It is observed from the study that the villagers have felt this programme is of utmost importance to them. Most of them were disappointed for discontinuing it and strongly favoured for its revival. They have also suggested that such programmes must also be introduced at local level i.e. with state ministers.

Recall of Political Events

Recall of any subject depends on personal interest in a given topic and secondly the effective presentation of a programme. An attempt was made to know how many of the respondents are able to recall the political events they watch on TV.

Out of the 200 respondents only 43(21.5%) could recall the political events immediately. If time was given, probably some more people would have recalled the programme. Among them women consist of a very less number. Among the forty-three respondents 27 could recall one event, 12 people two events and only four could recall three events. All of them recall the political events on the TV without any effort or hesitation or doubt. This can be attributed to the visual impact. Among the events easily recalled are the Prime Minister's Press Conferences, Gorbachev's visit to India, Sri Lanka and Punjab issues and Deal with Bofors.

Recollection of Bofors Deal as a news item reveals that an issue whether or not presented with much ado, strikes a note in the viewer's mind if that issue is already popular among the public. Forgetfulness has been observed to be one reason for inability to recall ; this was more in case of political programmes compared to other dramatized programmes, Women could recall some events mainly due to regular exposure to news on TV.

PART III

Influence of Subvariables on the Levels of Political Awareness

This part attempts to assess and analyze the association of subvariables like sex, age, caste, occupation, education and social participation on the political awareness attained by the rural masses through exposure to TV. It is mainly intended to know whether the different levels of awareness depend upon (or are independent of) the different categories of the subvariables determining the social status. And, if there is a dependence how is brought about ? i.e. which category has a greater level of awareness.

The possible influence of these factors while receiving a political message from TV has been discussed earlier in the third chapter. Taking into consideration the expected and observed influences the data collected was put to 'G' test (Sokal and Ralph) which is ad alternative to Chi-square test of the dependence in contengency data. 'G' test which is not as popular as the Chi-square test requires a brief description[2]. This method has some considerable advantages over the traditional Chi-quare test and the employment of the 'G' test does not require any special mathematical sophistication also. Though the 'G' test does not differ much from the Chi-square test the former has been found to be a more sensitive tool in assessing goodness of fit from small samples i.e. even when some of the expected frequencies are less than five. The 'G' value calculated as per formula given below,* follow a Chi-square distribution and hence its significance is judged by comparing with the corresponding tabuluated Chisquare value.

Due to the limitations discussed earlier in selecting the sample, the data contains more small figures which necessiates the application of the 'G' test rahter than the generally used Chi-square test. Further, in order to improve the efficiency of the test small frequencies were pooled with the adjacent classes wherever required.

The sub-variables were taken in rows and different levels of political awareness were arranged in columns. The computation, analysis and interpretation of each sub-variable is discussed in detail as follows.

Caste

Among the four categories of castes the sample did not have any scheduled tribe. Since the number of scheduled caste subjects is also very less it had to be pooled with backward classes. On the whole the table has only two categories i.e. BC and FC. The obtained values (Table No, 21) show that caste does not have much influence on the levels of awareness. The calculated Chi-square values are lesser than the tabulated values except in four areas where the difference is significant. These areas are International News, Budget, Janvani and Choice of the Media as a source of information etc.

It was not expected that caste as a variable directly influences the level of political awareness. Financial status also goes along with Caste, and it is understood that generally

---

*If 'fij' is the observed frequency in the (ij) the use of an r x s contingency table of r rows and s columns with f i., f j. being the corresponding marginal totals and f.. the grand totals. Then

$$G=2\left(\sum_i\sum_j f_{ij}\log f_{ij}-\sum_i f_{i.}\log f_{i.}-\sum_j f_{.j}\log f_{.j}+f_{..}\log f_{..}\right)$$

The quantity G follows a Chi-square distribution with (r—1) (s—1) degrees of freedom.

TABLE 21

Test of Association of Caste with the Levels of Awareness of different types of Political Programmes

Sl. No.	*Programme*	*X^2 Calculated*	*Degree of freedom*	*X^2 Tabulated*	*Level of significance*
1.	Economic News	3.068NS	3	7.815	5%
2.	International News	15.701**	3	11.341	1%
3.	News about political parties	1.812NS	3	7.815	5%
4.	Ministerial broadcasts	0.452NS	3	7.815	5%
5.	News about riots and violence	1.326NS	3	7.815	5%
6.	Assembly broadcasts	2.386NS	3	7.815	5%
7.	Party pre-election broadcasts	1.472NS	3	7.815	5%
8.	Programmes on vote casting	4.498NS	3	7.815	5%
9.	Election News	2.67NS	3	7.815	5%
10.	Budget broadcasts	7.858*	3	7.815	5%
11.	Messages by leaders	1.322NS	3	7.815	5%
12.	Janvani	8.578*	3	7.815	5%
13.	Choice of the Media	10.54*	3	7.815	5%

*Significant at 5% level—** Significant at 1% level—NS Not Significant

the forward caste sections are the more advantageous people. Hence it is not surprising that caste did not have much influence on the awareness except in the above four areas.

A look into the percentages of these areas where the association is observed shows that the Forward Castes are more at higher levels of awareness than the Backward castes.

The expected response for Budget and Janvani programmes is however less since those are occassional programmes and presented in English and Hindi and not in Telugu. Similarly, International news is mostly given in English News bulletins which is less comprehensible. As to the fourth area i.e. the Choice of the media, the percentages show that more number to BCs (35.63%) claimed Radio as their source of information where as only 15.93% FCs preferred the Radio. At the same time the difference between FC and BCs who selected TV as their source of information is less. This indicates that the appeal of TV to BCs is not less, though they did not possess TV sets as many as that of FCs.

It may be therefore concluded that caste as a sub-variable did not have much influence on the awareness of the sample. However, the level of understanding which goes along with the caste to some extent can influence the awareness in certain aspects.

Sex

When the data was analyzed according to sex it was found that the influence of sex on political awareness is very high, supporting the commonly held view that "women are politically backward" and "politics is men's affair". The obtained Chi-square values are very high compared to the tabulated ones. There is not even one area of political awareness where the influence of sex did not play it's role.

Though more women than men preferred TV as their choice of media for information it is seen from the figures (Table-22) that even this greater exposure to TV has failed to increase

TABLE 22

Test of Association of Sex with the Levels of Awareness of different types of Political Programmes

Sl. No.	*Programme*	*X^2 Calculated*	*Degree of freedom*	*X^2 Tabulated*	*Level of significance*
1.	Economic News	7.922*	2	5.991	5%
2.	International News	23.88**	3	7.815	5%
3.	News about political parties	42.234**	3	11.341	1%
4.	Ministerial broadcasts	18.406**	3	11.341	1%
5.	News about riots and violence	21.17**	3	11.341	1%
6.	Assembly broadcasts	64.667**	3	7.815	5%
7.	Party pre-election broadcasts	63.016**	3	11.341	1%
8.	Programmes on casting a vote	9.7 *	3	11.341	1%
9.	Election News	18.096**	3	11.341	1%
10.	Budget broadcasts	48.556**	2	9.210	1%
11.	Message by leaders	15.522**	3	11.341	1%
12.	Janvani	26.702**	2	9.210	1%
13.	Choice of the media	65.774**	2	9.210	1%

*Significant at 5% level—** Significant at 1% level

political awareness of women. The reasons that were discussed in earlier chapters may be valid here.

It is seen that women are quite heavy users of TV and they have no choice but to view even the political programmes. This kind of viewing gives them only a superficial knowledge of politics. For example, to identify few personalities in the political field and have only a vague impression of certain events. And that is all. They do not seem to have any knowledge about details in political affairs which they view on TV. This may be basically due to lack of deep concern for the subject. But one can hope that in the long run, the women, if their present liking for TV continues in the same line, may develop keen interest for political affairs.

Social Participation

Contrary to the assumption that social participation enhances one's level of political awareness the results (Table 23) show that there is no relation between political awareness and social participation. Here there is a minor exception in the area of news about political parties and party pre-election Broadcasts. In these two areas a slight association was noticed at 5% level but the same was not observed at 1% level of significance.

The reasons can be analyzed as below. In the 200 respondents 107 have social participation in various associations including political parties. A major portion of them (48 out of 107) are cooperative society members but this has only an indirect relevance to political activity. 18 respondents are participants in Educational, recreational, and welfare activities and 14 in other activities which cannot be considered as those directly connected with politics. 27 respondents have direct political participation. But the results show that there is no association between political participation and political awareness. The reasons could be :

(1) Though it is appreciable that 13 persons out of a hundred have political involvement other than simply talking

TABLE 23

Test of Association of Social Participation with the Levels of Awareness of different types of Political Programmes

Sl. No.	*Programme*	*X^2 Calculated*	*Degree of freedom*	*X^2 Tabulated*	*Level of Significance*
1.	Economic News	5,556^{NS}	6	12.592	5%
2.	International News	6.758^{NS}	6	12.592	5%
3.	News about political parties	16.078**	6	16.812	1%
4.	Ministerial broadcasts	10.872^{NS}	6	12.592	5%
5.	News about riots and violence	4.62 ^{NS}	6	12.592	5%
6.	Assembly broad-casts	8.25 ^{NS}	6	12.592	5%
7.	Party pre-election broadcasts	16.118**	6	16.812	1%
8.	Programmes on casting a vote	7.534^{NS}	6	12.592	5%
9.	Election News	5.298^{NS}	6	12.592	5%
10.	Budget broad-casts	12.412*	6	12.592	5%
11.	Message by leaders	6.252^{NS}	6	12.592	5%
12.	Janvani	7.944^{NS}	6	12.592	5%
13.	Choice of the Media	8.742^{NS}	6	12.562	5%

*Significant at 5% level—**Significant at 1% level—NS Not significant

about politics, this number does not sufficiently represent the varieties of political participation.

(2) The nature of rural political participation is limited to mere membership in one party or the other. There is a little activity during local elections. But there is no scope for these small numbers to expose themselves to the broader areans of political affairs.

(3) Apathy of the educated group towards politics is leading to their non-involvement in political activities.

Occupation

The values (Table-24) show that occupation has high influence on the political awareness of the villagers, except in three areas, namely, Ministerial broadcasts, Budget broadcasts and Janvani. It is observed that the villagers with owner cultivation followed by business have shown a higher level of awareness than the others i.e. agriculture labour and caste occupation (both were pooled as one) and service.

The reason for people with owner cultivation having higher level of awareness in villages may be that they are fairly rich people with many activities and advantages. Their financial and educational status is also high compared to others. This is the same in case of business category also.

A further exploration of figures reveals that the above two are at one level and agriculture labour, caste occupation and service categories broadly stood at a different level. Although the service category consists of a group of persons who are moderately educated the reason for their standing near the level of agriculture labour and caste occupation categories could be their low level of interest in state affairs. The agriculture labour and caste occupation category which showed lesser awareness can be justified by the fact that they spend most of their time in fields and at their work places and cannot concentrate on other things. The influence of occupation did not seem to be very significant when it comes to the actual

TABLE 24

Test of Association of Occupation with the Levels of Awareness of different types of Political Programmes

Sl. No.	*Programme*	*X^2 Calculated*	*Degree of Freedom*	*X^2 Tabulated*	*Level of Significance*
1.	Economic News	38.68**	8	15.507	5%
			8	20.090	1%
2.	International News	41.006**	12	26.217	1%
3.	News about political parties	56.774**	8	15.507	5%
			8	20.090	1%
4.	Ministerial broadcasts	19.192NS	12	21.026	5%
5.	News about riots and violence	102.078**	12	26.217	1%
6.	Assembly broadcasts	69.374**	8	20.090	1%
7.	Party pre-election broadcasts	65.172**	12	26.217	1%
8.	Programmes on casting a vote	20.466**	8	20.090	1%
9.	Election News	109.434**	12	26.217	1%
10.	Budget broadcasts	8.944NS	8	15.507	5%
11.	Message by leaders	34.182**	12	26.217	1%
12.	Janvani	6.164NS	8	15.507	5%
13.	Choice of the media	30.76**	12	26.217	1%

*Significant at 5% level—**Significant at 1% level—NS Not significant

casting of a vote since the procedure of voting was already familiar to them long before the invention of TV.

In the areas of Budget and Janvani also, no significant association with occupation was noticed i.e. the Chi-square values are lesser than the tabulated figures. The limitations of these two programmes were already discussed earlier (Part-II).

Though housewives were taken as separate category in the occupation group the level of their awareness has already been discussed under the category 'SEX'.

Occupation by its nature of work is expected to influence the political awareness of an individual. The observed results show that more than academic education the soundness in financial status seems to have a more direct impact on the level of political awareness. Here it may be mentioned that the villagers themselves said in as many words that they do not get enough time to see all the programmes as they spend the entire day in earning their daily bread. They even said that though the programmes shown are of utmost interest they simply could not ignore their regular duties. This group of people are ofcourse those striving for a firm financial background.

As to the choice of the Media as a source of information except the first category (owner—cultivation) others preferred TV as major source. The category-I preferred Radio as their Primary source. Agriculture labour selected Radio as second choice where as others ranked newspapers as second and Radio as third. It may be recalled here that many villagers stated that they carry with them Radio sets to the fields since they stay in the fields almost throughout of the day.

Education

Education as an influencing factor has a significant effect on the political awareness of the villagers. In certain critical areas of political awareness (the word critical here may be taken to mean where a little higher level of understanding is required) like International news, Political parties, Assembly,

Party broadcasts, Budget, Political events and Janvani, the difference of awareness was significant. In other areas where functional knowledge would have served the purpose, no difference between educated and uneducated was noticed.

Thus it can be inferred from the values (Table-25) that the more the Education the higher the level of understanding. Since no association was noticed between education and political awareness in certain aspects it may be said that a deep interest and motivation in the subject can compensate to some extent for the lack of formal education.

Except in International and Party broadcasts, the Chi-square values of association were not too high compared to tabulated values as observed in the case of sex, thus supporting the earlier discussions that apathy towards politics among the educated plays an important role in the level of their political awareness.

Similar to the case of occupation the limitation here is that the sample consists of :

(a) less number of highly educated people like Post-graduates and Professional degree holders ;

(b) among them also intellectuals like Professors, Doctors and Lawers are almost absent excepting one or two cases ;

(c) lack of Intellectual environment.

As regards to the choice of media no association was observed. However, Graduates and Postgraduates preferred Newspapers equally to TV.

Age

Age did not show any influence in the levels of political awareness of the villagers, except in understanding the Assembly proceedings. Assembly proceedings seem to have more appeal to villagers in the age group of above 40, whereas the respondents in the age groups of 21-30 and 31-40 mainly stood at first level i.e. the lowest (Table-26).

TABLE 25

Test of Association of Education with the Levels of Awareness of Different Types of Political Programmes

Sl. No.	*Programme*	*X^2 Calculated*	*Degree of freedom*	*X^2 Tabulated*	*Level of significance*
1.	Economic News	11.1 NS	6	12.592	5%
2.	International News	50.81 **	6	16.812	1%
3.	News about political parties	19.714**	6	16.812	1%
4.	Ministerial broadcasts	7.886NS	9	16.919	5%
5.	News about roits and violence	4.908NS	9	16.919	5%
6.	Assembly broadcasts	24.394**	6	16.812	1%
7.	Party pre-election broadcasts	35.776**	9	21.666	1%
8.	Programmes on casting a vote	11.9126NS	6	12.592	5%
9.	Election News	16.7 *	9	16.919	5%
10.	Budget broadcasts	22.388**	9	21.666	1%
11.	Message by leaders	21.506**	9	21.666	1%
12.	Janvani	24.618**	3	11.341	1%
13.	Choice of Media	8.054NS	6	12.592	5%

*Significant at 5% level— **Significant at 1% level—NS Not Significant

TABLE 26

Test of Association of Age with the Levels of Awareness of Different Types of Political Programmes

Sl. No.	*Programme*	*X^2 Calculated*	*Degree of Freedom*	*X^2 Tabulated*	*Level of significance*
1.	Economic News	5.096^{NS}	6	12.592	5%
2.	International News	8.892^{NS}	9	16.919	5%
3.	News about political parties	9.146^{NS}	9	16.919	5%
4.	Ministerial broadcasts	10.282^{NS}	9	16.919	5%
5.	News about riots and violence	7.93^{NS}	9	16.919	5%
6.	Assembly broadcasts	70.032**	9	21.666	1%
7.	Party pre-election broadcasts	20.444*	9	16.919	5%
8.	Programmes on casting a vote	8.432^{NS}	9	16.919	5%
9.	Election News	4.52^{NS}	9	16.919	5%
10.	Budget broadcasts	19.438*	9	16.919	5%
11.	Message by leaders	6.372^{NS}	9	16.919	5%
12.	Janvani	3.354^{NS}	6	12.592	5%
13.	Choice of Media	12.7*	6	12.592	5%

*Significant at 5% level—**Significant at 1% level—NS Not Significant

In pre-election and Budget broadcasts a slight association was noticed at 5% level. As thought earlier, older people with their maturity and experience and younger people with their enthusiasm to actually participate in politics were expected to have better understanding of politics.

The lack of appreciable difference between the different age groups in political awareness could be because;

(a) The sample consisted of a majority of youngsters whose level of awareness may be of the same order.

(b) Since persons of 21 years and above only were taken for the present study, all of them must have been exposed to political activity during elections as they were voting regularly.

(c) Again, contrary to the expectation, older people inspite of their experience were unable to perform better compared to the younger people. Although some older respondents were observed to be responding more out of their past experience than actually recalling exactly what they saw on TV. For example, they talked about assembly programmes which in fact had very short coverages only. Some people above sixty years of age confided their inability to follow the programmes due to their personal sight problems. Other reasons include frequent power failure and poor reception quality in case of villages situated more than 100 kilometres away from the city.

PART IV

A Quantitative Analysis of the Status of Awareness and its Relationship with the Viewers Background

This is yet another analysis in this study to see the nature of the sample sexwise and castewise and the relationship between political awareness, and certain selected aspects. For this purpose a particular score was given to each respondent for their socio-economic background, degree of exposure and political awareness and the data tabulated accordingly.

While fixing the score for each respondent, the rationale kept in mind is : the commonly accepted value plus the value of these different aspects in substantiating the purpose of the study, i.e. in influencing the awareness of the respondent. For example, with the exception of social participation, the entire socio-economic background was given the commonly accepted score. In case of social participation, since one cannot judge one's social activity as being better than another no definite score could be fixed. To overcome this problem only the type of activity connected to political awareness was considered for giving a gradation in scores i.e. political participation was given the higher score, as it is likely to influence more directly the political awareness. Activities relating to economics was rated second highest and so on.

Similarly, in case of programme preference also, respondent who rated political programmes as their first choice have been given the highest score (3) followed by educational (2) and recreational (1).

The same rationale was applied to all other questions where a similar problem was experienced. Thus, each person was given a particular score based on his/her response to different items. With the assistance of these total values the mean scores were calculated. (The interview schedule along with the scores given is presented at the end of the thesis as Appendix).

For the sake of convenience and reference the mean scores of different aspects have been identified as X for social status, Y for financial status etc. This may be further explained as below.

1. The total index of socio-economic background...Z

   This has been divided into two categories

   (a) Social status...X

   Education, occupation and social participation have been taken as indicators of social status.

(b) Financial status...Y

Income, land and home owned have been taken to consider the financial status of a person.

2. Degree of exposure to Television—Total index...U

(a) Degree of exposure of television...U_1

Owning a television set, viewing habits, time spent for viewing TV, suitability to timing, programme preference etc. were taken into consideration here.

(b) Impact of TV on other media...U_2

Radio listening, and movie going habits were considered here.

(c) Choice of media as a source of information...U_3

...Among Television, Radio, newspapers, friends, family members, neighbours and other sources.

3. Degree of exposure to political programmes—Total index...V

(a) Language preferred for news and language problem faced...V_1

(b) Type and content of news preferred...V_2

4. Level of political awareness...W

(a) Political awareness through regular programmes...W_1

(b) Political awareness through occassional programme...W_2

The level of awareness (W) was divided as above to find out whether there is any difference in the mean scores of the viewers of regular programmes and that of occassional.

The mean scores of the above parameters are given in Table-27. The nature of these mean values was analysed both independently and comparatively and the reasons were predicted as below.

As stated earlier this analysis consists of two parts.

(1) The nature of the sample, sex, and castewise and

TABLE 27

A Quantitative Analysis of the Status of Awareness and its Relationship with the Viewers Background

Sl. No.	Factor	Mean Scores of FC Men	BC Men	EC Women	BC Women
1.	X	11.90	10.12	5.05	4.25
2.	Y	7.84	4.32	8.90	6.71
3.	Z	27.01	20.84	10.57	15.14
4.	U_1	10.62	9.28	10.83	9.61
5.	U_2	1.99	2.02	2.45	2.21
6.	U_3	3.07	3.02	3.57	3.54
7.	U	15.67	14.32	16.86	15.36
8.	V_1	6.01	4.25	3.26	2.36
9.	V_2	6.05	5.60	7.43	7.00
10.	V	12.07	9.84	10.69	9.36
11.	W_1	18.16	18.56	15.02	13.79
12.	W_2	17.22	15.74	12.10	11.86
13.	W	35.38	34.30	27.12	25.64

X Social Status

Y Financial Status

Z Total index of socio-economic background

U_1 Degree of exposure to TV

U_2 Influence of TV on other media

U_3 Choice of media as a source of information

U Degree of exposure to TV-total index

V_1 Language preferred for news and language problem

V_2 Type and content of news preferred

V Degree of exposure to political programmes-total index

W_1 Political awareness through regular programmes

W_2 Political awareness through occassional programmes

W Levels of political awareness,

(2) The relationship between political awareness and certain selected aspects.

The analysis of the nature of the sample was mainly carried out to see whether there exists any difference sex and castewise in socio-economic status, exposure to media in general and TV in particular, exposure to political programmes and levels of political awareness of the respondents. Comparisons were made among the combinations given under.

The aim of comparing these means is to compare the degree of difference in mean scores of political awareness as per these social status categories. While the earlier analysis of association tested merely the presence of association, the present comparisons provide the quantitative differences in awareness levels.

1. Male and female
2. Forward caste male and forward caste female
3. BC male and BC female
4. FC male and BC male
5. FC female and BC female

The total index of the socio-economic background-(Z) of this sample shows that, the difference is greater castewise than sex-wise. The forward caste men stood at highest level, BC women at lowest and the difference between the BC men and FC women is very less. A look into the mean scores of social and financial status may reveal the reasons for these difference.

Social Status (X)

Mean scores of females is only half of that of males. This means that females rate very low in education, occupation and any social activity. Castewise there is not so much difference in the social status score of male and female, however, FC male and female score one point more than the BC male and female.

Financial Status (Y)

Scores show that there is a considerable difference in financial status taken castewise. In this sample females seem to have higher financial status than males. This may be because, while selecting the sample only one person (either male or female) was taken per house (to get a wider representation in socio-economic background). Probably the women who got included in the sample must be representing the richer sections of the society. Except in a few instances wives of the male respondents were not approached in this study.

BC women have shown a higher financial status than BC men. This is because, in addition to the above said reason, female respondents had to be approached in their houses (indicating ownership of houses giving them a better financial status), whereas men were available at all meeting points of the village like village panchayat office, community centre, hotels etc. representing different cross sections of the BC group i.e. different levels in financial status.

In case of FC women the Reddy caste persons form a higher percentage than other FC caste persons. The Reddy caste persons generally have always had a sound financial status in the Telangana districts. However, a point to be noted here is that in this sample women's high financial position is largely due to their parents'/husbands' property or income.

From the above it is observed that the reason for the BC men to score poorly than FC men in total index, inspite of their being almost equal in social status, is apparently their poor financial status. This also reflects one more point that their low score brings them closer to the score of FC women (with low profile in social status) the reason being the better financial position of FC women.

2. **Degree of Exposure-Total Index** (U)

Sex-wise men scored one point lesser than women. Castewise, BCs scored one point lesser than FCs.

A look into the three aspects (U_1, U_2 and U_3) that are covered under this category may give the reasons for the above findings.

Degree of Exposure to TV (U_1)

Caste-wise FCs have scored one point more than BCs. Owning a TV set could be the reason for this. Sex-wise females score slightly more than males. More leisure time in the hands of females could be the reason for this slight difference.

Impact of the Television on the other Media (U_2)

People who preferred to watch TV even when the Radio transmission is on were given higher score since the study is concerned mainly about knowing whether TV has influenced Radio listening.

Similarly, the sample whose movie going habit has been affected due to the influence of TV were also given higher score here.

In this FC women score more than BC women. Owning a TV may be one of the reasons for this. Among BC women, many of them do not own a set. Also some of them are in the fields from dawn to dusk. These women depend on the Radio more than TV. Coming to FC men, they score least in this respect. Because of their low score, it may be understood that they are not affected much with the influence of TV. This shows that FC men do not give a high priority to TV or to the media in general. They do keep in touch with the media for information but this is only when they are free. BC men score lesser than women. This is because they do not own a set and also they go out to the fields for work.

Choice of Media as a Source of Information (U_3)

...Among TV, Radio, Newspapers, movies and other sources. A point of clarification may be required here also.

Among these four sources of communication people who opted TV were given the highest score (4) followed by Radio (3), Newspaper (2) and others (1). In addition to the above discussed rationale while fixing the score, one more aspect was considered to be significant.

Keeping aside the criticism on reporting, Television experience can be regarded as almost all nearer to reality on account of its visual support. As such it was given the highest score. Radio which appeals to the auditory sense was considered as the next effective media of mass communication. Since newspapers' use is limited to only literates and less effective in presentation compared to broadcast media have been given the third place. The remaining category i.e. friends, family members and neighbours can be considered as secondary sources since they themselves depend for information on mass media and as such they have been given the last score.

Sex-wise, the difference is not much and the difference is only in small fractions. Women preferred TV to other source of information. The reasons have been discussed earlier. Caste-wise, there is only a negligible difference between FC and BC. The reasons may be owning a TV set and this has also been discussed earlier.

3. Degree of exposure to political programmes-total index-(V)

Caste-wise the difference between FC men and BC men is more (2.23) and between FC women and BC women the difference is lesser than men (1.33). Sex-wise the difference between FC men and women of both castes is more. In case of BC men and BC women there is no difference. BC men are at a lower level compared to FC women which again may be due to the caste influence. On the whole FC men stood at a higher level compared to the other categories. The reasons are discussed below.

(a) Language preferred for news and language problem faced (V_1)

Both sex and castewise the difference is evident. FCs score higher than BCs and males score higher than females.

Possession of TV set and other advantages in case of FCs, and a general interest for news and ability to follow news in different languages in case of men may be the reasons for the above difference. Women scoring less may be because of language problem to a large extent in following the news.

(b) Type and content of news preferred (V_2)

Scoring given to items is in the following manner.

Type of news : Regional (1), National (2), Global (3), All (4)
Content of News : Cultural (1), Economic (2), Political (3), All (4)

Sex-wise women show a greater difference than men. The reason for women scoring high is that in the questionnaire a high score was given for persons marking "All types preferred." And women generally liked all types of news without any specific concern (the question was originally meant to find out an overall interest and it was expected that only persons who had a considerable interest in preferring all types of news would prefer to mark against this question). Men are equally distributed in all four categories. Men scoring high in V_1 compared to women could not show the same level in total index since women have shown a big score in V_2 due to the above mentioned reasons.

4. Level of Political Awareness (W)

(a) Regular Programmes (W_1)

Caste-wise difference has been noticed in the females only. (FC women score higher than BC women). Sex-wise there is a notable difference between males and females.

(b) Occassional Programmes (W_2)

Both caste and sex-wise (between FC men and BC men and between FC women and BC women) and sex-wise in general there is difference in the levels of political awareness.

The total index of the levels of political awareness (W) shows that sex-wise there is an indication of greater difference. Caste-wise the difference is less. The reasons for the above differences in the two scores may be as follows :

Men. Better educational qualifications and financial position and a better aptitude [in general of FC men compared to BC men may be the reason for their higher score in the level of political awareness.

Women. FC women score higher than BC women. The reason here also may be the same as those in the case of men.

Thus far women have been showing higher scores in financial status, and degree of exposure to TV alongside of men. But the fact remains that with all these, women score very low in political awareness than men.

This is a point of concern. It shows that a sound financial status by itself does not contribute to a person's knowledge or awareness. But it would be agreed that it can indirectly influence a person's mind (if properly channelised) for his/her development. The sample being rural women, the first reason may be true, i.e. mere possession of property did not help in their personal development. Secondly, womens' high degree of exposure (than men) has also not given them a high score in political awareness. The reason for this has been discussed earlier. Women seem more entertainment oriented unlike men who seem equally if not better interested in the other programmes. Womens' degree of exposure to news (political programmes) according to their score is almost equal to men, but this does not seem to improve their awareness. This may be because of their lack of interest in political matters in general.

And hence, this may be taken to mean that social status and education in which women have scored poor is an important factor contributing to their low level in political awareness. Men who are better scoring in social status and education, are the better scoring group in political awareness too (although their scores are less in financial status and exposure to TV).

The low social status which was assumed to be the main factor contributing to the low level of political awareness of the rural women in this sample may need further explanation in detail.

The X factor (i.e, education, occupation and social participation) when analysed separately has revealed the following reasons :

Education. As discussed earlier (Ch. III) the historical background of Telangana region was the main cause for its low educational level as compared to other two regions of Andhra Pradesh. Though subsequently education facilities were provided, the cultural deprivation in the past is still felt in the remote areas of Telangana, In these circumstances of the low educational standards in general, the plight of womens education in particular can be imagined.

Occupation. Among the four categories the SC and ST women attend to fields as agricultural labourers. Among FCs (mostly Reddys) for many of them there is no necessity to go out for work since they belong to rich sections of the village society. On account of low education most of the BC women are contended as housewives. Hence, it can be understood that most of the rural women are housewives with very few exceptions.

The urban or educated or working women who move out in the society may sometimes feel a kind of conflict for not being in touch with the political affairs of the state/country. This conflict sometimes compels one to acquaint themselves with the day-to-day happpenings in their surroundings. But the rural women have both physical and mental involvement in their household chores unlike urban women.

Social Participation. Inspite of uneducated and being housewives, if interested, rural women can develop themselves through social participation.

The following reasons could be gathered from the conversation with the women for their inattentiveness towards political programmes and social participation.

An observation (though has no direct relevance to the study) may be made in this context. Unlike urban families, most of the rural families have more number of children varying between two and five. In some cases it is also observed that where the first three or four children are females the next child is invariably of the different sex. This shows their belief to compulsorily have a male child, in a family irrespective of the number of children to be reared. Because of this the rural women are overburdened with the family responsibilities than the urban women.

Some women were of the view that politics are of no use to them since no one expects them to talk about politics, whereas they are looked down if do not discharge their primary responsibilities as a housewife. Knowledge in politics according to them is not going to bring any change in their present life. The rural women do not seem to appreciate the role of politics in day-to-day life and are bothered only about their immediate problems.

Thus, whatever score they have shown in awareness as far as this study is concerned, may be said to be to some extent due to their extensive exposure to TV.

So far the observations made were limited to only FC and BC women sample. The SC and ST women in rural areas are in very pitiable conditions. Their ignorance and innocence are so high that even to talk about their political awareness in an ideal sense may be a futile exercise. To educate them in this regard through TV programmes, may require a minimum standard in their socio-economic status.

Relationship between Political Awareness and Certain Selected Aspects

The Second part of the analysis i.e. "The Relationship between Political awareness and certain selected aspects" was mainly carried out in order to further study the relationship between

(i) political awareness and owning a TV set

(ii) political awareness and time spent for viewing
(iii) political awareness and language preferred for news
(iv) political awareness and news content preferred
(v) political awareness and level of education.

The following salient findings are indicated by these mean values (Table-28).

(i) As mean scores of awareness among the groups owning and non owning a TV are almost same, we infer that owning a TV set does not show any relationship to political awareness. This reveals that the mere presence of an object (TV) may not increase one's knowledge in any field. In this sample people not owning a TV set are also keen on getting information even if it means going to their neighbours' homes or community centres to watch TV.

(ii) There is a slight relationship in the political awareness of people viewing TV for longer hours and those viewing for a limited time. That is, there is a small increase in the mean value of awareness when there is an increase in the time spent.

(iii) There is a considerable difference in the levels of awareness between people who watch only Telugu news and those who watch Hindi and English news also in addition to Telugu news. Persons watching news in all languages have shown a greater score in awareness, where as the score is a little less for people who watch news in any two languages only.

Since the scores show a relationship between language preferred for news and political awareness, it may be inferred that political news is being received in greater quantum in the national news bulletins. In this also the English news bulletins appear to provide more effective political news than the Hindi and regional news bulletins, perhaps because of the usually greater coverage of international news in the English bulletins. Taking the two national bulletins, only a small difference was observed between Hindi and English news. This small difference could be because the English news carries almost all that has been covered in the Hindi news except a few inclusions.

TABLE 28

A Quantitative Analysis of the Status of the Awareness and its Relationship with the Viewers Background

Sl. No.	Factors		Means scores Levels of Political Awareness W_1	W_1	W_1	Frequency number of persons
1.	Owning a TV set	.. No	17.46	15.04	32.5	74
		.. Yes	16.82	14.85	31.67	126
2.	Time spent for viewing	.. 1 hr.	16.91	14.45	31.37	115
		.. 2 hrs.	17.31	14.54	31.85	13
		.. 2 to 3 hrs.	17.14	15.75	32.89	56
		.. 4 to 5 hrs.	16.00	14.00	30.00	2
		.. 5 and above	17.07	16.64	33.71	14
3.	Language prferred for news	.. Telugu	15.84	13.49	29.33	82
		.. Hindi	14.5	9.5	24.00	2
		.. English	20.00	24.00	44.00	1
		.. Telugu & Hindi	17.34	15.78	33.12	50
		.. Telugu & Eng. .. Hindi & Eng.	18.00	15.82	33.82	11
		.. Tel. Hindi & Eng.	18.02	16.15	35.17	54

Contd.

4.	News content preferred	.. Cultural	16.5	15.00	31.5	4
		.. Economic	14.54	15.15	29.69	13
		.. Political	18.99	17.33	36.32	82
		.. All	15.73	13.03	28.76	101
5.	Level of Education	.. Illiterate	14.69	12.94	27.63	35
		.. Primary or literate	16.93	14.95	31.88	42
		.. Middle School	15.31	12.41	27.72	29
		.. High School	17.88	15.97	33.85	33
		.. Intermediate	18.41	15.97	34.38	32
		.. Graduation	19.18	18.00	37.18	22
		.. Postgraduation	18.71	16.71	35.71	7

(iv) The score obtained in case of persons who preferred political news is rather high than persons preferring other news items (36.32). This indicates that there is a direct relationship between viewers inclination and the programme's impact. The slight difference (0.93) between persons who preferred economic news and those who showed a neutral standpoint towards all types of news may be said to be due to the rural background of the respondents. Preference for economic news may be due to the direct relationship between rural economy and agriculture.

(v) A direct relationship was noticed between the level of education and that of political awareness. Graduates and postgraduates showed a higher score in their awareness among the respondents. The slightly higher level of awareness of persons with primary level of education than of persons with middle school level of education could be only a sampling variation. Moreover, as far as formal education is concerned there is not much difference between primary and middle school level. And this slight difference in the two levels does not seem to carry much weight after several years when it comes to measuring a person's political awareness based on his formal schooling.

Again the postgraduates in the sample taken showed slightly lesser score than the graduates. This may be due to the fact that only seven persons out of two hundred were postgraduates and this small number may not be a sufficient representation of all PGs. Also, as said earlier the lack of intellectual environment commensurate with their academic attainment may be one more reason for their not showing better awareness than the graduates.

To sum up, firstly, the mere presence of a piece of hardware does not enhance one's knowledge. Secondly, the possibility of having better awareness is more when the time spent for it is more. Thirdly, repeatedly hearing news items in different languages reinforces a point better on one's mind. The effective presentation of news in the National news bulletins has a greater impact on the viewers. Fourthly, specific interest in political matters makes one more receptive to information. Fifthly, education helps one to have a better understanding of whatever is received through the media.

PART V

Correlation-Regression Analysis

The fifth part of this chapter mainly concentrates on the analysis of Correlation and Regression Coefficients. In the mean score analysis attempt was made to find out the relationship between the quantitative level of status for different parameters and the respondents exposure to Television. While considering the dependence of awareness on several variables the tests of association reveals whether there exists any dependence or not. The present Correlation and Regression analysis indicates the degree of dependence i.e. how much is the dependence and which variable is more dependent on other variable. This analysis facilitates to assess the nature of the sample and also to predict the reasons for the same.

The scores which were fixed for the calculation of mean scores have also been used for the calculation of Correlation and Regression Coefficients.

Since many of the observations have been already discussed in the previous analysis, only additional findings of significance were discussed here to avoid repetation. The findings are as follows.

Among the three aspects i.e. socio-economic background, degree of exposure to TV in general and to political programmes in particular the last aspect has shown a higher degree of relationship to political awareness followed by socio-economic background. The degree of exposure to TV in general did not show much relationship to political awareness (Table-29).

The nature of the relationship between different variables may be explained in detail as below.

A higher correlation was noticed between the inclination to watch news and other programmes with political content and that of political awareness. The relationship (regression coefficient) is so high that a unit increase in political content is leading to three units of increase in political awareness. This gives an impression that the more the political content and inclination to watch the same the more is the political awareness.

Socio economic background of the sample has also shown a greater relationship to political awareness in this study. Among the three factors (education, social status and financial status) that were considered under socio-economic background, financial status stood first and shown the highest relationship followed by social status and education.

The nature of relationship is a bit less here than that of inclination to watch political programmes i.e. one unit increase in financial status or social status or education is leading to only one unit increase in political awareness. However, the relationship between socio-economic background of the sample and their political awareness in this study is of a significant importance.

Next to socio-economic background, language preferred for news and language problem faced (V_1) has shown a significant relationship to political awareness. This indicates that people who prefer to see news in three languages without any language problem are likely to have higher level of political awareness.

The nature of relationship (regression coefficient) is one unit increase in preference is leading to one unit increase in the level of political awareness.

The possibilities as to how these factors have influenced

TABLE 29

Correlation and Regression Coefficients of Awareness with Scores of Different Variables

Sl. No.	*Variables*	*Correlation Coefficient r*	*t ≠ value*	*Regression Coefficient ±*	*SE ±*
1.	Socio-economic background				
	Education	.4123**	6.3746	1.7993	.2951
	Social status (X)	.5467**	9.1875	1.0111	.1103
	Financial status (Y)	.6422**	11.7893	1.3185	.1209
	Total index (Z)	0.4439*	6.9704	0.4175	.0486
2.	Degree of exposure to TV (Genl)				
	Viewing habits (U_1)	0.1249	1.7716	0.4105	0.2333
	Influence of TV on other media habits (U_2)	0.3982	1.2945	1.0267	0.7395
	Choice of media (U_3)	0.1126	1.5947	0.9432	0.5909
	Total Index (U)	0.1424	2.0248	0.3702	0.1796
3.	Degree of exposure to political programmes				
	Language preferred for news and language Problem (V_1)	0.4119**	6.3621	1.1509	0.1809
	News content preferred (V_2)	0.8371**	21.5333	3.7834	0.1757
	Total index (V)	0.3926	6.0067	0.1939	0.0323

*Significant at 5% level— **Significant at 1% level ≠ t value has 198 degrees of freedom.

the political awareness have been already discussed in the previous analysis.

The relationship between the degree of exposure to Television programmes in general and political awareness is of not much significance. That means matters like owning a Television set, viewing habits, amount of time spent and other aspects have no influence on the political awareness. The slight relationship that is observed in the total index (U) is very less.

The analysis and interpretation of the present Chapter reveals that an overall exposure to television is satisfactory though there is some variation in the levels of understanding. The villagers' acceptance of Television as their companion explains how it has become a part of day-to-day life in the present day society. To quote Shirley Williams...

> "Broadcasting both Radio and TV has been a great mitigator of loneliness. People live longer and more of them live alone. Radio and Television act as friends, neighbours, sources of news and gossip, a surrogate village community. For the elderly unable to get about much, for the physically handicapped or for the isolated housewife, broadcasting is a lifeline. True. It can substisute for chat and talk within families and between neighbours, so that conversation dies when the set is switched on".

Hence the policy makers and planners must keep the effect of Broadcasting on the villagers in view while making programmes.

The major findings 'of the study are discussed in detail in the next and final chapter for their implications to the policy and programme makers etc.

REFERENCES

1. Tom Wicker *On Press*, (Prentice Hall of India Pvt. Ltd., New Delhi, 1979), pp 10, 15.

2. Robert R. Sokal and F. J. Ralf, *Biometry—The Principles and Practice of Statistics in Biological Research*, (W. H. Freeman and Co.: Sanfrancisco, USA, 1981), p 696.
3. Shireley Williams, Essay in *The Future of Broadcasting*, ed. Richard Hoggart and Jonet Morgan, (Macmillan : London, 1982), p 14.

CHAPTER FIVE

Summary and Conclusions

Broadcasting has a large net work. To demarcate its boundaries is difficult. The Radio and TV network is fast expanding day by day with various kinds of messages. The overall impact of TV cannot be assessed at one stretch. The fields which are influenced by this multifaceted institution are numerous. Among such fields, political education is one which deserves considerable importance both from media side as well as public. However, indepth research did not take place in this field of political broadcasting in our country due to many limitations. The research units of Doordarshan and other organizations have thrown some light in this area, but could not go in depth since they had to concentrate equally on other areas such as entertainment, commercials and agriculture programmes as well. Hence the present study has been conducted to explore this aspect. It was felt that the study is of importance to our country since our's is basically rural oriented and has adopted a democratic type of government where public opinion is the basis for the formation of the states policies. Mass media evidently plays a vital role in such a system in shaping public opinion.

In our country, it is observed that the print media is widely used to shape public opinion in political affairs. The electronic media which is presumed to be more powerful in covering large areas with an easy access to illiterates, is also contributing towards this end. While the broadcast media is in government's control, the film makers also, through cinema medium, are able to send political messages effectively to the masses now and then. However, all these media of mass communications are under criticism for their bias in coverage and each has its own place among the people, for example print media among literates etc.

The present study deals with the impact of TV on rural masses with reference to their levels of political awareness. The main objectives of this study are to assess the impact of TV on rural folk and to see how far the present political programmes on TV are useful to the masses in creating political consciousness among them. For this purpose, this study proposed a hypothesis that there exists a positive relationship between the degree of exposure to TV and political awareness of the rural masses. The influence of a number of other subvariables namely, age, caste, sex, education, social participation and occupation on the levels of political awareness is also considered while assessing the above relationship and the ultimate impact of TV. A structured interview schedule has been prepared as a tool for the study. A four point scale constructed to measure the levels of awareness in order to quantify it forms the main technical tool in the analysis of the results of the responses in the interview.

Ten villages of Ranga Reddy district have been taken as a sample to know the impact of political programmes that are broadcast from Doordarshan. Hyderabad. The sample consisted of 200 respondents of which seventy were women. The collected data have been analysed and put to statistical tests like chi-square, correlation and regression analysis, mean scores and testing of relationships. The results thus obtained, which were presented in the earlier chapters, are now discussed for the underlying factors that have influenced them and for their possible implications to the policy makers involved in media planning and education. The discussion is phased out over various major aspects. Though the study has its own limitations, the suggestions mentioned may provide some information useful for the effective functioning of the organization.

The major results of the study are listed out in a numbered sequence. Each result is shown in a small paragraph immediately followed by the discussion and conclusion before another result is taken up, as detailed under.

1. A good percentage of the respondents donot have TV sets of their own. However, owning a TV set doesnot seem to bear any direct relationship to political awareness as observed in this study.

Nevertheless, owning of TV sets is to be encouraged since this has been considered as a fundamental step in the development of TV as a medium of information. A good number of people are able to watch TV in their neighbours houses. It is noticed that in the village Gandeed almost all the people in the village are entertained by only one set in a private house. While the hospitality of the owner is appreciable, owning a TV set may be more desirable, comfortable and useful. It is observed that some of the people who may like to own a TV set are also habituated to depend on community TV sets due to the high cost. This dependence on neighbours or government may be reduced if a programme of providing TV sets at cheaper rates to the villagers is undertaken.

Since owning a TV set itself doesnot increase the levels of political awareness there is a necessity to draw the attention of the viewers to the programmes. Making programmes with attractive and captivating titles and using impressive music bits in the beginning of the programmes may draw the attention of the viewers to some extent. The techniques used in case of commercial advertisements may be kept in view in this context. A study of the TV programmes made in other countries may also give some ideas about the techniques that can be applied in this connection.

2. The study reveals that TV is not just an instrument for the entertainment of the viewers but it also makes them aware of many things provided they can sit before it for longer hours.

Many people are able to see TV for one hour daily with concentration. This duration is however very less when compared to the total transmission time of over five hours (morning transmission time not included). Only 20% of the transmission time is considered to constitute effective programme for the respective viewers. 40% of transmission time is viewed by very few (9.5%). There is also a difference between actual viewing and spending time before TV. The latest survey in this aspect conducted by Doordarshan in the twincities of Hyderabad and Secunderabad also says that the utilisation time out of a five hours transmission is only 18% (local-28%. National-12%, Network-25%)[1].

Here there is a necessity to study the viewing habits in detail i.e. whether they are dependent on the effectiveness of the programmes or on the physical and psychological conditions of the viewers. It is observed that many people switch the TV on for more time, but the actual viewing time is less. Some people do this due to lack of prior knowledge about the programme schedule. The effective viewing time can be increased to some extent if the programme schedule is published with full details well in advance and also by frequently highlighting the future programmes on TV. (It may be remarked here that the press is not providing full details of the programmes). Ofcourse the programme quality will always have an influence on increasing the viewing time. The viewing time may not be even to the extent observed in other areas of the state, where Hindi is not so popular. Hence increasing programmes in local language may also increase the effective viewing time.

.3 TV has weaned people away from Radio and Cinema. This was more in case of FC women than the others.

There is a considerable decline in Radio listening in case of villagers owning a TV set. These people usually tune to Radio in the morning or afternoon where there is no TV transmission mainly for film songs and other light entertainment. In case of Radio the first hypothesis i.e. TV can have greater impact when compared to other media of mass communications is supported by the study. It is observed that morning TV transmission is not so popular and many tune to Radio in the mornings even during TV transmission. This may be on account of several factors such as busy hours, inability to sit before TV during these hours and also non availability of programmes in regional languages etc. Hence, though TV could affect Radio to some extent it may not completely dominate Radio listening. While TV demands full attention of the viewers, the Radio is used even while working with casual attention. One more observation is that it is not possible to use all media of mass communication simultaneously, All the media give the same information with slight variation. Once the information is received from one source the necessity to get it from other sources in naturally reduced.

The study indicates that TV has affected movie going. In villages where the theatres are very less and people have to visit cities to watch movies this may be understandable. But one has to see whether the same atmosphere is prevailing in urban areas also, where the theatres are at a hand stretch. While the study supports the first hypothesis it is also seen that movies have not lost their attraction for youth and women. This may be attributed to a small difference between TV and movies. As observed by Patanjali, Television is a means of communication while cinema can be described as a vehicle of communion. Communion takes place at a deeper level where all men feel a kind of kinship. It is believed that TV viewers are in a position to make rational criticism, in the sense that they regard TV mainly as a means of disseminating real life information. The Cinema spectators on the other hand, by plunging as it were in to the film world seek to forget their own world and the reality of their world. The Cinema viewer knows that what he is being offered is only a dream.[2] It is also observed that film songs over Radio and feature films on TV are attractive to many villagers. Therefore it can be concluded that though TV is dominating the other media to a great extent the latter have also their own place among the people.

4. The present TV timings are suitable for a greater part of the sample.

The study shows that a majority of men and a higher part of women suitably adjust their routine work according to TV programme schedule to watch TV. The policy makers and programme people must keep this enthusiasm and interest of villagers in mind and prepare the programmes to the full satisfaction of the viewers. However, many agricultural labourers complained that they are missing some of the programmes telecast before 7.30 PM. A revised time schedule is suggested, so that the regional programmes can be seen by the agricultural labourers also who constitute a major part of the rural folk for whom such items are specially made.

5. The villagers are not passive viewers. Many of them discuss the programmes amongst themselves.

The programme makers should consider this aspect and make programmes which are thought provoking, of good quality and give no scope for any comments or criticism. It was pointed by some respondents, during personal discussions, that interviews and discussions and other such items that are telecast on TV lack depth. They are not well planned and are held in an uneasy and delicate atmosphere with a feeling of not hurting the interviewee by attacking from all the directions on the subject. Here the participants are expected to be efficient so as to go deep into the field and explore the maximum information from the discussions and satisfy the TV viewers.

6. (a) The preference for programmes among the villagers reveals that TV is not a mere tool of entertainment but it equally and effectively serve the fundamental purpose of educating the masses.

Recently many surveys were carried out regarding TV programmes especially of entertainment. The results of these surveys (published in newspapers) show that entertainment programmes are preferred to others. The present study while supporting the above findings concludes that a close look into the opinions of the villagers reveal that TV is not only entertaining the rural masses but is also equally educating them. As such the educationists can better utilise this medium without any hesitation for their non-formal educational programmes. Similarly the TV authorities also can transmit their educational programmes with confidence that they are useful for the target audience. In this context it is suggested to provide a separate channel for educational programmes wherein a portion of the time may be devoted for rural people.

6. (b) TV is the major source of information for majority of the villagers especially women.

Many villagers are happy in stating that they are able to know many things only because of TV. This also supports the first Hypothesis. In this aspect the present study supports the research made in Japan to know what media are the information sources not only for an election but for other various events in politics (Yoshimuras et al (1967) study on Hiratsuka city and research by the Komei Election league (Watanuki 1969). Regarding more women preferring TV, the author refers to TV as female type and newspapers as male type[3].

7. Telugu language is preferred for news by most of the villagers. However, persons watching news in all the languages have shown a greater score in awareness whereas the score is a little less for people who watch news in two languages only. Castewise BCs and Sexwise females found language as a barrier in understanding news.

Several suggestions made by the villagers that may be of interest to the TV authorities of Hyderabad Door Darshan include those such as :

—Increasing the number of regional news bulletins and raising their standard to the level of national bulletins.

—Increasing the number of visuals in news bulletins.

—Increasing the duration of the news bulletins.

—More coverage to local, village and district level news.

—Impartial coverage to all political parties.

8. A significant percentage, mainly consisting of men, is interested more in political news. They have also shown a high score in awareness. This is followed by economic news.

The preference for political news among men shows the inclination to receive more information of the nature among the villagers. It indicates that the existing political content appears to be not sufficient for them. Since the economic matters are closely related to their occupation than the others, the economic news is also preferred by the villagers. Therefore, the political and economic content in the news bulletins may be increased accordingly.

9. **Degree of Exposure to Political Programmes**

(a) Nine persons out of a hundred do not know the names or recognise the President, the Prime Minister, the Chief Minister or the Governor. The formal terminology of the designations was beyond the comprehension of some illiterates particularly among the scheduled castes.

For more than forty years we have adopted a democratic form of government. The mass media is giving lot of information everyday regarding government's activities. Many political parties are working actively to win the confidence of the villagers. Inspite of all these, it is surprising that nine out of a hundred donot even know the names of the above mentioned national leaders. If this is the plight in the villages that are very much nearer to the urban atmosphere, the situation in the remote villages and tribal and hill areas can be imagined. It is a poor index of our development. The study strongly suggests the educationists, political parties, intelligentia and government to prepare a timebound scheme wherein the people are educated of the fundamentals of state affairs.

The educationists must stress the need for more political education from the functional point of view in the school curriculum. Political parties simultaneously along with their party propaganda must also concentrate giving political education to the rural masses. The mass media and government must also take similar steps in raising the political consciousness of the villagers especially in respect of scheduled castes and tribal folk. The above institutions may start their education from the basic level including the terminology and the responsibilities of portfolios held by these leaders.

(b) TV is playing a significant role in familiarizing the national personalities to the villagers. A highest percentage of women folk could see these leaders only because of TV.

Familiarity of the political personalities may be considered as the first step to political education. Some times this may create interest in knowing further about politics. As Shirley Williams observes, TV creates an illusion of personal relationship between the viewer and the politician concerned, wherein the viewer feels that he or she knows the politicians intimately.[4] The studies in other countries have also revealed that TV news is drawing viewers who have been not exposed earlier to any media for news.

The following items of political broadcasting are mainly given through news which is a regular feature. Response to current affairs and such other programmes is completely blank which may be due to the non-availability of the programmes in the regional languages. It is observed that the regular ten minute daily news bulletin is not sufficient to impart political education to the rural masses. The study emphasizes the need to start supplementary programmes in regional language in addition to the political information presented through news. Talks, interviews, features, discussions, drama and other programmes that contain politics as a subject may be telecast to inculcate interest among the viewers and motivate them to receive political education. Though the effect of regular programmes is more than the occassional, these items could be telecast weekly once or twice keeping the available time in view. Hitherto there is no segregation as urban viewers and rural masses as far as the regional news is concerned. The supplementary programmes can (atleast some of them) keep rural masses as their target audience and may be prepared accordingly. These programmes should be strictly in local language for an easy and better understanding among them. If feasible rural participation may also be encouraged in TV programmes. An observation shows that the villagers are under the impression that their opinion has no weight and is not cared for. Such feelings may be eliminated by actively involving the rural masses in the programmes which make them self-confident and can express their opinions freely and frankly.

(c) *Economic News.* The news is received by both the sexes with equal interest and enthusiasm. The fact whether or not TV educates one in this regard does not seem to matter much for them.

The dissatisfaction among the villagers about the support price for their products and the higher purchase rate of the same product in the open market that they pay later is required to be removed by presenting factual details of the government policies and the tasks involved in this regard. The supplementary programmes should contain the details of the export import policies of the government, taxation and other reasons such as natural calamities, drought etc. that are beyond the control of the government which has a bearing on the prices, since many villagers have come to a conclusion that inflation is inevitable whether or not TV gives information in this regard. The villagers have absolutely no idea about the consumer societies, consumer movements, their rights etc. and peoples' involvement in this respect. Programmes are to be prepared to remove the helpless attitude among the villagers.

It is observed that there appears to be no difference in the presentation of economic news by TV and the Radio. TV has to present this news in a better manner by using visuals and film strips appropriately.

(d) TV is familiarising the international political personalities to the rural masses which could not be done earlier by the other media so effectively.

But the knowledge acquired through TV seems to be superficial since English news bulletin is the main source for such knowledge which proved to be difficult for villagers to understand. In addition to the effective presentation of international political information in regional news bulletins the supplementary programmes should aim at giving a basic ground as to the importance and need of the international news for the people in general. While giving coverage to international political personalities and affairs interests of the viewers must also be considered in addition to the preference and discretion of the programmers. To this end the research department of Doordarshan may conduct surveys and public opinion polls to know the interests of the people.

The adult educational programmes of TV may also concentrate on international matters which broadens the outlook of the people.

(e) *News about Political Parties.* There is a widespread criticism even among the villagers that the TV is being used for ruling party's publicity.

Some of the villagers have expressed indifference towards TV in this aspect. This to a considerable extent is damaging the credibility of this medium. It is the responsibility of the policy makers not to give any scope for such criticism. They must also keep in view while presenting the news, the opinion of the villagers that no coverage is being given to political parties other than the ruling one.

The importance and the positive role of the political parties for a healthy competition in a democracy needs to be highlighted through special programmes such as interviews, talks etc. by political leaders, intelligentia, educationists, statesmen etc. Since women's response to this news is very less, the women's programmes should impress upon the necessity, importance and use of such information. Educationists while preparing the curriculum for political education must also concentrate more on the role of opposition parties in a democracy.

(f) *Ministerial Broadcasts.* The villagers could recognise a few Ministers of Central Government on the screen. Earlier familiarity seems to help them in this regard.

Though these broadcasts are popular among rural masses the limited coverage in the news does not seems to give adequate knowledge about the ministers' activities, plans etc. The supplementary programmes can contain different categories of broadcasts by the ministers in their concerned fields instead of token coverages of inaugural functions and other ceremonies. Except central and state ministers, the ministers of other states are not much popular among the villagers. If occassional interviews with the ministers of other states are also arranged over TV the political atmosphere in these states is also known to the villagers, which gives scope for cooperative outlook of the political atmosphere in different states.

(g) *News about Riots and Violence.* The villagers' response to this news especially among women folk was emotional. Most of the sample deeply felt the necessity for such kind of news as it helps them in many ways.

It is observed that now-a-days politics and violence are interrelated. This is a peculiar phenomenon. Group rivalries particularly to prevent voting in favour of a particular group are frequently noticed. This sometimes makes villagers especially Harijans loosing interest in exercising their franchise. The political ignorance of these people is being exploited.

While covering such news of other states and abroad the situation at local level also needs to be given due importance. Since there is a danger of arousing emotions of adolescents by presenting such news the programme should be prepared in a manner so as to awaken the people to fight such anti-social elements. Different types of folk art that are popular among the villagers may be utilised in programme making.

(h) *Assembly Broadcasts.* While the exposure to this news is encouraging, Radio is preferred more to TV in this area since reporting of assembly proceedings is not very interesting on TV.

The proceedings of the legislature including the humour, wit etc. are to be reported in a more interesting manner over TV. Supplementary programmes throughout the year may be introduced to give the information about the governmental procedure and Assembly business as the present programmes are beyond the comprehension of some of the villagers especially women. Women's programmes should stress the need for such knowledge for the benefit of women viewers. These limited reports and reviews are not able to explain to the villagers what is actually happening in the Assembly. Hence the study suggests the live telecast or its edited session of Assembly/Parliamentary proceedings which can only give a complete education about the Assembly/Parliament procedure.

(i) *Party Election Broadcasts.* The villagers could recall these programmes because of their interest in party politics and due to visual impact.

Though they have realised the importance of these broadcasts their final decision as to whom to vote is not entirely based on this. Villagers watch these broadcasts just to know what is being said by different political parties. It may be fitting here to quote an observation by Lazarsfeld and his colleagues when the political impact of mass-media was under discussion.

> "Arguments enter the final stage of decision more as indicators than as influences. They point out like sign-boards along the road, the way to turn in order to reach a destination which is already predetermined. The political predispositions and group allegiances set the goal, all that is read and heard becomes helpful and effective in so far as it guides the voter towards his already 'chosen' destination. The clinching arguement thus does not have the function of persuading the voter to act. He furnishes the motive power himself. The arguement has the function of identifying for him the way of thinking and acting which he is already half aware of wanting."[5]

These party election broadcasts on our TV are just occassional programmes and are not sufficiently giving opportunity for the contesting parties to actually reach people through their policies and programmes. In advanced countries, TV has given scope to the leaders in reaching millions of people and winning their confidence. As McQuail says "an election is a special, infrequent, yet in a sense quite decisive event, one in which voters are invited to choose between political alternatives laid before them. It unleashes a more ample flood of overtly political materials onto the head of citizens than they are expected to cope with at any other moment of the civic calender."[6]

Keeping the importance of election time in view the request of the villagers for extending the party broadcasts to village and municipal level elections also may be considered.

In addition to this, regular features on major issues of the country involving major political personalities/parties in making some concrete suggestions to the government in overcoming the problems, for example, Sri Lanka problem, Punjab issues, border problem etc., can be telecast so that people may have an opportunity to know the view points of different groups. This is very helpful when the Assembly is not in session. No doubt all these telecasts must be in regional languages so that the villagers get a chance to understand them properly.

(j) *Programmes on Casting a Vote.* These programmes are very useful to the villagers.

When the small snippets and slogans have been so beneficial to the villagers, more regular programmes in this direction instead of only during election time, may create more awareness among them. Even the villagers who are already aware of the election procedures and the importance of a VOTE have also stressed the need for such programmes. The technique of DRAMA may be utilised here for making programmes more interesting.

(k) *Election News.* The response indicates that TV's role in this area is very laudable.

It is said that in an Election Year Broadcasting has a double opportunity, one, to inform the Electorate thoroughly and honestly and the other to display its technical virtuosity.[7]

The former observation was found to be true in case of the

present sample since majority of them have referred TV as a reliable source of information for Election results. However, the computer analysis between the special election bulletins did not have any appeal on the rural masses. This analysis can be telecaste in the regional language so that the actual trend of different political parties may be understood by the voters.

(l) *Budget Broadcasts.* Response to these programmes is not very overwhelming though the budget was presented over TV just before the study. Most of the respondents referred to Central budget only in comparison to state budget.

Instead of a limited coverage in the regional news, there should be a special budget bulletin in the local language in addition to English and Hindi. The information about the state budget should also be given in the form of a special bulletin. The presentation of budget bulletin in the regional language must be improved since at present there is no difference between TV and Radio. The study empahssises the need for a regular programme on this subject which gives basic information such as what is a budget, when and for what period it is presented, what are the budget estimates etc.

(m) *Messages by National Leaders.* These infrequent broadcasts are attracting the masses.

While the message delivered by the Prime Minister on Independence day is widely recalled, the President's and Chief Minister's messages on such occassions are not so popular. This necessiates programme people to present messages of President and Chief Minister also in an effective way with colour and gaiety.

(n) *Janvani.* This programme may be revived and such features are suggested in regional languages also with local ministers. Like news papers, TV also should reflect the public voice on various issues. Since public opinion is the backbone for the effective functioning of a democracy, people' involvement in media programmes is to be encouraged.

(o) *Recall of Political Events.* TV could impress certain events on the minds of the viewers with its visual impact.

Due to this, some people are able to recall the major political events covered by the TV. But entertainment programmes (serials) are recalled more compared to political events. This shows the effect of drama on the minds of the people. Though it is not advisable to make politics a drama, efforts can be made to use this sort of technique for giving political information effectively.

While making the above programmes the following aspects may be kept in mind :

—Language

—Age of the participants

—Experience of the participants in their respective fields

—Technique selected

—The target audience

—Content and the presentation style

Entertainment should be judiciously combined in the presentation of educative/message oriented programmes, rather than entertainment dominating the presentation, which is normally noticed in the present day programmes. Political satire is another technique that can be effectively used to convey the messages to the masses. Like political cartoons, political satires in the form of PRAHASANAS (such as Chilakamarthi and Panuganti fame in Telugu) may be utilised more in this area. Unfortunately Political satire has not been much used on the TV more so in the local language broadcasts.

The teaching process requires a lot of patience. With other responsibilities, TV may not be able to concentrate so much on the political programmes alone. However, a committed effort on the part of the programme people, may yield good results in creating political consciousness among the rural masses. For example, a recent study conducted by the MARG on the first programme in Doordarshan series of discussions on the Bofors issue revealed that the Broadcast was impartial for as many as 37% of the viewers interviewed whereas 45% are of the opinion that the Government's view is presented. However, 10% of the viewers actually believed that the opposition view was presented.[8]

Influence of Sub-variables on the Levels of Political Awareness

10. In case of caste and age the Hypothesis is rejected and regarding sex, occupation and education the hypothesis is supported.

The absence of relation between political awareness and social participation may be due to the reasons discussed earlier (Chapter-IV).

The study shows that the more the education the higher is the level of understanding. This indicates the advantages of formal education. However, the educated must also have a positive attitude towards politics since their apathy is making them less aware about some of the political matters.

Meanscore Analysis

11. Inspite of a high exposure to TV, women score very low in political awareness than men. Whatever score they have shown in awareness as far as this study is concerned may be said to be to some extent due to their extensive exposure to TV.

There is an urgent need to enhance the social status of rural women. Women's education must be given higher priority. The study emphasises the necessity for making additional efforts for women's education especially in rural areas.

TV which has proved to be a popular medium among rural women, only may impress upon them certain aspects which can raise their social status. The TV programmes especially of women need to encourage self-sufficiency among women. This does not apply to rural women who are agriculture labour. Programmes should also suggest suitable employment opportunities (part time) for women. Different self employment schemes under small scale industries are to be explained to rural women. Women participation in all types of social activities required to be encouraged by the mass media especially TV.

A self confidence must be created among women in facing social evils.

Taking part in all social or cultural benefit organisations such as cooperative societies, banks, recreation clubs, panchayats etc. must be encouraged through TV programmes. In raising the level of social status of women the men's role is more important and crucial than others. Men encouraging women for their participation in all the social and political activities including elections must be highlighted in the programmes.

12. In respect of financial status a wide gap is noticed between FC's and BC's.

Inspite of various efforts by the government for the upliftment of BC's there appears to be less improvement in the financial status of the BC's. It is also observed that the cultural deprivation that is carried on from many generations could not be filled by the government's schemes. This cultural deprivation is making our rural masses to enjoy literature and movies with low standard and the same is being exploited by the business people. The study observes that the classical dances and music telecast on TV has no appeal to the masses. TV as a cultural force may raise the standards of our villagers to some extent in this aspect. It may introduce, reinforce and impress upon the rural masses the rich heritage of the Indian culture. It is the responsibility of the policy and programme makers to keep this in mind while preparing the programmes. Well trained script writers, artists and programmers are required for this. TV can best utilize the local talent available to make programmes of good quality.

13. (a) Due to many advantages naturally the degree of exposure of FCs to TV is more than BCs.

(b) Men are unable to adjust their work schedule as compared to women to watch TV programmes. This shows that TV is more popular among women.

Correlation and Regression Analysis

14. The degree of exposure to TV in general did not show much relationship to political awareness. However, the degree of exposure to political programmes has shown a significant relationship to political awareness supporting the third hypothesis.

This shows that except news and current affairs the other categories of programmes i.e. educational and recreational are not giving much political education to the rural masses.

In this context it is suggested that the programmes of other categories may include politics as a subject and thereby educate the viewers. The study rules out the commonly held opinion that TV is for uneducated or semi-educated but not for the educated who can think and act independently. It positively indicates that the educated benefit more than the others during their exposure to TV since a direct relationship is noticed between the levels of education and that of political awareness.

The discussion can be concluded that regular exposure to political programmes is increasing the levels of political awareness. This shows that TV is certainly giving political education to the rural masses. Here also the more the inclination to watch political programmes the higher is the benefit of improving the political awareness. However, the socio-economic background also have its own influence to some extent.

Hence it is suggested that the political programmes may be presented effectively on TV to raise the levels of political awareness among the rural masses.

Limitations of the Study

There are no major earlier studies in the field of TV and political affairs in our country. Therefore, the study has to concentrate on some of the general aspects of Television also which made its scope broader, than was originally intended.

The study could not utilise the guidelines already available in the field of political communication research in other advanced countries as they are not quite applicable to our conditions. The allotted time for political programmes on our TV is very less. To assess their impact is a difficult task.

The villages of Ranga Reddy District may not represent typical remote villages of our country though all efforts have been made to eliminate the urban bias. The reasons that have compelled to select this particular district have been already discussed earlier. The other limitations in sampling and in data collection were discussed in the third and fourth chapters.

TV's role in politics may not be the same at all times. It varies according to the political atmosphere prevailing. This has been thoroughly studied by the researchers in other countries. It is observed that TV has raised the hopes of the political communication researchers when they could see no future to this particular field at one stage. Political broadcasting is a vast field that is open for research in our country. Each aspect of political broadcasting can be studied separately and in great detail. For example, experiments are conducted during the elections to study the political impact of mass media by many of the researchers. Likewise, proceedings of legislature, ministerial broadcasts, international broadcasts and budget broadcasts etc. have a wide scope for a separate and detailed study. The psychological factors that act in the political communication process have also got to be studied thoroughly. More sophisticated techniques can be utilized for the assessment of these factors.

All this is possible only when there is an effective political programming on our TV that gives scope for the researchers to go deep in this field. As Barry G. Cole says Television through the vivid reporting of actual events can incite new thoughts and emotions in the electorate. It also has the effect in many cases of heightening the sense of popular participation in public matters. If television would recognise an affirmative obligation to elevate the level of our politics and applied much thought it might play a great role in helping make our democracy more rational and responsible.[9]

REFERENCES

1. *A Survey (Report)* conducted by Research and evaluation cell, Doordarshan, Hyderabad (regarding the utilisation time of TV programmes).
2. V. Pathanjali, "Television : Towards meeting the challenge for change" in *Mass Media in India 1981-83* compiled by Research and Reference Division Ministry for Information and Broadcasting (Publication Division, I & B Ministry, New Delhi, 1982), p. 156.
3. Hiroshi Akuto, "Political process and public opinion voting behaviour and Mass-Communication," in *International Studies of Broadcasting with special reference to the Japanese Studies*, Edited by H. Egue Chie and H. Ichinohe (NHK Radio and TV Culture research Unit),(NHK : Tokyo, 1977), p. 119.
4 Shireley Williams, an Essay in *The Future of Broadcasting*, Ed. Richard Hoggart and Janet Morgan (Macmillan : London, 1982), p. 9.
5. Jay G. Blumler, *The Political Effects of Mass-Communication*, The Audience Unit 8, The Open University—Social Sciences a Third level course, (Walton Hall, Milton Keyness), p. 16.
6. *Ibid.*, p. 13.
7. Alfred 1. du pont, New York, Grosset and Dunlap, *Survey of Broadcast Journalism*, Ed. Barret Mervin 1968-69 (Coloumbia University, New York).
8. "Doordarshan Programme on Bofors," A survey conducted by MARG (Market Research Agency) in *Sunday Observer*, May 15, 1988, Bombay, p. 3.
9. *Television Today*, A closeup view—readings from T.V. guide, ed. Barry G. Cole (Oxford Univ. Press : New York, 1981), p. 482.

BIBLIOGRAPHY

Abshire David M., "International Broadcasting a new dimension of Western diplomacy, *The Washington papers*, (SAGE publications : London, 1976).

Alan P.L. Liu, *Communication and National Integration in Communist China*, (University of California Press : USA, 1971).

Alan Casty, *Mass Media and Mass-Man*, (Holt R and W. East Sussex, 1973).

Alwin J. Rubin Stein and Garold W. Thumm., *The Challenge of Politics, Ideas and Issues*, (New Jersey, Prentice Hall, 1963).

Alwin L. Bertrand, *Basic Sociology*, (Appleton-Century-Crofts, New York, 1973).

Alan W. Childs and Gary B. Melton, *Rural Psychology*, (Plenum Press, New York, 1983).

Alex S. Edeistein, *Comparative Communication Research* (SAGA : New Delhi, 1982).

Alan Ross, *Television the Ephimeral art.*

Anthony Smith Ed., *Television and Political Life-Studies in Six European Countries*, (Macmillan : London, 1979).

Arbind K. Sinha, *Mass Media and Rural Development*, A Study of village Communication in Bihar, (New Delhi, 1985).

Awasthy G.C., *Broadcasting in India* (Allied Publishers; Bombay, 1965).

Bary Cole (Editor), *Television Today, A close-up view—Readings from TV Guide*, (Oxford University Press : New York, 1981).

S. Bala Krishna, "Some demographic features of rural India," an essay in *Rural development in India—some facets*, (National Institute of Rural Development : Hyderabad, 1981).

Baruah U.L., *This is All India Radio* (Publication division, Ministry of Information and Broadcasting, New Delhi, 1983).

Barrie Stacey, *Political socialization in western society—An Analysis from a life span perspective* (Arnold Heinemann Publishers : New Delhi, 1978).

BBC Handbook, 1979, (Published by British broadcasting corporation : London, 1979).

Bernard Crick and Alex Porter, *Political Education and Political Literacy*, (Longman group limited : London, 1978).

Bhasker Rao, N., *Controlled Mass Communication*, (S. Chand &, Co., New Delhi, 1971).

Binod C. Agarwal and Arbind K. Sinha, *SITE to INSAT, Challenges of production and research for women and children*, (Concept : New Delhi, 1986).

Binod C. Agarwal and M.R. Malik, *Television in Kheda—A Social Evaluation of SITE*, (Concept : New Delhi, 1986).

Brown E.T., *Education and Politics—The Sovereign people—Analysis of an illusion*, (Melbourne : F.W. Cheshire, 1954).

Burton Paul, *British Broadcasting in Transition*, (University of Minnesota Press : Minneapolis, USA, 1956).

Carroll O. Meara., *Television Programme Production*, (Ronald : New York, 1955).

Caleb Gattegno, *Towards a visual culture, educating through television*, (Avon Books : New York, 1969).

Chatterjee R.K., *Mass Communication*, (National Book Trust, New Delhi, 1979).

Charles S. Steinberg, Ed., *Mass Media and Communication* (Hastings House Publishers : New York, 1972).

Chatterjee P.C., *Broadcasting in India*, (SAGE Publishers : New Delhi, 1987).

Charlene J. Brown, Trevor R. Brown and William L. Rivers, *The Media and the People*, (H. Holt and Co., New York, 1978).

Chalapathi Rao, *Journalism and Politics*, (Vikas Publishing House : New Delhi, 1984).

Claus Mueller, *The Politics of Communication--A Study in the political sociology of language, socialization and legitimation,* Oxford University Press : New York, 1974).

Coase R.H., *British Broadcasting,* (Longmans, New York, 1950).

Colin Leys, *Politics in Britain,* (Verso : London, 1986).

Colin Cherrey, *World Communication threat or promise,* A socio technical approach, (John Wiley and Sons : New York, 1978).

Daniel Blum, *Pictorial History of Television,* (Greenburg : New York, 1950)

David G. Clark and William B. Blankenburg, *You and mass-media—Mass communication and society,* (Harper and Row : New York, 1973).

Davison Phillips and Frederic T.C.Yu., (Edited), *Mass-Communication research, Major Issues and future directions,* (Praeger : New York, 1974).

Dewis Macshane, *Using the media* (*How to deal with the Press, Television and Radio*), (Pluto Press : London, 1979).

Dennis K. Davis and Stanley J. Baran, *Mass Communication and Everyday life,* (A perspective on theory and effects), (Wadsworth Publishing Co., California, 1981).

Desmond Devis, *The Grammer of Television Production* (Barrie and Jenkins London, 1974).

Dhawan B.D., *Economics of Television in India,* (S. Chand : New Delhi, 1975).

Douglas Cater and Richard Adler, *Television as a social force—New approaches to television criticism,* (Praeger : New York, 1975).

Douglas cater and Michale J. Nyhan, *The future of public broadcasting,* (Praeger Publishers : New York, 1976).

Douglas A. Hibbs, *Mass Political violence,* A cross-national casual analysis, (John Willey and Sons : New York, 1973).

Duggal K.S., *Indian Broadcast Media Year Book, 1982* (Marwah Publications, New Delhi, 1983).

Dua M.R., *Themes in Indian Communication*, (Metropolitan, New Delhi, 1980).

Edgar E. Wills, *Writing Television and Radio Programmes*, (Oxford University Press : New York).

Edward W. Ploman, *Broadcasting in Swedon-case studies on Broadcasting systems*, (SVERIGES Radio London Routledge and Kegan paul with International broadcast Institute, 1976).

Edwin Diamond, *Television, politics and the news Tin Kazoo*, (MIT Press, Cambridge, 1977).

Edwin Emergy, Phillip H. Ault and Warren K. Agee, *Introduction to mass communications*, (Vakils, Fetter and Simons Private Ltd. : Bombay, 1969).

Edwin Diamond and Stephen Bates, "The Spot" *The rise of political advertizing on Television*, (Massachuesetts Institute of Technology Press, Cambridge, 1986).

Eguchie H. and Ichninohe H. (Edited), *International studies of Broadcasting with special reference to the Japanese studies*, (NHK Radio and Television culture research Institute : Tokyo, 1977).

Elmo I. Ellis, *Opportunities in Broadcasting*, (VGM Career Horizons, Columbia, 1981).

Elihu Katz and George Wedell with Michale Pilsworth and Dovshinar, *Broadcasting in the third world, promise and performance*, (Macmillan: London, 1978).

Emery Smythe, *Readings in mass-communication concepts and issues in the use of mass media.* (Wm C. Brown, Iowa, 1986).

Erkki Olkinuora, *The effect of Television on personal norms.*

Eric Rowe, "Modern Politics," *An introduction to behaviour and Institutions*, (Humanities Press: London, 1969).

Erwin G. Krasnow and Lawrence D. Longley, *The politics of Broadcasting regulation*, (St. Martins Press, 1973).

Erik Barnouw, *Mass Communication*, (Holt, Rinehart and Winston, New York, 1961).

Francis Wheen, *Television,* The book of the major ITV Series, (Century, Hutchinsas, Irvine, 1986).

Franklin L. Burdette (Editor), *Education for citizen responsibilities.*

Gaye Tuchman, *Making news—A study in the construction of reality*, (The Free Press: New York, 1978).

George Gerbner (Edited by) *Mass media policies in changing cultures,* (John Wiley and Sons, Inc: New York, 1977).

Gisbert, P., *Fundamentals of sociology.*

Gladys Engel Loug and Kurt long, *Politics and Television reviewed,* (Quadrangle Books: Chicago, 1968).

Grace Jones, *The political structure* (Longman: London, 1976).

Gupta S.P., *Statistical methods,* (S. Chand and Sons: New Delhi, 1976).

Halliman E.S., and Hindley H., *Broadcasting in Canada-Case,* Studies on Broadcasting systems (Routledge: London, 1977).

Hadley Read, *Communications methods for all media,* (University Illinois Press Ltd.: Illinois, 1972).

Harvey Lesser, *Television and the Pre-school child,* A psychological theory of instruction and curriculum development, (Academic Press : New York, 1977).

Harlambus with R.M. Herald, Sociology-Themes and perspectives, (Tutor Prints, Sheridan England).

Heinz-Dietrich, Fischer and John C. Merill (Edited by), *International and Inter cultural communication,* (Hastings house Publishers, New York, 1977).

Heinz-Dietrich Fisher and Stefan Reinhard Melink, *Entertainment* (A cross-cultural examination), (Hastings House: New York, 1979).

Himmelweit, A.N. Oppenhein and Pamela vince, *Television and the child—An emprical study of the effect of TV on the young* (Books demand UMI, N. Zeeb Road, Ann Arbor, 1980).

Higgins A.P., *Talking about television*, (British Film Institute, London, 1966).

Hilda Matheson, *Broadcasting*, (Thornton Butterworth Ltd., London, 1933).

Hildic E.W., A close look at Television and sound broadcasting.

Horace New Comb (Edited by), *Television the critical view*, (Oxford University Press, New York, 1976).

Ivory Yorke, *The technique of Television News*, (Focal press: London, 1978).

James W. Markham, *Voices of the Red Giants*, (The Iowa State University Press: USA 1967).

James Martin, *The Wired Society*, (Prentice-Hall Inc., Englewood Cliffs : New Jersey, 1978).

Jain S.P., *The Art of Broadcasting*, (Intellectuals: New Delhi).

Jay G. Blumler and De nis Mcquail, *Television in Politics—Its uses and influence*, (Faber : London, 1968).

James R. Adams, *Media Planning*, (Brookfield : London, 1977).

James E. Fletcher, *Research procedure in audience programme* (Edited by), Hand book, (Rand McNally: Chicago, 1981).

Jay Black and Frederick C. Whitney, *Introduction to mass communication*, (Wm C. Brown: Iowa, 1987).

Jay G. Blumler (Editor), *Communicating to voters—Television in the first European parliamentary elections*, An international institute of communications project.

Jerome C. Singer and Dorothy G. Singer, *Television Imagination and Aggression a study of Pre-schoolers*, (Yale University).

Joseph F. Littel (Edited by) *Selected readings for libraries.*

Joseph F. Littel (Edited by) *Coping with the mass-media 1976.*

Jeffery Schrank, *Understanding mass media*, (Amphoto : New York, 1976).

Jnan E. Diaz Bordenave, *Communication and Rural Development*, (UNESCO : Belgium, 1977).

John Baggalcy and Steve Duck, *Dynamics of Television*, (Saxon House : England, 1976).

John A. Lent., *Broadcasting in Asia and the Pacific—A Continental survey of Radio and Television,* (Temple University Press, 1978).

John I. Spencer, Frank D. Alexander and Chester H. Freeman, *Audience evaluation of films produced for television.*

Kenneth S. David (Ed.), *Mass media and the Supream Court,* (Hastings House: New York, 1979).

Krishan Sondhi, *Problems of Communication in Developing Countries,* (Vision books: New Delhi, 1987).

Krishan Sondhi, *Communication and Values,* (Somaiya: Bombay, 1985).

Kurt Long and Gladys Engel Long, *Voting and non-voting implications of broadcasting returns before polls are closed,* (Columbia University Press: New York, 1983).

Kuppu Swamy B., *Communication and social development in India,* (Sterling: New Delhi, 1976).

Kurt FIN Sterbusch, *Understanding social impacts—Assessing the effects of public projects,* (Vol. 110), Sage Library of Social Research, (SAGE: London 1980).

Laurence Evans, *The communication gap.*

Lakshman Rao Y.V., *Communication and Development,* A study of two Indian villages, (University of Minnesota Press : Minneapolis, 1969).

Lord Windlesham, *Broadcasting in a free society,*(Basil Blackwell Publishers: Oxford; England, 1980).

Luthra H.R., *Indian Broadcasting,* (Publication division, Ministry of Information and Broadcasting, New Delhi, 1986).

Lucian W. Pye (Edited by), *Communication and Political Development,* (Studies in Political Development, Vol. I) (Princeton University Press : Lawrenceville, New Jersey, 1963).

Mankekar D.R., *Media and the third world;* (Indian Institute of Mass Communications, New Delhi, 1983).

Mathur J.C., *The studies in Broadcasting.*

Malhan P.N., *Communication media yesterday, today and tomorrow.* (Publications division, Ministry of Information and Broadcasting : New Delhi, 1985).

Martin Mayor, *About Television*, (Harper and Row : New York, 1972).

Mathur J.C. and Paul Neurath, *An Indian Experiment in Farm Radio Forums*, (UNESCO : Paris, 1959).

Martin D. Carter, *An Introduction to mass communications—problems in press and broadcasting*, (Macmillan : London, 1971).

May Katzen (Ed.), *Multimedia Communication*, (Frances Pinter Publishers : London, 1982).

Martin H. Seiden, *Who controls the Mass-Media*, Popular myths and Economic realities, (Basic Books (INC) Publishers : New York, 1974).

McGarry K.J. (Edited by), *Mass Communications*, (Clive Bingley : London, 1972).

McGarry K.J., *Selected readings for libraries*, (Bingley : London, 1972).

Mehra Masani, *Broadcasting and the people*, (National Book Trust : New Delhi, 1985).

Michael C. Emery and Ted Curtis Smythe, *Readings in Mass Communication, concepts and issues in the mass media*, (Wm C. Brown Co. : Iowa, 1975).

Michael Bland, *Executives guide to TV and Radio appearances.*

Mike Jervis., *An experiment in conference TV.*

Michale Oakesholt, *Rationalism in politics*, (Methuen and Co. : London, 1977).

Michale Gurevitch and Jay G. Blumler, *Linkage between the mass media and politics—a model for the analysis of political communication system*, (University of Leeds Press : Leeds, 1978).

Michale J. Robinson, *Television and American Politics 1956-1976*, (United States Information Service, New Delhi).

Morgan T.J., *The true book about Television and Radio*, (McDonald : London, 1958).

Mukhopadhyay A.K.. *Political Sociology*, (K.P. Bagchi and Co. : Calcutta, 1977).

Mukharjee B.N., *Mass media and political modernity : An empirical study of five developing countries*, (National psychological corporation : Agra, 1979).

Mullick K.S., Tangled tapes, *The inside story of Indian Broadcasting*, (Sterling Publishers : New Delhi, 1974).

Narayan Menon, *The communications revolution*, (National Book Trust : New Delhi, 1976).

Nippon Hoso Kyokai, *Studies of Broadcasting*, Institute for Radio and TV culture research, (NHK : Tokyo, 1977).

Norman Swallo, *Factual Television—Television and Party Politics*, (Focal Press : London, 1966).

Olle Findahl, *The effect of visual illustrations upon perception and retention of news programmes*, (SVERIGES Radio-Audience and Programme Research Department).

Peter Golding, *The mass media*, (Longman : London, 1974).

Peter H. Merkl, *Political continuity and change*, (Allied Publishers : New Delhi, 1975).

Peterson et al., *The mass media and modern society*, (Holt, Rinehart and Winston, New York, 1965).

Phillips Davison, James Boylan and Frederick T.C. Yu., *Mass-media systems and effects*, (Praeger : New York, 1976).

Phillips Davison and Frederic T.C. Yu., *Mass communications research major issues and future directions*, (Praeger : New York, 1975).

Ralf Berry, *Communication through the mass-media, a reader in communications*, (E. Aronold ; London, 1971).

Rao, B.S.S. and B.V. Sharma, *INSAT experiences—candid scenes from A.P.*, (Concept : New Delhi, 1986).

Reed H. Blake and Edwin O. Haroldsen, *A texonomy of concepts in communications*, (Hastings House Publishers : New York, 1979).

Richard Hoggart and Jannet Morgan, Ed., *The future of broadcasting*, (Macmillan : London, 1982).

Richard Bunce, *Television in the corporate interest*, (Praeger : New York, 1976).

Richard Clutter Buck, *The media and political violence*, (Macmillan : London, 1983)

Richard Adler and Douglass Cater, Ed., *Television as a cultural force*, (Praeger : New York, 1976).

Ronny Adhikarya et. al., *Broadcasting in Peninsular Malaysia*, (Routledge : London, 1977).

Ronald T. Farrar and John D. Stevens, *Mass media and the National Experience*, (Harper and Row Publishers : London, 1971).

Robert Stein, *Media Power*.

Roger Louis and Joseph Roven, *Television and Teleclubs in rural communities—An experiment in France*. (Reports and Papers on mass communications, UNESCO : Paris).

Robert Tyrrel, *The work of the television journalist* (Library of Film and Television Practice, Focal Press : London, 1981).

Robert T. Bower, *Television and the public*, (Columbia Univ. Press : New York, 1985).

Roy V. Peel and Joseph S. Roucek, *Introduction to politics*, (Thomas Y. Crowell Co. : 1941).

Robert L. Hilliard, Ed., *Television broadcasting, An Introduction*, (Communication Art Books : New York, 1978).

Robert R. Sokal and F.J. Ralf, Biometry *The Principles and Practice of Statistics in Biological Research*, (W.H. Freeman and Co., Sanfrancisco : USA, 1981).

Robert F. Arnove, Ed., *Educational Television*, A policy critique and guide for developing countries, (Praeger Publishers : New York, 1976).

Ruth Thomas, *Broadcasting and Democracy in France*, (Beekman Publishers : New York, 1976).

Sachdeva D.R. and Vidya Bhushan, *An Introduction to Sociology*, (Kitab Mahal, Allahabad, 1967).

Salvada Giner, *Mass-Society*, (Martin Robertson : Bristol, 1976).

Seshadri K. and S.P. Jain, *Panchayat Raj and Political perceptions of electorate—A study of electoral behaviour in the mid-*

term poll of 1971 in Hyderabad constituency, (National Institute of Community Development, Hyderabad, 1972).

Sitaram K.S. and Roy T. Cogdell, *Foundations of Inter-cultural Communications*, (A Bell and Howell Co. : Columbus, Ohio, 1976).

Sushila Mehta, *A study of rural sociology in India*, (S. Chand and Company, New Delhi, 1980).

Sydney W. Head, *Broadcasting in America*, Houghton Mifflin Co. : Boston, 1976).

Ted Tapper and Brian Salter, *Education and the Political Order*, (The Macmillan : London, 1978).

Tom Wicker, *On Press*, (Prentice Hall of India : New Delhi, 1979).

Trenaman J.M., *Communication and comprehension*, The Report of an investigation by statistical methods of the effective communication of educative material and an assessment of the factors making for such communication with special reference to Broadcasting, (Longmans Green and Co. : London, 1967).

Varavara Rao, *Telangana Vimochanodyamam—Telugu Navala, Samaja Sahitya Sambandhalu.*

Venkata Royappa K.N., *Rural Society and Change*, (Popular : Bombay, 1974).

Veldurthi Manikya Rao, *Hyderabad Swatantrodyama Charithra* (Published by Swatantra Samarayodhula Sangham, Gandhi Bhavan, Hyderabad, 1984).

Vivek Ranjan Bhattacharya, *Communication in a global village*, (Chetana publications : New Delhi, 1976).

Ward L. Quall and James A. Brown, *Broadcast management—Radio and Television*, (Hastings House : New York, 1979).

Warren K. Agee (Ed.), *Mass-media in a free society*, (Oxford and IBH Publishing Co., New Delhi, 1969).

Werner J. Severin and James W. Tankard Jr., *Communication Theories Origins methods uses*, (Hastings House Publishers : New York, 1979).

Whitby M.C. et al., *Rural resource development*, (Methuen and Co. : London, 1978).

William E. Mc Cavitt, *Broadcasting around the world*, (TAB BKS Blud Ridge Summit, 1985).

Wilbur Schramm, *Television reconsidered*, (Stanford University Press : Stanford, 1961).

Wilson P. Dizard, *Television a world's view*, (Syracuse-press : Syracuse, 1966).

Wilbur Schramm, *Mass-media and national development*, (Stanford University Press : Stanford, California, 1964).

Wilbur Schramm (Ed.), *The Science of human communication*, (Basic Books, (INC) Publishers : New York, 1963).

William L. Rivers, *The mass media reporting, writing; editing*, (Universal Book Stall : New Delhi, 1967).

Williams, Fredrick, *Communications revolution*, (SAGE : New Delhi, 1982).

Wilbur Schramm, *Men, Messages and Media—A look at human communication*, (Harper and Row Publishers : New York, 1973).

William L. Rivers, and Wilbur Schramme, *Responsibility in mass communication*, (Harper and Row Publishers : New York, 1917).

William Blueam A., *Documentary in American Television, form, function method*, (Hastings House : New York, 1965).

Willard D. Rowland Jr., *The politics of TV violence : Policy uses of communication research*, (SAGE : London, 1983).

William Bluem A., John F. Cox, Gene Ma Pherson, *Television in the Public interest—Planning, production and performance*, (Hastings House, New York, 1965).

William P. Lineberry, *Mass Communications*, (The W.H. Wilson Company : New York, 1969).

William Hawes, *The Performer in Mass-Media*, (In media profession and in community), (Hastings House : New York, 1978).

Wolf, *Television Programming for news and current affairs*, (Praeger Publishers : New York, 1973).

REPORTS, STUDIES, MAGAZINES, PERIODICALS ETC.

The practice of Mass Communication, some lessons from research, V. Lakshman Rao, Reports and papers on mass communication No. 65, UNESCO : Paris, 1975.

Planning for Satellite Broadcasting—The Indian Instructional Television Experiment by Romesh Chander and Kiron Kumar, Reports and papers on mass communication No. 78, UNESCO : Paris, 1976.

Space communication and the mass media, Reports and papers on mass communication, UNESCO : Paris.

The SITE Experience, Reports and papers on mass communication No. 91, UNESCO : Paris, 1983.

Broadcasting abroad, compiled by the Union Internationale-de Radio diffusion, GENEVA: Switzerland (A.R. Barrows—Secretary General).

Radio and Television, Report of the committee on Broadcasting and Information media, Ministry of Information and Broadcasting, Government of India : New Delhi, 1966, Ashok K. Chanda, Chairman.

International press clippings—Canadian broadcasting corporation, Variety-Wednesday-Jan 3rd, 1979.

United States to help strengthen third world media, International, Communication Agency official text, U.S.A., Nov. 6, 1978.

Role of the mass-media in American politics—The Annals—The American Academy of Political and Social Science, Vol. 427.

Television persuasive or merely pervasive, Edwin Diamond, TV's impact on Society, Horizons—USA—23.

Mass Communication and Society, The Audience Unit 7 and 8, The Open University Press : Stany Stratford, Walton Hall, Milton Keynes 1977.

Television in India – a perspective, Report on Seminar, Film and Television Institute of India, Pune.

Public Television a programme for action, The report and recommendations Carnegie commission on Educational Television, New York : Harper and Row, 1967.

A review of the Delhi pilot rural television project and its lessons, New Delhi.

Radio, Television in Malaysia, a report by Department of Broadcasting.

Radio and Television for the third world, A mass-media manual by Friedrich-Ebert-Stiffung.

Five Years of Scottish television, Scottish committee of the Independent television authority.

Seventh five year plan 1985-90 and annual plan 1985-86 of the Ministry of Information and Broadcasting by Planning Commission - Communication, Information and Broadcasting Division, New Delhi.

A study of the shift in aspiration of the rural community due to exposure to telecasts, Rajendra Prasad Yadav, a dissertation in Master of Sciences, New Delhi.

Production of T.V. Receivers in India, 22-3-1984, *Statesman*, New Delhi.

Daily Mirror 1950, From the Collections of Library of Mass Communication Centre, Jamia Milia Islamia, New Delhi.

Study of mass-media input into plan implementation (A research design), National level survey by Planning Commission, New Delhi.

A vision for Indian Television, Report of a feedback project-- Indian Television today and tomorrow-organized by NAMEDIA - Media foundation of the non-aligned, New Delhi.

Communicator, Quarterly Journal of the Indian Institute of Mass Communication, Vol. XX No. 1 January, 1985.

Communicator, Vol, XX No. 1, 2 and 3, April-June 1985.

Communicator, Vol. XI No. 2 and 3, April-July 1976.

Indian Television today and tomorrow, Regional seminars and national colloquium organized by NAMEDIA (Media foundation of the non-aligned, New Delhi, 1986).

Development of Television broadcasting in India, a note prepared by the Director General of Doordarshan, New Delhi.

Participation of women in politics, a case study of Andhra Pradesh, 1982 by Vijaya Tilakam K.J., M. Phil. dissertation in Sociology, O.U.

Study of pressure groups in Andhra Pradesh with special reference to I.N.T.U.C. The study has been made within the large framework of All India Pressure groups by Balaiah Kovuru, M.Phil. dissertation in Political Science, O.U.

Pressure groups and public policy, A case study of Telangana non-gazetted officers union in Andhra Pradesh, 1979 by Gopal, B., A Ph. D. thesis in Political Science, O.U.

Political participation of women in Andhra Pradesh from 1967 to 1978, by Lakshmi K., 1982, A Ph.D thesis in Political Science, O.U.

Role of Communist opposition in Andhra Pradesh Assembly 1972-78, by Mohana T.S., 1981, Ph. D thesis in Political Science, O.U.

Electrol politics in Andhra Pradesh — A case study of Vidhan Sabha election in Khamman district (1978), by Ramesh Babu J., 1982, A Ph.D thesis in Political Science, O.U.

Mass-Media in India 1984, compiled by Research and Reference division, Ministry of Information and Broadcasting, New Delhi, 1985.

Parliamentary and Political Broadcasting—Broadcasting from Parliament, BBC Handbook (Incorporating the Annual report and accounts), Published by BBC, London, 1979.

TV cuts audience for Cinema by Bede Perera (Sri Lanka), World Broadcast News, November 1985, Published by Broadcast Management/Engineering, New York.

Report : *Campaign and Voters choice, 1984—Parliamentary elections*, by J.S. Yadava, Indian Institute of Mass Communications, New Delhi.

INSAT-IB--Basic information, July 1984, Audience Research Unit, Doordarshan, New Delhi.

"*Television India*," Audience Research Unit, Directorate General, Doordarshan, New Delhi, 1986.

National TV ratings, A study report, 1986, from the files of Operations Research Group, a private organisation, New Delhi.

A study on viewing to newscasts, Audience Research Unit, Doordarshan, Bombay.

Printed and published by James A. McGinley for the United States Information Service, New Delhi...

"Guerrila Television," an article by Deirdre Boyle, originally published in *Transmission, 1985.*

"Distance Education : A unique blend of technology and pedagogy to train future special educators" an article by Marilyn Kay Johnson and Cheryl Amundsen in *Journal of Special Education Technology*, Vol. VI, Number 3, Summer 1983.

"Can the press tell the truth ?" an article in *Harper's, January 1985* (c) 1984 by the Harper's Magazine Foundation.

"A little bit of Heresy," an article by Anthony Serafini in *The Quill*, July/August 1984.

"News papers," An article by Walter Lippmann in *Media power in politics* Ed. Doris A. Graber, Macmillan: London.

"What's what in Corporate TV" an article by Gail Ablow and Barry Lynn in *Videography*, March 1985.

Liberal education in the Information Age," an article by George gerbner in *Current Issues in higher Education 1983-84*.

Printed and published by Jay W. Gildner for United States Information Service, New Delhi...

"The Media and the Presidency : An exchange analysis" an article by Michael Baruch Grossman and Francis E. Rourke in *Political Science Quarterly, Fall 1976*.

"The Politics of American Broadcasting : Public purposes and private interests" an article by Robert J. Williams in *Journal of American Studies*.

"Media Reformers," An article by William V. Thomas in *Editorial Research Reports*, December 23, 1977.

Strengthening third world media, address by Ambassador John E. Reinhardt to the 20th General Conference of the U.N. Educational, Scientific and Cultural organization in Paris, November 3, 1978.

"The President and the Press," Excerpt from the *Presidency Reappraised*, by Danil P. Moynihan, Ed. Thomas E. Cronin and Rexford G. Tugwell, 1977.

"Leaks" Excerpt from *The Power to Probe* : A study of Congressional Investigations by James Hamilton.

Communications policy making in Western Europe," an article by Roland S. Homet, Jr. in *Journal of Communication, Spring 1979*.

"Satellite broadcasting and communication policy," three articles by Rolf. T. Wigand, Marcellus S. Snow and Wilson P. Dizard in *Journal of Communication*, Spring, 1980.

"The Media's conflict of interests," an article by Donald McDonald in *The Center Magazine*, November/December 1976.

"The Mass media and Society," *An American View Point*, an article William G. Harley in *Courier*, April 1977, USA.

The American press and the law an enviable freedom, an excerpt from *The Economist of London*, 1977.

"Cave's Commandment" an article by Ray Cave in *The Quill*, July/August 1987.

Views on News : A survey on reactions to the telugu news telecasts from Hyderabad, November 1983, (Research and

Evaluation Cell Upagraha Doordarshana Kendra, Hyderabad).

A bunch of figures : Hyderabad Doordarshan Programmes in 1984 Research and evaluation cell, Upagraha Doordarshana Kendra, Hyderabad.

Backgrounder : "articles presented to the Conference on "World Communications : Decisions for the eighties," at the Annenberg School of Communications, University of Pennsylvania, Philadelphia, May 12-14, 1980.

"Global Communications in the Nineteen eighties : An American Perspective" by John E. Reinhardt.

"Toward a global communications policy for an independent world" by Anne W. Branscomb.

"Policy Issues in Global training and research in Mass Communication" by Robert, Lindsay.

"Information, Informatics, and International Information Flows : Predicates for new world law and policy by John M. Eger.

"World Communications : Public policies and private initiatives for the '80s by John L. McLucas.

The United States and the debate on the World Information Order by Academy for Educational Development (INC).

Published by Indian Institution of Mass Communications, New Delhi...

Report — Communication and Parliamentary Elections (1971), A study in a Haryana village by J.S. Yadava, 1972.

New Communication Technologies and Developing Societies, J.S. Yadava, 1983.

Resource Utilisation of Development Information Needs, A Study of Mandya district by Uma Narula and B.K. Kuthiala, 1984.

Communication and Development Information Needs, A study of Mahindergarh District (Haryana) by Nawal Singh, 1984.

Coverage and treatment of News in Different Media, J.S. Yadava and Zahoorul Haq, 1986.

Commonwealth Broadcasting Association, London, June and December, 1984 and September 1986 issues, (COMBROAD).

Indian Journal of Communication Arts, New Delhi, October '75 and May, June and July, 1976 issues.

The Impact of Television on a minority community, A case study of Muslims of Pahadi Bhojla by Smt. Abhilasha Kumari (an unpublished thesis).

Recall and learning from Broadcast News—Is print better, by John Stauffer, Richard Frost and William Rybolt from the Collections of Director General AIR Library, New Delhi.

Mass media — opportunities and threats, by Leonard R. Sussman. The Annals of the American Academy of Political and Social Science.

Alfred I. du pont, New York, Grosset and Dunlap, *Survey of Broadcast Journalism* Ed. Barret Mervin 1968-69 (Columbia University, New York).

The Report of the carnegie Commission on the future of public broadcasting -- Excerpts from a public trust, Harper and Row, New York.

The role of the Mass-media in Controlling opinion, An article in a Journal.

Wall Street Journal Vol. XCV No. 75. From the collections of American Library, Delhi.

Primary Census — Abstract General population, Part IIB(i) Series, *Census of India, 1981.*

An Indian Personality for Television, Vol. I and II. Report of the working group on software for Doordarshan publication division, Ministry of Information and Broadcasting, New Delhi, 1985.

Aakash Bharathi' National Broadcast Trust, Report of the working group on autonomy for Akashvani and

Doordarshan, Vol. I and II, Ministry of Information and Broadcasting, New Delhi, 1978.

Many voices — One world, Report by the International commission for the study of communication problems. Published by the United Nations Educational, Scientific and Cultural Organization (1980).

Mass-media in India 1980-81, Ed. Research and Reference Division, Ministry of Information and Broadcasting, New Delhi, 1982.

Mass-media in India 1981-83 – compiled by Research and Reference Division, Ministry of Information and Broadcasting, New Delhi, 1984.

Television India 1987, A report by the Audience Research unit, Doordarshan, New Delhi, 1987.

Manorama Year Book 1988, Kottayam, India, 1989.

States' rights over the media, *Newstime*, 30th July 1986, Hyderabad by Ashok Mitra.

Decontrolling the airwaves by Ramesh Thapar, Illustrated Weekly of India, Bombay, April (6-12), 1986.

Manorama Year Book 1986, Kottayam, India, 1987.

The advent of colour, Hyderabad Doordarshan in 1986, A report by Research and Evaluation Cell, Hyderabad Doordarshan Kendra 1987.

A.P. Year Book 1986, A data news feature publication, Hyderabad, 1987.

Television and behaviour - Ten years of scientific progress and implications for the eighties, Vol. I. Summary report by National Institute of Mental Health (from the collections of the American Library, New Delhi).

"The plight of foreign news in the United States Mass-Media—An Assessment," *Gazette-XXV*, No. 4, 1979, from the collections of All India Radio Library, New Delhi.

Content analysis of News Bulletins, A study by Audience Research Unit, All India Radio : New Delhi, 1986.

News from All India Radio - A cross-section of opinions in Vijayawada and suburbs, Audience Research unit, All India Radio, Hyderabad, 1982.

Chambers everyday Dictionary Ed. A. M. Macdonald and E.M. Kirkpatrick, Arnold-Heinemann : New Delhi, 1976.

A survey regarding the utilization time of T.V. programmes, Audience Research Unit, All India Radio, Hyderabad.

"Doordarshan programme on Bofors" - A survey conducted by MARG (Marketing Research Agency) in *Sunday Observer*, May 15, 1988.

Satellite Instructional Television Experiment - Technical Evaluation of the ground segment by Indian Space Research Organization : Bangalore, 1977.

Mass-communication and society, September 1977-80, Block 5. The Open University Social Sciences : A third level course. Uuits 13 to 15.

INDEX

हिन्दी के आंचलिक उपन्यासों में मूल्य-संक्रमण

डॉ. वेदप्रकाश अमिताभ

वाणी प्रकाशन

वाणी प्रकाशन का 'लोगो'
विख्यात चित्रकार मक़बूल फ़िदा हुसेन की
कूची से

ISBN : 81-7055-533-7

वाणी प्रकाशन
21-ए, दरियागंज, नयी दिल्ली-110002
द्वारा प्रकाशित

फोन : 0091#11#23273167, 23275710
फैक्स : 0091#11#23275710
ई-मेल : vaniprakashan@gmail.com
vani_prakashan@yahoo.com
वेबसाइट : www.vaniprakashan.com

प्रथम संस्करण : 1997
द्वितीय संस्करण : 2009

मूल्य : 250.00

जयभारत प्रिंटिंग प्रेस, शाहदरा, दिल्ली-110032
द्वारा मुद्रित

HINDI KE AANCHALIK UPANYASON
MEIN MULYA-SANKRAMAN
by Dr. Vedprakash Amitabh

जीवन संगिनी 'रंजना' को

अनुक्रम

अपनी बात

आंचलिक उपन्यासों को लेकर कई स्तरीय शोध प्रबंध और समीक्षा-ग्रंथ सामने आ चुके हैं। यह कृति भी आंचलिक उपन्यासों के मर्म तक पहुँचने और विशेषतः उनके मूल्यबोध को जाँचने का एक वस्तुनिष्ठ प्रयास है। बिना किसी पूर्वग्रह के हिंदी के आंचलिक उपन्यासों की वैचारिक शक्ति-सीमा की यह परख कितनी सार्थक है, इसका निर्णय हिंदी उपन्यास के अध्येता और सुधी समीक्षक ही कर सकते हैं। मैं सिर्फ इतना कह सकता हूँ कि इस कार्य को पूरा करके मुझे सुख मिला है।

इस कृति के लेखन की प्रेरणा डॉ. शांतिस्वरूप गुप्त (पूर्वकुलपति, आगरा विश्वविद्यालय) ने दी थी और मेरा सौभाग्य है कि मुझे कई वरिष्ठ कथाकारों और कथा-समीक्षकों का आशीर्वाद और सहयोग इस संदर्भ में बराबर मिला है। डॉ. राकेश गुप्त, यादवेन्द्र शर्मा चंद्र, डॉ. रामदरश मिश्र, डॉ. विवेकीराय, डॉ. त्रिभुवनसिंह, डॉ. मृत्युंजय उपाध्याय, डॉ. चंद्रेश्वर कर्ण, डॉ. गोपाल राय, डॉ. कुंदनलाल उप्रेती, डॉ. राजेन्द्र गढ़वालिया, डॉ. प्रेमकुमार और डॉ. अजयकुमार चतुर्वेदी के निर्देशों और उपालंभों ने इस प्रबंध की दिशा और स्वरूप को सुनिश्चित किया है। मैं इन सबके प्रति हृदय से आभारी हूँ। मूल्यों से संबंधित इस कार्य के समापन में मेरे परिवार ने भी बहुत कुछ मूल्य चुकाया है। अतः डॉ. रंजना शर्मा (पत्नी) और राजीव-अरविन्द-मनीषा का इस अवसर पर स्मरण स्वाभाविक है। विश्वविद्यालय अनुदान आयोग से प्राप्त अनुदान-राशि ने मेरी कई समस्याएँ हल की हैं। अतः मैं संबंधित अधिकारियों के प्रति कृतज्ञता ज्ञापित करता हूँ। भाई अरुण माहेश्वरी के सत्प्रयास से इसे प्रकाशित होने का सुयोग मिला है, मैं उनका भी आभारी हूँ।

यदि इस कृति से आंचलिक उपन्यासों के अनुसंधान और समीक्षा में कुछ नया जुड़ सका तो मेरा श्रम सार्थक होगा।

वेदप्रकाश अमिताभ

विषय प्रवेश

'आंचलिकता' केवल हिंदी उपन्यास की नहीं, समूचे भारतीय साहित्य की उल्लेखनीय प्रवृत्ति है। यह प्रवृत्ति जहाँ विदेशी साहित्य से प्रेरित और पोषित है, वहीं स्वातंत्र्योत्तर भारत के बदले हुए परिवेश का दबाव भी इसके उदय के मूल में है। मारिया एजवर्द, हार्डी तथा बहुत से रूसी उपन्यासकारों की कृतियों ने भारतीय उपन्यासों में 'आंचलिकता' की प्रवृत्ति के पल्लवन में महत्त्वपूर्ण योग दिया है।[1] आंचलिकता की प्रवृत्ति के पीछे सांस्कृतिक पुनरुद्धार की विश्वव्यापी मानसिकता सक्रिय है। "जिस प्रकार हार्डी में इंगलैंड का वेसेक्स अंचल, फाकनर में अमेरिका के दक्षिणी अंचल अपने समस्त रसगंधों के साथ उभरते हैं, उसी प्रकार रेणु में पूर्णिया अंचल, गणेश नारायण दाण्डेकर (मराठी) में बराड़ अंचल, सतिनाथ भादुड़ी में बंग-अंचल और झबेर चन्द्र मेघाणी (गुजराती) में सौराष्ट्र अंचल उजागर हो जाते हैं। यूरोप सहित विश्व और भारत के बीच आंचलिक साहित्य के निर्माणारंभ के बीच यद्यपि पूरी एक शताब्दी का अंतराल है तथापि आश्चर्यजनक रूप से सर्वत्र प्रवृत्तियों की एकरूपता पाते हैं।"[2] कतिपय आलोचकों ने 'आंचलिकता' के उदय के पीछे जनपदीय आंदोलन, बंगाली साहित्य के कल्लोल आंदोलन और प्रगतिशील लेखक संघ की स्थापना आदि आंतरिक कारणों की चर्चा की है। 'जनपदीय आंदोलन' का प्रस्ताव बनारसीदास चतुर्वेदी ने किया था और 'प्रगतिशील लेखक' संघ का समर्थन उसे प्राप्त था। प्रगतिशील लेखक संघ की स्थापना (1936 ई.) से पूर्व बंगाल में कल्लोल आंदोलन (1923 ई.) अस्तित्व में आ चुका था। "कल्लोल के माध्यम से कुछ विद्रोही बंगाली लेखक टैगोर के अंतर्राष्ट्रीय एवं विश्वमानव के विरुद्ध ऐसे मानव की प्रतिष्ठा करने का यत्न कर रहे थे, जिसे वे अपने भौगोलिक एवं समसामयिक सांस्कृतिक संदर्भ में पहचान सकें।"[3] हो सकता है, हिंदी उपन्यास-लेखकों को कल्लोल आंदोलन से अनजान और पिछड़े अंचलों की ओर मुड़ने की प्रेरणा

मिली है। लेकिन अधिक संभावना यह है कि स्वाधीनता के बाद भी गाँवों की स्थिति जस की तस रह जाने से संवेदनशील कथाकारों को क्षुब्ध और आहत किया होगा जैसा कि प्रभाकर माचवे ने लिखा है, "भारतीय जनमानस में गाँव के प्रति एक विशिष्ट प्रकार का भाव हे। यह भाव हार्डी के गाँव के दुखड़े का नियतिवाद नहीं है।"[4] जनतांत्रिक आकांक्षाओं और कुरूप वास्तविकताओं के द्वंद्व ने उपन्यासकारों को न केवल उद्वेलित किया है, अपितु उनके मूल्यबोध के निर्माण में गंभीर भूमिका निभाई है। मनोवैज्ञानिक उपन्यासों की एकांगिता और कथित प्रगतिवादी कथाकृतियों की वैचारिक और शैल्पिक सपाटता ने भी कुछ उपन्यासकारों को कथ्य और शिल्प की नई भंगिमाओं के तलाश की उत्तेजना दी है। यह गौरतलब है कि अधिकतर आंचलिक उपन्यासकार गाँव में जन्मे हैं और उनके पास इन अविकसित अंचलों की अनुभव-संपदा पर्याप्त है। इसलिए आंचलिक उपन्यास एक तरह से जिए हुए और कमाए हुए सत्यों की प्रस्तुति के प्रभावपूर्ण मंच बन गए हैं।

हिंदी में आंचलिक उपन्यासों के प्रादुर्भाव को लेकर पर्याप्त मतभेद है। कुछ आलोचकों के विचार में मन्नन द्विवेदी गजपुरी को इसके प्रवर्तन का श्रेय दिया जाना चाहिए।[5] उनकी कृति 'रामलाल' (1914 ई.) की पृष्ठभूमि ग्रामीण है। मधुकर गंगाधर ने 'बलचनमा' (1952 ई.) को पहला आंचलिक उपन्यास माना है।[6] बहुत से आलोचक 'रेणु' को यह श्रेय देते हैं क्योंकि उन्होंने 'मैला आँचल' की भूमिका में पहली बार 'आंचलिक उपन्यास' लिखने का दावा पेश किया। वस्तुतः 'रामलाल' और 'देहाती दुनिया' (शिवपूजन सहाय) में आंचलिकता की नींव पड़ गई थी। कालांतर में नागार्जुन और रेणु की कृतियों ने 'आंचलिक उपन्यास' की स्वतंत्र सत्ता को स्थापित कर दिया। किसी एक व्यक्ति को इसके प्रादुर्भाव का यश दिया जाना उचित नहीं है। यह निश्चित है कि इन नए उपन्यास-रूप का उदय एक ऐतिहासिक आवश्यकता के रूप में हुआ है। सामाजिक-आर्थिक परिवर्तन की हवा ने इसे पल्लवित और पुष्पित करने में महत्त्वपूर्ण योग दिया है।[7] इस स्थापना से रेणु के महत्त्व की उपेक्षा नहीं होती है, डॉ. मृत्युंजय उपाध्याय का यह अभिमत विचारपूर्ण है कि आंचलिकता और आंचलिक उपन्यासों के विकास और उसे एक निश्चित नाम देने में रेणु का स्थान सर्वोपरि है।[8] रेणु के उपन्यासों से पहले 'बलचनमा' प्रकाशित हो चुका था और इसके माध्यम से नागार्जुन आंचलिक उपन्यास का एक प्रारूप प्रस्तुत कर चुके थे। बकौल रामदरश मिश्र नागार्जुन के उपन्यासों की भूमि अंचल-विशेष है, हालाँकि बाद के आंचलिक उपन्यासों की सी समग्रता, जटिलता और विविधता उनमें नहीं है।[9] रेणु ने आंचलिक उपन्यास का जो मुहावरा विकसित किया है, उसमें परिवेश अधिक मुखर है। इस बात को ध्यान में रखकर डॉ. बच्चन सिंह का विचार है कि केवल 'रेणु' के उपन्यासों को ही आंचलिक माना जाना

चाहिए।[10] लेकिन यह आत्यंतिक विचार है। नागार्जुन, भैरव प्रसाद गुप्त, हिमांशु श्रीवास्तव के उपन्यासों का प्रारूप 'रेणु' के उपन्यासों से अलग है लेकिन उनमें अंचल-विशेष का सामाजिक-आर्थिक-सांस्कृतिक जीवन विविधता के साथ उभरा है। 'आंचलिकता' से आशय, अनुभव की सीमा में आनेवाले अंचल-विशेष के पात्रों, समस्याओं, संस्कृति, प्रगति आदि को अंकित करने की प्रवृत्ति है। यह प्रवृत्ति जितनी रेणु के 'मैला आँचल' और 'परती परिकथा' में है, लगभग उतनी ही 'बलचनमा' और 'सत्ती मैया का चौरा' आदि उपन्यासों में विद्यमान है। अंतर इनमें संरचनागत है। रेणु, राही मासूम रजा, रामदरश मिश्र, विवेकीराय, श्री चंद्र और शिवप्रसाद सिंह के उपन्यासों में एक ऊपरी किस्म का बिखराव दिखाई देता है। लेकिन इस बिखराव की आंतरिक संश्लिष्टता को ठीक से न देख पाने के कारण कतिपय समीक्षकों को यह लगता है कि वस्तु-विन्यास और कथा-सौष्ठव की दृष्टि से ये कमजोर रचनाएँ हैं। डॉ. महेन्द्र भटनागर ने 'मैला आँचल' को सामूहिक प्रभाव में बहुत कमजोर माना है।[11] यदि ऐसी बात होती तो रेणु की कृतियों की इतनी चर्चा न होती, न 'आधा गाँव', 'जल टूटता हुआ', 'अलग-अलग वैतरणी', 'राग दरबारी', 'सोना माटी', 'हजार घोड़ों का सवार' आदि कृतियाँ प्रशंसित और चर्चित होतीं। बल्कि वास्तविकता यह है कि स्वातंत्र्योत्तर हिंदी उपन्यास की अधिकतर उपलब्धियाँ आंचलिक कही जानेवाली कृतियों से जुड़ी हैं और उनमें से ज्यादातर कथित बिखराववाले शिल्प में रचित हैं। दलित जीवन पर लिखी गई अधिकतर औपन्यासिक रचनाएँ 'आंचलिकता' की प्रवृत्ति से युक्त हैं।

'मैला आँचल' के बहाने आंचलिक उपन्यासों की कई सीमाओं की ओर संकेत किया गया है। डॉ. त्रिभुवन सिंह ने 'मैला आँचल' के संदर्भ में लिखा है—"गाँवों में जो कुछ है, घृणित ही नहीं है, उसमें अच्छाइयाँ भी हैं, जिसकी ओर लेखक ने बहुत कम ध्यान दिया है। उसकी दृष्टि घिनौने प्रसंगों की ओर ही अधिक रही है...।"[12] वस्तुतः सभी आंचलिक उपन्यासों में 'शूल' के साथ 'फूल' भी विद्यमान हैं। अभाव, वैमनस्य, टुच्चापन ये सब आज के पिछड़े अंचलों की वास्तविकताएँ हैं, इनकी तुलना में सकारात्मक मूल्य ढूँढ़ने से मिलते हैं। इस सत्य का अनुसंधान कम महत्त्वपूर्ण नहीं होगा कि क्या 'मैला आँचल' आदि उपन्यासों में पिछड़े अंचलों के केवल 'घृणित' पक्ष को ही उद्घाटित किया गया है, या जीवन का शुभ पक्ष भी उभरा है ? कुछ अन्य आलोचकों के विचार में, असुंदरता और असंगतियों के चित्रण की व्यापकता के बावजूद आंचलिक उपन्यासों में 'मानवीय संवेदना' की छवि की उपस्थिति आश्वस्त करती है। डॉ. रामदरश मिश्र के शब्दों में—"पिछड़े हुए इलाकों को उपन्यास का क्षेत्र बनाकर उपन्यासकार उपेक्षित जीवन के प्रश्नों, आकांक्षाओं तथा गरीबी और अशिक्षाजन्य विषमता एवं असुंदरता का अंकन होता है और इन सबके बीच भी मानवीय संवेदना की छवि को अंकित कर उधर हमारा

ध्यान आकृष्ट करता है। इस प्रकार वह हमारे सौंदर्यबोध और संवेदना का विस्तार करता है। अनदेखी, जीवन-छवियाँ हमारे सामने उजागर हो उठती हैं।"[13] नवें दशक में प्रकाशित 'सोना माटी' (विवेकीराय) में बहुत से पृष्ठ विवाह संबंधी लोकाचारों के उल्लास को समर्पित हैं। 'जिंदगी नामा' (कृष्णा सोबती) के पहले खंड को पढ़कर भी यह नहीं कहा जा सकता है कि आंचलिक उपन्यासों में आया परिवेश और जीवन एकआयामी है।

आंचलिक उपन्यास के संबंध में यह लगभग सर्वसम्मत है कि इसमें 'क्षेत्रविशेष' का जीवन-सत्य उद्‌घाटित होता है। कुछ आलोचकों का विचार है कि यह क्षेत्र-विशेष या अंचल-विशेष गाँव भी हो सकता है, शहर भी हो सकता है।[14] लेकिन हिंदी के आंचलिक उपन्यासों को देखते हुए यह कहा जा सकता है कि 'आंचलिकता' का संबंध पिछड़े हुए ग्रामीण जीवन से ही है। नगर और कस्बे के जीवन पर आधारित बहुत से उपन्यास ऐसे मिल जाएँगे जिनमें चरित्रों की अपेक्षा आधारभूत अचंल कहीं अधिक मुखर होता है। ऐसी स्थिति में अधिकतर उपन्यास 'आंचलिक' मान लिए जाएँगे। डॉ. ज्ञानचंद गुप्त का यह कथन, इस संदर्भ में युक्तियुक्त है—"आंचलिक जीवन मुख्यतः ग्रामीण ही होता है और आंचलिक उपन्यास इस स्थानिक यथार्थ की सघनता एवं समग्रता के साथ अनुभव की प्रमाणिकता को लेकर प्रस्तुत हुए हैं।"[15] आंचलिक उपन्यासों के कालांतर में प्रभावहीन होते जाने के कारण को तलाशते हुए डॉ. विवेकीराय ने आंचलिकता में नगरबोध के प्रवेश और इसके फलस्वरूप उनमें सीधे टकराव की स्थिति को उत्तरदायी पाया है। उनके शब्दों में—"प्रकृत्या आंचलिकता और नगरबोध मूल की आधुनिकता की प्रवृत्तियाँ एक-दूसरे के विरोध में पड़ती हैं। आंचलिकता की सांस्कृतिक पृष्ठभूमियाँ, रागमयता और धरती के रसगंधों से जुड़ी संवेदनशीलता आधुनिकता को पसंद नहीं। उसकी कटी-छँटी और चकाचौंध भरी बुद्धिवादी यथार्थ की नगरभूमि अपने को संस्कृति से नहीं, राजनीति से दृढ़तापूर्वक जोड़कर चलती है।"[16] अतः यदि हिंदी में आंचलिकता के दौर को उपेक्षित गाँवों के सामूहिक जीवन को साहित्यचिंता के केंद्र में लाने से क्रांतिकारी[17] माना गया तो यह अनुचित नहीं है।

रघुवीर सहाय ने आंचलिकता के दौर की तुलना रूसी साहित्य की 'पोवेस्त्र' विधा से की है। उनके विचार में दोनों ही आंदोलन गाँव जाकर मानवीय अनुभव, न्याय और नैतिकता की खोज करते हैं। दोनों अपने निकट अतीत और वर्तमान के अत्याचार और सामाजिक-राजनीतिक हृदयहीनता के विरुद्ध घृणा व्यक्त करते थे। रेणु के 'मैला आँचल' और 'परती परिकथा' उपन्यासों की तुलना बलेंतीन रस्पूतिन के 'मत्योरा से विदाई और अंतिम घड़ी' से समानता दिखाते हुए रघुवीर सहाय ने लिखा है—"दोनों गाँव की ओर विश्राम या मनोरंजन के लिए नहीं जाते,

लोकतंत्र की जड़ों की खोज में जाते हैं। दोनों में आंचलिक होना ग्रामीण होकर रह जाना नहीं है, अधिक सार्थक जीवन जीना है।...दोनों जनजीवन और प्रकृति की शोषण से रक्षा को ही स्वाधीनता और लोकतंत्र की रक्षा मानते हैं। ये आंचलिक कहने को हैं, वास्तव में राष्ट्रीय हैं और इनके सरोकार मानवीयता के सरोकार हैं।''[18] इसमें संदेह नहीं कि आंचलिक उपन्यासों के केंद्र में जो गाँव है, वह रेल की खिड़की से देखा हुआ नहीं है। 'गोदान' में मालती-मेहता जैसे बुद्धिजीवी गाँव में सिर्फ आमोद-प्रमोद के लिए जाते हैं। आंचलिक उपन्यासकार 'गाँव' के प्रति ऐसा रवैया नहीं अपनाता। वह उपेक्षित गाँवों के मैले आँचल को, जो 'सोनामाटी' भी है, पानी के प्राचीरों से घिरा हुआ है, एक नहीं 'अलग-अलग वैतरणी' की उपस्थिति ने जिसे नरक बनाने में कोई कसर नहीं छोड़ी है, ऐसे गाँव के अस्तित्व संघर्ष और आजादी के बाद सामंती मूल्यों से जनतांत्रिक मूल्यों की टकहराहट को आंचलिक उपन्यासों में गंभीरता से अंकित किया है।[19] लोकजीवन और लोकसंस्कृति से आंचलिक उपन्यासों का नैकट्य भी उन्हें विशिष्ट बनाता है। इनकी लोकसंपृक्ति को 'अतीतग्रस्तता' की संज्ञा देना उचित नहीं है।

वस्तुतः नगर-केंद्रित उपन्यासों में लोकसंपृक्ति का स्पर्श नाम मात्र का होता है। इनमें लोकजीवन की रंगत, बिंब, प्रतीक और शब्दावली उसी रूप में आते हैं, जिस रूप में किसी ड्राइंगरूम में कोई 'शो पीस'। इसके अतिरिक्त अपनी सांस्कृतिक विरासत से गहरे जुड़े आंचलिक उपन्यासों में नए मूल्यों और पुराने मूल्यों के द्वंद्व और फिर मूल्य-संक्रमण के जो विस्तृत चित्र मिलते हैं, वे नगरबोधी उपन्यासों में कम हैं क्योंकि औद्योगीकरण आदि के फलस्वरूप नगरजीवन इस तरह के द्वंद्व को बहुत पहले झेल चुका है। इसलिए आंचलिक उपन्यास, उन्हीं उपन्यासों को माना जाना चाहिए जो मुख्यतः ग्रामीण पृष्ठभूमि पर आधारित हैं और जिनमें उस ग्रामीण अंचल या पिछड़े अचंल का वर्णन इतने विस्तार से हुआ हो कि वह 'अंचल' ही नायक लगे। डॉ. उषा डोगरा ने माना है कि आंचलिक उपन्यास में ''किसी जाति विशेष का परंपरागत जीवन''[20] चित्रित होता है। यह धारणा आंशिक तौर पर ही सत्य है। कुछ उपन्यास जैसे–'सूरज किरन की छाँव', 'हजार घोड़ों का सवार', 'धरती धन न अपना', 'आधा गाँव' निश्चय ही एक जाति विशेष के जीवन को विस्तार से उभारते हैं। लेकिन 'मैला आँचल', 'परती परिकथा', 'सोनामाटी', 'जल टूटता हुआ', 'अलग-अलग वैतरणी' आदि उपन्यासों में किसी जाति विशेष का जीवन केंद्र में नहीं है।

किसी आंचलिक उपन्यास का केवल अंचल विशेष पर आधारित होना पर्याप्त नहीं है। जिस कथित 'अनुभव की प्रामाणिकता' का शोर 'नई कहानी' के दौरान मचा था, वह नई कहानी के समानांतर चल रही आंचलिक उपन्यास धारा में अपने सीधे और स्पष्ट अर्थ में रचनाप्रक्रिया का अनिवार्य अंग बनी हुई थी। आंचलिक

उपन्यास 'सेकेण्ड हैण्ड' अनुभवों के सहारे नहीं लिखा जा सकता। युद्ध समस्या पर केंद्रित उपन्यास प्रायः ऐसे लेखकों ने लिखे हैं, जिन्होंने न तो युद्ध का प्रत्यक्ष अनुभव किया है और न युद्धजनित दुष्प्रभावों से उनका कोई निजी सरोकार रहा है। आंचलिक उपन्यास मात्र सूचनाओं और रपटों के आधार पर नहीं लिखा जा सकता। संभवतः इसीलिए डॉ. रामदरश मिश्र ने लिखा है–"आंचलिक उपन्यासों ने अनुभवहीन सामान्य या विराट् के पीछे न दौड़कर अनुभव की सीमा में आनेवाले अंचल विशेष को उपन्यास का क्षेत्र बनाया है।"[21] लेकिन केवल अनुभवशीलता और यथार्थ का हूबहू चित्रण ही किसी उपन्यास को आंचलिक बनाने में समर्थ नहीं है। मधुकर गंगाधर आंचलिक उपन्यासों की रचना में 'ऐतिहासिक एवं वैज्ञानिक धारणा' की उपस्थिति आवश्यक मानते हैं–'आंचलिक उपन्यासों' का आदर्श केवल किसी क्षेत्र की चित्रगत वास्तविकता प्रस्तुत करना नहीं, बल्कि संपूर्ण जीवन प्रणाली की ऐतिहासिक एवं वैज्ञानिक धारणा प्रस्तुत करना है।[22] ऐसी स्थिति में आंचलिक उपन्यासों का मूल्यबोध जहाँ एक ओर रचनाकारों द्वारा स्वतः अर्जित है, वहीं दूसरी ओर ऐतिहासिक विकास की प्रक्रिया को वैज्ञानिक दृष्टिकोण के तहत समझने से पुष्ट और प्रौढ़ हुआ है।

कुछ आंचलिक उपन्यासों में किसी प्रकार की राजनीतिक प्रतिबद्धता नहीं है, उनका दृष्टिकोण मानवतावादी है। उनके इस दलविहीन मानवतावाद को कुछ आलोचकों ने संदेह की दृष्टि से देखा है और इसकी कटु भर्त्सना की है। कृष्णप्रताप के शब्दों में–"दलविहीन मानवतावाद के इन आंचलिक दावेदारों ने पतनशील प्रवृत्तियों को नया भाववादी जामा ही नहीं पहनाया बल्कि मूर्खता और जहालत का आदर्शीकरण और उदात्तीकरण भी किया। समझ का अभाव सरलता का पर्याय नहीं हो सकता।"[23] 'मैला आँचल' के संदर्भ में डॉ. विजयमोहन सिंह का विचार है कि रेणु के पास कोई जीवनदृष्टि नहीं है।[24] अन्यत्र उनका विचार है कि आंचलिक कृतियों का भावबोध रोमांटिक सुधारवाद से ग्रस्त है–"एक दृष्टि वह थी जिससे गांधीजी ने गाँवों को देखा, परखा और जगाया था और दूसरी दृष्टि वह बनी जो यायावर अपने कैमरे की आँख से प्रत्येक अपरिचित स्थल और अंचल को देखता है।"[25] विजयमोहन सिंह के दोनों कथनों में अंतर्विरोध है। एक ओर वे 'मैला आँचल' में दृष्टिहीनता की चर्चा करते हैं, दूसरी ओर मैला आँचल आदि उपन्यासों में रोमांटिक सुधारवाद को रेखांकित करते हैं। आंचलिक उपन्यासों के कटु आलोचक रेणु की कृतियों पर विशेष आक्रमण करते दिखाई देते हैं। आंचलिक उपन्यास न तो रेणु की रचनाधर्मिता के पर्याय मात्र हैं और न स्वयं रेणु दृष्टिविहीन और अराजक हैं, जैसा उन्हें समझा गया है, राही मासूम रजा आदि के उपन्यासों में अतीत के जिस सम्मोहन और रोमांटिक 'इल्यजन' को खोजा गया है, वह आग्रही दृष्टि का परिणाम है। रेणु, रामदरश मिश्र, शिवप्रसाद सिंह आदि की कृतियाँ पढ़कर सामंतवाद

के श्वेतश्याम दोनों पक्षों का परिचय तो मिलता है, लेकिन सामंत वर्ग के साथ सहानुभूति जैसा भाव पैदा नहीं होता। बल्कि प्रबुद्ध पाठक को यह अनुभव होता है कि शोषण और अन्याय पर टिके सामंत वर्ग का नाश अवश्यंभावी था। इस बात का अध्ययन बहुत दिलचस्प और विचारोत्तेजक होगा कि 'अतीत' से आंचलिक कथाकारों का जुड़ाव 'नास्टेल्जिक' दृष्टि है या अंचल को अतीत और वर्तमान की समग्रता में देखने का परिणाम ? 'आधा गाँव' के संदर्भ में डॉ. आदित्य प्रसाद त्रिपाठी ने यह सिद्ध करने का प्रयास किया है कि 'नास्टेल्जिया' में रचनात्मक शक्ति भी होती है। नास्टेल्जिक मोह 'आधा गाँव' की मूल प्रेरणा और प्राण है।[26] देखना होगा कि यह मोह कहीं परंपरागत मूल्यों के प्रति मोह का दूसरा नाम तो नहीं है। यहाँ एक तथ्य गौरतलब है कि अधिकतर आंचलिक उपन्यासकार प्रगतिशील विचारधारा से संबंधित हैं। नागार्जुन, रांगेय राघव, राही मासूम रजा, रामदरश मिश्र आदि निर्विवाद रूप से वामपंथी हैं, यादवेन्द्र शर्मा 'चंद्र', 'रेणु', हिमांशु जोशी, शिवप्रसाद सिंह आदि भी समाजवादी या प्रगतिवादी विचारधारा के उपन्यासकार हैं। विवेकीराय, श्रीलाल शुक्ल आदि की दृष्टि मानवतावादी है। ऐसी स्थिति में आंचलिक उपन्यासों को रोमानी दृष्टि से प्रेरित और संचालित मानना निश्चय ही त्रुटिपूर्ण है। होफमन के साक्ष्य से डॉ. आदर्श सक्सेना ने 'आंचलिकता' को विश्वव्यापी स्वच्छंदतावादी आंदोलन से जोड़ा है।[27] लेकिन डॉ. सक्सेना ने इस विधा को आंचलिक यथार्थवाद और समाजवादी यथार्थवाद–दो श्रेणियों में विभक्त कर 'आंचलिकता' के रोमानी होने का स्वयं खंडन कर दिया है। डॉ. इंदुप्रकाश पांडेय का मंतव्य भी आंचलिक अपन्यासों के दृष्टिविहीन या रोमानी होने के विरोध में पड़ता है–"इन लेखकों का प्रमुख उद्देश्य पाठकों का मनोरंजन नहीं, बल्कि पीड़ित समाज के प्रति सहानुभूति प्रकट करना और उन्हें अपनी स्थितियों के विरुद्ध विद्रोह करने के लिए उभारना है।"[28]

'मैला आँचल' में रेणु ने डॉ. प्रशांत से कहलाया है कि मैं प्यार की खेती करूँगा।[29] और उनका जित्तन 'परती परिकथा' में गुलाब की खेती के लिए कृतसंकल्प है। गुलाब की खेती भी एक तरह से आत्मीयता और लगाव के वातावरण के निर्माण की सूचना है। प्यार और गुलाब की खेती के प्रति रेणु के इस आकर्षण को रोमानी माना गया है। जबकि 'मैला आँचल' की भूमिका में रेणु ने पहले ही कह दिया है कि इसमें जीवन के दोनों पक्ष हैं–शूल भी, फूल भी। यह समझना भूल होगी कि प्यार या गुलाब की खेती का संकल्प जनविरोधी या प्रगतिविरोधी है, बल्कि यह समाजवादी कलासंस्कृति का ही एक अंग है। यह शोषक व्यवस्था द्वारा पैदा की गई कुरूपताओं और सौंदर्यविरोधी अवस्थाओं का प्रतिकार है। हेनरिख हाइने ने एक सर्वांगपूर्ण व्यवस्था की चर्चा करते हुए लिखा था कि इसमें हर मुनष्य को खूब सारी रोटी ही नहीं, खूब सारे गुलाब भी उपलब्ध होंगे।[30] आब्नेर ज़ीस

ने इस कथन की व्याख्या करते हुए लिखा है कि साम्यवादी व्यवस्था में मनुष्य का सर्वांगीण विकास अभीष्ट है। समाजवादी समाज में मनुष्य और उसके मूल्य समाजवादी विकास का साधन नहीं, अपितु सर्वोच्च लक्ष्य होते हैं।[31] आंचलिक उपन्यासकार भी भूख, अभाव और शोषण की समाप्ति के साथ मानवीय मूल्यों की उपस्थिति को काम्य मानते हैं और यह निश्चय ही एक संतुलित दृष्टिकोण है। यादवेंद्र शर्मा 'चंद्र' सरीखे आंचलिक उपन्यासकार ने पुराने मूल्यों का चित्रण और नए मूल्यों के समर्थन को प्रासंगिक माना है। उनके विचार में, यदि कोई उपन्यासकार आज के मूल्यों को अपना समर्थन नहीं दे पा रहा है तो वह यथार्थ से पिछड़ा हुआ है।[32] रामदरश मिश्र ने भी माना है कि आधुनिकता-बोध ने आंचलिक उपन्यासकारों में सामंती रूढ़ियों और ठहरे हुए सोचविचार के विरुद्ध लड़नेवाली नई गतिशील चेतना उत्पन्न की है।[33] विवेकीराय ने एक बातचीत में साफ तौर पर कहा है कि यदि आंचलिक उपन्यासों में परंपरागत मूल्यों के प्रति मोह है तो यह निश्चित रूप से आधुनिकता-विरोधी दृष्टिकोण है।[34] इन सभी आत्मस्वीकृतियों से यह आभास मिलता है कि आंचलिक उपन्यासों का प्रस्थान बिंदु और गंतव्य एकआयामी या मनुष्य की सर्वांगीण प्रगति की विरोधी नहीं है। इन उपन्यासों में व्यक्त मूल्यों के संक्रमण के अनुशीलन से 'वास्तविकता' का ज्ञान किया जा सकता है।

आंचलिक उपन्यासों के अध्ययन में एक समस्या तब उठ खड़ी होती है, जब स्वयं उपन्यासकार अपनी कृति को अनांचलिक मानता है और प्रायः समीक्षक उसे 'आंचलिक' करार देते हैं। शिवप्रसाद सिंह कृत 'अलग-अलग वैतरणी' के साथ ऐसा ही हुआ है। शिवप्रसाद सिंह इसे आंचलिक नहीं मानते। आदित्य नारायण जैसे समीक्षक भी इसे आंचलिक नहीं मानते।[35] लेकिन अधिकतर समीक्षा कृतियों और शोधप्रबंधों में इसकी चर्चा 'आंचलिक उपन्यास' के रूप में हुई है। डॉ. अंजलि तिवारी के अनुसार—"यदि यह आंचलिक नहीं होगा तो बहुत ही विशृंखल कथाओंवाला, उद्देश्यहीन प्रभाववाला उपन्यास माना जाएगा।"[36] बलभद्र ठाकुर भी अपने उपन्यासों को आंचलिक कहा जाना अच्छा नहीं समझते। वस्तुतः अंचल-विशेष को जहाँ प्रमुखता प्राप्त है, किसी गाँव या अंचल को जहाँ समग्रता में उभारा गया है, वह उपन्यास निस्संकोच आंचलिक माना जाना चाहिए। यादवेंद्र शर्मा 'चंद्र' ने एक बातचीत में अपना मत इस रूप में व्यक्त किया है—"लेखक को इस विवाद में पड़ना ही नहीं चाहिए क्योंकि आप अपने बारे में कोई एक राय किसी से कायम नहीं करवा सकते। आलोचक, जिसकी जो दृष्टि होगी, वह उस प्रकार ही उसके बारे में बयान करेगा। रचना किसी अंचल से संबंधित है, फिर उसे आंचलिक उपन्यास कहलाना पसंद न हो तो वह लिखे ही नहीं।"[37] कुछ आलोचकों का मत है कि 'आंचलिकता' को कसौटी मान लेने से भी मूल्यांकन के स्तर पर एक समस्या

उठ खड़ी होती है। बहुत से आंचलिक उपन्यासों में आंचलिकता के अतिरिक्त भी बहुत कुछ है। इसलिए 'जल टूटता हुआ' के संदर्भ में डॉ. नरेन्द्र मोहन की यह चिंता वाजिब है कि 'आंचलिकता' के आधार पर इसका विवेचन करने पर उस यथार्थ की शायद खरोंच भर मिल सके जो इसमें अभिव्यक्त है।[38] इसके बावजूद 'आंचलिकता' को महत्त्व तो देना ही पड़ेगा। आंचलिक उपन्यासों का अनुशीलन करते समय यह देखना सर्वथा प्रासंगिक होगा कि 'कृति' में अंचल-विशेष के "लोकजीवन सहित उसकी आस्था, भाषा, कलारुचि, रूढ़ियाँ, गीत-नृत्य और तमाम-तमाम अतीतमुखी सांस्कृतिक बुनावटों"[39] को तरल रागबोध के स्तर पर सोद्देश्य भाव से प्रस्तुत किया गया है या नहीं। 'आंचलिक' होने का अर्थ, 'सीमित संवेदना' से नहीं है। आंचलिक उपन्यास अंचल-विशेष के व्याज से पूरे भारतीय ग्रामीण परिवेश की चर्चा करते हैं। 'असगाँव पसगाँव' के लेखक ने बल देकर कहा है कि यह संपूर्ण भारतीय ग्राम्य जीवन की त्रासदी भी है।[40]

डॉ. इंदुप्रकाश पांडेय ने के.ए. ज्वेलेबिल का मत उद्‌धृत किया है, जिसके अनुसार आंचलिक उपन्यासों का महत्त्व साहित्यिक न होकर समाजशास्त्रीय और नृतत्वशास्त्रीय अधिक है। इनका महत्त्व मूलतः एक दस्तावेज या संग्रहालय-मूल्य के रूप में है।[41] यह दृष्टिकोण अतिवाद ग्रस्त है। इन उपन्यासों में मानव जीवन की धड़कन है और धड़कन पर्याप्त कलात्मक रूप में व्यक्त हुई है। श्रेष्ठ आंचलिक उपन्यासों में समाजशास्त्रीय-नृतत्वशास्त्रीय संदर्भ रचना के अंग बनकर आए हैं। इनका नए ढंग का कथा-विन्यास, संश्लिष्ट एवं विशिष्ट परिवेश, अपने समय से जूझते हुए चरित्र, आंचलिक स्वरों से गूँथी गई भाषा और बिंबों प्रतीकों से समृद्ध अभिव्यंजना को देखते हुए ऐसा कतई नहीं लगता कि इनका साहित्यिक महत्त्व है ही नहीं।

राही मासूम रजा ने 'आधा गाँव' को "गंगौली में गुजरनेवाले समय की कहानी" माना है। 'आधा गाँव' ही नहीं ज्यादातर आंचलिक उपन्यास 'समय की कहानी' हैं। अपने युग का तेज संक्रमण—हर स्तर पर, पिछड़ों से पिछड़े अंचल को अपनी लपेट में ले चुका है। अशिक्षित और पुरा मूल्यों से चिपके जन-समुदाय के लिए 'नयेपन' को एकदम स्वीकार कर लेना यातना से कम नहीं है। बल्कि एक यातना से दूसरी यातना की ओर बढ़ना है। मूल्यों के इस द्वंद्व का स्वरूप सपाट नहीं है और इसकी साहित्यिक अभिव्यक्ति भी आसान नहीं है। आंचलिक उपन्यासकारों ने हर स्तर पर सक्रिय संक्रमण और अंततः मूल्यों के संक्रमण को कितनी निपुणता से, कितनी सफलता से व्यक्त किया है, यह विवेचन और अनुशीलन का विषय है।

आंचलिक उपन्यासों का शोधपरक अनुशीलन 'जीवन सत्य', 'आंचलिकता', 'भाषा', 'संस्कृति', 'शिल्पविधि' आदि कई दृष्टियों से हुआ है। आंचलिक उपन्यासकारों

पर अलग-अलग हुए शोधकार्य को छोड़ दिया जाए, तब भी लगभग दो दर्जन शोधप्रबंध सीधे आंचलिक उपन्यासों से संबद्ध हैं। डॉ. आदर्श सक्सेना, डॉ. जवाहर सिंह और डॉ. देवयानी प्रसाद ने क्रमशः 'हिंदी के आंचलिक उपन्यास और उनकी शिल्पविधि', 'हिंदी के आंचलिक उपन्यासों की शिल्पविधि' तथा 'हिंदी के आंचलिक उपन्यासों की शिल्पविधि' में अपना ध्यान मुख्यतः शिल्प पक्ष पर केंद्रित किया है। कुछ प्रबंधों में कथ्य और शिल्प के समन्वित अध्ययन का प्रयास हुआ है। 'आंचलिक उपन्यासों की तात्विक मीमांसा' (चित्रा तिवारी), 'हिंदी के आंचलिक उपन्यास कथ्य और शिल्प' (डॉ. कला मेहता) और 'हिंदी के आंचलिक उपन्यास' (डॉ. मृत्युंजय उपाध्याय) इसी प्रकार के प्रबंध हैं। डॉ. मृत्युंजय उपाध्याय ने उपन्यासों के समाजशास्त्रीय विवेचन के साथ-साथ भाषाशास्त्रीय अध्ययन भी किया है। 'आंचलिकता और हिंदी उपन्यास' (डॉ. नगीना जैन) 'स्वातंत्र्योत्तर हिंदी साहित्य में आंचलिक उपन्यासों का विकास' (आलोक कुमार सिंह), 'हिंदी के आंचलिक उपन्यास : उद्‌भव और विकास' (भोलाराम) आदि प्रबंधों में आंचलिकता के उदय को ऐतिहासिक संदर्भों में देखते हुए हिंदी उपन्यास को उसके प्रदेय की चर्चा की गई है। केवल 'भाषा-विवेचन' पर केंद्रित प्रबंधों की संख्या भी खासी है। 'हिंदी आंचलिक उपन्यास भाषा वैज्ञानिक भूमिका' (जे. माथुर), 'हिंदी भाषा के विकास में आंचलिक उपन्यासों का योगदान' (जयनारायण वर्मा) आदि प्रबंध इस संदर्भ में द्रष्टव्य हैं। डॉ. इंदु प्रकाश पांडेय ने आंचलिक उपन्यासों की 'सेटिंग' को लेकर 'हिदी के आंचलिक उपन्यासों में जीवन सत्य' शीर्षक शोधप्रबंध लिखा है। लोकतात्त्विक अध्ययन से संबद्ध प्रबंधों में 'आंचलिक उपन्यासों का सांस्कृतिक अध्ययन' (चित्रा पंचेरिया), 'हिंदी के आंचलिक उपन्यासों में लोकतत्त्व' (मालती केशरवानी), और 'हिंदी के आंचलिक उपन्यासों का लोकतात्त्विक विमर्श' (उषा डोगरा) मुख्य हैं। डॉ. एच.के. कडवे ने अपने प्रबंध 'हिंदी उपन्यासों में आंचलिकता की प्रवृत्ति' में हिंदी-मराठी उपन्यासों की तुलनात्मक समीक्षा की है। अन्य प्रबंधों में 'हिंदी के आंचलिक उपन्यास' (राधेश्याम कौशिक), 'हिंदी के आंचलिक उपन्यास' (प्रकाश वाजपेयी), 'हिंदी के आंचलिक उपन्यासों का अनुशीलन' (शकुंतला सिंह), 'हिंदी के आंचलिक उपन्यास' (आर.आर. दुबे), 'हिंदी के आंचलिक उपन्यासों में आधुनिकता' (रामवंदन पाठक) आदि उल्लेखनीय हैं। कथासाहित्य केंद्रित कई शोध-प्रबंधों में आंचलिक उपन्यासों को लेकर गंभीर विवेचन उपलब्ध है। ऐसे प्रबंधों में 'स्वातंत्र्योत्तर हिंदी कथा साहित्य और ग्रामजीवन' (विवेकीराय), 'स्वातंत्र्योत्तर हिंदी उपन्यास और ग्रामचेतना' (ज्ञानचंद गुप्त), 'हिंदी उपन्यास की प्रवृत्तियाँ' (डॉ. शशि भूषण सिंहल), 'हिंदी उपन्यास : शिल्प और प्रयोग' (डॉ. त्रिभुवन सिंह) आदि उल्लेखनीय हैं।

आंचलिक उपन्यासों पर आधारित समीक्षा कृतियों की संख्या खासी है। इनमें आंचलिक उपन्यास : 'संवेदना और शिल्प' (ज्ञानचंद गुप्त), 'हिंदी आंचलिक उपन्यास : उद्‌भव और विकास' (इंदिरा जोशी) और 'हिंदी के आंचलिक उपन्यास'

(सं. रामदरश मिश्र, ज्ञानचंद गुप्त) आदि में आंचलिक उपन्यास के विभिन्न पहलुओं पर गंभीर विचार विमर्श हुआ है। लेकिन उपर्युक्त सभी प्रबंधों और आलोचनाकृतियों में मूल्यों के संक्रमण के संदर्भ में आंचलिक उपन्यासों को विवेचित-मूल्यांकित करने का कोई स्वतंत्र प्रयास देखने में नहीं आया। इस दृष्टि से प्रस्तुत प्रबंध की नवीनता स्वयं सिद्ध है, इसमें उपन्यासों में व्यक्त मूल्य-संक्रमण को वास्तविक मूल्य-संक्रमण के समानांतर रखकर उनके गुणात्मक अंतर को भी रेखांकित किया गया है। तथ्यचेतना और मूल्यचेतना के अंतर का मूल्यांकन समाजशास्त्रीय अध्ययन और तुलनात्मक अध्ययन की प्राविधियों की सहायता से हुआ है। इसमें समाजशास्त्रीय शोधकार्यों की सहायता जहाँ-तहाँ ली गई है और कई आंचलिक उपन्यासकारों से हुई बातचीत का उपयोग भी कई स्थलों पर हुआ है। उपन्यासों में मूल्यों के द्वंद्व, संकट, उभार और नई दिशा में संक्रमण को लेकर उपन्यासकारों की वैचारिकता का निर्देश भी यथास्थान किया है। इस प्रबंध में प्रयास यही है कि वस्तुनिष्ठ एवं तथ्याधारित दृष्टि अपनाते हुए आंचलिक उपन्यासों के 'मर्म' और 'मूल्य' को उद्घाटित किया जाए। इस अध्ययन के दौरान यह ध्यान रखा गया है कि मात्र कुछ चर्चित कृतियों तक सीमित न रहकर कई कम चर्चित आंचलिक उपन्यासों को भी आधारभूत सामग्री का अंग बनाया जाए। इसी दृष्टि के तहत 'असगाँव-पसगाँव', 'दूब जनम आई' आदि कई कृतियों का समावेश किया गया है।

कुछ आलोचकों का विचार है कि आंचलिक उपन्यासों में 'मूल्य-निर्णय' अंचल के ब्यौरों के चित्रण के आग्रह में खो गया है। डॉ. शिवकुमार मिश्र ने इस आरोप को फैलाते हुए लिखा है—"मिट्टी महत्त्वपूर्ण बन जाती है, उस मिट्टी को अपने श्रम से सींचनेवाला मनुष्य गौण। और यह सब प्रकृतिवाद की रिपोर्ताज शैली में, समाचारपत्रों की संवेदनशून्य सूचनाओं के स्तर पर, कोरे विवरण और सूक्ष्मतम ब्यौरों के साथ रूपवादी प्रयासों से जुड़कर अलंकरण की शक्ल में सामने आता है।[42] प्रस्तुत शोधकार्य इस आरोप की परीक्षा के लिए विशेष रूप से प्रतिश्रुत है कि आंचलिक उपन्यासों में 'मिट्टी महत्त्वपूर्ण है या 'मनुष्य'।

संदर्भ

1. हिंदी के आंचलिक उपन्यास, डॉ. मृत्युंजय उपाध्याय, पृ. 15-16
2. हिंदी के आंचलिक उपन्यास, सं. रामदरश मिश्र-ज्ञानचंद गुप्त, विवेकीराय का ओलख, पृ. 19
3. हिंदी के आंचलिक उपन्यासों में जीवन-सत्य, पृ. 7
4. रचनाकार रामदरश मिश्र, सं. डॉ. नित्यानंद तिवारी, डॉ. ज्ञानचंद गुप्त, पृ. 152
5. हिंदी आंचलिक उपन्यास : उद्भव और विकास, पृ. 89

6. आलोचना, जनवरी 1966, पृ. 81
7. आंचलिकता और हिंदी उपन्यास, पृ. 26
8. हिंदी के आंचलिक उपन्यास, पृ. 26
9. वही, पृ. 12
10. आधुनिक हिंदी साहित्य का इतिहास, पृ. 387
11. हिंदी कथा साहित्य : विविध आयाम, पृ. 47
12. हिंदी उपन्यास और यथार्थवाद, पृ. 362
13. हिंदी के आंचलिक उपन्यास (सं.), पृ. 13
14. स्वातंत्र्योत्तर हिंदी उपन्यास, कांति वर्मा, पृ. 189
15. आंचलिक उपन्यास : संवेदना और शिल्प, पृ. 13
16. आलोचना, 69, पृ. 46
17. आलोचना, अक्टूबर-दिसंबर 1988, पृ. 55
18. वही।
19. वर्तमान साहित्य, जनवरी 1990, कृष्णप्रताप का आलेख, पृ. 7
20. हिंदी के आंचलिक उपन्यासों का लोकतांत्रिक विमर्श, पृ. 84
21. हिंदी उपन्यास : एक अंतर्यात्रा, पृ. 187
22. सुबह होने तक (उपन्यास), मधु प्रकाशन, ताशकंद मार्ग, इलाहाबाद, 85, पृ. 9
23. वर्तमान साहित्य, जनवरी 1990, पृ. 7
24. आधुनिक हिंदी उपन्यासों में प्रेम की परिकल्पना, पृ. 362
25. वही, पृ. 361
26. औपन्यासिक समीक्षा एवं समीक्षाएँ, पृ. 174
27. हिंदी के आंचलिक उपन्यास और उनकी शिल्पविधि, पृ. 63
28. हिंदी के आंचलिक उपन्यासों में जीवन-सत्य, पृ. 12
29. मैला आँचल, पृ. 16
30. कला के वैचारिक और सौंदर्यात्मक पहलू, पृ. 31
31. वही।
32. यादवेंद्र शर्मा चंद्र से वेदप्रकाश अमिताभ की बातचीत।
33. वेदप्रकाश अमिताभ से बातचीत।
34. विवेकीराय से शोधकर्त्ता की बातचीत।
35. औपन्यासिक समीक्षा एवं समीक्षाएँ, पृ. 145
36. हिंदी के आंचलिक उपन्यास, सं. रामदरश मिश्र, ज्ञानचंद गुप्त, पृ. 149
37. यादवेंद्र शर्मा 'चंद्र' से वेदप्रकाश अमिताभ की बातचीत।
38. हिंदी के आंचलिक उपन्यास, पृ. 159
39. हिंदी के आंचलिक उपन्यास, विवेकीराय, पृ. 18
40. 'असगाँव पसगाँव', पृ. 'घ'
41. हिंदी के आंचलिक उपन्यासों में जीवन-सत्य, पृ. 271
42. आलोचना, जनवरी-मार्च, 1986, पृ. 31

प्रथम प्रकरण

मूल्य-मीमांसा

डॉ. राधाकृष्णन के विचार में मुनष्य केवल भौतिक उपलब्धियों से संतुष्ट होनेवाला प्राणी नहीं है। उसका सर्वप्रथम ध्येय है–आत्म-साक्षात्कार।[1] यूनानी दार्शनिक सुकरात के अनुसार 'आत्म-साक्षात्कार' का अर्थ यह जानना है कि तुम्हारा मूल्य क्या है ? तुम्हारे मूल्य क्या हैं और महत्त्व की दृष्टि से उनका क्रम क्या है ?[2] आज भी अनेक विचारक मानते हैं कि मनुष्य के सामने एक बड़ी समस्या यह है कि वह नए और प्रासंगिक मूल्यों का अनुसंधान करे और जीवन के तथ्यों या वास्तविकताओं के साथ उनका तालमेल स्थापित करे।[3] मानव-जीवन के लक्ष्य से सीधा और प्रत्यक्ष संबंध होने के कारण मूल्यों की चर्चा और मीमांसा विश्वचिंतन का अंग बनी रही है। डॉ. मैत्र ने एक स्थान पर संकेत किया है कि भारतीय अध्ययन परंपरा मूल्यपरक रही है : "हमारी परंपरा है मूल्य-केंद्रित होना, न कि अस्तित्व-केंद्रित होना... ।"[4] आज मनुष्य के समस्त अनुभवों और विचारों में 'मूल्य' की स्थिति मानी जाती है और चिंतन के अधिकतर मानदंड मूल्य-मापदंड होते हैं। अतः ज्ञान-विज्ञान के विभिन्न क्षेत्रों से संबद्ध अर्थशास्त्र, दर्शन, मनोविज्ञान, समाजशास्त्र आदि में मूल्य-संबंधी विवेचन इतने परिमाण में उपलब्ध है कि उसका स्वतंत्र शास्त्र बन गया है। मूल्य संबंधी विवेचन को अंग्रेजी में 'एग्जियोलोजी' (Axiology) कहा गया है। इसके हिंदी पर्याय के रूप में 'मूल्य-विज्ञान' या 'मूल्य-मीमांसा' प्रस्तावित हैं। अनेक विचारक मूल्य-विवेचन को विज्ञान मानने में हिचकिचाते हैं। उनकी दृष्टि में 'मूल्य' का अर्थ किसी वस्तु के 'मूल्य' का 'भाव' या 'अभाव' है। लेकिन भाव-अभाव से परे 'मूल्य' तटस्थ भी हो सकता है। स्पष्ट है कि 'मूल्य' का कोई स्थिर, निश्चित सार्वभौमिक और सार्वकालिक मानदंड नहीं

है। अतः शुभ या अशुभ से जुड़े मूल्य-संबंधी सोच-विचार को मूल्य विज्ञान की संज्ञा देना उपयुक्त नहीं है।[5] इसे मूल्य-मीमांसा कहना अधिक युक्तिसंगत है। जैसा कि हेराल्ड एच. टाइटस ने स्पष्ट किया है, मानवीय आचरण और कला में मूल्यों का अध्ययन करना 'मूल्य-मीमांसा' के अंतर्गत आता है।[6]

मूल्य-मीमांसा : इतिवृत्त

पाश्चात्य-चिंतन में मूल्य-मीमांसा का स्रोत प्लेटो, कांट और फिश्टे की रचनाएँ हैं। प्लेटो द्वारा वर्णित प्रत्यय (IDEA) का मूल्य से बहुत निकट का संबंध है। बीसवीं शताब्दी में 'मूल्य-मीमांसा' का क्षेत्र नीतिशास्त्र और दर्शन से आगे बढ़कर मनोविज्ञान और समाजशास्त्र तक फैल गया। शुरू में मूल्य मुख्यतः नीतिशास्त्रीय प्रत्यय था और कुछ भिन्न अर्थ में अर्थशास्त्र में प्रयुक्त होता था। आज नीतिशास्त्र से विशिष्ट एक सामान्य मूल्य-सिद्धांत पर जोर दिया जाता है। आज के अर्थ में 'मूल्य' का प्रयोग बहुत पुराना नहीं है। प्रो. फिलिप ब्लेयर राइस के विचार में मूल्य-मीमांसा को पाश्चात्य दर्शन की शाखा के रूप में उन्नीसवीं सदी के अंत में ही स्वीकार किया जा सका था। समझा जाता कि मूल्यपरक अध्ययन का सुझाव हरमन लौत्जे ने 1885 ई. में दिया था और नीत्शे ने आजकल के अर्थ में 'मूल्य' का प्रयोग किया।[7] नीत्शे ने मूल्यों के मूल्यांतरण (ट्रांसवैलुएशन आफ वैल्यूज) पर बल दिया। बिडलबैंड ने प्रतिमानों और आदर्शों के अध्ययन को ही दर्शन माना। रिकर्ट और मुन्सटरबर्ग ने भी मूल्यों की स्थापना का समर्थन किया।[8] कालांतर में मूल्यों को लेकर इतना विवेचन और अनुशीलन हुआ है कि 'मूल्य-मीमांसा' का अच्छा-खासा शास्त्र निर्मित हो गया है।

मूल्य : भारतीय दृष्टि

प्राचीन भारतीय चिंतकों ने विधिवत् मूल्य-विवेचन नहीं किया है। पुरुषार्थों और आदर्शों को लेकर किए गए चिंतन को 'मूल्य-मीमांसा' के रूप में स्वीकार किया जा सकता है। प्रो. कृष्णनाथ ने 'मूल्य' की परिभाषा के सिलसिले में 'शुक्रनीति' की कुछ पंक्तियों को उद्धृत किया है। शुक्राचार्य ने जिन बातों को आर्थिक 'मूल्य' के संबंध में कहा है, वे काफी हद तक 'जीवनमूल्य' के लिए भी लागू हो सकती हैं। शुक्रनीति के अनुसार—"जो कुछ भी अप्रतिम है, बेजोड़ है, वह रत्न जैसा ही है। सब मनुष्यों का मूल्य देश-काल के अनुसार तय होना चाहिए। जो गुणहीन है और व्यवहार के योग्य नहीं है, उसका कोई मूल्य नहीं।...कामना के अनुसार पदार्थों का मोल हीन या अधिक, कमोबेश होता है।"[9] इस व्याख्या के अनुसार 'मूल्यवान' वह वस्तु है जिसके लिए व्यक्ति को अधिक से अधिक मूल्य चुकाना

पड़े। मूल्य देशकाल के अनुसार परिवर्तनशील है। प्रो. कृष्णनाथ ने 'मूल्य' की परिभाषा देते हुए उपनिषदों का साक्ष्य भी दिया है—"जो है", वह तो तथ्य है और "जो होना चाहिए" वह मूल्य कहा जाता है। "जो होना चाहिए" के लिए उपनिषदों की परिभाषा में दो शब्द आए हैं—श्रेय-प्रेय। अब अगर इन पारिभाषिक शब्दों का इस्तेमाल करें तो 'मूल्य' अन्य बातों सहित श्रेय-प्रेय है।" [10] इस विवेचन से यह अर्थ निकाला जा सकता है कि जो श्रेयस्कर है, कल्याणकारी है, वह भी मूल्य है और जो प्रीतिकर है, रुचिकर है, वह भी मूल्य है। सत्यं, शिवं और सुंदरम् की स्वीकृति भी इसी कथन को प्रमाणित करती है।

आधुनिक भारतीय विचारकों में डॉ. राधाकमल मुखर्जी, डॉ. देवराज, यशदेव शल्य, संगमलाल पांडेय आदि ने भी मूल्यों के स्वरूप पर विचार किया है। राधाकमल मुखर्जी ने अपने मूल्य-विवेचन में पाश्चात्य विचारों का भरपूर उपयोग किया है और उनका विवेचन मुख्यतः 'समाजशास्त्रीय' है। डॉ. देवराज की 'एप्रोच' दार्शनिक है। वे यह मानते हैं कि मानवीय विद्याएँ अनिवार्यतः मूल्यानुप्राणित होती हैं। [11] मूल्य-निर्मित के संदर्भ में उनका विचार है—"मनुष्य एक लक्ष्यान्वेषी अथवा प्रयोजनवान् प्राणी है, वह विश्व की असंख्य वास्तविकताओं को साध्यों और साधनों, मूल्यों और मूल्याभावों के रूप में ग्रहण करता है, ताकि वह उन्हें पाने अथवा दूर रखने की कोशिश कर सके।"[12] यशदेव शल्य ने नैतिक मूल्यों के संकट पर खास तौर से विचार किया है। उनकी अपनी दृष्टि संतुलित है। आधुनिकता को स्वीकारते हुए भी वे मुक्त भोग या यौन स्वच्छंदता को स्वीकार नहीं कर पाते। [13] अन्य भारतीय चिंतकों और समाजशास्त्रियों का मूल्य-विवेचन प्रायः पाश्चात्य विवेचन के अनुरूप है।

मूल्य : पाश्चात्य दृष्टि

पाश्चात्य विचारकों द्वारा 'मूल्य' का विवेचन बहुत विशद है। दार्शनिकों, मनोवैज्ञानिकों, समाजशास्त्रियों और नृतत्वशास्त्रियों ने अपने-अपने ढंग से 'मूल्य' के विविध पक्षों का अनुशीलन किया है। प्रारंभ में 'मूल्य' की दार्शनिक अवधारणा बहुत लोकप्रिय रही, लेकिन कालांतर में 'मूल्य' का समाजशास्त्रीय प्रत्यय अधिक महत्त्वपूर्ण माना जाने लगा।

(क) मूल्य : दार्शनिक अवधारणा

'मूल्य' की सर्वसम्मत दार्शनिक परिभाषा नहीं हो पाई है। बल्कि कैम्ब्रिज स्कूल के विचारकों जी.ई. मूर, डब्ल्यू.डी. रास आदि का विचार है कि 'मूल्य' अखंड और अनिर्वचनीय होने के कारण अपरिभाषेय है। फिर भी अधिकतर दार्शनिक इस बात

पर थोड़ा-बहुत सहमत हैं कि 'मूल्य' को किस प्रकार पारिभाषित किया जाए। वे यह मानकर चलते हैं कि मूल्य-निर्णय मूल्यांकन (एप्रैजल) के निर्णय होते हैं।[14] ये मूल्य-निर्णय दो प्रकार के माने गए हैं–(1) वस्तुनिष्ठ (2) आत्मनिष्ठ।

(1) वस्तुनिष्ठ दृष्टिकोण : डोलाल्ड बालहूट और एस. एलेक्जेंडर के अनुसार वस्तुगत वह है, जो एक व्यक्ति के नियंत्रण में न होकर अनेक चेतनाओं की संपत्ति होता है।[15] डॉ. देवराज के शब्दों में : ''मूल्यों को वस्तुपरक कहने से हमारा मतलब यह है कि सामान्य संवेदना तथा कल्पना से उत्पन्न सभी मुनष्य उन्हें चेतनजीवों के सुख के साधनों अथवा उपादानों के रूप में ग्रहण कर सकते हैं।''[16] मध्यकालीन पाश्चात्य चिंतन में भी मूल्य की चर्चा प्रायः उसे वस्तुगत मानकर की गई है। रोमन कैथोलिक दर्शन इसका साक्षी है।[17] जान एड्वर्ड मूर, जान लेयर्ड, सल्फबर्टन पेरी, जान डेवी आदि ने मूल्य की वस्तुनिष्ठता का समर्थन किया है।

मूर और लेयर्ड के विचारों में साम्य है। इन दोनों का मत प्रशस्तावाद (टिनोलौजीकल थ्योरी आफ वैल्यू) कहलाता है क्योंकि इन्होंने जिस गुणविशेष को मूल्य माना है, वह प्रशस्तता (एक्सीलैन्स और वर्थ) है।[18] डोरोथी ली ने 'मूल्य' को एक ऐसा आधार माना जिससे एक व्यक्ति, एक वस्तु (कोर्स) को दूसरे की तुलना में वरीयता देता है और अच्छे-बुरे, सही-गलत का चुनाव करता है।[19] ई. जी. स्पाल्डिंग के अनुसार मूल्य मनुष्य की इच्छा और चुनाव से परे हैं, वे हमारे बाह्य-विश्व में ही ढूँढ़े जा सकते हैं।[20] ऊपरी तौर पर डोरोथी ली और स्पाल्डिंग की मान्यताएँ परस्पर विरोधी लग सकती हैं। जबकि 'ली' ने भी उन वस्तुओं और परिस्थितियों पर ही बल दिया है, जिनके बारे में मूल्यात्मक निर्णय लिए जाते हैं।

मूल्यों की वस्तुनिष्ठता का विरोध कम नहीं हुआ है। आत्मनिष्ठतावाद, तर्कमूलक भाववाद आदि के अंतर्गत इसे कड़ी चुनौती दी गई। बहुत बल देकर कहा गया कि मूल्यात्मक वक्तव्यों का व्यवस्थित और वस्तुपरक अध्ययन संभव नहीं है। इसके अतिरिक्त 'मूल्य' को 'इच्छा' से परे मानना भी अनुचित समझा गया। वेस्टर मार्क ने इस पर टिप्पणी करते हुए लिखा कि नैतिक मूल्यों की तथाकथित वस्तुनिष्ठता का अर्थ यह होगा कि वे मूल्य मानवीय मस्तिष्क की निरपेक्षता में भी अस्तित्ववान हो सकते हैं। डॉ. देवराज ने उस विचारधारा को इस शताब्दी में अधिक प्रभावशाली माना है, जो यह मानती है कि मूल्यों के संबंध में मनुष्य का मंतव्य अनिवार्यतः आत्मपरक होगा।[21]

(2) आत्मनिष्ठ दृष्टिकोण : अनेक दार्शनिक 'मूल्य' को बाह्य परिवेश के स्थान पर मानव के अंतर्मन से संबद्ध करते हैं। उनके विचार में 'मूल्य' इच्छा के विषय हैं। यदि एडगर एस. बाइटमैन 'मूल्य' को किसी वांछित वस्तु या गतिविधि के उपभोग का वास्तविक अनुभव मानते हैं[22] तो बकौल डी.एस. पार्कर 'मूल्य' को मानव-इच्छा और इच्छा के परितोष के आश्रित मानते हैं।[23]

हैरिस ने भी मूल्य को वस्तुनिष्ठ न मानकर वैयक्तिक अनुभूति का विषय माना है।[24] अरबन ने 'मूल्य' को आत्मानुभूति का विषय मानते हुए उसकी तीन संक्षिप्त व्याख्याएँ की हैं। प्रथम व्याख्या के अनुसार मूल्य वह है जो मनुष्य की इच्छा को संतुष्ट करे। द्वितीय व्याख्या के अनुसार जो जीवन को सदैव विकास की ओर ले जाए, वह मूल्य है। तृतीय व्याख्या से वह वस्तु 'मूल्य' है, जो व्यक्तियों को विकास अथवा आत्मविकास या आत्मानुभूति की ओर ले जाती है।[25] लगता है अरबन 'मूल्य' को चेतनानिष्ठ मानते हैं। लेकिन हर्टमैन जैसे विचारक मूल्यों को भावना, विचार या चेतना से निष्पन्न नहीं मानते।

वस्तुनिष्ठता और आत्मनिष्ठता का संतुलन

दार्शनिकों का एक वर्ग 'मूल्य' को न तो 'वस्तुगत' न 'आत्मगत' मानते हैं। बहुत पहले जार्ज संत्याना ने 'मूल्य' के भावनात्मक और क्रियात्मक दोनों पक्षों पर समान बल दिया था।[26] टाइटस ने भी संकेत किया कि 'मूल्य' न सर्वथा वस्तुनिष्ठ है और न केवल वस्तुगत। वह वैयक्तिक और निर्वैयक्तिक तत्त्वों के मध्य घटनेवाली अंतःक्रिया का सहयोगात्मक निर्णय है।[27] प्रो. कृष्णनाथ[28] ने 'मूल्य' की परिभाषा के संदर्भ में 'शुक्रनीति' की कुछ पंक्तियाँ उद्धृत की हैं, जिनमें 'मूल्य' को गुण पर आश्रित होने के साथ-साथ मूल्य-निर्धारक की 'कामना' पर आधारित बताया गया है। 'शुक्रनीति' के अनुसार—जो कुछ भी अप्रतिम है, बेजोड़ है, वह रत्न जैसा ही है। मूल्य देशकाल के अनुसार तय होना चाहिए। जो गुणहीन है और व्यवहार के योग्य नहीं है, उसका कोई मूल्य नहीं। और जितने व्यय से मिले, उतना उसका मूल्य होता है। सुलभ होने और असुलभ होने और उसमें निहित गुण या अगुण से मूल्य तय होता है। कामना के अनुसार पदार्थों का मोल हीन या अधिक, कमोबेश होता है।[29] शुक्राचार्य का यह अभिमत निश्चय ही मूल्य की आर्थिक अवधारणा को सामने लाता है। लेकिन इससे 'मूल्य' या 'जीवनमूल्य' के आधुनिक अर्थ में भी समझा जा सकता है। तब 'मूल्य' वह होगा जिसके लिए व्यक्ति को अधिक से अधिक मूल्य चुकाना पड़े। श्रेय-प्रेय को एक साथ महत्त्व देनेवाली भारतीय विचारधारा भी 'मूल्य' के प्रति संतुलित दृष्टि अख्यार करती है। श्रेय अर्थात्, वस्तुगत मूल्य और प्रेय अर्थात् इच्छित या आत्मनिष्ठ मूल्य। इन सभी मतों को देखते हुए डॉ. विश्वंभरनाथ उपाध्याय का यह कथन सार्थक ठहरता है कि मूल्य न तो पूर्णतः वस्तुगत होते हैं और न पूर्णतः व्यक्तिगत। वे वस्तु, व्यक्ति के परस्पर संबंधों, क्रिया-प्रतिक्रियाओं, संघर्षों-संगतियों के फल होते हैं।[30]

(ख) मूल्य और सामाजिक विज्ञान

अर्थशास्त्र, समाजशास्त्र, मनोविज्ञान, नृतत्वशास्त्र आदि 'मूल्य' उतना ही महत्त्व देते हैं, जितना शुद्ध विज्ञान-भौतिकी, रसायनविज्ञान, जीवविज्ञान आदि प्राकृतिक नियमों को।[31] व्यक्ति के व्यक्तिगत, समूहगत एवं संस्थागत संबंधों तथा उसके आदर्शों-मूल्यों और नैतिक आदतों में अत्यंत घनिष्ठता होती है। इसलिए मूल्यों और नैतिक आदतों की पड़ताल किए बगैर, सामाजिक क्रियाओं और समस्याओं से सीधा और सही साक्षात्कार संभव नहीं। सामाजिक विज्ञानों की दुनिया में मूल्य-चर्चा की शुरुआत थामस और जैनिनकी की पुस्तक 'पोलिश पीजेन्ट इन यूरोप एण्ड अमेरिका' से मानी जाती है। लेकिन सन् 1930 ई. तक इस प्रकार का अध्ययन अस्पष्ट और धूमिल सा रहा। कालांतर में बेबर, मानहीम, ओवेन, राधाकमल मुखर्जी, फेयर चाइल्ड, राल्फ लिंटन आदि के उद्योग से सामाजिक विज्ञानों ने भी 'मूल्य' के महत्त्व को स्वीकार किया।

(ग) मूल्य : अर्थशास्त्रीय दृष्टि

'इन्साइक्लोपीडिया ब्रिटेनिका' के अनुसार अर्थशास्त्र में किसी वस्तु का मूल्य उसके विनिमय में प्राप्त होनेवाली वस्तुओं की मात्रा में निर्धारित होता है।[32] प्रो. टी.एन. के विचार में अर्थशास्त्रीय मूल्य 'आवश्यकता' और 'अभाव', इन दो चीजों पर निर्भर होता है।[33] मूल्य का श्रम-सिद्धांत मूल्य संबंधी पुराने सिद्धांतों में सर्वाधिक महत्त्वपूर्ण है। इसके समर्थकों और पोषकों में स्मिथ, रिकार्डो और मिल उल्लेखनीय हैं। इस सिद्धांत के अनुसार 'श्रम' ही किसी वस्तु के मूल्यांकन का एकमात्र और वास्तविक प्रतिमान है।[34] माल्थस जैसे अर्थशास्त्री जहाँ 'वस्तु' का 'मूल्य' उसके उत्पादन-व्यय से निर्धारित करते हैं, वहीं मेंजर, वालरस और जेवंस का विचार है कि वस्तु का मूल्य उसकी उपयोगिता पर आधारित होता है। प्रो. मार्शल ने लिखा है कि कुल माँग और कुल पूर्ति ही वस्तु के मूल्य को शासित करती है। मार्शल ने अपने मूल्य-सिद्धांत में समय-तत्त्व के प्रभाव का भी विवेचन किया है। कुन (Kuhn) के अनुसार 'मूल्य' प्राथमिकता क्रम पर आधारित किसी वस्तु की सापेक्षिक स्थिति है। यह सापेक्षिक स्थिति जितनी ऊँची होगी, वस्तु का मूल्य भी उतना ही महत्तर होगा।[35] माँग-पूर्ति और उत्पादन-व्यय पर 'मूल्य' के आधारित होने के मत जहाँ 'मूल्य' की वस्तुनिष्ठता पर बल देते हैं, वहीं 'उपयोगिता' से जोड़कर इसे मनुष्य की इच्छा से संबद्ध किया जाता है। जब 'मूल्य' की वस्तुनिष्ठता का आग्रह छोड़ दिया जाता है तब 'मूल्य' संबंधी एक अर्द्ध-मनोवैज्ञानिक सिद्धांत सामने आता है। उस दशा में मूल्य वस्तु और उपयोगिता के संबंध को दर्शानेवाली प्रक्रिया मात्र होता है या उसे मनुष्य की इच्छा की संतुष्टि कहा जा सकता है।[36]

कार्ल मार्क्स ने 'मूल्य' को श्रम से संबद्ध माना है। वे मानते हैं कि सामाजिक दृष्टि से श्रम की आवश्यकता वस्तु के मूल्य का निर्धारण करती है।[37] मूल्यों के बदलाव को मार्क्स ने उत्पादन के साधनों के बदलने से आर्थिक-सामाजिक संबंधों में आए बदलाव से जोड़ा है। उत्पादन के ढंग बदलने पर मनुष्य की कला-संस्कृति सब बदलते हैं। श्रम का विभाजन नए तरीके से होता है और नए मूल्य बनते हैं।[38] इस प्रकार अर्थशास्त्रियों के मतों का निचोड़ यह है कि किसी वस्तु का मूल्य माँग और पूर्ति के संतुलन की अवस्था में उस वस्तु के बदले में प्राप्त होनेवाला पदार्थ है। यह पदार्थ मुद्रा भी हो सकती है और कोई अन्य वस्तु भी। श्रम-मानवीय श्रम इस 'मूल्य' के निर्धारण में अहम भूमिका निभाता है। हालाँकि अर्थशास्त्रीय 'मूल्य' समाजशास्त्र आदि में उल्लिखित मूल्य-जीवनमूल्य से कुछ पृथक् है, तथापि इस अवधारणा से मूल्यों के अध्ययन में पर्याप्त सहायता मिलती है।

(घ) मूल्य : समाजशास्त्रीय संदर्भ

कभी समाजशास्त्रियों का विचार था कि 'मूल्य' दर्शन और नीतिशास्त्र के अध्ययन का विषय है। कालांतर में समाजशास्त्रियों ने अनुभव किया कि मूल्यों के अध्ययन के अभाव में समाजशास्त्र एक निर्जीव शास्त्र बनकर रह जाता है। अतः यह माना जाने लगा कि समाजशास्त्र मूल्यपरक समस्याओं से भी घनिष्ठ संबंध रखता है।[39] जॉन ई. ओवन के विचार में, जिस प्रकार नैतिक धर्म के अनुभवात्मक (Empirical) तत्त्व हैं, उसी प्रकार परिपक्व समाजशास्त्र के लिए सामाजिक मूल्य भी अनुभवात्मक तत्त्व है।[40] सामाजिक तथ्यों, संबंधों तथा सामाजिक परिस्थितियों का सर्वाधिक महत्त्वपूर्ण 'कथ्य' अन्य मनुष्यों के मूल्य हैं, जिनसे किसी व्यक्ति का 'स्व' संघर्ष या सहयोग करता है। डॉ. राधाकमल मुखर्जी ने व्यक्ति, समाज और मूल्यों में क्रमशः बत्ती, तेल और लौ का संबंध माना है।[41] जिस प्रकार बिना लौ के प्रकाश और गर्मी की प्राप्ति संभव नहीं, उसी प्रकार मूल्यों की परख के अभाव में व्यक्ति और समाज का अध्ययन असंभव है।

समाजशास्त्रियों ने प्रायः 'मूल्य' को सामाजिक जीवन के अंतःसंबंधों को पारिभाषित करने में सहायक सामाजिक मान के रूप में स्वीकार किया है। थामस और जेनिनकी की दृष्टि में 'मूल्य' वह लक्ष्य है, जिसकी अंतर्वस्तु तथा अर्थ तक एक सामाजिक समूह के सदस्य पहुँच सकते हैं। पेरी मूल्य को मानवीय अभिरुचि का विषय मानते हैं।[42] पेपर के अनुसार कोई भी अच्छी या बुरी चीज मूल्य है। इसी से मिलता-जुलता अभिमत आर.एम. विलियम्स (जूनियर) का है। उनके अनुसार मूल्य 'काम्य' (डिजायरेबल) की वे धारणाएँ हैं जो व्यक्ति के व्यवहार को प्रभावित करती हैं।[43] इमाइल दुर्खीम ने मूल्य की दो विशेषताओं की ओर संकेत किया

है–(1) बाह्यता (Exterority) और बाध्यता (Constraint)। दुर्खीम के विचार में मूल्य की विवेचना, सामाजिक तथ्य (Social fact) के रूप में होनी चाहिए। मूल्यों पर विस्तार से विचार करनेवालों में राधाकमल मुखर्जी अग्रगण्य हैं। सैमुअल हार्ट सदृश पाश्चात्य विचारकों ने उनके मूल्य-विवेचन की भूरि-भूरि प्रशंसा की है। डॉ. मुखर्जी के अनुसार "मूल्यों को सहअस्तित्व एवं परंपरा की भावनात्मक स्वीकृतियाँ कहा जा सकता है। भौतिक जगत् में प्राकृतिक नियमों के समान ही वे सामाजिक तथ्यों के संदर्भ में एक 'स्वीकृति', 'अनिवार्यता' और 'आवश्यकता' को व्यक्त करते हैं।"[44] एक अन्य स्थान पर वे 'मूल्य' को मानव के संपूर्ण व्यक्तित्व से संबद्ध मानते हैं और उसे 'एक जटिल संपूर्णता' कहकर संबोधित करते हैं।[45] डॉ. मुखर्जी लक्ष्य, 'आदर्श' और 'मूल्य' में अंतर करते हैं। विशिष्ट आवश्यकताओं के अनुरूप व्यक्ति या समाज अपने लक्ष्य का निर्धारण करता है। विभिन्न लक्ष्यों में टकराहट होने पर लक्ष्यों में सर्वोत्तम अर्थात् 'आदर्श' का चुनाव होता है। आदर्शों को पूर्णता देने के लिए समाज कुछ आदर्श-नियमों का निर्धारण करता है। ये आदर्श नियम उस अवस्था में मूल्य बन जाते हैं, जब वे समाज के सदस्यों के अंतःकरण और विश्वास के रूप में एक आंतरिक तत्त्व हो जाते हैं और सामाजिक संबंधों तथा संस्थाओं आदि के माध्यम से प्रकट होते हैं। 'मानवीय मूल्य' को उन्होंने विज्ञान की जननी कहकर संबोधित किया है।[46]

(ङ) मूल्य : मनोवैज्ञानिक अवधारणा

कुछ विचारकों के अनुसार आज मूल्य-सिद्धांत 'दार्शनिक' अधिक है, मनोवैज्ञानिक कम।[47] लेकिन 'मूल्य' के समाजशास्त्रीय रूप को देखते हुए यह नहीं कहा जा सकता कि 'मूल्य' मात्र दार्शनिक अर्थ में ग्राह्य है। इसके अतिरिक्त मानवीय इच्छा से संबंधित होने के कारण 'मूल्य' के मनोवैज्ञानिक पहलू की एकदम उपेक्षा नहीं की जा सकती। हालाँकि कुछ मनोवैज्ञानिक उपपत्तियों से 'मूल्य' की अवधारणा बाधित होती है। जैसे, मनोविश्लेषणकर्ता बच्चों के मूल्य-निर्णय में पशु रूप की अभिव्यक्ति मानते हैं। लेकिन इन अपवादों के बावजूद 'मूल्य' की सत्ता के कई आयाम मनोवैज्ञानिकता से संपृक्त हैं। मूल्य हमारी उस अंतश्चेतना का निक्षेपण है, जो हमारे व्यक्तित्व की पीठिका होती है।[48] आई.ए. रिचर्ड्स ने भी माना है कि मूल्य की सत्ता हमारी अनुक्रियाओं और अभिवृत्तियों के सूक्ष्म विशेषों (माइन्यूट पर्टिकुलर्स ऑफ रेस्पांस एण्ड ऐट्टीट्यूड) में है। लेकिन इस तथ्य को नहीं समझने के कारण कुछ लोग 'मूल्य' को आचार के सामान्य नियमों और विधि-निषेधों के साथ जोड़ते आए हैं।[49] स्वयं रिचर्ड्स ने 'मूल्य' को निम्नलिखित शब्दों में पारिभाषित किया है :

"कोई भी ऐसी वस्तु मूल्यवान है, जो किसी दूसरी समान या अधिक महत्त्वपूर्ण एषणा को कुंठित किए बिना हमारी किसी एषणा की संतुष्टि करे।"[50]

'मूल्य' को इच्छा की संतुष्टि मानते हुए रिचर्ड्स ने संकेत दिया है कि मूल्यों में आपसी टकराव के अवसर कम होते हैं। जीवन में अधिकाधिक मूल्यों की प्राप्ति आवेगों के सामंजस्य पर निर्भर होती है। लेकिन किसी भी व्यक्ति के जीवन में आवेगों का सामंजस्य करनेवाली मनोव्यवस्था बदलती रहती है। जिस मनोव्यवस्था में मानवीयता जितनी अधिक होती है, वह उतनी ही उत्कृष्ट होती है।[51]

कुछ विचारकों ने 'मूल्य' को व्यक्ति की अभिवृत्ति (Instinct) से जोड़कर देखा है। "अभिवृत्तियों और मूल्य के संबंध में दो प्रकार के मत हैं। एक मत के अनुसार तो अभिवृत्तियों के स्थायित्व में ही मूल्य निहित है और दूसरे मत के अनुसार अभिवृत्तियाँ 'नार्म' बनने पर ही मूल्य का स्वरूप धारण करती हैं।"[52] 'नार्म' बनने का अर्थ है किसी अभिवृत्ति की एक ऐसे प्रतिमान के रूप में प्रतिष्ठा, जो निर्णय करने में एक मानक या सिद्धांत के रूप में प्रयुक्त हो सके। 'इन्साइक्लोपीडिया ब्रिटेनिका' में 'मूल्य' को 'रुचि' और 'अनुभव' से जोड़कर देखा गया है।[53] इस व्याख्या के अनुसार 'मूल्य' और मूल्यानुभव दोनों एक ही हैं। कुछ मनोवैज्ञानिकों ने 'मूल्य' को व्यक्ति की नैतिक शक्ति माना है, जिसकी सहायता से वह अच्छे-बुरे तथा उचित-अनुचित में अंतर समझ पाता है। व्यक्ति मूल्यों को अपने परिवेश से सीखता है। जब वे भली-भाँति अंगीकृत हो चुकते हैं, तब वे व्यक्ति की नैतिक विशेषताएँ बन जाते हैं। इंगलिश एण्ड इंगलिश ने स्पष्ट किया है कि 'मूल्य' व्यक्ति की निजी मूल्यांकन-क्षमता पर निर्भर नहीं होते, बल्कि समाज उन्हें 'व्यक्ति' पर आरोपित करता है।[54] इससे स्पष्ट है कि 'मूल्य' को मात्र व्यक्ति के संदर्भ में नहीं समझा जा सकता है। समाज-मनोविज्ञान की नई खोजों के संदर्भ में भी 'मूल्य' की आत्यांतिक वैयक्तिकता के लिए अधिक अवकाश नहीं रह गया है। वस्तुतः राधाकमल मुखर्जी ने सही पहचाना है कि मूल्य-अनुभव सदैव सामाजिक अनुभव में होते हैं।

(च) मूल्य : नृतत्वशास्त्रीय व्याख्या

नृतत्वशास्त्रियों ने 'मूल्य' को संस्कृति में विद्यमान सामाजिक अंतःक्रिया के परिणाम के रूप में देखा है। राल्फ लिण्टन के अनुसार मूल्य वह तत्त्व है, जो परिस्थितियों की एक शृंखला में समान रूप से हो और जो व्यक्ति को अप्रत्यक्ष रूप से प्रेरित कर सके।[55] क्लाइट क्लुखान मूल्य को ऐसा मानक मानते हैं, जो समय के साथ प्रायः बदल नहीं पाता। क्लुखान के विचार में मूल्य, एक व्यक्ति की विशिष्टता या एक समूह के गुण का द्योतक एक अप्रत्याशित प्रत्यक्ष या अप्रत्यक्ष, संबोधन

है, जो कार्य के उपलब्ध ढंगों, साधनों और उद्देश्यों से संबंधित होता है।[56]

इस प्रकार विभिन्न सामाजिक विज्ञान 'मूल्य' के अनेक पहलुओं को देखते-भालते हैं। जहाँ मूल्यों की अर्थशास्त्रीय अवधारणा मानवीय मूल्यों के उद्भव को समझने में सहायक है, वहीं 'मूल्य' की मनोवैज्ञानिकता उपेक्षणीय नहीं है। मूल्यों की समाज-सापेक्षता स्वयंसिद्ध है ही। मैकडूगल की यह धारणा अनुचित नहीं कही जा सकती कि मूल्यों का समुदाय ही समस्त सामाजिक विज्ञानों के लिए मौलिक तथ्य हैं और इन्हें मनोवैज्ञानिक रूप से समझना ही सामाजिक विज्ञानों को स्थिरता प्रदान करने के लिए आवश्यक है। आर.एम. विलियम्स (जूनियर) के अनुसार यह संदेहास्पद है कि कोई परिभाषा मूल्य के साथ न्याय कर सकेगी। फिर भी वे सामाजिक विज्ञानों में व्यापक रूप से स्वीकृत परिभाषा प्रस्तावित करते हैं :

"मूल्य जो भी इच्छित है, उसकी धारणाएँ हैं जो व्यक्ति के चयनप्रधान व्यवहार को प्रभावित करती हैं।"[57]

मूल्य संबंधी समूचे चिंतन का निचोड़ यह है कि 'मूल्य' कुछ विशिष्ट धारणाएँ हैं, जिनके लिए व्यक्ति या समाज कुछ न कुछ जोखिम उठाता है। यह किसी दबाव से नहीं, स्वेच्छा से स्वीकृत अवधारणा है, जिसमें उपयोगिता का भाव कम, अभिरुचि की प्रेरणा अधिक होती है। शांति जोशी की निम्नलिखित परिभाषा अत्यंत सरल शब्दों में 'मूल्य' को पारिभाषित करती है :

"मूल्य उस सत्य को कह सकते हैं, जिसके लिए व्यक्ति या समाज जीवित रहता है और जिसके लिए आवश्यकता पड़ने पर वह संघर्ष करने, दुःख सहने तथा मृत्यु को स्वीकार करने के लिए भी तत्पर होता है।"[58]

'आदर्श', 'मूल्य' और 'नार्म'

प्रायः 'आदर्श' और 'प्रतिमान' (नार्म) 'मूल्य' के मिलते-जुलते अर्थ में प्रयुक्त होते हैं। वस्तुतः 'मूल्य' की सत्ता इनसे पृथक् है। मानवजीवन के कतिपय लक्ष्य होते हैं। लक्ष्यों में सर्वोत्तम आदर्श होता है। आदर्श से जुड़े नियम नार्म्स या प्रतिमान कहे जाते हैं। जब प्रतिमान समाज के सदस्यों के एक समूह के विश्वासों के रूप में जीवन के आंतरिक तत्त्व बन जाते हैं, तब इन्हें मूल्य कहा जाता है। 'आदर्श' और 'मूल्य' को अलगाते हुए कहा गया है : "आदर्श बने बनाए और स्थिर होते हैं, मूल्य अन्वेष्य और परिवर्तनशील होते हैं।"[59] वस्तुतः यह कोई स्पष्ट अंतर नहीं है। कुछ 'मूल्य' भी स्थिर (शाश्वत) होते हैं। मुख्य अंतर 'व्यवहार' का है। आदर्श के लिए कुछ मूल्य चुकाने या जोखिम उठाने पर आदर्श 'मूल्य' में परिवर्तित हो जाता है।

कुछ विद्वान् 'मूल्य' और 'प्रतिमान' में अभेद करते हैं। प्रभाकर माचवे ने

दोनों को एक माना है।[60] कुमार विमल भी यही मत व्यक्त करते हैं।[61] मूल्य और प्रतिमान में निकट का संबंध होने के बावजूद पर्याप्त अंतर है। प्रतिमान वह है, जो निर्णय करने के संदर्भ में एक सिद्धांत के रूप में प्रयुक्त होता है, जबकि 'मूल्य' निर्णय की उपलब्धि है। डॉ. रमेश कुंतल मेघ ने 'मूल्य' और 'प्रतिमान' के सूक्ष्म अंतर को रेखांकित किया है। वे मूल्य को काम्य की धारणाएँ मानते हैं और प्रतिमान को काम्य आचरण का रूपबंध या पैटर्न कहकर संबोधित करते हैं।[62] 'इंटरनेशनल इन्साइक्लोपीडिया आफ द साइंसेज' में इस भिन्नता को भलीभाँति स्पष्ट किया गया है। प्रतिमान व्यवहार के नियम हैं जबकि 'मूल्य' 'काम्य' के वे मानक हैं जो विशेष परिस्थितियों में भी अप्रभावित रहते हैं।[63]

मूल्यों का वर्गीकरण

कुछ विचारकों ने किसी अभाव की पूर्ति या जीवन की उपयोगिता के आधार पर मूल्यों का वर्गीकरण किया है। जीवन की आवश्यकताओं को ध्यान में रखकर अरबन ने मूल्यों को आठ वर्गों में बाँटा है–(1) शारीरिक मूल्य (2) आर्थिक मूल्य (3) मनोरंजनात्मक मूल्य (4) सामाजिक मूल्य (5) चरित्रात्मक मूल्य (6) सौंदर्यात्मक मूल्य (7) बौद्धिक मूल्य (8) धार्मिक और ईश्वरविषयक मूल्य।[64] इस वर्गीकरण में व्यापकता के बावजूद वर्गों की संख्या आवश्यकता से अधिक है। शारीरिक, आर्थिक और मनोरंजनात्मक मूल्यों को मिलाकर केवल एक वर्ग–भौतिक वर्ग बनाया जा सकता है। आगे चलकर अरबन ने स्वयं अपने वर्गीकरण की स्फीति को समझा और केवल दो वर्गों–साधनात्मक, साध्यात्मक को मान्यता दी। जे.एस. मैकेंजी भी इन्हीं वर्गों के समर्थक हैं। मैकेंजी ने रोटी के मूल्य की चर्चा करते हुए लिखा है–"रोटी का मूल्य जिंदगी कायम रखने या भूख की पीड़ा शांत करने के साधन रूप में या भोजन की सुखद अनुभूति देनेवाले साधन के रूप में ही है। तो इस प्रकार रोटी का मूल्य वास्तव में इस बात पर निर्भर है कि हम जिंदगी को या सुख को या पीड़ा के अभाव को मूल्यवान मानते हैं। ऐसे मूल्य को कभी-कभी 'साधन मूल्य' (Instrumental values) कहते हैं और 'स्वतः मूल्य' (Intrinisic value) से इसका विभेद मानते हैं।"[65] डॉ. देवराज ने 'अरबन' और मैकेंजी का समर्थन करते हुए लिखा है–"मूल्य दो प्रकार के होते हैं, आंतरिक या साध्यात्मक और साधनात्मक...यह कहने की जरूरत नहीं कि विभिन्न सदंर्भों में एक ही मूल्य साध्यात्मक अथवा साधनात्मक हो सकता है।"[66] जो मूल्य जीवन के लक्ष्य होते हैं, वे स्वतःमूल्य या साध्यमूल्य कहलाते हैं और जो उस लक्ष्य के साधन रूप होते हैं, उन्हें साधनमूल्य कहा जा सकता है।

स्वतःमूल्य की व्याख्या करते हुए जे.एस. मैकेंजी ने उसे 'तर्कनापरक चुनाव

का निर्भ्रांत लक्ष्य' कहा है।[67] कांट ने 'शुभ संकल्प' (good will) को स्वतःमूल्य माना था। सौंदर्य, प्रेम, सत्य आदि भी इसी प्रकार के मूल्य हैं। जार्ज संतायना के विचार में तो सारे मूल्य अंततः स्वतःमूल्य ही होते हैं।[68] लेकिन रिचर्ड्स 'साधन' और 'साध्य' के भेद को समझने पर बल देते हैं। उनके विचार में, साधनात्मक मूल्य और साध्यमूल्य में अंतर न देख पाने के कारण ही मानवीय मूल्यधारणा में इतनी विभिन्नता दिखाई देती है।[69] स्वतःमूल्यों को 'शाश्वत' या 'प्रकृत' भी कहा गया है। हालाँकि ये मूल्य काफी हद तक विशिष्ट सांस्कृतिक विशेषता, चिंतन की परिणति और व्यवहार की क्षमता का प्रतिनिधित्व करते हैं, फिर भी इन्हें 'शाश्वत' मान लेना अधिक उपयुक्त नहीं है। ऐसा करना उनके सामाजिक उद्देश्यों को अस्वीकृत करना होगा।[70] स्वतःमूल्यों को रूढ़ियों के रूप में स्वीकार नहीं किया जा सकता और न इनकी प्रकृति यथास्थितिवादी होनी चाहिए। जब वे दूषित सामाजिक व्यवस्था के स्थान पर समाज के सच्चे श्रेयों को व्यक्त करते हैं, मानवीय आदर्शों की प्राप्ति के लिए संघर्ष में सहायक होते हैं तभी प्रासंगिक करार दिए जा सकते हैं। जिस कृति में इन मूल्यों की परिणति जितनी अधिक होगी, उतनी ही कृति क्लासिक और मानवतावाद से भरपूर होगी।[71] प्रायः स्वतःमूल्य एक प्रकार की आध्यात्मिकता से मंडित हैं।

साध्यमूल्य जीवन या अनुभव की किसी दशा से संबंधित होते हैं जबकि साधनात्मक मूल्य उन वस्तुओं और स्थितियों में पाया जाता है जो उस दशा को उत्पन्न करती हैं।[72] दोनों प्रकार के मूल्यों में विनिमय भी होता है। कोई साधनमूल्य कभी-कभी साध्यमूल्य भी बन जाता है। जैसे—स्वास्थ्य, सौंदर्य आदि। मानविकी पारिभाषिक कोश (साहित्य खंड) में पाँच प्रकार के मूल्यों का उल्लेख है–(1) आनंदमूलक (2) कलात्मक (3) सांस्कृतिक (4) नैतिक अथवा धार्मिक (5) व्यावहारिक।[73] कुछ विचारकों ने समस्त मूल्यों को समेट कर तीन मूल्यों–सत्य, शिव और सुंदर में समाहित किया है।[74] उनके अनुसार 'सत्य' विज्ञान और दर्शन का मूल्य है, 'शिव' में धर्म आ जाता है और 'सुंदर' में 'कला' और साहित्य के मूल्य विद्यमान हैं। मूल्यवत्ता की मात्रा से 'अस्तिमूल्य' (पौजीटिव वैल्यूज) और 'नास्तिकमूल्य' (निगेटिव वैल्यूज) जैसे वर्ग भी बनाए गए हैं। जो शुभ या श्रेयस् है, वह ऐसी कोई भी वस्तु है, जिसका 'अस्ति-मूल्य' हो, इसके विपरीत जिस वस्तु का नास्तिमूल्य है उसे अशुभ कहा जाता है।[75] 'सत्य' अस्तिमूल्य है, मिथ्या नास्तिमूल्य। सौंदर्य शुभ है, असुंरदता अशुभ। नास्तिमूल्यों से व्यक्ति का जुड़ाव उसकी समझ की कमी और अनुकूलन की असफलता को व्यक्त करता है।[76]

आज मान लिया गया है कि मूल्यों के नियामक व्यक्ति और समाज हैं। अतः मूल्यों के दो भेद किए जाते हैं—(1) व्यक्तिगत या वैयक्तिक मूल्य (2) सामाजिक मूल्य।

व्यक्तिगत मूल्यों के अंतर्गत शारीरिक और बौद्धिक मूल्य आते हैं। जान लेयर्ड ने माना है कि व्यक्तिगत मूल्यों का आर्थिक प्रकार्य न्यूनतम हो सकता है, लेकिन वे उपयोगी अवश्य हैं। हैरिस के विचार में मूल्य-निर्णय तभी महत्त्वपूर्ण होते हैं, जबकि वे व्यक्ति-केंद्रित होते हैं।[77] व्यक्तिगत मूल्यों को अलग करके समाज, संस्कृति की कल्पना करना असंभव है। ''व्यक्तिगत मूल्यों की स्थापना व्यक्ति की समाज में विशिष्ट रुचियों अथवा व्यक्तित्व की आत्मान्वेषी आस्थाओं स्मृतियों, प्रतीतियों द्वारा होती है। इसमें सामाजिक परिष्कार से नियमित व्यक्ति मुक्त भी हो सकता है और स्वेच्छापूर्ण बंदी भी।''[78] डॉ. रमेशकुंतल मेघ ने व्यक्तिगत और व्यक्तिवादी मूल्यों में अंतर माना है। व्यक्तिगत मूल्य इंद्रिय-बोध, भावनात्मक विकास, जीवन-संघर्ष का परिणाम हैं और प्रायः समाजविरोधी नहीं होते। व्यक्तिवादी मूल्य व्यावहारिक रूप में विकृत और मानवद्रोही तक हो जाते हैं।[79]

कुछ विचारक 'मूल्य' की सत्ता को सामाजिक मानते हैं। दुर्खीम ने मूल्यों की सामाजिकता पर बल दिया। बाद में मार्क्स ने भी यही धारणा व्यक्त की। हैरिस के अनुसार सामाजिक मूल्य संयुक्त उपलब्धि हैं।[80] डॉ. विश्वंभरनाथ उपाध्याय ने 'मूल्य' के सामाजिक पक्ष को उभारते हुए लिखा है–''मूल्य एक प्रकार का निर्णय होता है–प्रशंसापरक निर्णय और इसमें सर्वदा कोई सामाजिक सुझाव निहित रहता है। अतः मूल्य-निर्णय हमेशा सामाजिक होता है, व्यक्तिगत नहीं।''[81] सेवा, उपकार, सहयोग, न्याय, सांप्रदायिक सहिष्णुता आदि मूल्य सामाजिक कहे जाते हैं। जातिगत एवं वर्णगत मर्यादाएँ भी इनके अंतर्गत आती हैं।

मूल्यों की उच्चावचता पर भी पर्याप्त विचार हुआ है। यह माना जाता रहा है कि स्वतःमूल्य, साधनभूत मूल्यों से उच्चतर होते हैं और स्थाई मूल्य परिवर्तनशील मूल्यों से बेहतर हैं। फलदायक या अस्तिमूल्यों को निष्फल या नास्तिमूल्यों से श्रेष्ठ माना जाता है। लेकिन आज की यथार्थवादी विचारधारा इस क्रम से मतभेद रखती है। चूँकि स्वतःमूल्य या स्थाई मूल्य निरपेक्ष सत्य नहीं है, इसलिए आवश्यकता पड़ने पर साधनभूत मूल्य अधिक अनुकूल पड़ते हैं। बल्कि कभी-कभी साध्यमूल्य ही साधनमूल्य बन जाते हैं। इसके अतिरिक्त कुछ शाश्वत या स्थाई कहे जाने वाले मूल्य यथास्थितिवाद को प्रश्रय देते हैं, अतः उस स्थिति में इनकी अवहेलना भी हो जाती है। सतीत्व, पतिनिष्ठा वगैरह स्थाई मूल्य हैं लेकिन 'ध्रुवस्वामिनी' में प्रसाद ने इन पर परिस्थिति विशेष में प्रश्नचिह्न लगाया और नारी की 'स्वतंत्रता' को महत्तरमूल्य घोषित किया। अतः मूल्यों की उच्चावच स्थिति सापेक्षता में देखी जानी चाहिए। यहाँ यह स्मरणीय है कि साध्य और साधन मूल्यों में विरोध नहीं, पूरकता का भाव है।[82]

मूल्य-निर्मिति अथवा मूल्य-सृष्टि

ग्रीन ने मूल्यों के तीन स्तर माने हैं–(1) अमूर्त संवेग (2) नैतिक प्रतिमान (3) अहं।[83] इसका अर्थ यह हुआ कि संवेग, स्थापित नैतिकता और व्यक्ति का इगो, समवेत रूप में 'मूल्य' की उत्पत्ति करते हैं। डॉ. कुमार विमल ने मूल्य के पाँच तत्त्वों की चर्चा की है–व्यवस्था, परिस्थिति, संभावना, आचार और तोष।[84] व्यवस्था से परंपरा, नई परिस्थितियाँ, भावी संभावनाएँ, आचार संबंधी नियम और मनुष्य का आत्मिक संतोष मिलकर नए मूल्यों को जन्म देते हैं। मूल्य-सर्जक के लिए जहाँ यह आवश्यक है कि वह 'लकीर का फकीर' न हो, क्रांतदर्शी हो, आचार को आत्यंतिक महत्त्व न देता हो। इस प्रकार मूल्य-सृष्टि एक ऐसी प्रक्रिया है, जिसकी शुरुआत विश्लेषण से होती है और जिसका समापन 'संश्लेष' में होता है। केंद्रगामिता उसका धर्म है, प्रभावान्विति उसका लक्ष्य।[85]

महावीर दाधीच ने मूल्य-सृष्टि की दार्शनिक व्याख्या करते हुए लिखा है कि 'मूल्य' की उत्पत्ति के लिए द्वैत अनिवार्य है क्योंकि 'एक' मूल्यातीत ही नहीं, निर्मूल्य होता है। 'एक' का अर्थ है 'पूर्ण' और 'पूर्णता' में मूल्यों की स्थिति तो दूर मूल्यीय चेतना भी नहीं होती।[86] मूल्य-सृष्टि का संबंध मनुष्य की चेतना से है, जो अनुभूति को 'प्रत्यय' और 'प्रत्यय' को अनुभूति बनाने की क्षमता रखती है। चेतना का एक पक्ष शारीरिक है, जिससे शरीर-संबंध साधनात्मक मूल्य पैदा होते हैं। चेतना के यथार्थ पक्ष से जहाँ व्यवस्थागत मूल—राजनीति, वर्ण, वर्ग विभाजन संबंधी मूल्य पैदा होते हैं, वहीं चेतना के भावात्मक पक्ष से प्रेम, स्वातंत्र्य, आत्मसम्मान आदि मूल्य उभरते हैं। चेतना के अतिक्रमणशील (Transcendental) पहलू से ईश्वर और धर्म से संबद्ध मूल्य उपजते हैं। सत्य, विनय, प्रेम, सद्भाव, समन्वय, नैतिकता, पुण्य आदि मूल्य इसी कोटि में आएँगे।[87] इस चेतना के वस्तुमुखी रुख से वैज्ञानिक प्रत्यय उत्पन्न होते हैं, लेकिन मूल्यों का विधान नहीं होता।[88]

आई.ए. रिचर्ड्स ने मनोविज्ञान का सहारा लेकर अपने मूल्य-सिद्धांत का निर्माण किया है। इसके अंतर्गत माना गया है कि इच्छाएँ आवेशों को विशिष्ट ढंग से संगठित करती हैं। प्रभावशाली आवेश-गुच्छ (सेट आफ इंपलसेज) ही मूल्य की समस्या पैदा करते हैं। आवेश 'काम्य' और 'विकर्षक' होते हैं। वह वस्तु मूल्यवान् है, जो किसी 'काम्य' को संतुष्ट करे।[89] आर.टी. हैरिस ने भी इच्छा-अनिच्छा को मूल्य-सृष्टि में महत्त्वपूर्ण माना है। 'इच्छा' को संतुष्ट करनेवाला 'आलंबन' भी इसमें महत्त्वपूर्ण भूमिका निभाता है।[90] सी. जानसन ने धर्मों, सामाजिक मिथकों, नैतिक व्यवस्थाओं और विश्वासों को मूल्यों की जड़ में माना है।[91] नए मूल्यों के निर्माण के पीछे मनुष्य की इच्छाएँ और आवश्यकताएँ सर्वप्रमुख भूमिका निभाती हैं। बाहरी दबाव उन्हें प्रेरित या प्रभावित करते हैं। मनुष्य का

मन एक खास दिशा में कई उत्तेजकों और इच्छाओं को एक साथ महसूसता और संतुष्ट करता है। यह कार्य चेतन रूप में भी होता है और अचेतन रूप से भी। यही इच्छाएँ-वृत्तियाँ बाद में मूल्यों का रूप धारण करती हैं। लेकिन इच्छाओं की संतुष्टि में व्यक्ति के तर्क-चुनाव कम, समाज के निर्णय अधिक प्रभाव डालते हैं। समान प्रथाओं, रीतिरिवाजों, संस्थाओं आदि के जरिए मानवीय इच्छाओं और आवश्यकताओं को इस तरह संयोजित करता है कि वे मूल्यों में स्थानांतरित हो जाती हैं।[92] मुक्तिबोध ने मूल्यों की सृष्टि को व्यक्तित्व के गुणों के विकास के रूप में देखा था। मुक्तिबोध ने मूल्यों को मूर्त्त माना है, जो केवल भावुक और वैचारिक धरातल पर 'मूल्य' कहलाकर 'व्यक्तित्व' का गुण बनने का प्रयास करते रहते हैं—"नई परिस्थितियाँ जब व्यक्तित्व को इष्ट दिशा में संपूर्ण रूप से मोड़ देती हैं—अपने तकाजों की पूर्ति के लिए आवश्यक कार्यों की शक्ति जब व्यक्तित्व में पैदा कर देती है, यानी उस परिस्थिति के लिए आवश्यक गुणों का जन्म और विकास जब उस व्यक्तित्व में हो जाता है, तब वे मूल्य साकार हो उठते हैं।"[93] व्यक्ति का नए मूल्यों के लिए आग्रह प्रायः अपने आसपास की स्थितियों से संबद्ध होता है। यदि यह आग्रह बहुत आंतरिक है, तो उसके लिए अशांति और चिंता का कारण बनेगा। इसके फलस्वरूप नए पुराने मूल्यों का संघर्ष तीव्र होता है।[94] पुराने मूल्यों की अप्रासंगिकता नए मूल्यों की सृष्टि के लिए वातावरण तैयार करती है।

मूल्य-संकट, मूल्य-विघटन, मूल्य-विपर्यय और मूल्यहीनता

बीसवीं शती में प्रतिष्ठित जीवनमूल्यों के ध्वंस या उनकी अस्वीकृति को विचारकों ने चिंता की दृष्टि से देखा है। आज का व्यक्ति मूर्तिभंजक महमूद की तरह बड़ी निर्ममता से मूल्य प्रतिमाओं को खंडित कर रहा है।[95] निश्चय ही मानव-संस्कृति विराट् और व्यापक परिवर्तनों में से होकर गुजर रही है, उसके मूल्य-मानों में अमूल उखाड़-पछाड़ हुई है। किंतु इन महान् परिवर्तनों को संकट कहना कहाँ तक उचित है ? परिवर्तन विरोधी शक्तियाँ ही इन्हें संकट के रूप में आँकती और प्रचारित करती हैं।[96] 'मूल्यहीनता' और मूल्य-अराजकता का ढोल भी यथास्थिति के समर्थकों द्वारा अधिक पीटा जाता है।[97] मूल्य-संकट की स्थिति में समाज और व्यक्ति के सामने वैचारिक धुँधलापन तो होता है लेकिन मूल्यों के नए क्षितिज भी उभर रहे होते हैं। बगैर मूल्यों के विघटन के नए मूल्यों की सृष्टि संभव नहीं है। इसके अतिरिक्त पुराने मूल्यों को टूटने से बचाए रखना संभव नहीं है। मनुष्य अपनी विरासत में मिले मूल्यों को मजबूती से पकड़े रखता है, लेकिन वे उसकी गिरफ्त से दूर जाकर ही रहते हैं। वह चाहकर भी पुराने मूल्यों को जीवित नहीं रख पाता

क्योंकि उन्हें जीवित रखने का अर्थ है स्वयं मृत्यु का वरण।[98] यह समझना गलत है कि किसी देश में किसी 'आचार' या 'विचार' को सदैव 'मूल्यवान्' माना जाता रहेगा। बदलते हुए संदर्भों में मूल्यों के अर्थ बदल जाते हैं। आज यह विडंबनापूर्ण स्थिति है कि पुराने मूल्य अप्रासंगिक लग रहे हैं, लेकिन उनकी जगह लेनेवाले नए मूल्य अभी संख्या में कम हैं। यही मूल्य-संकट की स्थिति है।

कुछ विचारकों की दृष्टि में संकट मानव-मूल्यों पर उतना नहीं है, जितना मूल्यों को निर्मित और संक्रमित करनेवाले सामाजिक संबंधों और स्थितियों (परिवेश) पर है। वस्तुतः संबंधों पर संकट आने का अर्थ यही है कि 'मूल्य' संकटग्रस्त हो गए हैं। इसमें कोई बुनियादी अंतर नहीं है। इस मत से यह अवश्य ध्वनित होता है कि 'मूल्य-संकट', 'मूल्य-विघटन' परिवेश के बदलाव पर आश्रित हैं।

'मूल्य-विघटन', 'मूल्य-संकट' को जन्म देनेवाले प्रेरक कई हैं। प्रायः 'विज्ञान' को इसके लिए जिम्मेदार ठहरा दिया जाता है। निश्चय ही विज्ञान ने हमारी धारणाओं और विश्वासों की चूल हिला दी है। लेकिन विज्ञान सीधे तौर पर न पुराने मूल्यों का विघटन करता है न नयों का निर्माण।[99] विज्ञान मनुष्य को भौतिक वास्तविकता का ज्ञान कराकर चिंतन की नई दिशाएँ खोलता है। यह दो स्तरों पर मूल्य-विघटन या परिवर्तन में सहायक होता है। पहला स्तर है, विज्ञान का बौद्धिक रूप और दूसरा है यांत्रिकी (टेकनोलॉजी) का निरंतर बढ़ता दबाव। विज्ञान का बौद्धिक या सैद्धांतिक पक्ष रूढ़िवादी चिंतन को धक्का देता है। विज्ञान ने न केवल रहन-सहन बल्कि जीवन-दृष्टि को भी गंभीरता से प्रभावित किया है।[100] विज्ञान ने सबसे कड़ी चुनौती धर्म और अध्यात्म से जुड़े मूल्यों को दी है। आस्तिकता, भक्ति आदि को अस्वीकारते हुए विज्ञान ने पारलौकिक सत्ता के अस्तित्व को नहीं माना। फ्रायडवाद, अस्तित्ववाद, विकासवाद, साम्यवाद, वर्गसां का जिजीविषावाद आदि विज्ञान प्रेरित सिद्धांतों ने मानव-चिंतन को नई दिशाएँ दीं। लेकिन विज्ञान पर यह दोषारोपण भी किया जाता है कि वैज्ञानिक दृष्टिकोण ने प्राचीन धर्म और दर्शन-जन्य मूल्यों का नाश तो किया लेकिन मानवजाति को निश्चित मूल्य नहीं दिए।[101] अतः टायनबी, नेव्हूर, मनहेम, इलियट आदि विचारक 'विज्ञान' को अस्वीकार करते हुए धर्म या प्रत्ययवादी दर्शन की स्थापना करना चाहते हैं। इसके विपरीत रसेल, आयर, हक्सले आदि वैज्ञानिक दृष्टिकोण को स्वीकारते हुए नई मूल्य-व्यवस्था का जन्म संभव मानते हैं। लारेंस और हेमिंग्वे जैसे कुछ विचारक संस्कृति, धर्म और विज्ञान की असंगतियों पर चोट करते रहे। इस विचार-वैभिन्नय के बावजूद यह निश्चित है कि आज 'विज्ञान' को मानव-जीवन से बाहर नहीं किया जा सकता।[102] वह आज मूल्यों को प्रभावित कर रहा है और भविष्य में भी करता रहेगा। यांत्रिकी बौद्धिक धरातल पर कोई संकट नहीं पैदा करता। यह व्यावहारिक जीवन पर प्रभाव डालती है। नगरीकरण, आर्थिक प्रतियोगिता, संपत्ति का

विक्रेंद्रीकरण, तीव्रगामी संचार व्यवस्था और विध्वंसात्मक अस्त्र आदि यांत्रिकी के तत्त्व मानवजीवन में क्रांतिकारी परिवर्तन ला चुके हैं। इनके प्रभाव से जीवन-स्तर ऊपर उठा है, शोषण के नए तरीके सामने आए हैं, नैतिकता के रूढ़ मानदंडों को गहरा आघात लगा है, पारिवारिक संबंध कठोर आजमाइश में पड़ गए हैं। विध्वंसात्मक अस्त्रों ने संपूर्ण मानवता के लिए भयंकर संकट खड़ा कर दिया है। लोग सोचने लगे हैं कि चतुर्थ विश्व-युद्ध शायद ईंट-पत्थरों और नाखूनों-दाँतों से लड़ा जाएगा। पिछले दो विश्व-युद्धों में 'यांत्रिकी' के दुरुपयोग का फल यह हुआ कि संपूर्ण यूरोप अजनबीपन, अकेलापन और अनास्था से गुजरता हुआ 'मूल्यहीनता' की दहलीज तक पहुँच गया था।

मूल्यहीनता और अराजकता की स्थिति में जनसाधारण अपने अनुकूल मूल्यों का एक काल्पनिक संसार बना लेता है, जो एक ओर वर्गहितों का पोषण करता है, दूसरी ओर सार्वजनिक हितों को बढ़ाता है। मूल्यों के पुराने साँचे को तोड़ने से एक हानि भी हुई कि मनुष्य की पाशविक प्रवृत्तियों और आवेगों पर से नियंत्रण हट गया।

यांत्रिकी के अतिरिक्त व्यक्ति को जीवन के विभिन्न चरणों में प्राप्त होनेवाले नए अनुभवों के विस्तार तथा उसकी सामाजिक-आर्थिक भूमिकाओं में आनेवाले परिवर्तनों से भी मूल्य परिवर्तित होते हैं।[103] मार्क्स, काडवेल, प्लेखानोव आदि विचारक 'मूल्य' को जीव-अस्तित्व और वातावरण के संबंध का प्रतिबिंब मानते हैं।[104] आधुनिकता के संचरण को भी मूल्यों के परिवर्तन के लिए उत्तरदायी ठहराया गया है।[105] इन्द्रनाथ मदान ने आधुनिकता को एक जीवन-बोध के रूप में देखा है, जिसमें प्रश्नचिह्न की निरंतरता है और मध्यकालीन तथा रोमैंटिक बोध का अस्वीकार है।[106] आधुनिकता को जीवन-बोध के अर्थ में लेने से इसमें एक ओर विज्ञान और यांत्रिकी से संबद्ध चिंतन समाहित हो जाता है, दूसरी ओर मार्क्सवाद, अस्तित्ववाद, गांधीवाद आदि आधुनिक विचारधाराएँ भी इसके अंतर्गत आ जाती हैं। आधुनिकता को परिवर्तन में सहायक मानने का एक अर्थ यह निकलता है कि 'दृष्टि' बदलते ही मूल्यों के बदलने की शुरुआत होने लगती है।[107] लेकिन मूल्य-परिवर्तन तभी माना जाना चाहिए, जब किसी न किसी 'मूल्य' की उपस्थिति हो। पुराना उखड़ जाए, नया उगे नहीं अर्थात् कोई मूल्य न हो तो यह 'मूल्य-परिवर्तन' की स्थिति नहीं है।[108] इस स्थिति में या तो मूल्य-शून्यता के प्रति मूल्य-बोध का आक्रोश होता है या मूल्य-शून्यता अथवा मूल्यहीनता के प्रति सामान्य क्षोभ मात्र व्यक्त होता है। यह क्षोभ किसी मूल्य-दृष्टि से अनुशासित नहीं होता। मानसिक दुर्बलताओं या सामान्यतः अनुचित माने जानेवाले अनैतिक व्यवहार को 'मूल्य' के रूप में प्रस्तुत करना कुछ विचारकों की दृष्टि में मूल्य-परिवर्तन न होकर मूल्य-विपर्यय या मूल्यबोध का द्योतक है।[109] यदि कोई उन्मुक्त यौनाचरण,

डाकाजनी आदि को 'ग्लोरीफाई' करता है तो निश्चय ही वह मूल्य-विपर्यय को प्रोत्साहित कर रहा है।

इस प्रकार मूल्य-संकट जहाँ मूल्य-परिवर्तन की भूमिका है, वहीं मूल-विघटन नई मूल्य-दृष्टि के उदय में महत्त्वपूर्ण योग देता है। मूल्य-विघटन के साथ ही मूल्य-संक्रमण जुड़ा हुआ है। मूल्य संक्रमण के बाद या तो नई मूल्य-दृष्टि जन्म लेती है या मूल्य-शून्यता अथवा मूल्यहीनता की स्थिति आ जाती है। हालाँकि कुछ विचारकों के खयाल में मूल्यों का एकदम अभाव कभी नहीं होता।[110] भीष्म साहनी ने जोर देकर कहा कि पुराने मूल्यों की अप्रासंगिकता के बावजूद मूल्यहीनता की स्थिति नहीं आती।[111] जब हम भ्रष्टाचार की बात करते हैं तब इसके विपरीत किसी दूसरे आचार की धारणा हमारे मन में होती है। मूल्यहीनता केवल इस अर्थ में समझी जाती है कि अपेक्षित मूल्यों पर आचरण नहीं हो पा रहा है।[112]

मूल्य-संक्रमण : प्रकृति और प्रेरणा

मानक हिंदी कोश में संक्रमण शब्द के आठ अर्थ दिए गए हैं।[113] इनमें प्रमुख हैं—आगे की ओर बढ़ना, अतिक्रमण, एक अवस्था से दूसरी अवस्था में पहुँचना, सूर्य का एक राशि से निकलकर दूसरी राशि में प्रवेश करना आदि। प्रो. सिद्धेश्वर प्रसाद जैसे विद्वानों ने 'संक्रमण' को संक्रांति का पर्याय मानते हुए इसी विशिष्ट अर्थ में संक्रमण के प्रयोग की चर्चा की है—"...संक्रांति शब्द सूर्य का एक राशि से दूसरी राशि में प्रवेश करने के समय का वाचक होने के साथ-साथ, जो भारतीय ज्योतिष परंपरा में बड़ा पुनीतकाल माना जाता है, दो युगों के बीच के उस संधि-काल का भी वाचक हो गया है, जब पुराने मूल्यों में आस्था तो हिलने लगती है, लेकिन नए मूल्य उनका स्थान नहीं ले पाते हैं। ऐसी स्थिति में संक्रांति काल दो मूल्यबोधों के संघर्षकाल का वाचक हो गया है और अब ज्योतिष के बाहर इसी अर्थ में इसका प्रचलन हो गया है।"[114] 'मानविकी पारिभाषिक कोश' में 'संक्रमण' अंग्रेजी शब्द—Transition के पर्याय के रूप में प्रयुक्त हुआ है। वहाँ इसे दो रूपों में समझाया गया है—"(1) किसी एक विषय से, अथवा कृति के किसी एक अवस्थान से, दूसरे में प्रवेश करने की क्रिया या कार्य अथवा वे युक्तियाँ, जो विचार को विकास की एक अवस्था से अगली अवस्था में ले जाती हैं। (2) किन्हीं दो पूर्वापर अवस्थाओं अथवा युगों के बीच में पड़नेवाली स्थिति जिसमें दोनों की ही विशेषताएँ परिलक्षित होती हैं अथवा जिसमें दोनों के संघर्ष का सूत्रपात होता है।"[115] मूल्य-प्रक्रिया के संदर्भ में संकट, विघटन आदि शब्दों का भी प्रयोग हुआ है लेकिन 'संक्रमण' शब्द इन सबका विकसित रूप है।[116] इन स्पष्टीकरणों को 'मूल्यों' के संदर्भ में लागू करने पर लगता है कि मूल्य-संक्रमण की दो प्रमुख स्थितियाँ हैं। जब कोई उच्चतर

मूल्य स्थानच्युत होता है, उसका स्थान अपेक्षाकृत हीन मूल्य लेता है अथवा साध्यमूल्य और साधनमूल्य अपनी जगह बदल लेते हैं, तब मूल्य-संक्रमण की एक स्थिति सामने आती है। इससे ज्ञात होता है कि मूल्यों का विकास किस दिशा में हुआ है ? दूसरी स्थिति तब पैदा होती है, जब पुराने मूल्य एकदम समाप्त नहीं होते और उनका स्थान लेनेवाले मूल्य पूरी तरह नहीं उभर पाते हैं। 'सूर्य का यद्यपि नहीं आना हुआ, किंतु समझो रात का जाना हुआ' से मिलती-जुलती स्थिति होती है। फर्क इतना है कि जहाँ कुछ ही क्षणों में सूर्य का आविर्भाव निश्चित है, वहीं नए मूल्यों का स्वरूप और जन्म-समय निश्चित नहीं है। इस अंतराल में परंपरागत और आधुनिक मूल्यों की युगपत् स्थिति होती है। आधुनिकता, जिसमें विज्ञान वगैरह की अनेक धारणाएँ निहित हैं, के दबाव से यह असमंजस की स्थिति पैदा होती है।[117] परंपरागत मूल्यों को कड़ी चुनौती मिलती है और वे विचलित हो जाते हैं। यह विचलन और परिवर्तन सामाजिक-आर्थिक परिस्थितियों से आता है, लेकिन आधुनिकता परिवर्तन की प्रक्रिया तेज बनाती है। आधुनिकता के प्रसार से समाज का एक वर्ग विशेष आधुनिक दृष्टि-संपन्न होकर नए मूल्यों को प्रश्रय देता है, लेकिन समाज का एक बड़ा वर्ग आधुनिकता के अल्पांश से भी परिचित नहीं हो पाता।[118] यही नहीं, नए मूल्यों का हामी वर्ग भी पुराने मूल्यों को अपने व्यवहार से बाहर नहीं कर पाता। विचार या बोध के स्तर पर 'अस्पृश्यता' को प्रबुद्ध व्यक्ति नहीं स्वीकारता, लेकिन रोटी या बेटी का संदर्भ आने पर वह जातिगत ऊँचनीच के कठघरों में कैद हो जाता है। 'सांप्रदायिकता' के साथ भी यही बात है। इसलिए आधुनिकीकरण के समानांतर संस्कृति की मानवीय सदंर्भों में पुनर्व्याख्या भी होती रहती है।[119] अर्थात् परंपरा का पुनर्नवीकरण होता रहता है। विज्ञान इसमें सर्वाधिक सहायता करता है। नए मूल्यों के उदय और पुरामूल्यों की पुनर्व्याख्या में धार्मिक-सामाजिक आंदोलन और क्रांति आदि का योगदान कम नहीं है। वे कभी-कभी संस्थाओं और अधिकारों, कर्तव्यों, नियमों वगैरह के आंतरिक संबंधों में निहित 'सामाजिक संतुष्टि' में परिवर्तन उपस्थित कर नई सामाजिक मूल्य-दृष्टि को जन्म देते हैं।[120] ''कभी-कभी विभिन्न जातियों के सम्मिश्रण से (सामाजिक संबंधों में परिवर्तन आने के फलस्वरूप) नए विचारों का आवागमन होता है अथवा नई सामाजिक व्यवस्था अथवा नए आचार-विचार उदित होते हैं और नई मान्यताएँ स्थापित होती हैं।''[121] भारतीय परिवेश में आर्य समाज, ब्रह्मसमाज, स्वातंत्र्य आंदोलन और यूरोप में फ्रांस तथा रूस की क्रांतियों ने मानवीय चिंतन में बुनियादी फर्क पैदा किया है।

आधुनिकता के दबाव से पूर्व मूल्य किसी पारलौकिक सत्ता से संबद्ध थे। लेकिन वैज्ञानिक अवधारणाओं ने धर्म को खासी चुनौती दी। सबसे पहले 'यूरोप' में पुरामूल्यों के स्थान पर नई मर्यादाओं को प्रतिष्ठित करने की बेचैनी दिखाई दी।

भारत के रूढ़िवादियों ने पश्चिम और पूर्व की नियति को अलग मानते हुए हमेशा यही चाहा कि 'नई रोशनी' का प्रभाव यहाँ न पड़े।[122] लेकिन वे परिवर्तन के चक्र को न रोक पाए। आज मूल्यों की स्वीकृति और निर्धारण के पीछे उपयोगिता की कसौटी विद्यमान होती है। जो मूल्य अव्यावहारिक और अनुपयोगी होते हैं, उन्हें क्रमशः उपेक्षित कर दिया जाता है। बहुत से पुरामूल्यों के साथ यह कठिनाई है कि वे इतनी ऊँचाई पर स्थित होते हैं कि मनुष्य उन्हें अपने जीवन में उतार नहीं पाता।[123] परिणाम यह होता है कि कथनी और करनी में अंतर दिखाई देता है। वैचारिक स्तर पर पुरामूल्यों की स्वीकृति बनी रहती है लेकिन 'व्यवहार' में उनकी उपेक्षा की जाती है। 'अपरिग्रह' और 'ब्रह्मचर्य' आदि मूल्य-मर्यादाओं के साथ यह विडंबना प्रायः देखी जाती है। ऐसी स्थिति में 'व्यक्ति' अंतरात्मा की आवाज के नाम पर व्यक्तिगत निर्णयों को 'मूल्य' की सी गरिमा देने लगता है। एक परिचर्चा में भाग लेते हुए मराठी नाटककार विजयतेंदुलकर ने स्पष्ट किया था कि अंतरात्मा की आवाज पर किसी विवाहित स्त्री के साथ सोता हूँ तो यह पाप नहीं है। यदि सामाजिक दबाववश मैं ऐसा नहीं करता, तब 'पाप' है।[124] यदि सभी अंतरात्मा की आवाज की दुहाई देने लगें तब तो डकैती, हत्या आदि भी पाप नहीं है। निश्चय ही मूल्य-निर्धारण का महत्त्वपूर्ण कार्य व्यक्ति-विशेष की अंतरात्मा की आवाज पर नहीं छोड़ा जा सकता।

मूल्य-संक्रमण की स्थिति वहाँ भी पैदा होती है, जब एक समुदाय या संस्कृति का सदस्य दूसरे समुदाय या संस्कृति के संपर्क में आता है और समायोजन नहीं कर पाता।[125] एक आदिवासी बस्ती के व्यक्ति को नई सभ्यता से तालमेल बिठाने में बहुत कठिनाई होती है। इसी तरह ठेठ गाँव के लोग महानगरीय जीवन के मूल्यों को गले नहीं उतार पाते। हिंदू आदर्शों से जुड़े 'व्यक्ति' के लिए 'मुसलमान' या 'ईसाई' मानसिकता के परिवेश में समायोजित होने में समय लगेगा। नैतिक मूल्यों के संक्रमण का एक पक्ष भी एक समुदाय की मूल्य-व्यवस्था से दूसरी मूल्य-व्यवस्था में प्रवेश से उत्पन्न द्वंद्व या संघर्ष से संबद्ध है। पति के परमेश्वरत्व में विश्वास रखनेवाली नारी के लिए 'तलाक' को सहज रूप में मान्यता देनेवाली मूल्य-व्यवस्था शीघ्र ही स्वीकार्य नहीं हो सकती। आचरण से जुड़े मूल्यों में उलटफेर का आयाम समाज और देश का नियमन करनेवाले कर्णधारों से संबंधित है। जिन व्यक्तियों से अपेक्षा की जाती है कि वे उच्चादर्शों का पालन करेंगे, वे ही जब निम्न स्तर पर उतर आते हैं तो जनसाधारण भी उनकी देखा देखी अपनी नई आचार संहिता गढ़ने लगता है। स्पष्ट है कि आचार के नियम ऊपर से नीचे की ओर चलते हैं।[126]

परिवर्तन जीवन और विश्व की अनिवार्यता है। इसलिए विचारों और मनोभावों में परिवर्तन आकस्मिक नहीं है। इस 'तथ्य' को न समझने के

परिणामस्वरूप कुछ लोग किसी भी बदलाव के लिए तैयार नहीं होते। लेकिन उनके न चाहते हुए भी परिवर्तन का रथ आगे बढ़ जाता है और मूल्यों में आमूलचूल बदलाव के संकेत मिलने लगते हैं। परिवर्तन के संबंध में यह जान लेना अपेक्षित है कि मात्रात्मक परिवर्तन से गुणात्मक परिवर्तन और गुणात्मक परिवर्तन से मात्रात्मक परिवर्तन संभव होता है। ''यदि इसे आइन्स्टाइन की भाषा में कहें तो चेतन तत्त्व से भूततत्त्व और भूततत्त्व से चेतन तत्त्व उत्पन्न होता है।''[127] संक्रमण की प्रक्रिया चलती रहती है, लेकिन उसका बोध तभी होता है, जब मात्रात्मक परिवर्तन गुणात्मक परिवर्तन का रूप ले लेता है।[128]

इस प्रकार मूल्य-संक्रमण के अंतर्गत पाँच प्रमुख स्तर इस प्रकार हैं :

(1) आधुनिकता के दबाव से पुरातन मूल्यों की अप्रासंगिकता का बोध। (2) नए-पुराने मूल्यों का संघर्ष और असमंजस की स्थिति। (3) कुछ पुरामूल्यों की पुनर्व्याख्या और संशोधनों के साथ स्वीकृति। (4) अस्तिमूल्य, साध्य मूल्य, उच्चतर मूल्यों का क्रमशः नास्तिमूल्य, साधनमूल्य और हीनतर मूल्यों में पर्यवसान और इसकी विपरीत स्थिति भी। (5) कतिपय नए मूल्यों की प्रतिष्ठा।

विचार या धारणा के स्तर पर होनेवाला हर परिवर्तन मूल्य-संक्रमण नहीं है। क्षणिक आवेश में आकर किसी धारणा या मूल्य को नकारना विक्षोभ या किसी असहज स्थिति का सूचक है। यह आवश्यक नहीं कि इससे मूल्य-संक्रमण की कोई स्थिति उत्पन्न हो ही। पुरामूल्यों के अप्रासंगिक होने के बोध के साथ कर्तृत्वाभिमान (मैं कर्ता हूँ) का अहसास भी आवश्यक है। कांट का विचार था कि 'कर्तव्य' विवेकशील संकल्प का विधान होने से 'सार्वभौतिक उत्तरदायित्व' है।[129] चूँकि कांट शुभ संकल्प के अतिरिक्त कुछ भी शुभ (मूल्य) नहीं मानते, अतः स्पष्ट है, ''मूल्य भी एक तरह से सार्वभौतिक उत्तरदायित्व हैं। जब उनकी प्रासंगिकता में संदेह उत्पन्न होता है और व्यक्ति या बहुत से व्यक्ति स्थापित मूल्य-व्यवस्था को संदेह की दृष्टि से देखने लगते हैं, तब विचलन और संक्रमण की स्थिति सामने आती है।''

सोरोकिन ने सामाजिक गतिशीलता के दो प्रमुख प्रकार माने हैं[130] :

(1) क्षैतिज सामाजिक गतिशीलता

(2) उदग्र सामाजिक गतिशीलता

मूल्य-संक्रमण की दिशा गतिशीलता के इन दोनों आयामों के अनुरूप है। जब एक ही स्तर के मूल्य एक समूह से दूसरे समूह में स्थानांतरित होते हैं तब मूल्य संक्रमण की दिशा 'क्षैतिज' होती है। जब युवा पीढ़ी के मूल्य बूढ़ी पीढ़ी को स्वीकार्य होने लगें या वर्गसंघर्ष की धारणा विभिन्न जातियों में संक्रमित होने लगे, तब क्षैतिज संक्रमण होगा। जब मूल्यों का स्थानांतरण एक सामाजिक स्तर से अन्य सामाजिक स्तर पर होता है तो मूल्य संक्रमण उदग्र होता है। यह संक्रमण उच्च

सामाजिक-आर्थिक स्थिति से निम्न सामाजिक स्थिति की ओर भी हो सकता है। अनुसूचित जातियों में ऊर्ध्वगामी दोनों दिशाओं में होनेवाला संक्रमण आर्थिक कारणों–विशेषतः उत्पादन संबंधों से प्रभावित होता है। एक निश्चित आर्थिक नींव के ऊपर अनिवार्य रूप से एक निश्चित विचारात्मक ढाँचा खड़ा होता है।[131] मार्क्स ने इतिहास को मानव-विकास की चक्करदार कमानी में एक तरह की कुंडली मानते हुए दूसरी और तीसरी मंजिल की जो व्याख्या की है, उससे विचारों के संक्रमण पर प्रकाश पड़ता है। तीसरी मंजिल–व्यक्तियों के सर्वमुखी विकास पर आधारित व्यक्तित्व का स्वातंत्र्य[132] आज विकासशील देशों की जनता का लक्ष्य है। इस लक्ष्य से वे पुरामूल्य, जो पूँजीवादी संबंधों और श्रमविभाजन से उपजे हैं और वे जो पिछली सामंती व्यवस्था के अवशेष हैं, बाधा उत्पन्न करते हैं। फलस्वरूप संक्रमण की प्रक्रिया तेज होती है।

मूल्यों को संवेदना, संवेग या आवश्यकता से अनुशासित अवधारणों के रूप में देखा गया है। ये प्रारंभ में अनुभवों से निचोड़े गए अमूर्त्त तथ्य होते हैं। समाजशास्त्री ग्रीन ने मूल्यों के तीन स्तर–'अमूर्त्त संवेग', 'नैतिक प्रतिमान' और 'अहम्' माने हैं।[133] जब कोई नई मूल्य-मर्यादा उभरती है तो पहले उसका रूप बहुत स्पष्ट नहीं होता है। बाद में वह नैतिक प्रतिमान के रूप में स्वीकार होने लगता है। उसकी समग्र स्वीकृति तब होती है जब वह व्यक्ति के अहम् का अंग बन जाता है। तदनंतर उसकी सामाजिक स्वीकृति की स्थिति बनती है।

संदर्भ

1. पूर्व पश्चिम, पृ. 91
2. 'Know what you really value, know what your values are and know them in their order of importance.'–Social Ethics, Robert T. Harris, p. 4
3. The great task before man today is to discover a new the genuine values of life and to share them with his fellow must learn to unify and harmonize the world of facts with the world of values.–Living issues in Philosophy, H.A. Titus, p. 347
4. संस्कृति का दार्शनिक विवेचन, डॉ. देवराज, पृ. 31 से उद्‌धृत
5. विश्वकोश, हृदयनाराण मिश्र, पृ. 365
6. Living issues in Philosophy, p. 333
7. कल्पना, अप्रैल 1964, 'मूल्य की परिभाषा', पृ. 28
8. नीतिशास्त्र का सर्वेक्षण, संगमलाल पांडेय, पृ. 346
9. शुक्रनीति-2, 48-49

10. कल्पना, अप्रैल 1964, पृ. 35

11. संस्कृति का दार्शनिक विवेचन, पृ. 96

12. वही, पृ. 122

13. आलोचना, जनवरी-मार्च 1970, पृ. 76

14. "In general, we can say that value judgements are judgement of appraisal" —Living issues in Philosophy, p. 334

15. संस्कृति का दार्शनिक विवेचन, डॉ. देवराज, पृ. 49 के आधार पर

16. वही, पृ. 21

17. Living issues in Philosophy, P. 337

18. नीतिशास्त्र का सर्वेक्षण, पृ. 345

19. 'By human values, by a value or a system of values, I mean the basis upon which an individual will choose one course rathor than another judged as better or worse, right or wrong'.—From, Living issues in Philosophy, p. 335

20. Ibid, p. 337

21. "मूल्यों के संबंध में मनुष्य कोई भी मंतव्य क्यों न बनाए, वह अनिवार्य रूप में आत्मपरक होगा। इसका मतलब यह है कि ऐसे कोई वस्तुपरक अर्थात् वास्तविक मूल्य नहीं हैं, जिनके लिए मानव-जीवन को जिया जाय।"—संस्कृति का दार्शनिक विवेचन, भूमिका, पृ. 8

22. In the most elemently sense, value means whatever is actually liked, prized, esteemed, desired, approved or enjoyed by anyone at any time. It is the actual experience or enjoying a desired object or activity. Hence value is an existing realization of desire. —Living issues in philosophy, p. 335

23. नई कविता : स्वरूप और समस्याएँ, जगदीश गुप्त, भारतीय ज्ञानपीठ, प्रथम सं. पृ. 13 के आधार पर।

24. '"""but come into relation to one another and become realized as values only in personal experience.'—Social Ethics, p. 15

25. आधुनिक काव्य में नवीन जीवनमूल्य, हुकुमचंद राजपाल, पृ. 63

26. कल्पना, अप्रैल 64, मूल्य की परिभाषा, कृष्णनाथ, पृ. 30

27. Value is the co-oprative result of an inter action between personal and impersonal elements. —Living issues in Philosophy. p. 340

28. कल्पना, अप्रैल 64, पृ. 35

29. रत्नभूतं तु तत्तत् स्याद यद्यप्रतिमं भुवि
यथादेशं यथाकालं मूल्यं सर्वस्य कल्पयेत्
न मूल्यं गुणहीनस्य व्यवहाराक्षमस्य

x x x

येन व्ययेन संसिद्धस्तव्ययस्तस्य मूल्यकम्
सुलभासुलभ त्वच्चागुणात्वगुण संश्रयः
यथाकामात् पदार्थानाधर्म हीनाधिकं भवेत्–शुक्रनीति, 2-48/49

30. जलते-उबलते प्रश्न, बोहरा प्रकाशन जयपुर (1969), पृ. 23
31. The social structure of values, S. Chand Company, New Delhi (1965), R.K. Mukerjee, p. 2
32. Encyclopaedia Britanica, p. 961
33. Encyclopaedia Americana, p. 867
34. Encyclopaedia Britanica, p. 961
35. International Encyclopaedia of the social sciences, Ed. by David L. Sillis, Volume 16, p. 285
36. The Social structure of values, p. 231
37. "...किसी भी उपयोग-मूल्य अथवा उपयोगी वस्तु में मूल्य केवल इसलिए होता है कि उसमें अमूर्त मानव-श्रम निहित होता है, या यूँ कहिए यह कि उसमें अमूर्त मानव श्रम भौतिक रूप धारण किए होता है।" पूँजी, खंड-1, प्रगति प्रकाशन, मास्को, दूसरा संस्करण (1975), पृ. 53
38. हिंदुस्तानी भाग 29, अंक 1-4, 'मूल्य-स्तबक की वैयक्तिकता तथा परस्परस्पर्धा', रमेशकुंतल मेघ, पृ. 190
39. The Social structure of values, p. 31
40. The Frontiers of social sciences, (Ed. B. Singh), P. 167
41. 'Between man and society, the floating wick and the deep oil, there is a never ending give be take, producing the bright, steady flame of value experience that enternally radiates light and warmth on our bleak, dreary universe.'–The social structure of values, page XII
42. International Encyclopaedia of the social sciences, p. 283.
43. Ibid
44. Dynamics of Morals, p. 201
45. "A value is a complex gestalt, a conscious vital-social ideal situation." –The social structure of values, p. 107
46. Human value is the mother of the sciences. Dynamics of morals, P. 216
47. Encyclopaedia Britanica, p. 963
48. "मूल्य की सत्ता के कई आयाम मनोवैज्ञानिकता से संपृक्त हैं, क्योंकि कभी-कभी उसका संबंध किसी बहिर्निष्ठ वस्तु की अपेक्षा छायावेष्टित रहःस्थलों की निगूढ़ताओं

से अधिक रहता है। ऐसी अवस्था में मूल्य का आधार हमारी उस अन्तश्चेतना का निक्षेपण है, जो हमारे मूल व्यक्तित्व की पीठिका बनी रहती है।''—'मूल्य और मीमांसा', कुमार विमल, पृ. 7

49. रिचर्ड्स के आलोचना-सिद्धांत, शंभुदत्त झा, पृ. 61
50. वही, पृ. 54
51. वही, पृ. 56
52. बीसवीं शताब्दी की हिंदी कहानी में जीवनमूल्य, रमेश चंद्र लवानियाँ, (अंकित प्रति), पृ. 7
53. "...Value is a determination or quality of an object which envolves any sort of appreciation or interest such appreciation however envolves feeling and ultimatly desire or tendencies underlying the feeling."—Encyclopaedia Britanica, p. 962-963
54. ''परंतु कोई मूल्य किसी व्यक्ति-विशेष के निजी मूल्यांकन की क्षमता पर आधारित नहीं होता, बल्कि वह समाज द्वारा उसके ऊपर लादा जाता है, जिसे वह धीरे-धीरे ही ग्रहण कर पाता है और अंततोगत्वा उसे अपने आचरण की निजी कसौटी बना लेता है।''—मानव विकास का मनोविज्ञान, डॉ. जगतनारायण लाल, पृ. 270 से उद्धृत
55. ज्ञानोदय, जुलाई 1968, गोपालशरण, समाजगत मूल्यों की परख नृतत्व के संदर्भ में, पृ. 90
56. वही, पृ. 90
57. "...values to be conceptions of the desireble, influncing selective behaviour." —International Encyclopaedia of the social sciences, P. 283
58. नीतिशास्त्र, पृ. 546
59. समकालीन कहानी : दिशा और दृष्टि, सं. (धनंजय), बच्चनसिंह, 'गुमशुदा पहचान की तलाश की प्रतिक्रिया', पृ. 89
60. ''मूल्य और प्रतिमान समानार्थी शब्द हैं, दोनों ही मानव-निर्मित निकष या कसौटियाँ हैं...''—हिंदी साहित्य कोश, पृ. 604
61. ''मूल्य का अर्थ है जीवन-दृष्टि या स्थापित वैचारिक इकाई, जिसे हम सक्रिय नार्म (NORM) भी कह सकते हैं।''—काव्यानुशीलन : आधुनिक : अत्याधुनिक, पृ. 151
62. बिंदु, वर्ष 6 संयुक्तांक विशेषांक (3-4) 'आधुनिकता बोध और जनचित्त', पृ. 573
63. 'Values are not the same as norms for conduct. Norms are rules for behaving, they say more or less specifically what should or should not be done by particular types of actors in given circumstances. Values are standards of deserability that are more nearly independent of specific situations. —International Encyclopaedia of

the social sciences, p. 284

64. आधुनिक काव्य में नवीन जीवनमूल्य, पृ. 65 के आधार पर
65. नीति प्रवेशिका, अनुवादक—गोवर्द्धन भट्ट, गंगारत्न पांडेय, शशिप्रभा त्रिपाठी, पृ. 190
66. संस्कृति का दार्शनिक विवेचन, पृ. 73-74
67. "स्वतःमूल्य वह है, जो एक तर्कनापरक व्यक्ति द्वारा शांतिपूर्वक विचार किए जाने पर स्वतःमूल्य प्रतीत हो। इस प्रकार स्वतःमूल्य उसे कहा जा सकता है, जो एक तर्कनापरक चुनाव का निर्भ्रांत लक्ष्य हो।"—नीति प्रवेशिका, पृ. 191
68. The sense of beauty, Dover Publication, New Yark, p. 28
69. रिचर्ड्स के आलोचना-सिद्धांत, पृ. 53
70. सौंदर्य मूल्य और मूल्यांकन, रमेशकुंतल मेघ, पृ. 45
71. वही।
72. संस्कृति का दार्शनिक विवेचन, पृ. 74
73. मानविकी पारिभाषिक कोश, साहित्य खंड
74. "जीवन के प्रायः सर्वमान्य, सार्वभौम या सार्वकालिक मूल्य (श्रेष्ठ पर ही दृष्टि रखती) हैं—त्याग, दया, सहानुभूति, कर्त्तव्यपरायणता, सत्य, प्रेम, शौर्य, सेवा आदि, जिन्हें समेटकर तीन मूल्यों में रखा जा सकता है—सत्य, शिव और सुंदर।"—जयशंकर प्रसाद, वस्तु और कला, रामेश्वरलाल खंडेलवाल, पृ. 423
75. नीति प्रवेशिका, पृ. 191-192
76. The negative values-error, ugliness and moral evil-bring us some where up against an obstacle and cause a failure of understanding and adjustment.—The frontiers of social sciences (Ed. B. Singh), Haridas Bhattacharya, p. 425
77. Value judgements, if they are to have any living significance, must be those of the individual"'—Social Ethics, p. 4
78. हिंदुस्तानी भाग 29, अंक 1-4, 'मूल्य स्तबक की वैयक्तिकता तथा परस्परस्पर्धा', रमेश कुंतल मेघ, पृ. 184
79. सौंदर्य मूल्य और मूल्यांकन, पृ. 46
80. Social values are values jointly held. These also can be clarified by experience and reflection.—Social Ethics, p. 50-51
81. जलते-उबलते प्रश्न, पृ. 24
82. आधुनिकता और भारतीय परंपरा, महावीर दाधीचि, पृ. 17
83. 'व्यक्ति और समाज', निगम और हेलेन, पृ. 459 के आधार पर।
84. मूल्य और मीमांसा, पृ. 1
85. वही, पृ. 4
86. आधुनिकता और भारतीय परंपरा, पृ. 9

87. वही, पृ. 14

88. "इससे मूल्यों को विधान नहीं होता क्योंकि 'यह है' 'और कैसे है' तक सीमित है। 'होना चाहिए' अथवा 'क्यों है' पर विचार नहीं करती। फलतः यह मूल्य-निरपेक्ष है। इससे उत्पन्न प्रत्यय वस्तु की भौतिकता से घनिष्ठतः बद्ध रहते हैं।"—वही, पृ. 15

89. सौंदर्य मूल्य और मूल्यांकन, पृ. 25

90. "The two major poles of every value situation are abvious : (1) There will be some object, generally an external thing or event that pleases or displeases us, attracts or repels us. (2) There will be our liking or disliking itself; the second pole is our inner and personal, felt response to the object. It may be a feeling of repulsion or attraction."—Social Ethics, p. 14

91. Revolutionry change, p. 21

92. 'Society through its customs, traditions and institutions, disciplines, cordinates and integrates the desires and wants of man in a manner that will serve it. This is the transformation of wants into values.'—The Social structure of values, p. 77

93. नई कविता का आत्मसंघर्ष तथा अन्य निबंध, पृ. 46

94. वही, पृ. 45

95. चिंतन अनुचिंतन, नेमनारायण जोशी, पृ. 68

96. "संकट मानव मात्र के लिए अहितकर, विनाशकारी और भयकारी होता है, परंतु उपर्युक्त मूल्य-अराजकता मानव-समाज के स्वाभाविक विकास का परिणाम है। पुराणवादी, रूढ़िवादी दृष्टियाँ ही उन्हें संकट के रूप में देखती हैं क्योंकि वे परिवर्तन विरोधी होती हैं, उनसे डरती हैं और समाज को यथास्थिति (Status quo) में रहने देना चाहती हैं।"—'नई कविता : सीमाएँ और संभावनाएँ', गिरिजाकुमार माथुर, पृ. 63

97. नई कहानियाँ : मई 1971, 'सामाजिक चुनौतियाँ' : 'आज की कहानी', धनंजय वर्मा, पृ. 122

98. समकालीन हिंदी साहित्य : समालोचना को चुनौती, बच्चनसिंह, पृ. 106

99. वही, पृ. 131

100. "इस दृष्टिकोण के कारण न केवल रहन-सहन, खान-पान के तरीके ही बदले हैं बल्कि आंतरिक स्तर पर जीवन की प्रत्येक घटना का अर्थ ही बदल गया लगता है—मानवी जीवनदृष्टि में मूलगामी परिवर्तन आया है।"—'कहानी संवेदनशीलता : सिद्धांत और प्रयोग', पृ. 182

101. आधुनिकता और भारतीय परंपरा, पृ. 22

102. "एक बात स्पष्ट है कि विज्ञान को हटाया नहीं जा सकता। हमें इसके साथ रहना

होगा—इसे स्वीकार करना होगा। मानव-चेतना और सभ्यता के विकास को 'न-हुआ' करना संभव नहीं है, मशीनों की करामात, उनका सुख और उनका भय यथार्थ है, जीवनांश हो गया है। उनसे आँख नहीं मूँद सकते।"—आधुनिकता और भारतीय परंपरा, पृ. 24

103. The social structare of values, p. 10

104. जलते-उबलते प्रश्न, पृ. 22-23

105. "आधुनिकता के संचरण के साथ-साथ मूल्य-परिवर्तन भी अनिवार्यतः घटित होता है। यदि यह कह दिया जाए कि आधुनिकता और मूल्य-परिवर्तन एक-दूसरे से उत्प्रेरित अथवा अन्योन्याश्रित है तो अनुपयुक्त नहीं होगा।"—संचेतना (जून 1980) 'आधुनिकता और मूल्य-संक्रमण', पुष्पपालसिंह, पृ. 23

106. हिंदी उपन्यास पहचान और परख, पृ. 79

107. "वास्तव में मूल्यों की और संपूर्ण मानवीय वस्तुस्थिति की यह विशेषता है कि इसके संबंध में दृष्टि इसमें परिवर्तन घटित कर देती है।"—आलोचना, जनवरी-मार्च 1970, परिवर्तित नैतिक मूल्य और साहित्यकार की स्थिति, यशदेव शल्य।

108. वही, पृ. 77

109. आलोचना, जनवरी-मार्च 1970, पृ. 76

110. "इतिहास ऐसी एक भी स्थिति का साक्षी नहीं है और यदि ऐसी स्थिति आ जाए तो भयंकर अराजकता के मध्य समाज ही नहीं, स्वयं व्यक्ति का भी अस्तित्व संदिग्ध हो उठे। मूल्यों की ध्वंस-क्रिया से मूल्य-हीनता की स्थिति का परिणाम निकालना वस्तुतः भ्रामक है।"—'चिंतन और अनुचिंतन', नेमनारायण जोशी, पृ. 69

111. "हमारे सभी मूल्य समाज-जनित हैं। ज्यों-ज्यों समाज बदलता है, हमारे मूल्य बदलते जाते हैं। न इंसान समाज से अलग हो पाता है और न ही कभी मूल्यहीनता की स्थिति आ पाती है।"—आलोचना, अक्टूबर-दिसंबर, 68, 'संत्रास का आतंक', पृ. 11

112. आलोचना, अक्टूबर-दिसंबर, 68, 'संत्रास का आतंक', पृ. 11

113. संक्रमण-पुं. (सं. सम/क्रम) चलना (+ल्युट-अन) (1) आगे की ओर बढ़ना। विक्रमण का विपर्याय। (2) अतिक्रमण। लाँघना। (3) घूमना-फिरना (4) एक अवस्था से धीरे-धीरे बदलते हुए दूसरी अवस्था में पहुँचना। जैसे—संक्रमण काल (5) एक के हाथ या अधिकार से दूसरे के हाथ या अधिकार में जाना। (पासिंग) (6) सूर्य का एक राशि से निकलकर दूसरी राशि में प्रवेश करना। (7) एक स्थिति पार करते हुए दूसरी स्थिति में जाना या पहुँचना। (8) कीटाणु, रोग आदि का फैलते हुए एक से दूसरे को होना।—मानक हिंदी कोश, पाँचवाँ खंड, पृ. 210

114. अनुवाक् (वर्ष 1, 1977, रांची विश्वविद्यालय), ('संक्रमण की प्रक्रिया और कविता की भूमिका'), पृ. 1

115. मानविकी पारिभाषिक कोश, सं. नगेन्द्र, 1965, पृ. 258
116. कविता और मूल्य-संक्रमण, कमलेश गुप्ता, पृ. 18
117. "आधुनिकीकरण के द्वारा मूल्य-संक्रमण की प्रक्रिया के दो पहलू स्पष्ट होते हैं। प्रथम, आधुनिकीकरण मूल्य-दृष्टि को परिवर्तित करता चलता है और दूसरे पारंपरिक मूल्य आधुनिक दृष्टि से बिल्कुल समाप्त नहीं हो जाते हैं, वे नए मूल्यों के साथ विद्यमान रहते हैं।" —संचेतना-54, 'आधुनिकता और मूल्य-संक्रमण', पुष्पपालसिंह, पृ. 23
118. संचेतना-54, पृ. 25
119. "वस्तुतः संस्कृति में संक्रांति की वजह संस्कृति का आधुनिकीकरण भी है और संस्कृति की मानवीय संदर्भों में पुनर्व्याख्या भी है। विज्ञान, तकनीकी विकास और मनुष्य की विज्ञान के प्रति संचेतनता इस पुनर्व्याख्या की दृष्टि का पूर्ण निर्माण करती है।"—आधुनिकता : साहित्य के संदर्भ में, पृ. 113-114
120. The social structure of values, R.K. Mukerjee, p. 10-11
121. सौंदर्य मूल्य और मूल्यांकन, पृ. 38
122. "औद्योगिक क्रांति के बाद उन्नीसवीं शती में समस्त यूरोप में समानता, प्रजातंत्र मानवीय अधिकारों का जो आंदोलन उठ खड़ा हुआ था, जिसके अंतर्गत स्वतंत्र चुनाव, मजदूर संगठन और सामाजिक सुधारों की जो लहर पश्चिम में चली थी उससे वे पूर्व को मुक्त रखना चाहते थे।" —पश्यंती, धर्मवीर भारती, पृ. 146
123. "सामाजिक आचरणों का निर्धारण करनेवाले ये मूल्य उच्चादर्शों की प्रतिष्ठापना की कल्पना से अभिप्रेरित थे किंतु सामाजिक उच्चादर्श भौतिक सत्य से इतने दूर थे कि कर्म और विचार दो भिन्न स्थितियाँ लगती थीं।"—आधुनिकता : साहित्य के संदर्भ में, गंगाप्रसाद विमल, पृ. 119
124. धर्मयुग, 12 मार्च 1962, परिचर्चा, 'पाप-पुण्य का सवाल और आधुनिक मानस', आयोजिका—सरोज सरुक्कै, पृ. 29
125. "प्रायः एक समुदाय का सदस्य किसी अन्य संस्कृति के मूल्यों के साथ और एक संस्कृति में पलनेवाला व्यक्ति किसी अन्य संस्कृति के मूल्यों के साथ उचित समायोजन नहीं स्थापित कर पाता। जब तक वह नए सामाजिक वातावरण के मूल्यों को स्वीकृत नहीं कर लेता, उसे मानसिक द्वंद्व का अनुभव होता रहा है।" —मानव विकास का मनोविज्ञान, पृ. 273
126. "⋯क्योंकि आचरण के नियमों का यह स्वभाव है कि वे कभी नीचे से ऊपर की ओर नहीं, ऊपर से नीचे की ओर, छोटे से बड़े की ओर नहीं, बड़े से छोटे की ओर चलते हैं। जिस समाज में सत् को दंडित और असत् को पुरस्कृत किया जाता हो, वहाँ ये सब आचार के मूल्य अगर उलट-पुलट जाएँ तो इसमें आश्चर्य की कोई बात नहीं है।"—आधुनिक भावबोध की संज्ञा, अमृतराय, पृ.67

127. अनुवाक्-1, (1977), पृ. 2
128. वही-1, पृ. 5
129. आलोचना, अप्रैल-जून 68, नैतिक मूल्य, यशदेव शल्य, पृ. 35 के आधार पर।
130. सामाजिक विचारधारा : कामू से मुखर्जी तक, रवीन्द्रनाथ मुखर्जी, पृ. 319 से उद्धृत
131. इतिहास के अद्वैतवादी दृष्टिकोण का विकास, प्लेखानेव, पृ. 251
132. समाजवाद और संस्कृति, पृ. 447
133. व्यक्ति और समाज, निगम और हेलेन, पृ. 459 के आधार पर।

द्वितीय प्रकरण

आंचलिक उपन्यास : व्यक्तिगत मूल्यों के संक्रमण का संदर्भ

मूल्य का पहला संबंध व्यक्ति से है, अतः मूल्य का एक आयाम व्यक्तिगत है। मूल्य में 'व्यक्तिगत' होने का अर्थ समाजविरोधी होना नहीं है। अंततः वे ही व्यक्तिगत मूल्य प्रधान और उल्लेखनीय होते हैं जो सामाजिक मूल्यों के पोषक होते हैं।[1] व्यक्तिगत मूल्य और व्यक्तिवादी मूल्य दो अलग चीजें हैं। रमेश कुंतल मेघ के अनुसार व्यक्तिवादी धारा के मूल्य समाजविरोधी होते हैं जबकि व्यक्तिगत मूल्यों में सामाजिक दायित्व की उपेक्षा नहीं होती। व्यक्तिगत मूल्य में सामाजिक परिष्कार से नियमित व्यक्ति मुक्त भी हो सकता है और स्वेच्छापूर्ण बंदी भी।[2] व्यक्तिगत मूल्यों से अलग होकर साहित्य, समाज और संस्कृति की कल्पना करना असंभव है। "यदि व्यक्तिगत मूल्य संस्कृति की परंपराओं से समृद्ध समाज के संबंधों से विकासशील तथा सृजन की अनगूँजों से नई कृति-वंशियों से मुखर होनेवाले मूल्य नहीं बनते तो वे व्यक्तिगत न रहकर व्यक्तिवादी धारा के पोषक होते हैं।"[3] मूल्य के व्यक्तिगत या व्यक्तिवादी होने का निर्णय सापेक्षता में होता है। प्रेम, स्वास्थ्य, व्यक्ति-स्वातंत्र्य, सौंदर्य आदि मूल्य सामाजिक मूल्यों के विरोधी होने की स्थिति में व्यक्तिवादी कहे जाते हैं। समाज-सापेक्ष व्यक्ति मूल्य 'व्यक्तिगत मूल्य' हैं।

व्यक्तिगत मूल्यों के नियामक और प्रभावक तत्त्व

व्यक्तिगत मूल्य-व्यवस्था पर विचार करते हुए गार्डनर मर्फी ने जिन चार स्तरों[4] का उल्लेख किया है, उनमें से पहले दो मनुष्य के शरीर और इंद्रिय जगत् से हैं।

'मूल्य' का अनुभव उत्तेजकों से प्राप्त तनाव और उस तनाव की संतुष्टि में है। लेकिन इस तनाव की समाप्ति का बहुत हद तक स्थाई और उत्तेजक का स्थिर होना आवश्यक है।[5] रमेश कुंतल मेघ ने व्यक्तिगत मूल्यों को 'आत्मनिष्ठा के मूल्य' मानते हुए इनके निर्माण में मूलवृत्तियों के योगदान को महत्त्वपूर्ण माना है–"इन मूल्यों के उद्‌भव में हमें मूलवृत्तियों का सक्रिय भाग भी नहीं विस्मृत कर देना चाहिए क्योंकि अभिरुचि, निष्ठा, मौलिकता के प्रेरणास्रोत वे ही हैं, उन्हीं के संवेगों या भावों से शुभ या अशुभ का संघर्ष होता है, कलाकार अपने सुख-दुख से ऊपर उठता है और युग में घुल-मिल जाता है।"[6] न केवल व्यक्तिगत अपितु सामाजिक मूल्यों के उद्‌भव में भी मूल प्रवृत्तियों का योगदान महत्त्वपूर्ण होता है। मूल्य तब तक महत्त्वपूर्ण और प्रासंगिक नहीं बनते, जब तक उनका सामाजिकीकरण नहीं हो जाता। इस तरह मुखबोध का प्रारंभ इंद्रियबोध से होता है और रचनाकार के जीवन-संघर्ष से प्राप्त अनुभवों और वैचारिकता के संयोग से वह स्थायित्व को प्राप्त होता है। कतिपय आंचलिक उपन्यासकारों के अंतःसाक्ष्य से इस तथ्य की पुष्टि होती है।

विवेकीराय ने अपनी एक रचना 'मेरा लेखक' में दिखाया है कि गरीबों की पक्षधरता के पीछे उनका स्वयं अपना अभावग्रस्त जीवन और उसके कटु अनुभव हैं। उन्होंने लिखा है–

"शायद कहानियों में मैं अधिक अभिव्यक्त हो जाता रहा। मेरी कुछ कहानियों को पढ़ने के बाद एक पाठक ने हँसी-हँसी में कहा, 'अरे यार तुम्हारे पास रजाई वगैरह ओढ़ने की सामग्री की कमी है क्या, जो तुम्हारे पात्र जाड़े में काँपते-ठिठुरते होते हैं।' में ठक् हो गया। बात सही थी।"[7]

अपने जीवन की कठिनाइयों से श्री राय का लेखन कुंठित नहीं हुआ है, बल्कि उससे उनके बोध को उत्तेजना मिलती है। पारिवारिक समस्याओं के अतिरिक्त गाँव का यथार्थ उनके मूल्यबोध के निर्माण में महत्त्वपूर्ण भूमिका निभाता है। गाँव की नियति को लेकर निराशा का भाव उनके अपने अनुभवों की देन है–"भारत के लाखों गाँवों की भाँति अभी मेरा गाँव भी बिजली और सड़क से वंचित है। ऐसे गाँवों में उक्त वस्तुओं के पहुँचने की जो वर्तमान दुर्गतिपूर्ण प्रगति है, उसे देखते हुए इक्कीसवीं सदी में कोई आशा भी नहीं। सम्प्रति इसी निराशा को लेकर, 'सोनामाटी' के बाद मैं नया उपन्यास लिख रहा हूँ।"[8] यह उपन्यास 'समर शेष है' नाम से छपा है। विवेकीराय के उपन्यासों में 'प्रेम', 'सेक्स', 'व्यक्ति स्वातंत्र्य' आदि संदर्भ मुखर नहीं है, इसका एक कारण यही है कि अपने जीवन-संघर्ष के मध्य वे अन्य बड़े सवालों और समस्याओं के जितने भयावह अनुभव उन्हें हुए, उतने प्रेम आदि के नहीं। श्री राय मार्क्सवादी नहीं हैं, लेकिन मार्क्सवादी चिंतन ने उन्हें प्रभावित किया है।[9]

फणीश्वर नाथ 'रेणु' की संस्मरणात्मक रचनाओं और उनके अपने जीवन-संघर्ष से पता चलता है कि न केवल प्रेम, यौन संबंध आदि से संबद्ध मूल्य अपितु उनका समग्र मूल्यबोध उनके विराट् और गहन अनुभवों से निर्मित हुआ है। उनकी मृत्यु के पश्चात् लतिका रेणु ने एक संस्मरण में लिखा है—"उपन्यास के पात्र प्रशांत की कल्पना, उन्होंने डॉ. प्रसूनबनर्जी (डॉ. टी.एम. बनर्जी के लड़के, जो उन दिनों हाउस सर्जन थे) के व्यक्तित्व—चलने-हँसने-बोलने के अंदाज से ली। ममता के रूप में मुझे खींचा और कमली के रूप में गाँववाली पत्नी, पद्मा जी को।"[10] अपनी एक रचना 'अपनी कथा' में रेणु ने संकेत दिया है कि प्रशांत-कमली की कहानी उनकी अपनी कहानी है।[11] फर्क बस इतना है कि वास्तविक कहानी में कमली मर जाती है और प्रशांत से उसका मिलन नहीं हो पाता।[12] रेणु की राजनीतिक प्रतिबद्धता दबी-ढँकी नहीं है। उनके समाजवादी विचारों का भी उनकी मूल्य-व्यवस्था के निर्माण में सहयोग होना स्वाभाविक है। 'सागर लहरें और मनुष्य' के लेखक उदयशंकर भट्ट ने विस्तार से बताया है कि किस तरह वे बरसोवा नामक मछुआरों की बस्ती में रहे और रुचि-अरुचि को ताक में रखकर मछुआरों के जीवन को देखा। उनके साथ नाव में समुद्र की जानलेवा यात्रा के अनुभव भी प्राप्त किए। उन्हीं के शब्दों में—"छोटी नाव, अगाध जलराशि, तेज लहरें नागिन की तरह फुँफकारती—यह सब दृश्य आज भी जब याद करता हूँ तो डर लगता है। फिर नाव में मछली की बू, मेरे दिमाग में जो बसी तो हफ्तों नहीं निकली।" उदयशंकर भट्ट ने यह दावा किया है कि इस उपन्यास के सभी पात्र उनके देखे-सुने और जाने-पहचाने हैं।[13]

रामदरश मिश्र ने अपनी आत्मकथात्मक कृतियों—'जहाँ मैं खड़ा हूँ', 'रोशनी की पगडंडियाँ', 'टूटते-बनते दिन' में उन स्थितियों, प्रेरणाओं, बाधाओं आदि का विस्तारपूर्वक बयान किया है जो उनकी जीवनयात्रा और रचनायात्रा को बराबर प्रभावित करते रहे। मिश्रजी ने अपनी आस्थामूलक दृष्टि और मानवीय मूल्यों में दृढ़ विश्वास को अपने जन्म के समय की एक घटना से जोड़कर व्यक्त किया है। उनको एक पड़ोस की महिला ने जन्म के तुरंत बाद कीड़ों से बचाया था। मिश्रजी के अनुसार—"मेरी जीवन यात्रा में कीड़े-मकोड़े भी खूब मिले लेकिन मुझे उनसे बचानेवाली शक्तियाँ भी मिलती ही गईं। कीड़े-मकोड़े तो सबको मिलते हैं, किसी न किसी को साफ ही कर जाते हैं, उनकी जिजीविषा, उनके जीवन-मूल्य सभी को चट कर जाते हैं लेकिन मुझे जिजीविषा मिली है जीवन के प्रति अगाध विश्वास, निष्ठा और मूल्य मिला है तो इसीलिए कि कीड़ों-मकोड़ों के बावजूद जीवनदायक कोई न कोई शक्ति, कोई न कोई रस मुझे देर-सबेर मिलता ही रहा है। इसलिए जीवन के प्रति आस्था को खंडित करनेवाले साहित्य में मेरी आस्था जम नहीं पाती। अपने लेखन से मैं जीवन-आस्था को जिलाए रखने की कोशिश

करता हूँ।" [14] मिश्रजी ने मार्क्सवाद के प्रति अपने रुझान की चर्चा भी की है–"यह झुकाव भी धीरे-धीरे हुआ, भीतर से हुआ, मार्क्सवाद की चेतना अंदर उतरी तब हुआ–मार्क्सवादियों के कहने से या समझाने-बुझाने से नहीं हुआ।"[15] भैरवप्रसाद गुप्त, अर्जुन अरोड़ा, पी.सी. जोशी आदि के संपर्क और सोवियत साहित्य के अध्ययन से मार्क्सवादी बने[16] और इससे उनका सोच प्रगतिशील और मानवीय होता गया। यादवेंद्र शर्मा चंद्र ने अपने एक साक्षात्कार में बताया है कि उन्हें अपने पिता को यह विश्वास दिलाने के लिए बहुत मेहनत करनी पड़ी कि ये सामंती तत्त्व बुरे लोग हैं। उन्हें सामंती उत्पीड़न का सामना भी करना पड़ा–"मैं आपको बताऊँ कि मुझे उन लोगों ने मारने की धमकी तक दे दी। आप यह सोचिए कि उन उपन्यासों की सार्थकता सामंती विरोध है।"[17] स्पष्ट है कि यादवेंद्र शर्मा 'चंद्र' की सामंत-विरोधी और जनधर्मी वैचारिकता उनके जिए हुए सत्य का ही विकास है।

इन सभी आंचलिक उपन्यासकारों के अंतःसाक्ष्य से उनके 'मूल्यबोध' और 'मूल्य-संक्रमण' को पढ़ने की अंतर्दृष्टि के निर्माण में उनके जीवन-परिवेश और कटु-मृदु अनुभवों का योगदान गौरतलब है। चाहे व्यक्तिगत मूल्यों का संदर्भ हो या सामाजिक मूल्यों का, प्रायः उपन्यासकारों के संवेगों से अशुभ और अप्रिय के संघर्ष के फलस्वरूप मूल्यों का निर्धारण हुआ है। अधिकतर उपन्यासकार अपने समय की हलचलों के न केवल साक्षी रहे हैं, अपितु उन्होंने सामाजिक-राजनीतिक गतिविधियों में सक्रिय भागेदारी भी की है। अतः उनके उपन्यासों में आए न्याय, सत्य, ईमानदारी, कर्तव्य आदि मूल्यों के अनुभव 'फर्स्टहैण्ड' तथा कमाए हुए 'सत्य' के रूप में स्वीकार किए जा सकते हैं। अधिकतर उपन्यासकारों की मूल्य-दृष्टि को माँजने में प्रगतिशील चिंतन विशेषतः समाजवादी एवं मार्क्सवादी विचारधारा ने गंभीर भूमिका निभाई है, ऐसा इन अंतःसाक्ष्यों से प्रमाणित होता है। इद्रिंयबोध, अनुभवजगत् और विचारधारा की यह संश्लिष्टता व्यक्तिगत मूल्यों के संक्रमण को पढ़ने और आँकने में किस हद तक सफल हुई है, इसका निर्णय आंचलिक उपन्यासों में व्यक्त प्रेम, सेक्स, व्यक्ति स्वातंत्र्य आदि अवधारणाओं के समग्र अनुशीलन से किया जा सकता है।

प्रणय बनाम सेक्स

(क) प्रणय : उच्चतर दिल में संक्रमण : प्रणय को आंचलिक उपन्यासों में पर्याप्त गरिमा मिली है। प्रेम केवल शारीरिक संपर्क या मानसिक लगाव मात्र नहीं। उसमें एक ऊँचाई होती है। वह देवता का वरदान या प्रसाद है।[18] इसके बिना जीवन नहीं–"फिर औरत की जिंदगी वह तो प्यार के सतरंगे इंद्रधनुष पर ही जीती है। जिस दिन उसे प्यार नहीं मिलेगा, वह या तो खत्म हो जाएगी या बाज के मुँह

में दबे पक्षी की तरह छटपटाएगी। इस दूसरी हालत में उसका अंत पास ही समझना चाहिए।"[19] 'जल टूटता हुआ' के अमलेश जी भी प्रेम की इसी दिव्यता के समर्थक हैं।[20] प्रेम को किसी प्रकार के बंधन जातिगत, वर्गगत आदि से मुक्त रखने[21] की यह दृष्टि जहाँ एक ओर 'प्लेटोनिक लव' की सीमा का संस्पर्श करती है, वहीं स्वच्छंदतावादी दृष्टिकोण के बहुत निकट पड़ती है। 'कब तक पुकारूँ' में जिस नट समाज का चित्रण है वहाँ शारीरिक पवित्रता का कोई अर्थ नहीं बचता। पुलिस और सम्पन्न वर्ग की हविश के आगे नटनी का सतीत्व या शील शेष नहीं रहता। लेकिन सुखराम-प्यारी, सुखराम-कजरी का प्रेम हर तरह की जघन्यता और अपवित्रता से ऊपर उठा हुआ है।[22] सर्वाधिक महत्त्वपूर्ण यह है कि इस प्रेम में एकाधिकार नहीं होता।[23] इसी प्रकार नरेश-चंदा का प्रेम ऊँच-नीच की मर्यादा के विरोध में खड़ा है।

'परती परिकथा' में दो पीढ़ियों के प्रणय प्रारंभ के उल्लेख से संक्रमण की उस स्थिति को उभारा गया है जिसमें 'प्रेम' साध्य न रहकर साधन बन जाता है। जितेन्द्र के पिता शिवेन्द्र मिश्र और रोज उड की प्रेम कहानी आत्मसमर्पण, एकनिष्ठ प्रगाढ़ता और परम नैकट्य के धागों से बुनी हुई है। जितेन्द्र के प्रति ताजमनी के प्रेम में समर्पण है, लगाव है, लेकिन जितेन्द्र के लिए वही सब कुछ नहीं है। यह प्रेम उसके अकेलेपन का भागीदार नहीं बन पाता क्योंकि वह इस प्रेम को 'आउट ग्रो' कर गया है।[24] उसके सामने मुख्य लक्ष्य डेढ़ हजार बीघे परती को हरा-भरा देखना है। 'प्रेम' से जुड़े संक्रमण का एक पक्ष इरावती की वासदी से उभरा है। भारत-विभाजन की विभीषिका का शिकार हुई इरावती 'प्यार' करने की ताकत खो चुकी है—"मेरे प्यार को लकवा मार गया है। दिन-रात मैं इसी चेष्टा में रहती हूँ, मेरा प्यार फिर पनपे।...इतना सब कुछ देखने और सहने के बाद किसी औरत का दिल-दिमाग प्यार करने के काबिल कैसे रह सकता है ?"[25] अभिजात वर्ग के सुवंश का हरिजन कन्या मलारी से प्रणय और परिणय न केवल रूढ़ नैतिकता को झटका देता है, अपितु 'प्रेम' को बहुत से दबावों और स्वार्थों से ऊपर उठाने की प्रासंगिकता को स्वीकारता भी है। रेणु ने 'मैला आँचल' में प्रणयगत संक्रमण को उभारा है, किंतु वह उतना खुला और स्पष्ट नहीं है जितना 'परती परिकथा में'। प्रशांत-कमली, कालीचरण-मंगला, बालदेव-लछिमी आदि युग्मों का प्रणय सपाट या साधारण नहीं है। ये सभी प्रेम के लिए कुछ न कुछ मूल्य चुकाते हैं। इनके प्रेम में मार्टिन जैसा पागलपन भले ही न हो, समर्पण का वैभव भरपूर है। ये सभी युग्म प्रणय के संदर्भ में यौन अतृप्ति से प्रगाढ़ आस्था तक का रास्ता तय करते हैं। कमला, लछिमी और मंगला अपनी दमित भावनाओं की अभिव्यक्ति के लिए उचित आलंबन पाते ही पूरी तरह समर्पित हो जाती हैं। लेकिन 'मैला आँचल' में आज के प्रेम की बदली हुई भंगिमा को पिछली पीढ़ी के प्रेम बोध के समानांतर

रखकर नहीं देखा गया है। यह काम 'परती परिकथा' अच्छी तरह करती है। 'आधा गाँव' में भी इस अंतर को दृष्टिपथ में रखा गया है। सुलेमान चा–झंगटिया बो तथा मिगदाद–सैफुनिया के युग्म 'प्रेम' के पीढ़ीगत अंतर को सामने लाते हैं। सुलेमान चा झंगटिया बो के लिए जोखिम मोल लेते हैं।[26] लेकिन प्रेम के साथ आभिजात्य का ढोंग भी बना रहता है। मजहबी सुलेमान चा पत्नी के हाथ का बना खाना नहीं खाते। मिगदाद इस तरह के ढोंग को प्रश्रय नहीं देता। उसके लिए उच्चतर मूल्य 'प्रेम' है, कुल मर्यादा और परंपरागत नैतिकता उसके लिए विशेष अर्थ नहीं रखती। सैफुनिया से ब्याह का उसका निर्णय एक 'अनहोनी'[27] से कम नहीं है। मिगदाद का कदम स्वस्थ मूल्यधर्मिता का द्योतक है। स्पष्ट है कि संक्रमण हीन मूल्यमर्यादा की स्थिति से उच्चतर मूल्य-स्थिति की ओर हुआ है।

'अलग-अलग वैतरणी' में दो पीढ़ियों के प्रेम प्रसंग यह स्पष्ट करते हैं कि समय के साथ 'प्रेम' को लेकर भावुकता का उबाल कम होता गया है। अब प्रेम एक भावुक प्रतिक्रिया के बजाय 'बौद्धिक निर्णय' अधिक हो चला है। देवपाल-राजमती का प्रसंग एक-दूसरे के लिए मर मिटनेवाले लोककथात्मक प्रेम के करीब है। दो परिवारों की दुश्मनी के बीच पनपा हुआ यह 'प्रेम' अंततः मनुष्य की नीच वृत्तियों के आगे अपना अस्तित्व नहीं बचा पाता। देवपाल और राजमती मरकर प्रेम का मोल चुकाते हैं।[28] प्रेम का यह रोमानी स्वरूप विपिन-पुष्पा के प्रणय-प्रसंग में दुहर सकता था लेकिन अन्यमनस्क विपिन 'प्रेम' को चरम मूल्य के रूप में नहीं ले पाता। 'सिर्फ दूसरों के लिए जिंदगी कुर्बान करने के लिए' अभिशप्त विपिन मन के भीतर छिपे मिथ्या प्रतिष्ठा और खानदानी बड़प्पन के डोम से हार जाता है।[29] जग्गन मिसिर ने इस सत्य को अच्छी तरह पहचाना है कि आज 'प्रेम' का अवमूल्यन हो गया है। पहले का चलन था कि जो किया उसे अंत तक स्वीकार किया जाता था।[30] आज प्रेम बैठे-ठाले का शगल हो गया। शशिकांत इस अवमूल्यन के लिए गरीबी को जिम्मेदार मानता है। चूँकि गरीबी ने व्यक्ति को बीमार बना दिया है अतः अनैतिक काम संबंधों में उसे वही तुष्टि मिलती है, जो कुत्ते को सूखी हड्डी चिचोरने पर।[31] स्पष्ट है कि आर्थिक-सामाजिक कारणों से 'प्रणय' का संक्रमण इधर-उधर के हल्के-फुलके रोमानी प्रसंगों में होता गया है। शिक्षित व्यक्ति के लिए भी 'प्रणय' में कोई गरिमा नहीं बची। 'प्रेम' के इस अवमूल्यन को नगरीय संवेदना के संदर्भ में अमृतलाल नागर ने भी 'मार्क' किया है।[32] इसका अर्थ यह हुआ कि यह अवमूल्यन बहुत व्यापक स्तर पर घटित हुआ है। लेकिन इसका यह अर्थ नहीं कि 'प्रेम' की मूल्यवत्ता खंडित हो गई है और किसी अन्य अवधारणा में उसका विलीनीकरण हो गया है। बहुत पिछड़े और असभ्य समझी जानेवाली जातियों से लेकर आधुनिकता के संघात से चौंकते अंचलों के व्यक्तियों में 'प्रेम' प्रायः एक मूल्यवान्, वस्तु भावना के रूप में ग्राह्य है।

'जंगल के फूल' में बस्तर के आदिवासियों की 'प्रेम' के प्रति निष्ठा देखी जा सकती है।[33] यह निष्ठा अतीत में भी कम नहीं थी। हिरमे-मुंदरी की प्रणय कथा यही व्यक्त करती है। समाज के नियमों को तोड़कर दोनों विवाह करते हैं।[34] नियमों और रूढ़ियों को तोड़ने का साहस 'जल टूटता हुआ' के कुंजू-बदमी, उमाकांत-शारदा में भी है। कुंजू एक झटके में गाँव, पड़ोस, जमीन वगैरह का मोह त्याग कर बदमी को अपना लेता है।[35] उमाकांत के लिए दीनदयाल की संपत्ति मूल्यवान नहीं है। मूल्य है तो केवल शारदा के प्रति पूजा के फूल जैसे पवित्र प्रेम का।[36] ये सभी उदाहरण उच्चतर मूल्य की ओर प्रयाण के साक्षी हैं। 'वरुण के बेटे' में इस प्रयाण का संदर्भ दूसरा है। वहाँ प्रेम को सामंती अय्याशी के मुकाबले समाज-सापेक्ष और पर्याप्त जिम्मेदार ठहराया गया है, "हमारा प्रेमनगर कहीं समाज से अलग या संसार से बाहर आबाद हुआ है ? सुनती हूँ बड़े आदमी जब और कामों से ऊब उठते हैं तो दिल के टुकड़े इधर-उधर फेंका करते हैं और दसियों घर बरबाद कर छोड़ते हैं··· ।"[37] इन सभी उदाहरणों में प्रणय का मूल्य न केवल कर्त्ता पक्ष में 'तथ्य' पर एक आरोपित प्रतिक्रिया है अपितु वह प्रपत्तिमूलक अवधारणा भी है, जिसे घटनाओं या अनुभवों की तुलना द्वारा प्राप्त किया गया है। 'तथ्य' के प्रति भोक्ता या गृहीता की दृष्टि पर्याप्त संतुलित और साहसिक है।

आंचलिक उपन्यासों में 'प्रेम' का जो स्वरूप उभरा है, वह परंपरा-विरोधी न होते हुए भी रूढ़ियों, वर्जनाओं और निषेधों के विरोध में है। यह न तो प्राचीन शौर्यपूर्ण प्रेम (शिवेलियर्स लव) के मेल में है और न प्रेम के उस पुराने मिथक को समर्थन देता है कि पुरुष वृक्ष है और नारी लता। प्रायः प्रेम के साथ समानता, त्याग, बलिदान, संघर्ष की अवधारणाएँ भी जुड़ी हुई हैं। आंचलिक उपन्यासकार के लिए प्रेम न केवल विचार, अपितु अनुभव और व्यवहार के स्तर पर भी मूल्यवान है। प्रेम को वह न तो 'सेक्स' तक सीमित करने के पक्ष में है, न प्रेम उसके लिए 'मिचली' की तरह घृणित और निरर्थक है। विजयमोहन सिंह का यह आरोप आंशिक तौर पर ही सत्य है कि आंचलिक उपन्यास रचनात्मक स्तर पर परंपरागत या प्रचलित प्रेम धारणा का कोई विकल्प नहीं ढूँढ़ पाए।[38] वस्तुतः अधिकतर आंचलिक उपन्यासों में प्रणय के दो या दो से अधिक 'मॉडेल' आमने-सामने रखकर प्रेम-संक्रमण के स्वरूप को रेखांकित करने के साथ-साथ प्रचलित प्रेमधारणा को चुनौती भी दी गई है। प्रशांत, मिगदाद, कुंजू, नरेश आदि के प्रणय प्रसंग हर तरह की संकीर्णता से उबरने के साक्षी हैं। वे विवाह की मर्यादा के विरोधी नहीं हैं, लेकिन विवाह पूर्व यौन-संबंध स्थापित करने में उन्हें कोई हिचक नहीं होती। उनका प्रेम 'प्लेटोनिक लव' नहीं है। सर्वाधिक महत्त्वपूर्ण है कि 'प्रेम' का आधार पाकर संबद्ध चरित्र टूटने या बिखरने से बच जाते हैं। इसके अतिरिक्त शायद ही कहीं

'प्रेम' का अमानवीयकरण होने की स्थिति आती हो। बल्कि रांगेय राघव जैसे उपन्यासकारों की धारणा है कि प्रेम ने ही उन्माद, अत्याचार और विषमता की लहरों में मनुष्यता के जहाज को बचाए रखा है—"स्त्री का प्रेम और बच्चों का प्यार इसी कठोरता में जीवित रहा है। उसने ही पुरुष का उन्माद बार-बार झुकाया है, और उसी की सहायता से विजय मिली है, और यह विषमता जो आज मानवीयता के नए मूल्यों के लिए काटी जा रही है उसका भी आधार यही है।"[39] जहाँ कहीं प्रेम 'सर्वोच्च' मूल्य के रूप में उभरा है वहाँ भी वह 'व्यक्तिगत' अधिक है, व्यक्तिवादी कम। वह कहीं भी है सामाजिक सरोकारों से सदैव संबद्ध है।

बर्ट्रेंड रसेल ने रोमांटिक प्रेम को जीवन के उल्लास का स्रोत ठहराया है।[40] रोमांटिक प्रेम के साथ यह मान्यता बद्धमूल रही है कि विवाह रोमांटिक प्रेम का परिणाम होना चाहिए। लेकिन आंचलिक उपन्यासों ने 'प्रेम' के रोमानी रूप को बहुत कुछ महत्त्व देते हुए भी उसकी अनिवार्य परिणति विवाह में नहीं मानी है। आगे हम देखेंगे कि 'विवाह' भी आंचलिक उपन्यासकारों के लिए अनिवार्य नहीं है। प्रेम में उत्कटता, कल्पना और कोमलता का बराबर समर्थन करते हुए वे जीवन की ठोस जमीन पर बराबर बने रहते हैं। रोमानी प्रेम का आनंद उनके लिए जीवन का एक अंग है, उसका मुख्य प्रयोजन कभी नहीं बनता। इस तरह प्रेम का संक्रमण पक्ष दर्शाते हुए आंचलिक उपन्यासकारों ने बहुत संतुलित मूल्यबोध का परिचय दिया है। उनका प्रणय न तो 'बंद गली के आखिरी मकान' पर ठहरा हुआ है और न 'अँधेरे बंद कमरे' तक ही सीमित है। इसमें खुलापन है, संयम है, त्याग-उत्सर्ग की तड़प है और टूटने-बिखरने के बजाय जुड़ने-जोड़ने-सँवारने की शक्ति है।

(ख) सेक्स : जैवीय आवश्यकता बनाम मानसिक-शारीरिक विलासिता : परंपरागत मूल्य दृष्टि 'प्रेम' को 'सेक्स' से अलग मानती आई है। आंचलिक उपन्यासों में प्रेम के संदर्भ में यौन-तुष्टि या संभोग को नहीं नकारा गया, लेकिन केवल यौन-तुष्टि उनका अभीष्ट कभी नहीं रही। इसके लिए प्रणय वासना का पर्याय नहीं। 'सेक्स' को एक जैवीय आवश्यकता मानते हुए भी आंचलिक उपन्यासकार यौन उच्छृंखलता को कहीं अपना समर्थन नहीं देते। स्वच्छंद यौनाचार में संलग्न चरित्रों की कटु भर्त्सना हुई है। शील और मर्यादा को महत्त्व देनेवाली परबतिया शरीर का सौदा करनेवाली युवतियों के भौतिक सुख को देखकर पथ-च्युत नहीं होती।[41] नारी के लिए 'पत' का बहुत मोल है।[42] एक षोडशी की सेक्स अपील से विचलित मौलवी बेदार सबकी भर्त्सना का आलंबन बनते हैं।[43] बुझारथ (अलग-अलग वैतरणी), बांके, लारेंस (कब तक पुकारूँ), महंत (मैला आँचल), धीरूवाला (सागर, लहरें और मनुष्य), विलियम कपूर (सूरज किरन की छाँव) आदि के कुकृत्य गलीज वासना से प्रेरित हैं और हीनतम मूल्यों का प्रतिनिधित्व करते हैं। कनिया जैसी पत्नी की उपेक्षा कर अन्य युवतियों को अपनी हविश का शिकार

बनानेवाला बुझारथ गाँव में लुच्चा और बदमाश व्यक्ति माना जाता है।[44] बलात्कार एक प्रकार का अपहरण है, क्रूर सामंती प्रवृत्ति है। बलात्कारी स्नेह के समर्पण और सहिष्णुता का अनुभव नहीं कर सकता।[45] संभोग जैवीय आवश्यकता है, पाप नहीं है, लेकिन जहाँ स्त्री का जबरन उपभोग करने की पाशविकता है, वह जघन्य है।[46] यह पाशविकता तब और गंभीर और गुरुतर अपराध बन जाती है, जब समाज को नैतिकता और धर्म का पाठ पढ़ानेवाले व्यक्ति इसमें संलग्न होते हैं। महंत सेवादास (मैला आँचल), पुजारी सर्वजीत चौबे (परती परिकथा) वासना के आगे सारा धर्म कर्म भूल जाते हैं। अपनी बेटी की तरह रखने का आश्वासन देकर भी महंत लक्ष्मी के साथ बरसों बलात्कार करता रहा।[47] पुजारी वासना विह्वल होकर अपने कथित धर्म की अवहेलना करने को तैयार होता है।[48] इस तरह के नकारात्मक मूल्यों के संवाहक व्यक्तियों के पास अपने दुराचरण के समर्थन में हास्यास्पद तर्क भी हैं जो उनकी दुहरी नैतिकता की असंगति को रेखांकित करते हैं।[49] प्रायः नारी अपनी सुरक्षा की खोज में कुछ व्यभिचारी भेड़ियों का शिकार बनती है। आर्थिक पराधीनता इस तरह की दुर्घटनाओं में महत्त्वपूर्ण भूमिका निभाती है। रत्ना[50] बंजारी[51] की विडंबनापूर्ण नियति इस संदर्भ में द्रष्टव्य है।

जहाँ संभोग केवल 'सेक्स' की भूख है, वहाँ व्यभिचार है।[52] इस बात को आंचलिक उपन्यासों ने बहुत बलपूर्वक स्थापित किया है। 'नदी फिर बह चली', 'मैला आँचल', 'कब तक पुकारूँ', 'सूरज किरन की छाँव', 'आधा गाँव', 'अलग-अलग वैतरणी', 'राग दरबारी' आदि में इस तथ्य को चिंता के साथ देखा गया है कि व्यभिचार का रोग तेजी से बढ़ रहा है। दीनदयाल (जल टूटता हुआ), सूरजसिंह, बुझारथ (अलग-अलग वैतरणी), वैद्य जी (राग दरबारी), सहदेव मिसिर (मैला आँचल), विलियम कपूर (सूरज किरन की छाँव), छंगामल, धीरूवाला (सागर लहरें और मनुष्य), चौधरी (धरती धन न अपना), शिया जमींदार (आधा गाँव) आदि यानी कि समूचा उच्चवर्ग बहुत सी स्त्रियों से यौन संबंध स्थापित करना अपना पुनीत कर्तव्य समझता है। वासना इनके लिए कुल-मर्यादा, स्वाभिमान, लोकलाज आदि से कहीं मूल्यवान है। इनकी वासना-तुष्टि प्रायः यौन-शोषण का पर्याय है।

कुछ उपन्यासकारों ने दो विरोधी मॉडल आमने-सामने रखकर 'सेक्स' से जुड़े सोच के दो सिरों को उभारा है। 'जल टूटता हुआ' में कुंजू-बदमी का सहवास सामाजिकता के विरोध में होते हुए भी एक स्वस्थ मूल्य दृष्टि की ओर प्रयाण का सूचक है जबकि दीनदयाल जैसों के गुपचुप यौन संबंध 'व्यभिचार' की हद नहीं फलाँग पाते। 'सूरज किरन की छाँव' में विलियम द्वारा छली गई बंजारी के बहकने और वासना की अंधी घाटी में खो जाने के अवसर अधिक थे, लेकिन वह कभी मन से व्यभिचार को स्वीकार न कर सकी। इसके विपरीत रूबी की मानसिकता उसे चरित्रहीन की कोटि में पहुँचा देती है। 'आधा गाँव' में अब्बास-सितारा का

संबंध मात्र सेक्स-केंद्रित है, उसके साथ किसी तरह की नैतिक जिम्मेदारी या गहरी रागात्मकता संबद्ध नहीं है। मिगदाद-सैफुनिया, सफिखा बछनिया के साहचर्य में आपसी लगाव के साथ उसे रिश्ते को स्वीकारने का साहस मौजूद है। 'मैला आँचल' की फुलिया का आचरण उसे गिरी हुई औरत करार देता है। लेकिन यही बात कमला और लक्ष्मी के संबंध में नहीं कही जा सकती। कमला और लक्ष्मी के आचरण में ठहराव है और उसका केंद्र एक व्यक्ति है। आर्थिक कारणों के बावजूद फुलिया में भ्रमर की वृत्ति है। इसी तरह उपन्यासकारों ने यौन तुष्टि को एक अराजक आचरण न मानकर उसे एकनिष्ठता, गहरे लगाव और नैतिक जिम्मेदारी से संबद्ध किया है। इनसे रहित यौन संबंध कोरी देह की भूख या विलासिता का संस्करण मात्र है। समाज में मूल्य-संक्रमण की दिशा प्रेम की शुचिता से यौन-उच्छृंखलता की ओर है लेकिन आंचलिक उपन्यासकार इस प्रवाह को उल्टी दिशा में मोड़ने के लिए उत्सुक है। वह अपने कुछ चरित्रों के माध्यम से अस्वस्थ वासना या यौन तुष्टि को नकारते हुए स्वस्थ यौन संबंधों की निर्मिति की दिशा की ओर इंगित करता है। समाज में जिस यौन-स्वच्छंदता का प्रचार बढ़ रहा है, वह कथित आधुनिक और गुमराह व्यक्तियों के लिए ही 'मूल्य' हो सकती है।

(ग) प्रेम की वैवाहिक परिणति : कुछ प्रसंगों में 'प्रेम' विवाह की समाजिक मर्यादा में परिवर्तित हुआ है। सुवंश-मलारी का प्रेम इसी प्रकार का है।[53] उमाकांत-शारदा भी विधिवत् परिणय सूत्र में बँधनेवाले हैं।[54] मिगदाद-सैफुनिया का निकाह मौलवी बेदार ने पढ़ाया है।[55] लेकिन ऐसे संदर्भ अपेक्षाकृत अधिक हैं, जहाँ प्रेम को विवाह का जामा पहनाने की आवश्यकता महसूस नहीं की गई। कुंजू-बदमी बगैर विवाह के एक साथ रहने का निर्णय करते हैं।[56] प्रशांत-कमला के संबंध को बाद में भले ही सामाजिक स्वीकृति दिला दी गई[57] वस्तुतः वहाँ विवाह की औपचारिकता का निषेध ही है। जित्तन ताजमनी भी विवाहहीन साहचर्य का उपभोग करते हैं।[58] हालाँकि सबके सामने जित्तन ने ताजमनी को 'रक्षिता' की संज्ञा दी, 'पत्नी' नहीं कहा, फिर भी ताजमनी उसकी सब कुछ है। भंडार घर की चाबी और तुलसी चौरे पर दीप जलाने का काम उसके हाथ में है। लेकिन यह सच है कि उसकी हैसियत शरत् की राज्यलक्ष्मी और चंद्रमुखी से बढ़कर नहीं है।[59] अनपढ़ आदिवासियों में भी विवाह को अनिवार्य न मानने का सोच उभर रहा है। अपनी आजादी के लिए लड़ रहे युवक के लिए पेंडुल (विवाह) बहुत महत्त्वपूर्ण नहीं है।[60] सुलक-महुआ समाज के सामने एक नई मिसाल रखते हैं—''हम अपनी जाति के ढंग से विवाह नहीं करेंगे। अनबिहाए रहकर भी हम एक रहेंगे और इस तरह घोटुल की जिंदगी भर सेवा कर सकेंगे।''[61] यहाँ प्रेय और श्रेय का सही समीकरण बिठाया गया है। बंजारी का कंगला के साथ गाँव लौटने का निर्णय[62] भी परंपरागत विवाह के विरोध में है। बंजारी का अपना कटु अनुभव है कि विवाह समाज के जड़ बंधनों

में एक है।[63] 'दूबजनम आई' की अनुराधा सामाजिक मान्यताओं को चुनौती देकर जग्गू के साथ रहने को तैयार है।[64] फुन्ननमियाँ और कुलसूम का लंबा सह-अस्तित्व साक्षी है कि लगाव और रागात्मकता से भरपूर साहचर्य के लिए विवाह की वैधानिकता अनिवार्य नहीं होती।[65] जग्गन मिसिर और उनकी भाभी का सहवास इसी किस्म का है।

ये सभी उदाहरण वे हैं, जहाँ पूरे विवेक के साथ विवाह की अनिवार्यता चुनौती दी गई है। ये युग्म विवाह की संस्था के विरोधी नहीं हैं लेकिन अपने लिए विवाह की कथित औपचारिकता को आवश्यक नहीं मानते हैं। ये निश्चय ही 'गोदान' के मालती-मेहता की परंपरा का विकास सूचित करते हैं। कुछ स्थितियों में 'प्रेम' की परिणति विवाह में इसलिए नहीं हो पाती कि सामाजिक मूल्य और पुरातन रूढ़ियाँ बहुत सशक्त सिद्ध होती हैं। संबद्ध चरित्र मूल्य-संघर्ष की प्रक्रिया से गुजरते हैं, लेकिन लक्ष्मण रेखा का उल्लंघन नहीं कर पाते और चाह कर भी अपने मन का चाहा नहीं कर पाते। पुष्पा-विपिन (अलग-अलग वैतरणी) और नरेश-चंदा (कब तक पुकारूँ) के प्रेम-प्रसंग इसी प्रकार के हैं। विपिन की कायरता पुष्पा को दूसरे की अर्द्धांगिनी बना देता है। नरेश-चंदा के मिलन में थोथी कुलमर्यादा और आभिजात्य का दंभ बाधक है। जो समाज के रूढ़ सोच की दृष्टि से 'श्रेय' है, 'प्रणय' अर्थात् प्रेय उसके विरोध में पड़ता है। विपिन के लिए 'प्रेम' मूल्य नहीं है, नरेश-चंदा के लिए बेहद मूल्यवान। नरेश का विक्षिप्त होना इस बात का प्रमाण है कि वह समाज-स्वीकृत मर्यादाओं से तालमेल नहीं बिठा पाता।

चूँकि आंचलिक उपन्यासकार वैवाहिक विधिविधान को अनिवार्य नहीं मानता, अतः उसके लिए 'विवाह-विच्छेद' का प्रश्न बहुत महत्त्वपूर्ण नहीं रह जाता। यही वजह है कि विवाह-विच्छेद के प्रसंग आंचलिक उपन्यासों में कम हैं। विवाह हो जाने के बाद आपसी लगाव, एकनिष्ठता, सतीत्व आदि को प्रायः स्वीकारा गया है। पति की निरंकुशता आदि कारणों से क्षुब्ध नारी बहुत अनिवार्य होने पर ही विच्छेद की ओर बढ़ती है।

व्यक्ति-स्वातंत्र्य की चेतना और सामूहिक मुक्ति

स्वतंत्रता एक आधारभूत मानव मूल्य है। स्वतंत्रता शून्य में प्रतिष्ठित नहीं होती। कुछ विचारक स्वतंत्रता को व्यक्ति केंद्रित मानते हुए भी उसे व्यक्ति तक सीमित नहीं मानते।[66] वे उच्चावच क्रम के अनुसार व्यक्ति को समाज और व्यवस्था की तुलना में अधिक गौरव देते हैं।[67] मूल्यों के संदर्भ में व्यक्ति समाज की परस्थरता के समीकरण की व्याख्या करते हुए वात्स्यायन ने बल दिया है कि मूल्यों की अवधारणा व्यक्ति करता है और उन मूल्यों के अनुरूप सामाजिक आचरण का

नियमन, मूल्यांकन और संशोधन समाज के जिम्मे रहता है।[68] इस तरह स्वतंत्रता के धरातल पर मूल्य-संक्रमण व्यक्ति की इच्छा से सामाजिक स्वीकृति की दिशा में होता है। बहुत से समाजवादी विचारक व्यक्ति को आत्यंतिक महत्त्व देने के पक्ष में नहीं हैं। हालाँकि व्यक्ति-स्वातंत्र्य में दायित्व का आंतरिक विकासोन्मुख[69] माना गया है, फिर भी इस तरह का चरम स्वातंत्र्य एक अतिवाद है।[70] लेनिन ने यदि इसे पूँजीवादी मुहावरा कहा है तो यह बहुत कुछ सही है।[71] यह कहना सतही तौर पर ही सच है कि जीवन में अपने चुनाव से अलग मूल्यवान कुछ और नहीं है।[72]

आंचलिक उपन्यासों में व्यक्ति-स्वातंत्र्य का समर्थन बहुत सीमित और सशर्त है। 'कब तक पुकारूँ' में उस स्वतंत्रता को जीवन की शक्ति माना गया है, जो दूसरों को कुचलती नहीं है।[73] जाहिर है, यह स्वतंत्रता 'व्यक्ति' तक सीमित नहीं होगी। रांगेय राघव ने इस विडंबना को भी व्यक्त किया है कि चरम स्वातंत्र्य को भोगने की आकांक्षा अंततः स्वतंत्रता के अपहरण में सहायक होती है 'हमने ही अपनी स्वतंत्रता को मिटाया है, ताकि हम अपनी स्वतंत्रता को भोग सकें।'[74] इस सत्य को 'अलग-अलग वैतरणी' में भी रेखांकित किया गया है कि निरंकुश स्वतंत्रता उसी तरह खतरनाक होती है, जिस तरह बंदर के हाथ में चाकू।[75] केवल व्यक्ति की स्वतंत्रता या चरम-स्वातंत्र्य की माँग बेमानी ठहरती है। इसीलिए कुछ उपन्यासकारों ने व्यक्ति की स्वतंत्रता को उसके वर्ग की आजादी से जोड़ दिया है। 'बलचनमा' के लिए आजादी का अर्थ किसान की आजादी है।[76] जिसके लिए जिंदगी जैसी अनमोल चीज भी कुर्बान की जा सकती है। अधिकतर आंचलिक उपन्यासों में एक की मुक्ति के स्थान पर सबकी मुक्ति का आह्वान मुखर हुआ है। 'गंगा मैया' में सत्ताविहीन और शोषणमुक्त समाज की स्थापना का यूटोपिया इस अर्थ में प्रासंगिक है। स्वतंत्रता शोषणमुक्ति का पर्याय बन गई है। अब शोषित जन इस जुए को उतार फेंकने के लिए कृत संकल्प हैं।[77] 'सागर लहरें और मनुष्य' तथा 'सूरज किरन की छाँव' में व्यक्ति की स्वतंत्रता नारी-स्वातंत्र्य के व्यापक प्रश्न से जुड़ी हुई है। रत्ना की मुक्ति केवल माणिक नहीं अपितु समूची पुरुष प्रधान व्यवस्था के गुंजलक से मुक्त होने की दिशा में है।[78] बंजारी का यह सोच यथार्थ के मेल में है कि इस दुनिया में औरत बनना सबसे बड़ा पाप है। औरत को 'मनुष्य' भी नहीं समझा जाता।[79] कपूर की 'जेल' में बंजारी को 'सरकस के सिखाए जानवरों की तरह'[80] अपनी इच्छा के विरुद्ध कुकर्म करने पड़ते हैं। 'जंगल के फूल' में साम्राज्यवादी विस्तारवाद के विरुद्ध आदिवासियों के मुक्ति-अभियान को मूर्त्त रूप दिया गया था। 'सूरज किरन की छाँव' में भी बंजारी की स्वतंत्रता सबकी मुक्ति के साथ जुड़ी हुई है।[81] यह मुक्ति-चेतना व्यक्ति, वर्ग से भी आगे बढ़कर मानव मात्र की स्वाधीनता से जुड़ जाती है। विध्वंसक, संहारात्मक और पाशविक शक्तियों

के प्रकोप से मानवता कराह रही है। लेकिन हिंसा और संहार का यह अँधेरा हमेशा नहीं रहेगा। मनुष्य प्रचंड शक्तिशाली बमों से आक्रांत नहीं हो सकता।[82] बंजारी की तरह प्रशांत (मैला आँचल) भी गाँव से जुड़ता है। वह आँसू से भीगी धरती पर प्यार की खेती करना चाहता है।[83] तभी अज्ञान, फूट और घृणा में फँसा मनुष्यत्व उबरेगा शोषण की बरसात रुकेगी–''मानवता पर से यह बरसात एक दिन अवश्य दूर होगी और तब नई शरद में नए फूल खिलेंगे···।''[84]

आंचलिक उपन्यासों में सामाजिक प्रतिमानों के विरुद्ध व्यक्ति की अभिरुचि को वहीं समर्थन दिया गया है, जहाँ व्यक्ति की प्रगति और विकास में बाधा आने की संभावना लगती है। अनुराधा-गोबिन (सोनभद्र की राधा), कुंजू-बदमी (जल टूटता हुआ), मिगदाद-सैफुनिया (आधा गाँव) आदि के विवाह व्यक्तिगत निर्णय हैं और रूढ़ियों के विरोध में पड़ते हैं। 'कथा कहो उर्वशी' में सोना का रासलीला में राधा बनना कुल मर्यादा के मूल्य को चुनौती देता है और वह अंततः अपने चुनाव की स्वतंत्रता पर अडिग रहती है।[85] 'दूब जनम आई' की विधवा अनुराधा जग्गू के पास बिना विवाह के रहने को प्रस्तुत है, हालाँकि उसे मालूम है कि समाज इस अनहोनी को नहीं स्वीकारेगा।[86]

यह आकस्मिक नहीं कि व्यक्ति-स्वातंत्र्य की चर्चा आंचलिक उपन्यासकारों ने प्रायः नारी-मुक्ति के संदर्भ में की है। वस्तुतः आज भी नारी सर्वाधिक शोषित वर्ग है। जो केवल नारी होने के कारण अत्याचार का शिकार होना पड़ता है।[87] इसीलिए रामविलास शर्मा जैसे विचारक नारी की गुलामी को महज नारी की समस्या तक सीमित न रखकर वर्ग संघर्ष की समस्या के रूप में देखने के हामी हैं।[88] नारी के व्याज से आंचलिक उपन्यासकारों ने प्रायः समूचे दलित-शोषित वर्ग की मुक्ति का आह्वान किया है। 'सागर लहरें और मनुष्य' की 'रत्ना' की नियति इस संदर्भ में द्रष्टव्य है।[89] 'सोना माटी' में 'कोइली' और 'सुनरी' के माध्यम से यही व्यंजित किया गया है कि नारी सबके लिए नरम चारा है, शोषण का सर्वाधिक आसान शिकार है। कभी बाली, कभी साड़ी का प्रलोभन देकर सुनरी जैसी नारियों का शीलहरण संपन्न वर्ग के लिए खिलवाड़ है। इस यौन-शोषण से मुक्ति के लिए सुनरी को आत्मघात के अलावा और कोई मार्ग नहीं जँचता।[90] कोइली की व्यथा अलग है। वह बार-बार बेची जाती है। बेटी कहनेवाले लोग उसके साथ मुँह काला करते हैं।[91] आखिर वह एक वृद्ध के साथ अपने को हमेशा के लिए बाँध लेती है–''अब यही हमारा सासुर है और यही हमारा गंगा नैहर है।''[92] कोइली का यह निर्णय विवशताजन्य होते हुए भी लीक से हटकर है। न तो वह आत्महत्या करती है और न वह सबके यौन-शोषण का शिकार बनने को तैयार है। 'ग्रामदेवता' में किशोरी को निमित्त बनाकर नारी के शोषण का अमानवीय रूप दर्शाया गया है। गाँव की नारी-स्वतंत्रता की प्रतीक 'किशोरी' आखिर में पागल हो जाती है।

गर्भवती किशोरी को उसका सगा भाई आश्रय नहीं देता। वह भाई जो स्वयं भी व्यभिचार के आरोप में पकड़ा जा चुका है। उसके साथ पकड़ी गई लड़की पुरुषों के नैतिकता संबंधी दुहरे प्रतिमानों की पोल करारे शब्दों में खोल देती है। अपने पिता से उसका दो-टूक कथन है–"खबरदार जो हाथ उठाया। चुपचाप चले जाओ, नहीं तो इसी दम कस्बे से चिल्लाकर कहूँगी कि मेरे भाई को पढ़ने के बहाने शहर भेजकर अपनी पतोहू के साथ रंगरेलियाँ मनाते हो।"[93] लेकिन छुटपुट आक्रोश-प्रदर्शन के बावजूद नारी की वरण की स्वतंत्रता का प्रश्न इन उपन्यासों में सामूहिक आक्रोश बनकर नहीं उभरा है। वैसे मूल्य-संक्रमण की दिशा नारी की निजी स्वतंत्रता से समूची नारी जाति की आजादी की तड़प की ओर प्रवाहमान है। सर्वाधिक महत्त्वपूर्ण यह है कि वरण की स्वतंत्रता या व्यक्ति स्वातंत्र्य की माँग नारी की उच्छृंखलता या देहभोग की आजादी का रूप लेते नहीं दिखाई गई है। 'सागर लहरें और मनुष्य' में वंशी का विट्ठल को पीटना[94] श्रमजीवी समाज में एक नए मूल्य की ओर संकेत है, जो पुरुष की परंपरागत निरंकुशता के अधिकार के पक्ष विरोध में उगा है। रत्ना भी मातृसंस्कारों के आधार पर अपने मार्ग का चुनाव स्वयं करती है। "रत्ना की स्वतंत्र चेतना उसे ठोंक-पीटकर माणिक के विरुद्ध खड़ा करती है अंततः पूँजीवाद के प्रति विद्रोह की शिथिल भंगिमा में वह माणिक का त्याग करती है।"[95] 'कब तक पुकारूँ' में प्यारी और कजरी को अंग्रेज कन्या सूसन की अपेक्षा अधिक वरण की स्वतंत्रता प्राप्त है। बलात्कार का शिकार होकर निर्दोष सूसन को यह आजादी नहीं प्राप्त है कि वह अपने बच्चे को जन्म दे सके और पाले। इस दृष्टि से कसट जाति की कजरी अधिक उन्मुक्त है। वह अनजाने ही शिक्षित और पाश्चात्य नारी की कथित स्वतंत्रता पर प्रश्नचिह्न लगा देती है–"पर यह भी क्या दुनिया है। इतना सब कुछ है, पर फिर भी आपको आजादी नहीं, आपके लिए तो सब कुछ होकर भी नहीं के बराबर है।"[96] भारत के उच्च वर्ग की महिलाओं की स्थिति और भी दयनीय है।[97] 'गंगा मैया' में वैधव्य के संदर्भ में उनकी पराधीनता वर्णित है।[98] नगरबोध के उपन्यासों में एक विशिष्ट प्रकार की आधुनिक दृष्टि नारी के संभोग की स्वतंत्रता में ही मुक्ति मानती है, लेकिन 'कब तक पुकारूँ' में इस तरह की स्वतंत्रता को पाशविकता करार दिया गया है–"वह सतीत्व को रूढ़ि से तोड़कर अलग करते समय जब नारी को मुक्त कर रहा था, तब वह भूल गया था कि संभोग अपने आप में भले ही पाप नहीं हो, किंतु स्त्री को पशु बनाकर उसका भोग करने की प्रवृत्ति पाशविकता ही है और जघन्य है क्योंकि वह स्त्री को समान स्वतंत्रता देना नहीं है, वरन् उसे दासी से भी बदतर बना देना है।"[99] 'नदी फिर बह चली' की परबतिया श्रमजीवी है और वह अपनी सीमाओं के बावजूद गलीज शर्तों पर समझौता प्रायः नहीं करती है। इन उपन्यासों से स्पष्ट है कि जिन वर्गों और जातियों में नारियाँ कर्मक्षेत्र में सक्रिय हैं, अपने पैरों पर खड़ी हो रही हैं, वहाँ

उन्हें वरण की स्वतंत्रता अधिक मिली हुई है।

कुछ विचारकों ने व्यक्ति-स्वातंत्र्य की उपलब्धि न होने की स्थिति में व्यक्ति के अजनबी, अकेले और आत्मनिर्वासित होने की चर्चा की है और इन नकारात्मक पहलुओं को 'मूल्य' के स्तर पर प्रतिष्ठित करना चाहा है। वस्तुतः अजनबीपन और अकेलापन मूल्य-बोध की स्थितियाँ या मनःस्थितियाँ अधिक हैं, इन्हें 'मूल्य' नहीं कहा जा सकता है। अजनबीपन की अस्तित्ववादी धारणा के अनुसार, समूह में व्यक्तिगत अस्तित्व का लोप निंदनीय है। ऐसी स्थिति में व्यक्ति एक पदार्थ या वस्तु हो जाता है तथा अपनी निजता खो बैठता है। कॉलिन विल्सन ने इसे एक सामाजिक समस्या माना है। कार्ल मार्क्स ने इसे अजनबी श्रम की समस्या से संबद्ध किया है और इसे एक आर्थिक विसंगति के रूप में व्याख्यायित किया।[100] 'लोहे के पंख', 'बलचनमा', 'गंगा मैया' आदि कुछ उपन्यासों में मार्क्स द्वारा व्याख्यायित श्रम संबंधी अजनबीपन की आंशिक अनुभूति व्यक्त हुई है। आंचलिक उपन्यासों में स्वतंत्रता परवर्ती मोह भंग से जुड़ा अजनबीपन और अकेलेपन का बोध उभरा है। 'बावनदास' (मैला आँचल), 'जित्तन' (परती परिकथा), 'सतीश' (जल टूटता हुआ) 'रामरूप' (सोना माटी), 'हरखू' (ग्राम देवता), 'हकीम साहब' (आधा गाँव), 'जग्गू मिसिर, विपिन' (अलग-अलग वैतरणी) आदि चरित्र अपने-अपने अकेलेपन में टूट रहे हैं। आंचलिक उपन्यासकारों ने 'अजनबीपन' को वैभव के रूप में प्रस्तुत न कर त्रासदी के रूप में रेखांकित किया है।

यह द्रष्टव्य है कि कुछ आंचलिक उपन्यासों में देशी किस्म का अकेलापन और अजनबीपन वर्णित है। इस तरह के बोध के अंकन में न अस्तित्ववादी सूत्रों की सहायता ली गई है, न मार्क्सवादी उपपत्तियों का कोई योगदान है। यह बोध पिछड़े हुए ग्रामांचल की परिस्थितियों के प्रत्यक्ष अनुभव से जन्मा है। कई उपन्यासों के सकारात्मक चरित्र स्वयं को आपाधापी और मूल्य-विघटन के इस माहौल में 'मिसफिट' पाते हैं और निरंतर अकेले होते चले जाते हैं। प्रायः ऐसे संवेदनशील चरित्रों की यह विवशता है कि वे गलत बातों या अवमूल्यों से समझौता नहीं कर पाते हैं। अतः गाँव को छोड़ जाना उनकी अंतिम परिणति है। उनका ग्रामांचल को छोड़ने का निर्णय उनकी नहीं, मानवीय मूल्यों की पराजय है और नास्ति मूल्यों के वर्चस् की सूचना भी।

'मैला आँचल' में बावनदास और कालीचरन कतिपय सकारात्मक मूल्यों के लिए संघर्षरत है। न केवल गाँव अपितु पार्टी, शहर और यहाँ तक कि पूरे देश में 'स्वार्थ' का सर्वोच्च मूल्य के रूप में स्थापित हो जाने से उनका त्याग, संघर्ष और ईमानदारी उपेक्षित होते हैं। कालीचरन अपराध की दुनिया की ओर धकेल दिया जाता है और बावनदास का अंत बहुत करुण होता है। 'सब चौपट हो गया' की पीड़ा लिए बावनदास प्राणपण से बेईमानी और अन्याय रोकना चाहते हैं और

तस्करों द्वारा मार दिए जाते हैं।[101] बावनदास का अंत गांधीवादी मूल्यों की अप्रासंगिकता की आहट देता है। 'अलग-अलग वैतरणी' के विपिन और देवनाथ, 'रागदरबारी' के रंगनाथ, 'सत्ती मैया का चौरा' के मन्ने के साथ बावनदास जैसा हादसा तो नहीं होता, लेकिन ये सब अपने परिवेश की भद्दगियों से त्रस्त होकर पलायन करने को विवश होते हैं। 'जल टूटता हुआ' का सतीश और 'सोनामाटी' का रामरूप हालाँकि गाँव नहीं छोड़ते, लेकिन वे बराबर हाशिए पर कटे हुए हैं, उस परिवेश से निराश, हताश और स्तब्ध। दूसरों की दृष्टि में वे सनकी से कम नहीं हैं क्योंकि वे कतिपय मूल्यों के लिए संघर्षरत हैं, आसानी से समझौता नहीं कर पाते हैं। सतीश 'सत्य' और 'न्याय' की रक्षा के लिए कृत संकल्प है, लेकिन वह एकदम अकेला रह जाता है। भ्रष्ट शक्तियों के समीकरण भारी पड़ते हैं।[102] उपन्यासकार ने दर्शाया है कि गाँव का अकेलापन शहर के कथित अकेलेपन से कहीं अधिक जटिल और भयावह है। अनजान राय के अनुसार "शहरों में अकेले रहकर आप चैन की साँस तो ले सकते हैं, वहाँ अकेलेपन के तमाम साथी हैं। वहाँ तो आप अकेले हैं मगर चाहकर भी अकेले नहीं रह सकते, न सार्वजनिकता का सुख है यहाँ, न अकेलेपन का। कोई सहायता नहीं करता लेकिन आपके अकेलेपन को छोड़ने के लिए अनेक आलोचनाएँ, गालियाँ, शिकायतें और आक्रामक कार्यवाइयाँ टूट पड़ती हैं...।[103] यह कथन न केवल सतीश अपितु रामरूप (सोनामाटी) पर भी मौजूद है। रामरूप के अकेले पड़ते जाने के कारण गाँव में सिद्धांतविहीन राजनीति का प्रसार है। उपन्यासकार ने चुनावों को ध्यान में रखकर इस कटु सत्य को रेखांकित किया है कि लोकतंत्र ने और कुछ दिया हो या नहीं, 'अलगाव' [104] के सारे सामान जुटा दिए हैं। भुवनेश्वर के चुनाव के समय रामरूप अपने घर में भी अकेला अनुभव करता है—"क्या रामरूप अपने ही घर में दूध की मक्खी की भाँति निकालकर फेंक दिया गया ? परम अवांछित अनावश्यक व्यक्ति बन गया ? क्यों ऐसा हुआ ? कैसे ऐसा हो गया ?"[105] रामरूप गाँव जवार और अपने स्कूल में भी अकेला ही है। उसकी संवेदनशीलता और कुछ मूल्यों की पक्षधरता उसे आज के स्वार्थी और तिकड़मी परिवेश में उपेक्षित बना देती है। लेकिन आंचलिक उपन्यासकारों ने सतीश, रामरूप आदि को हताश एवं एकदम परास्त नहीं दिखाया है। वे गाँव छोड़कर भागते भी नहीं हैं। इससे स्पष्ट है कि उनका अकेलापन 'सत्य', 'साहस', 'न्याय' 'ईमानदारी' आदि कुछ स्वस्थ मूल्यों से संबद्ध है। लेकिन यही बात 'आधा गाँव' के भूतपूर्व जमींदारों के अकेलेपन के विषय में नहीं कही जा सकती है। यह अकेलापन शोषण, विलास आदि सामंती मूल्यों के प्रति मोह से ग्रस्त है सबकी आलमे तनहाई अपनी है। ऐसी तनहाई कि सपने भी दुश्वार हो गए।[106]

नैतिक मूल्यों का बदलता संसार

नैतिकता के दो रूप बताए गए हैं[107]--कर्तव्यपालन (ड्यूटी) और साधुता (वरच्यू) कर्तव्य पालन से जुड़े नैतिक व्यवहार का अर्थ 'सभ्य व्यवहार' है और इस दृष्टि से नैतिकता का स्थान सामाजिक प्रथाओं, नियमों और जीवन के साधनों में होता है। साधुता से संबद्ध नैतिकता एक तरह से व्यक्तिगत नैतिकता है। व्यक्तिगत नैतिकता के अंतर्गत सच्चाई, ईमानदारी, स्वार्थहीनता आदि के साथ यौन-शुचिता का समावेश किया जा सकता है।

नैतिकता के समाजव्यापी अवमूल्यन के संदर्भ में 'रागदरबारी' के गंगादीन की नेक सलाह है—"नैतिकता का नाम न लो मास्टर साहब, किसी ने सुन लिया तो चालान कर देगा।"[108] वह नैतिकता के स्वार्थ संकुल और सुविधानुसार परिवर्तित होनेवाले रूप[109] पर व्यंग्य करता है। आंचलिक उपन्यासकार नैतिकता के अवमूल्यन से न केवल चिंतित हैं, अपितु नैतिक मूल्यों को महत्त्व भी देते हैं।[110] नैतिकता में गिरावट का मुख्य कारण देशव्यापी भ्रष्टता और मूल्य मूढ़ता है। सभी स्तरों पर उच्च मूल्यों से हीन मूल्यों की दिशा में संक्रमण हुआ है। व्यक्ति की नैतिकता में गिरावट का एक पहलू यह है कि 'स्वार्थ' जबर्दस्त मूल्य बनकर उभरा है। ऐसा नहीं है कि यह स्वार्थभावना नई है। हमेशा इसे महत्त्व दिया गया है। धौली गाँव (उड़ीसा) के बड़े-बूढ़े मानते आए हैं—"चोरी, चुगली और व्यभिचार से बचे रहो तो मामला ठीक है। बाकी स्वार्थ के लिए तो खुली छुट्टी है।"[111] 'देहाती दुनिया' में बूढ़ी पीढ़ी की प्रतीक नानी 'स्वार्थ' को जीवनमूल्य के रूप में प्रतिष्ठित करती है।[112] वैद्यजी (राग दरबारी), दीनदयाल (जल टूटता हुआ), हनुमान प्रसाद (सोना माटी) आदि चरित्र स्वार्थपरता की प्रतिमूर्ति हैं। गरीबों की संपत्ति हो या सरकारी अनुदान सब इन लोगों की लिप्सा में होम होते रहते हैं। 'स्वार्थ' इनके लिए इतना प्रमुख हो जाता है कि नजदीकी रिश्ते भी बेमानी हो जाते हैं। वैद्यजी अपने बेटे रुप्पन और हनुमान प्रसाद अपने दामाद रामरूप को भी अपमानित करने में पीछे नहीं रहते। 'स्वार्थ' जैसे हीनतम मूल्य को स्वीकारने का रोग कुछ विशिष्ट व्यक्तियों तक ही सीमित नहीं है। समूचा ग्रामांचल इसकी पकड़ में है। औसत बुद्धिजीवी भी इससे बचा नहीं है।[113]

व्यापक स्वार्थपरता के माहौल में 'सत्य', 'ईमानदारी' और परहित यदि कुछ व्यक्तियों तक सीमित रह गए हैं तो यह आश्चर्य का विषय नहीं है। उपन्यासकारों ने विरल होते जा रहे इन मूल्यों को अपना भरपूर समर्थन दिया है।

आंचलिक उपन्यासों में 'सत्य' को सूर्य कहा गया है। धन का गर्व रखनेवाले, स्वार्थ और अहंकार में मदमस्त लोग इसके आलोक को सह नहीं पाते।[114] सत्य के लिए मूल्य चुकाना पड़ता है। लेकिन किसी एक के मूल्य चुकाने का कोई अर्थ

नहीं। सबको संगठित होकर 'सत्य' की रक्षा करनी पड़ेगी।[115] सत्य, बुद्धि, प्रेम, समता आदि ईश्वर के प्रतिरूप हैं।[116] सत्य की रक्षा से जुड़ी ईमानदारी भी एक धनात्मक मूल्य है। 'जल टूटता हुआ' में अनजानराय और 'दूब जनम आई' में रामपाल ईमानदारी को मूल्य चुकाते हैं। अनजानराय बेईमानी से समझौता न कर त्यागपत्र दे देता है और रामपाल अपने स्थानान्तरण पर दुखी नहीं होता।[117] रामपाल के विचार में–"मैंने आज तक ऐसा कोई काम नहीं किया, जिसके लिए मुझे ग्लानि हो...अच्छी राह कभी सुखद नहीं होती। नया काम भयंकर विरोध झेलने के बाद ही शुरू किया जा सकता है।"[118] बेईमानी के गले तक डूबे हुए लोग भी ईमानदारी के मूल्य को स्वीकार करते हैं। वास्तविकता को नकार नहीं पाते।[119]

'स्वार्थ' के स्थान पर–'परहित' के मूल्य को आंचलिक उपन्यासों में बलपूर्वक स्थापित किया गया है। 'परमार्थ' मानव जीवन का पुण्य है।[120] परहित के लिए जीना ही वास्तविक जीवन है।[121] मटरू (गंगा मैया), प्रशांत (मैला आँचल), सुखराम (कब तक पुकारूँ), 'बलचनमा' (बलचनमा) आदि चरित्र इस मूल्यबोध को व्यवहार में परिणत करते दिखाई देते हैं। प्रशांत का कहना है–"मैं साधना करूँगा, ग्रामवासिनी भारतमाता के मैले आँचल तले। कम से कम एक ही गाँव के कुछ प्राणियों के मुरझाए ओठों पर मुस्कराहट लौटा सकूँ, उनके हृदय में आशा और विश्वास को प्रतिष्ठित कर सकूँ...।[122] 'कब तक पुकारूँ' का गोरखी माली की जान बचाने के एवज में कुछ नहीं लेता। वह पैसे को अपनी विद्या की कीमत नहीं मानता। इसकी तुलना में पश्चिम का व्यवसायी और स्वार्थी दृष्टिकोण सूसन को बहुत तुच्छ लगता है–"वह गरीब माली था। उसने इनाम लेने से इनकार कर दिया। यदि यूरोप में किसी को यह दवा मालूम होती तो वह इसे पेटेण्ट करवा लेता, लाखों कमा लेता, दुनिया में नाम कर लेता।"[123]

यौन नैतिकता के संदर्भ में आंचलिक उपन्यासकारों का मूल्यबोध एकांगी नहीं है। आज कथित आधुनिकता से प्रेरित प्रभावित विचारकों और बुद्धिजीवियों को यौन-उच्छृंखलता प्रगतिशीलता का प्रमाण लगती है। यशदेव शल्य के अनुसार–"आज बहुत से लोग यौन नैतिकता को पिछड़ेपन का पर्याय मानते हैं और यौनवृत्तिता को उचित और प्रगति का पर्याय मानते हैं। ये मूल्य-परिवर्तन नहीं हैं, मूल्य-विपर्यय हैं अथवा कहें मूल्यबोध हैं।"[124] आंचलिक उपन्यासकार इस मूल्य-विपर्यय को 'मूल्य' के रूप में स्थापित नहीं करते। 'बंजारी' (सूरज किरन की छाँव), 'मिगदाद-सैफुनिया' (आधा गाँव), 'कुंजू-बदमी' (जल टूटता हुआ) आदि अनेक पात्र परंपरागत यौन नैतिकता का उल्लंघन करते हैं लेकिन यौन स्वच्छंदता के हामी नहीं हैं। आंचलिक उपन्यासकारों ने स्वयं को पिछड़ा घोषित किए जाने का जोखिम उठाकर भी देह-संबंधों से जुड़ी यौनशुचिता, एकनिष्ठता आदि का समर्थन किया है। जहाँ देह-शुचिता का उल्लंघन है, वहाँ भी 'भोग' या व्यभिचार

की मनःस्थिति नहीं है। वहाँ किसी न किसी सामाजिक रूढ़ि को चुनौती देने का भाव प्रमुख है। प्रायः ऐसी स्थिति में नैतिक अहं (सुपर इगो) कौमार्य या सतीत्व के खंडन का विरोधी होता है लेकिन अंततः संवेगशीलता और तर्क का गँठजोड़ उन्हें नया कदम उठाने के लिए बाध्य कर देता है। इस तरह स्पष्ट है कि यौनवर्जनाओं और यौन नैतिकता का उल्लंघन आंचलिक उपन्यासों में सशर्त है और अपेक्षा है कि नैतिक मूल्यों का संक्रमण उच्चतर स्थितियों की ओर हो।

संदर्भ

1. ''...अंततः वे व्यक्ति मूल्य ही प्रधान हैं, जो समाज के मूल्य के विरोधी न होकर उनके पोषक हों। वे ही सच्चे मानवीय मूल्य हैं।'' –प्रभाकर माचवे, हिंदी साहित्य कोश, पृ. 605
2. हिंदुस्तानी (त्रैमासिक), भाग-29, अंक 1-4, लेख 'मूल्य स्तबक की वैयक्तिकता और परस्पर स्पर्धा', पृ. 184
3. वही, पृ. 185
4. The frontiers of social sciences, Ed. B. Singh, p. 191
5. The social structure of values, p. 72
6. सौंदर्य मूल्य और मूल्यांकन, पृ. 10
7. आम रास्ता नहीं है, पृ. 97
8. वही, पृ. 99
9. वही, पृ. 100
10. रेणु स्मृति तीर्थ स्मारिका 1987, पृ. 46
11. एक श्रावणी दोपहर की धूप, पृ. 46
12. वही, पृ. 42
13. उदयशंकर भट्ट : व्यक्ति और साहित्यकार, पृ. 144
14. जहाँ मैं खड़ा हूँ, पृ. 7-8
15. रोशनी की पगडंडियाँ, पृ. 147
16. मार्क्सवाद दर्शन संस्कृति और साहित्य, सं. अरुण माहेश्वरी, पृ. 256
17. नवीन दुनिया, 12-8-1990
18. ''...प्यार एक वरदान है। वह एक देवता के मंदिर का ऐसा अनोखा प्रसाद है, जो साधक को ही मिलता है। वह प्रसाद पाना सबकी बिसात नहीं।''–सूरज किरन की छाँव, पृ. 97
19. वही
20. ''प्रेम ब्रह्म के अखिल आनंद का रहस्य है...जिसके अंतर में प्रकाश नहीं हुआ वह

हतभाग्य मनुष्य सृष्टि के अंधकार में छटपटाता हुआ अपदार्थ वस्तु ही तो है।" –जल टूटता हुआ, पृ. 284

21. वही
22. "...जहाँ संभोग नारी पर बलात्कार नहीं रहता, सृष्टि के सृजन के पवित्र और महान् कार्य का पर्याय हो जाता है, जहाँ प्रेम और वात्सल्य का उत्तरदायित्व पुरुष और नारी साथ-साथ उठाते हैं और फिर कोई जघन्यता नहीं बच रहती।"–कब तक पुकारूँ, पृ. 418
23. आधुनिक हिंदी उपन्यास (सं. नरेन्द्र मोहन), विश्वंभरनाथ उपाध्याय, पृ.175
24. "...ताजमनी का प्रेम अपने समर्पण के बावजूद उसके अकेलेपन का भागीदार बनने में असमर्थ है। वह इस प्रेम को 'आउट ग्रो' कर गया है। वैसे ही जैसे माँ का प्रेम शिशु को सुरक्षा तथा आश्वासन दे सकता है किंतु वयस्क बेटे को नहीं।"–आधुनिक हिंदी उपन्यासों में प्रेम की परिकल्पना, विजय मोहन सिंह, पृ. 266-267
25. परती परिकथा, पृ. 308
26. आधा गाँव, पृ. 42
27. "लेकिन मिगदाद तो एक अनहोनी बात कर रहा था। इसीलिए वह डर रही थी।...अब तक ऐसा नहीं हुआ।"–आधा गाँव, 10/97
28. अलग-अलग वैतरणी
29. वही, पृ. 630
30. वही, पृ. 444
31. वही, पृ. 444-445
32. "यह विद्रोहों और मानसिक विस्फोटों का युग है। आज हर पुराने कोहेनूर का भाव घटाया जा रहा है, तब प्रेम ही को उसके सर्वोच्च आसन से क्यों न गिराया जाय।"–अमृत और विष, पृ. 395
33. "प्रेम उनके लिए व्यापार नहीं। प्रेम उनके लिए नया पाठ नहीं। न उसे वे पाप समझतीं। प्रेम उनका देवता है। प्रेम उनकी जिंदगी है।"–जंगल के फूल, पृ. 30
34. वही, पृ. 40
35. जल टूटता हुआ, पृ. 534
36. "आप, आपकी संपत्ति और प्रतिष्ठा तो मेरे जैसे आदमी के लिए सड़े गोबर से अधिक मूल्यवान नहीं है...मैंने आपकी बेटी से प्यार किया है, वह आपकी बेटी होकर भी आपसे बिल्कुल अलग है, पूजा के फूल की तरह पवित्र, सुगंधित और सुंदर।"–जल टूटता हुआ, पृ. 554
37. वरुण के बेटे, पृ. 50-51
38. आधुनिक हिंदी उपन्यासों में प्रेम की परिकल्पना, पृ. 374
39. कब तक पुकारूँ, पृ. 455
40. "...रोमांटिक प्रेम जीवन के सर्वोत्तम उल्लास का स्रोत है। स्त्री-पुरुष एक-दूसरे को

प्रेम करते हों और उस प्रेम में उत्कटता, कल्पना और कोमलता हो तो उसका अमूल्य महत्त्व है।"—विवाह और नैतिकता, पृ. 49-50

41. "अब चाहे जो हो, मुझसे इज्जत देते पार नहीं लगेगा।"—नदी फिर बह चली, पृ. 324
42. कब तक पुकारूँ, पृ. 267
43. आधा गाँव, पृ. 123
44. अलग-अलग वैतरणी, पृ. 49
45. "उसकी क्रूर वासना ने जीवन में कभी अपने स्नेह को आदान-प्रदान की सहिष्णुता से स्वीकार नहीं किया था। वह लुटेरे की प्रवृत्ति का आदमी था। वह आज तक जो कुछ करता था, उसकी राय में वह सब अपहरण करने पर ही उसे प्राप्त होता था।"—कब तक पुकारूँ, पृ. 268
46. "…संभोग अपने आप में भले ही पाप नहीं हो, किंतु स्त्री को पशु बनाकर उसका भोग करने की प्रवृत्ति पाशविकता ही है और जघन्य है…"—कब तक पुकारूँ, पृ. 508
47. "कहाँ वह बच्ची और कहाँ पचास बरस का बूढ़ा गिद्ध। रोज रात में लक्ष्मी रोती थी।… ।"—मैला आँचल, पृ. 27
48. परती परिकथा, पृ. 238
49. 'धरम' तो कमर के ऊपर होता है।—कब तक पुकारूँ, पृ. 217
50. सागर लहरें और मनुष्य, पृ. 181
51. सूरज किरन की छाँव, पृ. 22 और पृ. 174
52. "…जिस यौन स्वतंत्रता की आवश्यकता है, वह है प्रेम करने की आवश्यकता, न कि किसी अज्ञात स्त्री के साथ शारीरिक आवश्यकता की पूर्ति करने की भद्दी स्वतंत्रता।"—बर्ट्रेंड रसेल, विवाह और नैतिकता, पृ. 201
53. परती परिकथा, पृ. 265
54. जल टूटता हुआ, पृ. 563
55. आधा गाँव, पृ. 291
56. जल टूटता हुआ, पृ. 534
57. (पाँच पंच को जना कर जब जब सादी की बात पक्की हुई, एक न एक विघ्न पड़ गया। इसीलिए कासी के पंडितों ने गंधारब विवाह कराने को कहा।)—मैला आँचल, पृ. 330
58. परती परिकथा
59. राजेन्द्र यादव, अठारह उपन्यास, 'परती परिकथा' की ताजमनी, पृ. 146
60. "अरे बिहाव तो एक पड़ाव है। जब आदमी चलते-चलते थक जाता है तो किसी मेंड का आसरा ले लेता है, बस। हम अभी थके थोड़े हैं।"—जंगल के फूल, पृ. 223
61. जंगल के फूल, पृ. 224

62. सूरज किरन की छाँव, पृ. 190
63. ''शादी ब्याह भी क्या किसी खेल से कम है ? बचपन में हम गुड़ियों का ब्याह रचाते थे। शादी भी तो यही गुड़ियों का ब्याह ही है।...समाज के ये जड़ बंधन न जाने कब से चले आ रहे हैं...।''—सूरज किरन की छाँव, पृ. 158-159
64. ''शादी की रस्म तो सामाजिक स्वीकृति को प्रकट करने के लिए होती है और समाज हम लोगों के इस संबंध को स्वीकृति देने से रहा। हाँ, मैं साथ रहने को तैयार हूँ।''—दूब जनम आई, शिवसागर मिश्र, पृ. 195
65. आधा गाँव, पृ. 267
66. ''स्वतंत्रता निःसंदेह व्यक्ति की है और व्यक्ति की होकर ही अर्थवान है, लेकिन वह न तो व्यक्ति तक सीमित है, न ही व्यक्ति को शून्य में स्थापित करके किसी सार्थक रूप में उसके साथ जोड़ी जा सकती है।''—सच्चिदानंद वात्स्यायन, 'व्यक्ति और व्यवस्था', पृ. 9
67. वही, पृ. 10
68. वही
69. धर्मवीर भारती, मानवमूल्य और साहित्य, पृ. 127
70. गंगाप्रसाद विमल, आधुनिकता : साहित्य के संदर्भ में, पृ. 16
71. ''और यह परम स्वातंत्र्य एक पूँजीवादी अर्थात् एक अराजकतावादी मुहावरा है (क्योंकि दर्शन के रूप में अराजकता उलटी हुई पूँजीवादी विश्व दृष्टि ही है)।''—आलोचना, जुलाई-सितंबर 1969, स्तेफान मोराठस्की के लेख का अनुवाद, अनु. गिरधर राठी, पृ. 12
72. ''यह कहना कि हम मूल्यों का आविष्कार करते हैं, इसका इसके सिवाय कोई अर्थ नहीं है कि जीवन का कोई अर्थ नहीं है। यह तुम्हारे ऊपर है कि तुम इसको अर्थ दो। अर्थ जिसका चुनाव करते हो।—उससे अलग मूल्य नाम की कोई दूसरी चीज नहीं है।''—सार्त्र का कथन, विद्याशंकर राय, आधुनिक हिंदी उपन्यास और अजनबीपन, पृ. 20 से उद्धृत।
73. कब तक पुकारूँ, पृ. 570
74. वही, पृ. 39
75. ''अब आदमी सचमुच स्वतंत्र है। बिल्कुल स्वतंत्र। पर लोग यह भूल जाते हैं कि बंदर के हाथ में चाकू का रहना कितना खतरनाक है। स्वतंत्रता बिना अक्ल के आदमी के हाथ में दुधारी तलवार की तरह होती है...।''—अलग-अलग वैतरणी, पृ. 444
76. ''किसान की आजादी आसमान से उतरकर नहीं आएगी...।''—बलचनमा, पृ. 192
77. ''तुम्हारे साथी अपने खून की आखिरी बूँद तक इनकी रक्षा करेंगे। जिस तरह गुजरा जमाना फिर वापस नहीं आता उसी तरह जमींदारों के उखड़े पैर यहाँ फिर कभी न जम पाएँगे।''—गंगा मैया, पृ. 141
78. सागर लहरें और मनुष्य

79. "यदि औरत को भी मनुष्य समझा जाता तो मेरे साथ यह सब न होता।"—सूरज किरन की छाँव, पृ. 173
80. वही, पृ. 179
81. "गाँव की और गाँववालों की सेवा कर अपने पाप-मोचन करूँगी और देखूँगी कि वहाँ की किसी बंजारी को निर्वासित होकर फिर मिसेज बेंजो जोसेफ न बनना पड़े।"—सूरज किरन की छाँव, पृ. 190
82. "विधाता की सृष्टि में मानव ही सबसे बढ़कर शक्तिशाली है। उसको पराजित करना असंभव है, प्रचंड शक्तिशाली बमों से भी नहीं।...पागलो ! आदमी आदमी है, गिनी पिग नहीं।...सबारि ऊपर मानुस सत्य।" —मैला आँचल, पृ. 3
83. "आँसू से भीगी हुई धरती पर प्यार के पौधे लहलहायेंगे। मैं साधना करूँगा, ग्रामवासिनी भारतमाता के मैले आँचल तले। कम से कम एक ही गाँव के कुछ प्राणियों के मुरझाए ओठों पर मुस्कराहट लौटा सकूँ।"—मैला आँचल, पृ. 334
84. कब तक पुकारूँ, पृ. 576
85. "मैं कोई द्रोपदी हूँ कि पाण्डव मुझे जुए में हार जाएँ।...कोई मुझे कौन सा बाण मारेगा ? रासलीला में राधा बनना कुलमर्यादा पर सात घड़े पानी डालने जैसा कैसे हुआ था।"—कथा कहो उर्वशी, पृ. 119
86. दूब जनम आई, पृ. 195
87. "अबला नारी हर जगह अबला ही है। रूप और जवानी...यह भी गलत। औरत होना चाहिए, रूप और उम्र की कोई कैद नहीं।"—मैला आँचल, पृ. 165
88. कथन, जनवरी-फरवरी 1983, 'भारतीय परिवार और समाज में नारी की स्थिति', पृ. 26
89. सागर लहरें और मनुष्य, पृ. 181
90. "अब वह कहाँ जाएगी ? कितना सहेगी ? ये मर्द उसका रहा-सहा मांस भी नोचकर खा जाएँगे।...बस अब मर जा। कोई रास्ता नहीं।"—सोना माटी, पृ. 365
91. "अपने गरीब बाप के घर जवान हुई तबसे हर आदमी हमारे पास खास काम के लिए भी आया है। मास्टर जी। यहाँ एकदम एकांत है। कहिए सेज लगा दूँ, अपने को सौंप दूँ ? एक बेटी और क्या कर सकती है ?"—सोना माटी, पृ. 133
92. वही, पृ. 105
93. ग्राम देवता, पृ. 98
94. "हमको ऐसा आदमी नई पाहिजे। समझ ले बिट्ठल तेरे कूँ मार-मार ठीक करना होयेगा।"—सागर लहरें और मनुष्य, पृ. 31
95. अतुलवीर अरोड़ा, आधुनिकता के संदर्भ में आज का हिंदी उपन्यास, पृ. 146
96. कब तक पुकारूँ, पृ. 541
97. "इधर किसी पर मन आ गया तो हम तो अपने पहले नाते को तोड़ देती हैं।...बड़ी जातों में ऐसा नहीं होता। वहाँ तो एक-एक की कई-कई औरतें होती हैं।...बड़ी साँसत है सरकार, बड़ी जात का होना भी पूरा आफत ही समझो।"—कब तक पुकारूँ,

पृ. 484

98. "यह कैसा रिवाज है, मालकिन आपकी बिरादरी का। इस मामले में तो हमारी ही बिरादरी अच्छी है जो कोई बेबा इस तरह अपनी जिंदगी खराब करने को मजबूर नहीं"—गंगा मैया, पृ. 51

99. कब तक पुकारूँ, पृ. 508

100. "मनुष्य के श्रम द्वारा उत्पादित वस्तु और उसका उत्पादन अजनबी करनेवाली वस्तु के रूप में उसके सामने आने लगता है। इस प्रकार वस्तु की दूसरों के लिए बढ़ती उपयोगिता उसके लिए अजनबीपन के रूप में उभरती है।...यह अजनबी श्रम मनुष्य को उसके मानव शरीर से, प्रकृति से, उसके अपने आत्मिक तत्त्व मनुष्यत्व से अजनबी कर देता है।"—आधुनिक हिंदी उपन्यास और अजनबीपन, पृ. 16 के आधार पर

101. मैला आँचल, पृ. 318

102. जल टूटता हुआ, पृ. 450

103. वही, पृ. 473

104. सोनामाटी, पृ. 295

105. वही, पृ. 309

106. "बिस्तर की तनहाई से लेकर दिलों की तनहाई तक।...लेकिन ख्वाबों की टेढ़ी-मेढ़ी पगडंडियों पर कोई अकेला नहीं जा सकता...।"—आधा गाँव, पृ. 306

107. देवराज, संस्कृति का दार्शनिक विवेचन, पृ. 309

108. राग दरबारी, पृ. 129

109. "नैतिकता समझ लो कि यही चौकी है। एक कोने में पड़ी है। सभा सोसाइटी के वक्त केवल इस पर चादर बिछा दी जाती है। तब बड़ी बढ़िया दीखती है। इस पर चढ़कर लेक्चर फटकार दिया जाता है। यह उसी के लिए है।"—राग दरबारी, पृ. 129

110. जिसके लिए दुनिया में नैतिकता नाम की वस्तु का अस्तित्व नहीं, जिसके लिए कुछ पाप नहीं, कुछ पुण्य नहीं।"—सोना माटी, पृ. 406

111. कथा कहो उर्वशी, पृ. 146

112. "भर पेट कमा लो, नहीं तो पछताओगे, कुछ हाथ न लगेगो। तहसीलदार और पटवारी जहाँ कहीं जाते हैं, नोच-नोचकर खा-चबा जाते हैं, पर तुमको न जाने भगवान् कब सुबुद्धि देंगे।"—देहाती दुनिया, पृ. 95

113. "फिर हमारे जैसे बुद्धिजीवी का सोच भी दीनदयाल से आगे कहाँ पहुँचता है ? सबको अपनी-अपनी लगी है।"—सोना माटी, पृ. 125

114. "...तर्क और सत्य के उज्ज्वल आलोक को सह सकना उनके लिए असंभव है, क्योंकि उसमें उनके स्वार्थों का पर्दाफाश होता है और एक की पोल में दूसरे की पोल घुसी हुई है कि सब उस पर पर्दा डाले रहना चाहते हैं।"—कब तक पुकारूँ, पृ. 454

115. "सत्य के लिए मूल्य तो देना ही पड़ता है। और जब तक कुछ लोग संगठित होकर मूल्य देने को तैयार नहीं होंगे और दूसरों की देखा देखी असत्य की ओर उन्मुख

होते रहेंगे, तब तक गाँव का क्या देश का और पूरे विश्व का उद्धार नहीं होगा।"—जल टूटता हुआ, पृ. 473

116. हजार घोड़ों का सवार, पृ. 159

117. जल टूटता हुआ, पृ. 474

118. दूब जनम आई, पृ. 190

119. "कहीं भीतर से मन कितना डाँटता फटकारता है। लगता है, बेईमानी-शैतानी का चक्कर पाप है, बुरा है।"—सोना माटी, पृ. 95

120. "मानुस जन्म पाकर हम परमारथ के बदले सोआरथ देखें तो इससे बढ़कर क्या पाप हो सकता है ?"—मैला आँचल, पृ. 30-31

121. "जीने के लिए जीना, जीना नहीं है, परोपकार के लिए जीना ही जीना है। अगर मेरी मृत्यु जनसाधारण के लिए लाभप्रद हो तो नहीं चाहिए मुझको यह जीवन।"—बाबा बटेसरनाथ, पृ. 17

122. मैला आचँल, पृ. 334

123. कब तक पुकारूँ, पृ. 474

124. आलोचना, जनवरी-मार्च 1970, पृ. 76

तृतीय प्रकरण

आंचलिक उपन्यासों में मूल्य-संक्रमण : सामाजिक परिपार्श्व

आंचलिक उपन्यासकारों ने स्वयं स्पष्ट किया है कि उनके उपन्यासों में व्यक्त मूल्य क्षेत्र विशेष के न होकर पूरे समाज के हैं। रामदरश मिश्र ने 'पानी के प्राचीर' के 'पूर्वाभास' में लिखा है—"इस प्रदेश की व्यापक पृष्ठभूमि पर जो मानव मूल्यों और उच्चतर सत्यों के रूप उभरे हैं, वे एकदेशीय न होकर पूरे समाज के हैं।"[1] यही मानसिकता अन्य उपन्यासकारों की भी है। उन्होंने ग्रामीण जीवन में घट रहे बहुआयामीय मूल्य-संक्रमण को इस प्रकार प्रस्तुत किया है कि वह पूरे भारतीय समाज में परिवार, जाति, वर्ग, संप्रदाय आदि के स्तर पर हो रहे मूल्य-संक्रमण का साक्ष्य बन गया है।

पारिवारिक मूल्य : परंपरा और आधुनिकता का द्वंद्व

इन उपन्यासों में औद्योगीकरण, शहरीकरण, शिक्षा का प्रचार, राजनीति की घुसपैठ आदि अनेक कारणों से परंपरागत मूल्यों के विचलन को बहुत विस्तार के साथ प्रस्तुत किया है। परंपरा और आधुनिकता के द्वंद्व के परिणाम अच्छे-बुरे दोनों हैं। कहीं आधुनिकता ने रूढ़ियों को तोड़ने में महत्त्वपूर्ण भूमिका निभाई है तो कहीं आपसीपन और सद्भाव को आँच भी आई है। आंचलिक उपन्यासकारों ने इन सभी परिवर्तनों को तटस्थ भाव से नहीं लिया है। देखना होगा कि सामाजिक मूल्यों का संक्रमण कहाँ उन्हें आहत करता है और कहाँ आश्वस्त करता दिखाई देता है।

श्रद्धा, सम्मान, आज्ञाकारिता आदि का अवमूल्यन

संयुक्त परिवार से संबद्ध परंपरागत मूल्य-व्यवस्था में बड़ों का अधिकार और परंपरा की पवित्रता सर्वाधिक महत्त्वपूर्ण माने जाते हैं।[2] स्वतंत्रता के बाद के भारतीय समाज में संयुक्त परिवार का विघटन होने पर न तो बड़ों के अधिकार सुरक्षित रहे और न परंपरा ही सुरक्षित रही। पारिवारिक स्तर पर मूल्य संक्रमण की प्रक्रिया नगर-महानगर में जितनी तीव्र रही, पिछड़े अंचलों में उतनी तेज नहीं रही। फिर भी पारिवारिक व्यवस्था को हिला देनेवाले परिवर्तन को स्पष्ट लक्ष्य किया जा सकता है। आंचलिक उपन्यासों में श्रद्धा, सम्मान, अनुशासन, सहयोग आदि मूल्यों के इस अवमूल्यन को उसकी संपूर्णता में प्रस्तुत किया गया है।

अर्थाभाव, नई रोशनी, पीढ़ियों का अंतराल आदि अनेक कारणों से माता-पिता को आज वह सम्मान प्राप्त नहीं है जो कभी आचरण के प्रतिमानों में प्रमुख था। 'श्रवणकुमार', 'राम' आदि के मिथक बहुत से युवकों को प्रभावित नहीं करते। 'रागदरबारी' के छोटे पहलवान अपने को श्रवणकुमार की हालत में नहीं देखना चाहते। बल्कि वे जब-तब अपने पिता कुसहर प्रसाद को मार बैठते हैं। जब उन्हें समझाया जाता है कि आखिर कुसहर ने तुम्हें पैदा किया है, तब छोटे पहलवान बिगड़ उठते हैं—"कोई हमने स्टाम्प लगाकर दरखास्त दी थी कि हमें पैदा करो। चले साले कहीं के पैदा करनेवाले।"[3] श्रवणकुमार का अनुकरण करना[4] 'अलग-अलग वैतरणी' के हरिया को भी रुचिकर नहीं।[5] हरिया द्वारा पिता के अपमान के कारण शुद्ध आर्थिक हैं। जब तक खेतों में उत्पादन सही था, हरिया के परिवार में सुख-शांति थी। लेकिन प्रकृति के प्रकोपवश जब भरपूर परिश्रम के बावजूद घर की स्थिति नहीं सुधरती तब घरेलू संबंध गड़बड़ा जाते हैं। शहर में काम करनेवाला ग्रामीण युवक मुरतिया अपने पिता भजन के अनुशासन को कतई नहीं मानता। वह अपशब्दों का जवाब अपशब्दों से देता है।[6] पिता के प्रति अवज्ञा का भाव न केवल छोटे, हरिया, मुरतिया जैसे अशिक्षित युवकों में है अपितु कुछ पढ़ी-लिखी युवा पीढ़ी भी पितृभक्ति के आदर्श से विचलित हो उठी है। रुप्पन, ब्रदी (राग दरबारी) जैसे युवक इस संदर्भ में देखे जा सकते हैं। लेकिन उपर्युक्त उदाहरणों से यह समझना भूल होगी कि आंचलिक उपन्यासों में श्रद्धा सम्मान आदि मूल्यों को नेस्तनाबूद होते दिखाया गया है। बल्कि अधिकतर उपन्यासों में माता-पिता और संतति के पारस्परिक लगाव और निकटता के बहुत से प्रमाण मिल जाते हैं। 'जसौंतसिंह' (हौलदार) 'मँगरू' (लोहे के पंख), 'परबतिया' (नदी फिर बह चली), 'गीधू' (हजार घोड़ों का सवार), 'सतीश' (जल टूटता हुआ), 'भोलानाथ' (देहाती दुनिया), 'नीलकंठ' (कथा कहो उर्वशी) आदि चरित्र कहीं भी माता-पिता की अवज्ञा करते नहीं दिखाई देते। सौतेली माताओं को छोड़ दें तो माँ-बाप भी इनसे असंतुष्ट

नहीं हैं। जसौंतसिंह स्पष्ट रूप में पिता को श्रेष्ठ करार देता है।[7] रमुवा (हौलदार), रतिनाथ (रतिनाथ की चाची) और 'मिगदाद' (आधा गाँव) जैसे चरित्र यदि क्रमशः अपनी माँ और पिता से असंतुष्ट नजर आते हैं तो यह साभिप्राय और साधार है, रमुवा अपनी माँ की 'अति' को नहीं सह पाता। चूँकि रतिनाथ ने पिता को माँ की गर्दन रेतते हुए देखा है, अतः वह पिता को श्रद्धा की दृष्टि से नहीं देख पाता।[8] रतिनाथ की चाची पिता-पुत्र के संबंध को लेकर तत्कालीन समाज में प्रचलित धारणा को पूरे विश्वास के साथ प्रस्तुत करती है।[9] पर लोक, तर्पण और सद्गति आदि में विश्वास रखनेवाले बहुसंख्यक जनसमुदाय में यह मान्यता आज भी निश्शेष नहीं हुई है। मिगदाद का विरोध वस्तुतः परंपराभंजन का एक रूप है, इसलिए उसे उपन्यासकार की सहानुभूति प्राप्त है।

संबंधहीनता की स्थितियाँ

आंचलिक उपन्यासों में माँ को नकारने के संदर्भ कम़ हैं। 'रतिनाथ की चाची' में उमानाथ का वीतश्रद्ध होना सकारण है। अपने माँ से संबद्ध प्रवाद को सुनकर वह न केवल कुपित होता है, अपितु माँ पर हाथ भी उठा देता है। इस प्रकार के पुत्र इने-गिने ही हैं। 'असगाँव-पसगाँव' की बासमत्ती अपनी माँ के व्यवहार पर क्षुब्ध होती है लेकिन किसी प्रकार की अश्रद्धा का भाव उसमें नहीं उगता।[10] चूँकि पितृसत्तात्मक समाज में 'पिता' की स्थिति नियामक की होती है, अतः माता की तुलना में 'पिता' को अधिक प्रहार सहने होते हैं। लेकिन कुल मिलाकर आंचलिक उपन्यासकार पिता की अवज्ञा या अवहेलना करने के पक्ष में नहीं हैं। उन्होंने उन चरित्रों को प्रायः महिमामंडित किया है, जो कतिपय मतभेदों के बावजूद पिता के प्रति श्रद्धावनत हैं। इससे स्पष्ट होता है कि व्यापक स्तर पर माता-पिता से जुड़े मूल्यों के हेरफेर को दिखाने के बावजूद आंचलिक उपन्यासकार पुरानी मूल्य-मर्यादाओं को खारिज नहीं करता है।

आंचलिक उपन्यास में न केवल माता-पिता के प्रति श्रद्धा, सम्मान अपितु अन्य बड़ों की प्रतिष्ठा, बंधुत्व, पातिव्रत, आपसी नातेदारी आदि पर गहराते संकट को भी पढ़ा गया है। इस मूल्य संकट का कारण प्रायः आर्थिक है। 'रतिनाथ की चाची' में गौरी और कमलमुखी अर्थात् सास-बहू के संबंध खराब होने के कारणों में एक आर्थिक भी है। गौरी चाहकर भी सड़क निर्माण के लिए दो रुपये चंदा नहीं दे पाती।[11] 'लोकऋण' की आजाद बहू अपनी चचिया सास की खुली अवज्ञा करती है।[12] 'अलग-अलग वैतरणी' का विपिन सदैव 'बबुआन की मर्यादा' का हामी रहा, लेकिन अपने भतीजे बुद्ध की लाठी का प्रहार झेलने के बाद उसे पुरानी परंपरा भहराती हुई लगती है।[13] 'बलचनमा' में दिखाया गया है कि किस प्रकार बड़े-बूढ़ों

की मृत्यु का समाचार पाकर नई रोशनी के नवयुवक सिर मुड़ाने के भय से उल्टे पाँव लौट जाते हैं।[14] विपिन और उसके बड़े भाई के संबंध अच्छे न होते हुए भी खुले तौर पर सामान्य लगते हैं क्योंकि विपिन मूल्यों की लक्ष्मण रेखा को नहीं लाँघना चाहता।[15] लेकिन परती परिकथा के लालचन बाबू 'लैण्ड सर्वे' के दौरान थोड़ी सी जमीन की खातिर अपने सगे भाई सरबन का सिर फोड़ देते हैं। सरबन बाबू भरी कचहरी में लालचन को अपना भाई मानने से इनकार कर देते हैं।[16] जमीन बंदोबस्ती के समय किस प्रकार आपसी संबंधों पर स्वार्थपरता की परत जम जाती है, इसका ब्यौरा 'मैला आँचल' में भी उपलब्ध है। भजू महतो की जमीन उसी का भगिना सरूप महतो लेना चाहता है और सोबरन की जमीन पर उसका चाचा रामेसर नजर लगाए बैठा है।[17] आर्थिक कारणों से ही 'असगाँव-पसगाँव' के सुखई को अपने भाइयों के अविश्वास का सामना करना पड़ता है। हरखू जहाँ अलगाव के लिए तैयार बैठा है, वहाँ सुखई किसी भी मूल्य पर घर में अलग चूल्हा नहीं चाहते।[18] दो विरोधी मूल्यबोध टकराते हैं और उपन्यासकार परिवार को टूटने से बचा लेता है। 'असगाँव-पसगाँव' में पारिवारिक द्वंद्व के दौरान 'सुखई' को पड़ोसियों और नातेदारों की सहानुभूति बराबर प्राप्त होती है लेकिन 'कभी न छोड़े खेत' में स्थिति कुछ जटिल है। बंचित सिंह के कुल को संतानहीन देखकर उसके निकट के संबंधी भीतर ही भीतर खुश होते हैं कि भविष्य में जमीन जायदाद पर उनका अधिकार हो सकेगा। मेला सिंह तो अपने परिवार का एक बच्चा गोद लेने की पेशकश भी कर देता है।[19] इस तरह के व्यवहार से क्षुब्ध जसवंत कौर का बद्दुआ देना असंगत नहीं है–''मोये शरीकों के सूल निकले। मेरे बेटे की मौत पर उन्होंने घी की पूरी खाईं। मुकदमा हारे तो शराबें पी। मोये⋯तुम्हारे जीते जी हमारी जमीन जायदाद के वारिस बन रहे हैं।''[20]

अस्ति मूल्यों और नास्ति मूल्यों का द्वंद्व

आर्थिक कारणों के अतिरिक्त कुछ निहित स्वार्थों के हस्तक्षेप से भी संबंधों में बिगाड़ आता है। 'जल टूटता हुआ' में बड़े भाई कुंजू के प्रति बिरजू का बैर भाव इसी प्रकार का है। बिरजू न केवल बड़े भाई की पवित्रता पर संदेह करता है अपितु उसकी बाँह मरोड़ कर बुरी तरह अपमानित भी करता है।[21] इसी उपन्यास में सतीश और चंद्रकांत का आदर्श बंधुत्व भी प्रदर्शित है। वस्तुतः कुछ आंचलिक उपन्यासकारों ने संबंधों में बिगाड़ के फलस्वरूप मूल्यों के संक्रमण का लिपिबद्ध करते समय जहाँ एक ओर नास्ति मूल्यों के 'मॉडल' खड़े किए हैं, वहीं उनके मुकाबले में अस्ति मूल्यों के चरित्र भी विद्यमान हैं। उपन्यासों से स्पष्ट है कि संक्रमण की दिशा अस्ति मूल्यों से नास्ति मूल्यों की ओर है किंतु उपन्यासकारों ने अस्ति मूल्यों को अपना

भरपूर समर्थन दिया है। 'जल टूटता हुआ' में मुरतिया यदि एक मूल्यबोध का प्रतिनिधि है तो सतीश दूसरे का। 'बिरजू' और 'चंद्रकांत' की मूल्यगत मानसिकता परस्पर विपरीत है। 'रतिनाथ की चाची' में जहाँ जयकिशोर में माँ के प्रति श्रद्धा है, वहीं उमानाथ माँ के प्रति दुर्व्यवहार करता है। असगाँव-पसगाँव में हरखू और सुखई की मूल्य मर्यादाएँ पृथक्-पृथक् हैं। 'हौलदार' में डूँगर सिंह का चरित्र नकारात्मक है और पारिवारिक विघटन को जन्म देता है। उसकी तुलना में उसके दोनों भाइयों का बिंब आश्वस्त करता है। डूँगर का बड़ा भाई प्रेमवश नहीं चाहता कि वह पलटन में भर्ती होकर आँखों से ओझल हो जाए। डूँगर सिंह की भर्ती की सूचना उसे सुखद नहीं लगती।[22] इसके विपरीत डूँगर सिंह को विश्वास नहीं कि भाई-भौजियों से उसका कल्याण हो सकेगा।[23]

'हौलदार' में ही एक ओर खिमुली और भिमुली जैसी बहुएँ हैं, जो परिवार की एकता को बनाए रखना चाहती हैं, स्वार्थ की भावना उन्हें आक्रांत नहीं करती। दूसरी ओर लछमा थोकदार की सारी जमीन पर अपने बालकों के हल चलते देखना चाहती है।[24] अपनी विधवा देवरानी और छोटे देवर के प्रति लछमा का व्यवहार उचित नहीं कहा जा सकता। स्वयं थोकदार इस स्थिति से भली-भाँति अभिज्ञ है।[25] परिवार की संयुक्तता की तुलना में व्यक्तिगत स्वार्थ हीनतर मूल्य है। आंचलिक उपन्यासों में संयुक्त परिवार के विघटन को यथार्थ मानते हुए भी प्रायः उसके बिखरने का समर्थन नहीं किया गया है।

मार्क्सवादी दृष्टिकोण के तहत उत्पादक-शक्ति और उत्पादन संबंधों के संपूर्ण योग से समाज की आर्थिक संरचना निर्मित होती है। इसी नींव पर समाज की संरचना खड़ी होती है। जब हाथ की चक्की थी तब सामंतवादी आर्थिक संरचना थी जब भाप से चलनेवाली चक्की आई तब पूँजीवादी व्यवस्था आ गई। आर्थिक संरचना के बदलने का प्रभाव पारिवारिक संबंधों पर बहुत स्पष्ट दिखाई देता है। सामंतवादी युग में घर का वयोवृद्ध व्यक्ति मुखिया और सर्वशक्ति संपन्न था, इसलिए सेवा, श्रद्धा, आदेशपालन, विनय आदि मान्यताएँ महत्त्वपूर्ण थीं। पूँजीवादी संरचना में महत्त्व कमानेवाले का हो गया और 'स्वार्थ' असहिष्णुता आदि का बोलबाला हो गया। इस तरह पारिवारिक व्यवस्था में मूल्यों की निम्न स्थिति की ओर स्थानांतरण के पीछे आर्थिक संरचना के दबाव की भूमिका पर्याप्त उल्लेखनीय है। उपर्युक्त उदाहरण इस कथन की पुष्टि करते हैं।

आंचलिक उपन्यायों में व्यक्त पीढ़ी-अंतराल वस्तुतः दो तरह के मूल्यों की टकराहट को व्यक्त करता है। कहीं यह टकराहट सकारात्मक और नकारात्मक मूल्यों के बीच है और कहीं सामंती मूल्यों से आधुनिकबोध से निष्पन्न मानवीय मूल्यों की टक्कर हो रही है। आंचलिक उपन्यासों में यह तथ्य विशेषतः ध्यान आकृष्ट करता है कि शोषक वर्ग की दो पीढ़ियों में मूल्यों का फर्क कुछ अपवादों को छोड़

देता नाम मात्र का है। विपरीत प्रकृति के मूल्यों की टकराहट मध्यवर्ग और निम्नवर्ग के स्तर पर अधिक तीव्र है और इसका मुख्य कारण आर्थिक है। शोषक वर्ग के पिता-पुत्र प्रायः एक जैसा सोचते हैं और करते हैं। हनुमान प्रसाद भुवनेश्वर (सोनामाटी), पिताजी-भाई जी (जंगली सूअर), जैपाल सिंह-बुझारथ (अलग-अलग वैतरणी), त्रिभुवन-आजाद (लोकऋण), वैद्यजी-रुप्पन (राग दरबारी) आदि के उदाहरणों से इस तथ्य की पुष्टि की जा सकती है। हनुमान प्रसाद अपार जायदाद और धन का स्वामी है। अधिकतर संपत्ति दूसरों को छलकर या दलकर हथियाई हुई है। वह दया, परोपकार, आदि मूल्यों से शून्य है।[26] शायद ही कोई ऐसा दुर्गुण होगा जो हनुमान प्रसाद में न हो। भुवनेश्वर भी अपने पिता के पद चिह्नों पर चला है। भाई जी के पिताजी (जंगली सूअर) दूसरों की जमीन के अहेरी थे।[27] मरने के समय तक उनकी इच्छा थी कि गाँव में जहाँ-जहाँ पैर रखूँ, मेरे पैर अपनी जमीन में पड़ें। भाई जी ने उनके सपने को पूरा करना प्रारंभ किया...''उनके मरते ही भाई जी को जमीन हड़पने का नशा छा गया था। आज तक वे उसी दिशा में बढ़ते रहे हैं।''[28] जैपाल सिंह (अलग-अलग वैतरणी) का अपनी प्रजा से बाघ और मेमने का संबंध था।[29] उसके पुत्र बुझारथ के व्यक्तित्व में अवमूल्यों की भरमार है। बुझारथ का पुत्र बुट्टू जिस तरह का आचरण करता है[30], उससे लगता है तीसरी पीढ़ी में भी नकारात्मक मूल्यों का संक्रमण नकारात्मक मूल्यों में ही हुआ है। वैद्य जी (राग दरबारी) स्वार्थ के पुतले और राष्ट्रीयता, सेवा, त्याग आदि मूल्यों से रहित व्यक्ति हैं।[31] उनका पुत्र रुप्पन उनसे किसी भी तरह कम नहीं है। सबको तुच्छ समझना और स्वयं हर प्रकार की अनियमितता से संबंधित रहना उनका स्वभाव है।[32] 'लोकऋण' के पिता-पुत्र त्रिभुवन और आजाद की मूल्य-मानसिकता में गहरा साम्य है। सभापति त्रिभुवन जबर्दस्ती सार्वजनिक पोखर को अपना खेत और धर्मशाला को डेरा बना लेता है।[33] वह 'धर्म', 'पुण्य', 'सत्य' आदि अवधारणाओं का खुला उल्लंघन करता है और गाँव का कोई व्यक्ति उसका हाथ नहीं पकड़ पाता। उसका बेटा आजादकुमार एकदम आजाद है। वह श्रद्धा, सम्मान, कुल मर्यादा आदि मूल्यों की कतई परवाह नहीं करता। उसका पिता भी उससे डरता है क्योंकि उसके कई मोर्चे आजाद के कारण तेज रहते हैं।[34]

कुछ उपन्यासों में शोषक वर्ग के पिता-पुत्र तो नहीं हैं लेकिन किसी रूप में दो पीढ़ियाँ अवश्य हैं और थोड़े-बहुत ऊपरी भेद को छोड़ दें तो दोनों की मानसिकता एक सी है। 'बलचनमा' के फूल बाबू यों तो सामंती वर्ग से वर्गच्युत होने का भ्रम देते हैं, लेकिन वास्तविकता यही है कि वे अपने फूफा के वर्ग से अलग नहीं हो पाए हैं। बलचनमा इस रहस्य को आखिरकार समझ ही जाता है—''साफ-साफ दीखने लगा था कि बाबू-भैया लोग वहीं तक हमारा पक्ष लेंगे, जहाँ तक कि उनका अपना मतलब रहेगा।...अरे भैया, फूफा और सर बेटा का रिश्ता

बाप-बेटा का रिश्ता समझो।...सोराजी हो गए थे क्या थे तो आखिर बाबू भैया ही न। गरीब-गुरवा का दुख ये लोग क्या जानें।''[35] लेकिन 'परती परिकथा', 'कब तक पुकारूँ' और 'अलग-अलग वैतरणी', 'जिंदगीनामा' आदि उपन्यासों में शोषकवर्ग की युवा पीढ़ी में पिछली पीढ़ी की अमानवीयता और क्रूरता को नकारने का साहस: स्वस्थ और मानवीय मूल्यों की दिशा में विचार-संक्रमण की गवाही देता है। जित्तन का पिता शिवेन्द्र मिश्र दूसरों की जमीन हड़पने के लिए कितनी ही जालसाजियों से गुजरता है। उसने रोज उड से कहा था कि जमींदारों के वंश-परिचय में कोई न कोई डकैत अवश्य होगा। 'अपहरण', 'शोषण', अत्याचार आदि सामंती मूल्यों के पक्षपाती पिता का पुत्र जित्तन उससे एकदम अलग है। वह सामंती मूल्यों को निरस्त करते हुए 'परोपकार', 'समानता' आदि मूल्यों के पक्ष में है। गरीबों को जमीन देना[36] और अपराधियों को पुलिस के हवाले कर देना[37] इस संदर्भ में द्रष्टव्य है। 'कब तक पुकारूँ' का नरेश जिस तरह जाति और वर्ण की रूढ़ मर्यादाओं को तोड़ देना चाहता है, वह उसकी रूढ़िवादी माँ और कथित उदार पिता के मूल्यबोध से न केवल अलग है, अपितु क्रांतिकारी भी। 'अलग-अलग वैतरणी' का विपिन अपने पिता और बड़े भाई की तरह अन्याय और उत्पीड़न का समर्थक नहीं है। दरोगा को डाँटने पर खलील मियाँ ने 'विपिन' के माध्यम से नई मूल्य मर्यादा के उदय की संभावना को पढ़ा है। यह नया मूल्य 'इंसाफ' के रास्ते में रुकावट बननेवाली दीवारों को गला देने में सक्षम है।[38] 'जिंदगीनामा' (पहला भाग) में छोटा शाह शोषण को अनुचित मानता है—''बेचारे गरीब जट्ट किसान को इतना दोहना कहाँ तक वाजिब है भ्राजी।''[39] जित्तन, नरेश छोटा शाह और विपिन, काजल की कोठरी में रहते हुए भी कालिख से बचे हुए हैं। उपन्यासकारों ने दर्शाया है कि शोषक वर्ग के कुछ परिवारों में नई पीढ़ी नकारात्मक और अमानवीय मूल्यों को नकार कर स्वस्थ मूल्य-मर्यादाओं को अंगीकार कर रही है। अर्थात् एक पीढ़ी से दूसरी पीढ़ी में मूल्यों का संक्रमण हीनतर मूल्यों से उच्चतर मूल्यों की ओर हुआ है। उपन्यासकार इस कोटि के संक्रमण को वांछित और सार्थक मानते हैं।

निम्नवर्गीय, निम्नमध्यवर्गीय परिवारों में मूल्यों और विचारों के स्तर पर 'पीढ़ी-अतंराल' विस्तृत और निर्विवाद है। शिक्षा, नई विचार सरणियाँ, कार्य-कारण-संबंध का ज्ञान आदि कई बातों से यह अंतराल निर्मित हुआ है। 'जिंदगीनामा' में फरमान अली अपनी गरीबी के लिए तकदीर को दोषी मानता है, लेकिन उसका बेटा मेहरअली इसके लिए जमींदारों को उत्तरदायी मानता है। वह अपने संघर्ष में सफल होता है जब शाह जमीन पर उसकी मिल्कियत मानने को तैयार हो जाते हैं।[40] बलचनमा का बोध भी अपनी पिछड़ी पीढ़ी के मूल्यों से अलहदा है। निम्न और निर्धन वर्ग में पीढ़ियों का मतभेद प्रायः 'शोषण' को स्वीकारने या अस्वीकारने को लेकर है, जबकि मध्यवर्ग में यह अंतर 'श्रद्धा-सम्मान' आदि मूल्यों की अवज्ञा के

रूप में प्रायः आया है। कारण, दोनों के आर्थिक हैं। अपनी आर्थिक कठिनाइयों के कारण ही नई पीढ़ी उग्र और उद्दंड दिखाई देती है और अधिकतर स्थलों पर वह अपनी दुर्गति के लिए पुरानी पीढ़ी को जिम्मेदार मानती है। इस तरह का मूल्य-द्वंद्व स्वाभाविक है और कुछ स्थितियों को छोड़ दें तो संक्रमण सही और सकारात्मक मूल्यों की दिशा में सक्रिय है। यदि युवा पीढ़ी शोषण को एकदम नकार रही है तो यह एक शुभ लक्षण है।

'अलग-अलग वैतरणी' में पुरानी पीढ़ी के 'सम्मान' के संकट में पड़ जाने के दो उदाहरण ध्यान आकृष्ट करते हैं। हरिया और जगेसर दोनों अपने 'पिता' के प्रति बहुत कटु और असभ्य जान पड़ते हैं। हरिया कठोर श्रम के बाद भी घर में खुशहाली नहीं ला पाता तो उसके स्वभाव में एक तीखापन आ जाता है, जो पिता की भर्त्सना के रूप में व्यक्त होता है।[41] उपन्यासकार ने इस भर्त्सना को स्वाभाविक माना है, लेकिन थोड़ा सा धन कमाकर अहंकार में फूले हुए जगेसर का अपने पिता को कुली बनाना[42] और माँ के पैर न छूना, उसे नहीं रुचता। पुरानी पीढ़ी के प्रति अश्रद्धा, अवज्ञा और अपमान को आंचलिक उपन्यासकारों ने अपना समर्थन प्रायः नहीं दिया है। 'तथ्य चेतना' यही है कि श्रद्धा, सम्मान आदि मूल्यों का विघटन हो रहा है। लेकिन उपन्यासकारों को लगता है कि यह विघटन अभी व्यापक रूप में 'अमूर्त्त संवेग' की स्थिति में ही है। यह अभी नैतिक प्रतिमान नहीं बन पाया है। यही कारण है कि कई उपन्यासों में युवापीढ़ी के चरित्र बड़ों के प्रति सम्मान-असम्मान के द्वंद्व में पड़े दिखाई देते हैं और अंततः परंपरागत मूल्यों की ओर ही झुकते हैं। 'जल टूटता हुआ' का सतीश अपनी आर्थिक विपन्नता के कारण के रूप में यदा-कदा पिता--अमलेश जी के प्रति क्षुब्ध होता है, लेकिन आखिरकार उसे अपने पिता पर गर्व ही होता है--"कभी वह पिता की निष्क्रियता के प्रति अजीब तरह से बेचैन हो जाता है, बड़ा तीखा-तीखा अनुभव करने लगता है, बरबादी देखकर छटपटाता है, किंतु पिता के प्रति कुछ ऐसा भाव है जो उसे खुलने नहीं देता, भीतर ही भीतर विचित्र प्रकार का द्वंद्व पीता रहता है।...बल्कि उसे सहज क्षणों में अपने पिता पर गर्व ही होता है।"[43] रामकुमार को लगता है कि खेती-बारी के नाश के लिए उसके बनवारी बाबा जिम्मेदार हैं। वह उन्हें घर से निकल जाने तक के लिए कह देता है लेकिन बनवारी बाबा को यह नहीं लगता कि उनकी जीवन-पद्धति सदोष है या उनके जीवनमूल्य गलत हैं। वे अपने बेटे से दबते नहीं हैं--"मैं लाख नालायक था, लेकिन मैंने किसी का अहित नहीं किया, सबसे प्रेम किया। एक तुम हो कि सबके साथ राजनीति खेल रहे हो, धोखे धड़ा से सबका खेत लिखाने के चक्कर में हो, एक-एक अभद्द काम कर धरम बदनाम किया।"[44] यह कथन स्पष्ट करता है कि पुरानी पीढ़ी जहाँ 'हित', 'प्रेम', 'सद्भाव' और 'धर्म' को जीवन मूल्यों के रूप में मान्यता देती रही, वहीं गाँव की युवा पीढ़ी

में 'धोखा', 'राजनीतिक कुटिलता', 'स्वार्थ' आदि अवमूल्य पसरते गए हैं। युवा पीढ़ी से सहानुभूति के बावजूद मूल्यधर्मिता की दृष्टि से उपन्यासकार पुरानी पीढ़ी के साथ है। बंसी-महावीर दुबे प्रसंग में भी वह पुरानी पीढ़ी के मूल्यबोध को प्रासंगिक पाता है। बंसी का कर्मशील होना अवमूल्यों पर श्रम, श्रद्धा, ममत्व आदि की जीत का द्योतक है।[45] दोनों उदाहरणों से स्पष्ट है कि जहाँ रामकुमार के स्तर पर पुरानी पीढ़ी के मूल्यों का संक्रमण लगभग नास्ति मूल्यों के रूप में हुआ है, वहाँ बंसी के स्तर पर ये नास्ति मूल्य पुनः स्वस्थ और प्रासंगिक मूल्यों में परिवर्तित हो गए हैं। रामकुमार जैसे युवकों की मानसिकता जहाँ चिंता उत्पन्न करती है, वहीं बंसी का परिवर्तन आश्वस्त करता है। सोनामाटी के पिता-पुत्र का संबंध भी आश्वस्त करता है। हालाँकि विलास बाबा की संगीत-प्रियता ने घर के आर्थिक ढाँचे को अस्त-व्यस्त किया है, चकबंदी में एक मौजे में सब उनके कारण बिगड़ गया[46] लेकिन इस सबको लेकर रामरूप उन पर आरोप-प्रत्यारोप नहीं करता। विलास बाबा भी अपने पुत्र के कमासुत हो जाने के बाद निष्क्रिय और अकर्मण्य नहीं हो जाते—"कोई सोच भी नहीं सकता था कि सारी जिंदगी मौज मस्ती में काटकर बेटा जब कमासुत हुआ तो चौथेपन में इस प्रकार वे खेती की माया में फँस जाएँगे।"[47] विलास बाबा गाँव की सांस्कृतिक मुद्रा के प्रतीक भी हैं। आर्थिक कारणों से यह सांस्कृतिक मुद्रा आहत हो रही है, इसका प्रमाण झिरहिरी का जुलूस है। जुलूस तो तैयार हो जाता है, लेकिन आर्थिक अभाव के चलते पुराना उल्लास नहीं लौट पाता।[48] विलास बाबा सहयोग, आत्मीयता, सद्भाव आदि जिन मान्यताओं पर विश्वास रखते हैं, वे आज के स्वार्थ-संकुल यथार्थ से टकराकर लहूलुहान हो रही हैं। दीनदयाल जैसे 'स्वार्थ' और 'अनीति' के पथ पर चलनेवाले फल-फूल रहे हैं। इस तथ्यचेतना के विपरीत विवेकीराय आदि उपन्यासकार अस्ति और मानवीय मूल्यों की दिशा में संक्रमण को वांछित मानते हैं। उनकी पक्षधरता पीढ़ी-विशेष के प्रति कहीं नहीं है। पक्षधरता सदैव मूल्य-विशेष के प्रति है। जो पीढ़ी स्वस्थ, मानवीय और सकारात्मक मूल्यों को जीवनपद्धति का अंग बनाए हुए है, अधिकतर आंचलिक उपन्यासकार उसी के पक्ष में हैं।

एकपत्नीव्रत, सतीत्व आदि की प्रासंगिकता

नगर-महानगर जीवन पर लिखे गए बहुत से उपन्यासों में विवाह की प्रासंगिकता पर जिस तरह बार-बार प्रश्नचिह्न लगाया गया और नर-नारी के काम संबंधों को लेकर यौनवर्जनाओं को नकारने का साहस दिखाया गया वह आंचलिक उपन्यासों में विरल है। झूठा सच, अँधेरे बंद कमरे, एक पति के नोट्स और उखड़े हुए लोग आदि में पति-पत्नी के संबंधों में तनाव के समानांतर जिस तरह नई मर्यादाओं के

उन्मेष को रेखांकित किया गया है, उस तरह की चेतना 'धरती लहरें और मनुष्य' जैसे कुछ आंचलिक उपन्यासों में ही उपलब्ध है। स्यात् ही किसी आंचलिक उपन्यासकार ने 'विवाह' की सार्थकता और प्रासंगिकता को चुनौती दी हो। इन कृतियों में पति-पत्नी के संबंध से जुड़े पातिव्रत, सतीत्व, पति की एकनिष्ठा आदि मूल्यों को यथावत् स्वीकारा गया है। 'असगाँव-पसगाँव' की सुनयना के संदर्भ में कहा गया है--''हिंदू औरत अब भी सुहाग को अपना अनमोल धन मानती है।''[49] 'कभी न छोड़े खेत' में ठाकुर शीतल कौर की बातचीत से पति के प्रति पत्नी की अनन्य निष्ठा बहुत मूल्यवान पदार्थ के रूप में सामने आती है।[50] पति या सुहाग को सर्वोच्च मूल्य के तौर पर मान्यता का आग्रह 'नदी फिर बह चली' की अंतिम पंक्तियों में द्रष्टव्य है। मरणोन्मुख परबतिया जगलाल को वास्तविक 'मँगटीका' कहकर संबोधित करती है।[51] जगलाल में कई ऐब हैं, लेकिन उसके प्रति परबतिया का लगाव कभी समाप्त नहीं होता। सुगनी (बलचनमा), रामरूप की पत्नी (सोनामाटी) वासंती (जल टूटता हुआ) आदि नारियों की मानसिकता कमोबेश इसी प्रकार की है। विधवा धूपो सतीत्व को इतना मूल्यवान समझती है कि अपमानित होने के बाद आत्महत्या कर लेती है।[52] एकनिष्ठता का यह भाव अधिकतर पतियों में विद्यमान है। बलचनमा, सुखई, सतीश आदि किसी भी स्तर पर परनारी से जुड़ते नहीं दिखाई देते । आधा गाँव में सैयद परिवारों के पुरुष अवश्य बीवी के अलावा रखैल भी रखे हुए हैं। 'अलग-अलग वैतरणी' के सुरजूसिंह, बुझारथ सिंह, 'नदी फिर बह चली' का जगलाल, 'जल टूटता हुआ' का दीनदयाल, रागदरबारी के वैद्य जी आदि पुरुष भी एकाधिक नारियों--विशेषतः निम्नवर्गीय युवतियों से अपनी वासना की तृप्ति करते देखे जा सकते हैं। 'आधा गाँव' का मिगदाद इस प्रकार की हीनतर मर्यादाओं के विरोध में दुस्साहसपूर्ण निर्णय करता है।[53] वह कुल की श्रेष्ठता और ऊँच-नीच की धारणा को तिरस्कृत करते हुए सैफुनिया नाइन से विवाह करता है। अपने वर्ग के अन्य लोगों की तरह वह रखैल रखने के पक्ष में नहीं है। वह विवाह भी एक से अधिक नहीं करना चाहता।[54] इस प्रकार वह एक तरह से वर्गच्युत होता है, उसे बिरादरी बाहर कर दिया जाता है, लेकिन वह अपने निर्णय पर पश्चात्ताप नहीं करता।

आंचलिक उपन्यासों में जिन नारियों को पति के 'परमेश्वरत्व' और जन्मजन्मांतर के संबंध को नकारते दिखाया गया है, उनकी यह परंपरा-विरोधी धारणा अकारण नहीं है। या तो इसके पीछे आर्थिक विवशताएँ हैं या नई मूल्य मर्यादा को स्वीकारने का दुस्साहस है। केवल यौन-बुभुक्षा के लिए पर-पुरुषगामी नारियाँ आंचलिक उपन्यासों में कम हैं। कुछ पत्नियों की वितृष्णा का कारण अनमेल विवाह है।[55] और कुछ की एकनिष्ठता खंडित होने के पीछे कुछ विशिष्ट महत्त्वाकांक्षाएँ, रुचियों की टकराहट और संतानहीनता जैसी स्थितियाँ हैं। 'कथा

कहो उर्वशी' की कोइली को कवयित्री बनने की महत्त्वाकांक्षा उसे हरिपद से काट देती है।[56] लेकिन अंत में कोइली का घर लौटना इस बात का प्रमाण है कि उपन्यासकार इस प्रकार के स्वैराचार को अपना समर्थन नहीं देता। निम्न वर्ग की नारियों के पतन के पीछे प्रायः गाँव के सामंती तत्त्वों के प्रलोभन या दबाव का हाथ होता है। रमेसर की घरवाली बाबू देवराम सिंह के जाल में फँस जाती है।[57] 'देहाती दुनिया' की सुगिया को दरोगा की वासना का शिकार बनना पड़ता है। 'परती परिकथा' के महीचन चमार को संदेह है कि उसकी पत्नी और योगेन्द्र भूमिहर में अवैध संबंध हैं।[58] निश्चय ही यह संबंध सवर्ण द्वारा हरिजन के परंपरागत शोषण की एक कड़ी होगा। करनटों की बहू-बेटियों का उपयोग ये तत्त्व न जाने कब से करते चले आ रहे हैं। प्यारी और कजरी को विवश होकर दूसरों की अंकशायिनी बनना पड़ता है। अनूपी के पलायन के पीछे आर्थिक विवशता के साथ-साथ कुछ मनोवैज्ञानिक कारण भी हैं। अनूपी अपने पति में एक अधिकार भावना चाहती है। नथुनी पानवाले के हाथों पिटकर उसे तृप्ति मिलती है।[59] 'अलग-अलग वैतरणी' में कनिया बुझारथ के कुकृत्यों से क्षुब्ध है। पति-पत्नी के संबंध बस नाम भर के हैं।[60] लेकिन कनिया में कोई नकारात्मक प्रतिक्रिया नहीं जन्मती। गिरीश और उनकी पत्नी का संबंध भी समाप्त प्राय है लेकिन किसी प्रकार का स्पष्ट विखंडन वहाँ नहीं दिखाई देता।[61] जहाँ पति की निरंकुशता सीमा पार कर गई है, वहाँ उसके प्रति पत्नी का वीतश्रद्ध होना सर्वथा स्वाभाविक है। ऐसी स्थितियों में आंचलिक उपन्यासकार पति के अबाध और निरंकुश अधिकार को नकार कर किसी अन्य पुरुष से जुड़ने के साहस को मान्यता देते हैं। 'सूरज किरन की छाँव' में जोसेफ अपनी पत्नी बंजारी को बेच देता है।[62] अतः अंत में बंजारी का कांगला के साथ जाना सर्वथा नैतिक है। बदमी को अपने दो-दो पतियों से जो यंत्रणा मिलती है वह उसकी श्रद्धा और निष्ठा को तोड़ देने के लिए पर्याप्त है। दूसरा पति उसे अस्मत बेचने पर मजबूर करता है और इनकार करने पर मारता-पीटता है।[63] आखिर वह पिता के घर आकर उस नरक से मुक्ति प्राप्त करती है। रत्ना और माणिक के संबंध विच्छेद का आधार भी 'जेनुइन' है। माणिक में न तो पुरुषत्व है न रत्ना की महत्त्वाकांक्षाओं को पूरी करने की क्षमता। वह धन के लिए 'पत्नी' को इस्तेमाल करने से नहीं चूकता। संबंध विच्छेद के उदाहरण आंचलिक उपन्यासों में बहुत कम हैं। इससे स्पष्ट है कि अधिकतर उपन्यासकार, नए मूल्यबोध के हावी होते हुए भी पति-पत्नी के संबंध को सामान्यतः भंग होने देने के पक्ष में नहीं हैं। लेकिन जहाँ नारी की अस्मिता और शुचिता पर आघात होता है, वहाँ वे 'मुक्ति' या 'विच्छेद' का विरोध नहीं करते। आंचलिक उपन्यासकार मनुस्मृति की इस व्यवस्था को आँख मींचकर नहीं स्वीकारते कि पति का पत्नी पर पूरा अधिकार होना है। कालिदास ने भी पत्नी पर पति के सर्वतोमुख अधिकार की चर्चा की है।[64] 'सूरज

किरन की छाँव', 'जल टूटता हुआ', 'सागर लहरें और मनुष्य' आदि उपन्यास इस सर्वतोमुख अधिकार को स्वीकार नहीं करते हैं। इसके साथ वे विवाहिता नारी के स्वच्छंदाचरण को भी मान्यता नहीं देते हैं। यहाँ नगर-महानगर के जीवन पर आधारित उपन्यासों के मूल्यबोध से आंचलिक उपन्यासों की मूल्यचेतना का अंतर समझा जा सकता है। 'वैशाखियों वाली इमारत' (रमेश बक्षी), 'मित्रो मरजानी' (कृष्णा सोवती), 'एक पति के नोट्स' (महेन्द्र भल्ला) आदि कृतियों में यौन स्वच्छंदता का विरोध नहीं किया गया है। 'अमृत और विष' में मिसेज माथुर को नागर जी ने अत्याधुनिक नारी की मानसिकता का संवाहक बनाया है। मिसेज माथुर को दुख है कि पवित्रता की बीमारी हमारे जाहिल देश में ही क्यों है ?[65] 'वे दिन' (निर्मल वर्मा) की रायना परपुरुष से संबंध स्थापित करने में नहीं हिचकती।[66] आंचलिक उपन्यासों में पति-पत्नी के संबंधों में आए बदलाव के समानांतर मूल्यों के संक्रमण को समझते हुए अंततः शारीरिक पवित्रता, एक निष्ठा, पातिव्रत आदि मूल्यों को प्रायः प्रासंगिक ठहराया गया है। स्थिति विशेष में ही इनके उल्लंघन का औचित्य माना गया है।

यौन शुचिता का समर्थन

'भूल' या 'विवशता' में यौन शुचिता की लक्ष्मण रेखा का अतिक्रमण होने पर यदि पति-पत्नी अनैतिकता से उबरना चाहते हैं तो कई उपन्यासों में उनकी वापसी को शुभ माना गया है। कोइली के लौटने पर हरिपद उसे सहर्ष स्वीकारने के लिए तत्पर है।[67] हीतलाल भी अनूपी को अपनाने के लिए तैयार है।[68] जगलाल भी अंततः 'कुपथगमन' छोड़ देता है।[69]

आंचलिक उपन्यासों में अवैध यौन संबंधों की चर्चा विस्तार से हुई है। लेकिन परंपरा से वर्जित यौन संबंधों को नैतिक मूल्यों का विरोधी समझा गया है। मौसेरी बहन (मैला आँचल), अनुजवधू (रतिनाथ की चाची, जल टूटता हुआ, सूखता हुआ तालाब), भाभी (अलग-अलग वैतरणी), पुत्रवधू (वरुण के बेटे, जुलूस) आदि के साथ यौन संबंधों में थोड़ी बहुत सहानुभूति भाभी के साथ जग्गन मिसिर के संबंध को लेकर है। चूँकि यह संबंध दबा-ढँका न होकर खुलेआम है, अतः इसे समर्थन देकर उपन्यासकार नई मूल्य-मर्यादा का साथ देता है। 'अनुजवधू' 'भगिनी' 'सुतनारी' के प्रति उपन्यासकार का रवैया परंपरागत है। 'रतिनाथ की चाची' में एक बार पाँव फिसल जाने के बाद गौरी दुबारा अपने जेठ को मर्यादा का अतिक्रमण नहीं करने देती। 'जल टूटता हुआ' का कुंजू बिरजू की बहू के खुले आमंत्रण को नकार कर अपनी नैतिक सबलता का परिचय देता है। 'सूखता हुआ तालाब' के मोतीलाल का अपनी विधवा अनुजवधू के साथ संबंध 'व्यभिचार' की सीमा को

नहीं लाँघ पाता। 'वरुण के बेटे' की मधुरी अपने शराबी श्वसुर की हरकतों को नहीं सह पाती। 'जुलूस' के तालेवर गोढ़ी का अपनी पुत्रवधू के साथ संबंध सबकी निंदा का विषय बनता है।

कुलीनता और कुलमर्यादा

संयुक्त परिवार की व्यवस्था में कुलीनता और कुलमर्यादा का बोध एक नियंत्रक की भूमिका निभाता है। व्यक्ति की निजी अभिरुचियाँ केवल इसलिए भी दमित होती हैं कि वे कुलीनता या कुलाभिमान के विरुद्ध पड़ती हैं। कुल की यह 'मरजाद' संयुक्त परिवार के बिखर जाने पर भी बरी रहती है। इसी 'मरजाद' की रक्षा के लिए 'गोदान' का होरी अपने भाई हीरा के घर तलाशी नहीं होने देता। आंचलिक उपन्यासों में केवल 'कुल' के आधार पर श्रेष्ठता के दंभ को न केवल खारिज किया गया है, अपितु गुणों के आधार पर व्यक्ति के छोटे-बड़े होने की धारणा प्रतिपादित हुई है। अशरफ उल्लाह खाँ अशरफ ताजियेदारी में महज इसलिए शरीक हो लेते हैं कि बाप-दादा की परंपरा बनी रहे।[70] विपिन 'बबुआन की मर्यादा' की रक्षा के लिए बुझारथ के अनुचित कार्यों को अनदेखा करता है।[71] चूँकि स्वतंत्रता के बाद सामंत वर्ग का प्रत्यक्षतः खात्मा हो गया, अतः कुदम की ठसक जैसी चीज शेष नहीं रही। महीपसिंह को जनता के दरबार में हाजिर होना पड़ता है।[72] शिवेन्द्र मिश्र इस सत्य से अवगत है कि जमीदारों की कुलीनता लूटखसोट जैसे नीच कर्मों से बनी है। वह रोज उड से स्पष्ट कहता है कि हर जमींदार की वंशावली में कोई न कोई डकैत जरूर होगा।[73] कुलीनता के दंग के तहत न केवल दूसरों को बहुत तुच्छ समझने की भूल की जाती है, अपितु बेईमानी, छल, गर्भपात, बलात्कार आदि कुकर्म भी संपन्न होते हैं। गौरी की माँ से चमाइन के कहे गए इन शब्दों से लगता है कि नीची कही जानेवाली जातियाँ सवर्णों से कहीं बेहतर हैं—"माफ करना, बड़ी जातवालों की तुम्हारी बिरादरी बड़ी मलिच्छ, बड़ी निठुर होती है मलिकाइन।...हमारी बिरादरी में किसी के पेट से आठ-आठ, नौ-नौ महीने का बच्चा निकालकर जंगल में फेंक आने का रिवाज नहीं है।"[74] बदमी विवाह पूर्व के अपने गर्भ को नहीं गिराती और सवर्ण परिवारों पर सीधा आपेक्ष करती है।[75] 'हौलदार' में ब्राह्मण उमादत्त मानसिंह को धक्का देकर मृत्यु के कगार पर पहुँचा देता है। किसन मिस्त्री मानसिंह का पक्ष लेता है और उमादत्त से कहीं अधिक भला सिद्ध होता है।[76]

जातिगत, वर्णगत मूल्य-मर्यादाएँ : संपूर्ण अस्वीकार

डॉ. राममनोहर लोहिया की निश्चित धारणा थी कि वर्ण और यौन, इन दो कठघरों पर प्रहार करने से बड़ा कोई पुण्य नहीं।[77] वर्ण-व्यवस्था का विकृत रूप जातिप्रथा

है। समाज के खंडात्मक विभाजन, खान-पान सामाजिक सहवास और व्यवसाय में स्वतंत्र चुनाव पर प्रतिबंध आदि दुर्बलताओं से जुड़ी जाति-व्यवस्था जहाँ समाज को छोटे-छोटे वर्गों में बाँटती है और पारस्परिक कटुता, मतभेद और घृणा का प्रश्रय देती है, वहीं संकुचित मूल्यों या नास्ति मूल्यों को उभारती है। 'जाति-व्यवस्था' को बनाए रखने में एक ओर उच्च कही जानेवाली जातियों के वर्ग हित सक्रिय हैं, दूसरी ओर भारतीय जीवन विशेषतः ग्रामीण जीवन पर धार्मिक मान्यताओं की मजबूत पकड़ भी इसके लिए उत्तरदायी है। 'जाति-व्यवस्था' की मान्यता के पीछे बहुत पहले से ही अलौकिक सत्ता में विश्वास और रहस्यात्मक पवित्रता-अपवित्रता की धारणाएँ विद्यमान रही हैं।[78] जातिप्रभा की कुरूपता कभी जातिगत श्रेष्ठता का दंभ बनकर व्यक्त होती है, तो कभी जाति-निष्ठा के आगे राजनीति, राष्ट्र और मानवता के प्रति निष्ठाओं के दुर्बल होने की विसंगति के रूप में उभरती है। 'जातिवाद' का रूप धारण करके जाति-निष्ठा न केवल मानवीय मूल्यों और आदर्शों के विरोध में खड़ी होती है अपितु स्वार्थ, अन्याय, अत्याचार आदि को खुला समर्थन देती दिखाई देती है। आंचलिक उपन्यासों में दिखाया गया है कि आधुनिकता के दबाव और प्रगति की आहट के बावजूद जाति-प्रथा का गुंजलक और कसता गया है। यह आकस्मिक नहीं है कि 'मैला आँचल' के डॉ. प्रशांत को जाति-संबंधी सवाल का सामना करना पड़ता है[79] और 'परानपुर' (परती परिकथा) में 'अस्पताल' और 'हाईस्कूल' में क्रमशः डॉक्टर और 'हेडमास्टर' नहीं टिकते।[80] कायस्थ डॉक्टर सिर्फ कायस्थों को अच्छी दवा देता है अतः दूसरी जाति के लोग उसे टिकने नहीं देते। यही हाल हेडमास्टर का है। इन हादसों को देखते हुए 'रेणु' की यह टिप्पणी सार्थक लगती है कि मनुष्य का हृदय हमेशा से जातिवाद के दीमकों का मुख्य आहार रहा है।[81]

'मैला आँचल', 'परती परिकथा', 'अलग-अलग वैतरणी', 'राग दरबारी', 'कब तक पुकारूँ' और 'आधा गाँव' के अध्ययन के आधार पर डॉ. विश्वंभरदयाल गुप्त ने दिखाया है कि जहाँ 'अलग-अलग वैतरणी' और 'कब तक पुकारूँ' के कथा-आंचल में ठाकुरों का प्रभुत्व है, वहीं 'परानपुर' और 'शिवपालगंज' में ब्राह्मणों का वर्चस् है। 'मैला आँचल' में कायस्थ प्रभावी हैं जबकि 'आधा गाँव' में चमार प्रमुख हैं।[82] वस्तुतः 'आधा गाँव' में बहुमत और प्रभाव शिया मुसलमानों का है। 'धरती धन न अपना', 'कभी न छोड़े खेत' में चौधरियों की चलती है, 'जल टूटता हुआ', 'रतिनाथ की चाची', 'बाबा बटेसरनाथ' और 'लोकऋण' स्थित अंचलों में ब्राह्मणों का प्रभुत्व है। 'देहाती दुनिया', 'लोहे के पंख' और 'हौलदार' में गाँव पर क्षत्रियों का नियंत्रण है अर्थात् पिछड़े अंचलों में सर्वत्र ऊँची जातिवालों की तूती बोलती है। उत्पादन के साधन इनके अधिकार में हैं और निम्न कही जानेवाली जातियों का शोषण करना वे अपना जन्मसिद्ध अधिकार समझते हैं। इस अधिकार

की व्यापकता और शक्ति असीमित है।[83] इसी अधिकार के चलते वे नान्हजात की महिलाओं की बेइज्जती करते हैं। 'अलग-अलग वैतरणी' का सिरिपा सरूप भगत से साफ कह देता है कि ठाकुर और चमार की इज्जत एक नहीं हो सकती।[84] चूँकि हरिजनों के पास भूमि नहीं है, वे पूरी तरह से सवर्णों पर निर्भर हैं,[85] अतः उनकी विवशता स्वयंसिद्ध है। 'धरती धन न अपना' से स्पष्ट है कि चौधरियों के मुकाबले गलती हमेशा कमीन की होती है। जातिगत ऊँचनीच की इस विसंगति को निम्न वर्ग ने आधुनिक युग से पहले बहुत कम चुनौती दी बल्कि जनसाधारण ने इसे, विवशता में ही सही, स्वीकृति दे रखी है। यह मान्यता आज भी निर्मूल नहीं हुई है कि व्यक्ति का छोटा-बड़ा होना ईश्वर की कृपा पर निर्भर है।[86] बहुसंख्यक निम्नवर्ग जो पिछले अंचलों में जी रहा है, जातिप्रथा के संदर्भ में उसका मूल्यबोध गोदान के 'होरी'[87] से आगे नहीं बढ़ा है। 'रागदरबारी' में वैद्यजी को लंगड़ जिस तरह मुर्गा बनकर प्रणाम करता है, उससे उपन्यासकार को लगता है, आज भी शास्त्र सर्वोपरि है और जातिप्रथा को मिटाने की सारी कोशिशें अगर फरेब नहीं तो रोमांटिक कार्यवाइयाँ जरूर हैं।[88]

जातिप्रथा खान-पान, चुनाव आदि अवसरों पर अपने समूचे खुलेपन में प्रस्तुत होती है। खानपान की गड़बड़ी होते ही जाति-बिरादरी की अप्रियता मोल लेनी पड़ती है। 'मैला आँचल' में बिरंची को कायस्थ तहसीलदार का जूठा खाने की अफवाह मात्र पर कड़ा प्रायश्चित्त करना पड़ता है।[89] भंडारे की घोषणा होने पर जातियों के खानपान संबंधी दुराग्रह उभर कर सामने आते हैं।[90] उच्च वर्ग के पाखंडी निम्नवर्ग की औरतों के साथ सोते हैं, लेकिन उनका छुआ नहीं खाते। इसके पीछे तर्क यह है कि 'धर्म' तो कमर से ऊपर होता है।[91] चुनाव के दिनों में जातिवाद बुरी तरह उभरता है। यादव, यादव उम्मीदवार को वोट देने के लिए प्रतिश्रुत हैं[92], उम्मीदवार की योग्यता से कोई लेना-देना नहीं। जाति से जुड़े परंपरागत मूल्यों का संक्रमण तीन दिशाओं में हुआ है। एक ओर 'स्वार्थ' और 'अर्थ' के आगे जातिगत मर्यादाएँ विचलित होती दिखाई देती हैं, दूसरी ओर पढ़े-लिखे लोगों द्वारा इनके आगे प्रश्नचिह्न लगाया गया है या इन्हें झटका देने के लिए व्यक्तिगत स्तर पर कुछ कार्य किए गए हैं। अस्पृश्य कही जानेवाली जातियों में अपने 'हीनत्व' के विरुद्ध चेतना जाति-व्यवस्था के प्रति संदेह और गुस्से की मिली-जुली अभिव्यक्ति है।

'रेणु' की यह पकड़ सही है कि धन की ऊँचाई जाति के बुर्ज से भी ऊँची होती है।[93] 'जाति' का 'धन' के आगे झुकना पूँजीवाद के आगे सामंतवादी समाज व्यवस्था का झुक जाना सूचित करता है। स्वतंत्रता के बाद जातिगत दायरे में संस्कृतीकरण और असंस्कृतीकरण की प्रक्रिया तीव्र हुई है। ब्राह्मणों की देखा-देखी निम्न मानी जानेवाली जातियों ने भी यज्ञोपवीत धारण करना शुरू किया और क्षत्रियों की स्पर्द्धा में कितने ही नए 'क्षत्रिय' पैदा हो गए।[94] सालकन्ह अपने को राजपूत

घोषित कर देते हैं और यादव स्वयं को क्षत्रिय मानते हैं। 'लोहे के पंख' का अकलू कहार कहारजाति की पैदाइश जरासंध से मानकर खुद को राजपूत मान लेता है।[95] लेकिन आजादी के बाद असंस्कृतीकरण की प्रक्रिया चली। निम्न जातियों को मिलनेवाली सरकारी असुविधाओं ने आल्हा-ऊदल के वंशजों को 'अनुसूचित जाति' और 'अनुसूचित जनजाति' की फेहरिस्त में अपना नाम लिखाने के लिए प्रेरित किया।[96] राजपूत माने जानेवाले बुनियादी बाबुओं ने परिगणित जाति का होने के पक्ष में तर्क देने शुरू किए—"कौन कहता है कि हम लोग राजपूत हैं। देख लीजिए गाँव में जाकर हमारी जाति के लोग भेड़ चराते हैं। औरतें साल में तीन ही बार नहाती हैं, आज भी"[97] अजीब गिरगिटिया जमाना है और 'प्रजातंत्र' नहीं 'लघुजातंत्र' है।[98] लेकिन यह 'सत्य' है कि 'उच्च जातियों' में शामिल होने की घटनाओं की तुलना में असंस्कृतीकरण की घटनाएँ कम देखने में आती हैं।

जातिप्रथा की अस्वीकृति

समाज की सवर्ण और असवर्ण दोनों जातियों में एक समझदार तबका उभरा है जो तर्क और बौद्धिकता के आधार पर जातिप्रथा को अस्वीकार करता है। सवर्ण जहाँ एक प्रकार का बौद्धिक असंतोष व्यक्त कर चुप हो जाता है, वहीं अस्पृश्य की अस्वीकृति उग्र और आक्रामक भी दिखाई देती है। 'बबूल' में 'अस्पृश्यता' के प्रति बौद्धिक शंका 'नैरेटर' के इस सोच में निहित है कि अछूत उसके लोटे से पानी क्यों नहीं पी सकता है—"क्यों इसे अछूत समझें···यदि नियम, कानून और व्यवहार को चीरकर अलग कर दिया जाए तो मैं कितना तुच्छ हूँ, इसके सामने।"[99] न केवल हिंदुओं अपितु मुसलमानों में भी समझदार लोगों ने जान लिया है कि जातिगत, कुलगत मर्यादाएँ जमींदारी का चोंचला थीं।[100] 'सतीश' (जल टूटता हुआ) के विचार में जाति-पाँति अन्याय को सह लेने का एक मिथ्या संकोच सिखानेवाली रूढ़ि है।[101] जाति प्रथा के प्रति सवर्ण व्यक्तियों के विरोधी रवैये में फिर भी ठंडापन है, क्योंकि उन्होंने उस उपेक्षा और दमन के विष को नहीं पिया है, जो हरिजनों तथा अन्य दलितों को प्रायः पीना पड़ता है। फिर भी बौद्धिक स्तर पर ही सही जाति-पाँति और अस्पृश्यता को नकारना उस मूल्य-संक्रमण का द्योतक है, जो शिक्षा और विज्ञान प्रभाव से शिक्षित मध्यवर्ग में जन्मा है।

दलितवर्ग की उग्र प्रतिक्रिया

जाति-प्रथा के संदर्भ में दलित वर्ग के मूल्यों का संक्रमण केवल 'सोच' के स्तर पर घटित नहीं होता, अपितु 'व्यवहार' में हिंसा के सीमांत तक पहुँचता दिखाई देता है। कुछ थोड़े से हरिजन युवक बगैर किसी वर्ग-संघर्ष के अपने को ऊपर

उठाने में विश्वास रखते हैं।[102] लेकिन यह जानी हुई बात है कि दलितों का हित-साधन उच्चवर्गीय सवर्णों के वर्ग-हितों से टक्कर लिए बिना नहीं हो सकता। जहाँ 'बलचनमा' को विश्वास नहीं था कि वर्गभेद नहीं रहेगा।[103] वहीं 'धरती धन न अपना', 'अलग-अलग वैतरणी', 'जंगली सुअर', 'कब तक पुकारूँ' आदि उपन्यासों के दलित यह मानकर चलते हैं कि संगठित संघर्ष से ऊँच-नीच, छुआछूत की खाई पाटी जा सकती है। इसीलिए उनमें एक किस्म की आक्रामकता है। 'धरती धन न अपना' में काली के नेतृत्व में हरिजन चौधरियों से जमकर टक्कर लेते हैं। उन्हें आगाह कर देते हैं कि हम भी इंसान हैं।[104] लेकिन उन्हें संघर्ष में सफलता नहीं मिलती, क्योंकि उनमें वह चेतना नहीं थी जो स्थैतिक यथार्थ (स्टैटिक रीयलिटी) को प्रावैगिक यथार्थ (डाइनैमिक रीयलिटी) में बदल देती।[105] इसके बावजूद शोषण की मूक स्वीकृति के स्थान पर अन्याय के विरोध को 'मूल्य' के रूप में प्रतिष्ठित किया गया है। अब उच्चवर्ग के अत्याचारों को दलित वर्ग अपनी 'नियति' मानकर सहज भाव से नहीं स्वीकारता। एक जमाना था जब छोटी जाति के व्यक्ति को गाँव में घोड़े या ऊँट की सवारी करने की सजा लात-घूँसों से दी जाती थी।[106] ब्राह्मण-ठाकुर निकलने पर चमरही या चमरौठी के लोग हाथ जोड़कर खड़े हो जाते थे। हुक्के जमीन पर रख दिए जाते थे। चिलमें फेंक दी जाती थीं। "और महाराज चारों ओर आशीर्वाद लुटाते हुए और इस बात की पड़ताल करते हुए कि पिछले चार महीनों में किसकी लड़की पहले के मुकाबले जवान दिखने लगी और कौन लड़की ससुराल से वापस आ गई, त्रेता युग की तरह वातावरण पर सवारी गाँठते हुए निकल जाते थे।"[107] लेकिन आजादी के बाद के वर्षों में इतना बदलाव आया कि वैद्यजी (रागदरबारी) जैसे लोगों ने उधर से निकलना बंद कर दिया। लेकिन वैद्यजी जैसे व्यक्तियों के सोच में कोई फर्क नहीं आया। वे हरिजनों को 'पैर की जूती' से अधिक न तब समझते थे, न अब मानते हैं। 'सोनभद्र की राधा' में रामधनी सिंह हरभजन को खबरदार कर देते हैं—"ऐसी वैसी बातें यहाँ फैलाईं तो बनगाँव में रहना मुश्किल हो जाएगा। दादे जूती बनकर जिए हैं, तुम्हें भी बाबुओं की जूती बनकर रहना है।"[108] जाहिर है मूल्यों का संक्रमण वैद्यजी, रामधनी सिंह जैसों के चिंतन के स्तर पर नहीं हुआ है। यह कुछ समझदार सवर्णों और भुक्तभोगी हरिजनों की चेतना स्तर पर घट रहा है। महात्मा गांधी, अम्बेडकर के प्रभाव से हरिजनों में अपनी स्थिति से उबरने की छटपटाहट पैदा हो गई थी। वे मंदिर, कुएँ आदि पर लगी बंदिशों को तोड़ने लगे थे।[109] चाहे भीतर से उगी चेतना हो या अस्पृश्यता अधिनियम 1955 का प्रभाव हो, आजादी के बाद हरिजनों और दलितों को सवर्णों से बहस करते, तर्क करते और कभी-कभी आत्मरक्षार्थ लाठी उठाते देखा जा सकता है। उनमें यह 'सोच' प्रबल हो रहा है कि निम्न जाति में पैदा होने मात्र से कोई बड़ी जातिवालों का गुलाम नहीं हो जाता।[110] लवंगी (जल टूटता हुआ) ने अपने

भाई के पीटे जाने पर जो सवाल पूछा है, वह सामंती व्यवस्था में नहीं पूछा जा सकता था–"चमार का खून खून नहीं है, बामन का खून खून है। हमारी कोई इज्जत नहीं होती क्या, बामनों की ही इज्जत होती है।"[111] 'असगाँव-पसगाँव' के हरिजन जमींदारी के जमाने की मजदूरी पर काम करने से इनकार करते हैं और सुखई जैसे समझदार सवर्ण भी जानते हैं कि बँधे कुत्ते अहेर नहीं होनेवाला है।[112]

जाति वर्ण से जुड़े पूरे मूल्यों पर एक जबर्दस्त प्रहार अंतर्जातीय विवाहों–खासतौर पर प्रतिलोम विवाहों ने किया है। हालाँकि उपन्यासों में अनुलोम विवाह के उदाहरण ही अधिक हैं। समझदार सवर्ण युवक 'अस्पृश्यता' या 'ऊँचनीच' की लक्ष्मण-रेखा लाँघते हुए अन्त्यज युवतियों का हाथ थाम लेते हैं, जबकि उनके पूर्वज उनका यौन शोषण करना बहुत साधारण बात समझते थे। 'परती परिकथा' में सुवंश और मलारी[113] अग्निबीज में हरिजन छबिया और हुड़दंगी ब्राह्मण[114], 'जल टूटता हुआ' में कुंजुतिवारी और बदमी कहारिन[115], 'आधा गाँव' में मियाँदाद और सैफुनिया नाइन[116] के विवाह परंपरागत मूल्यों को खुली चुनौती देते हैं। प्रतिलोम विवाह के उदाहरण 'सोनभद्र की राधा' और 'मैला आँचल' में देखे जा सकते हैं। उच्चवर्ण की अनुराधा हरिजन युवक की अर्द्धांगिनी बनती है और अज्ञात कुलशील प्रशांत को तहसीलदार साहब जामाता के रूप में स्वीकारते हैं।[117] यदि उपन्यासकारों ने अंतर्जातीय विवाहों पर बल दिया है तो यह साभिप्राय है। एक सर्वेक्षण के अंतर्गत यह पाया गया कि अधिकतर व्यक्ति जहाँ छुआछूत, खानपान आदि के प्रति उदार थे, वहीं हरिजनों से विवाह के प्रश्न पर उनका रुख सकारात्मक नहीं था।[118] अतः सवर्ण-हरिजन विवाह दिखाकर उपन्यासकारों ने वस्तुस्थिति का अतिक्रमण करने और भावी यथार्थ को रेखांकित करने की कोशिश की है। लेकिन यादवेंद्र शर्मा चंद्र जैसे कुछ उपन्यासकार अंतर्जातीय विवाह को समस्या का हल नहीं मानते। 'हजार घोड़ों का सवार' के नायक गीधू का विचार है–"इससे कोई क्रांति नहीं होगी। सामूहिक रूप से आर्थिक समता ही वास्तविक वर्गहीन समाज की रचना का कदम है।"[119]

'मुक्ति' और सामाजिक मूल्यों के बीच जबर्दस्त तनाव होता है।[120] पुराने और यथास्थितिवादी मूल्य 'मुक्ति' के आड़े आते हैं। इसलिए प्रायः मुक्ति के लिए संघर्ष अनिवार्य हो जाता है और हमेशा यह संघर्ष अहिंसक ही नहीं होता। हरिवंश और अनुराग चतुर्वेदी के साथ बातचीत में समाजशास्त्री आंद्रे बेते ने स्वीकार किया है कि मानव इतिहास से मालूम होता है, पद दलित वर्ग और सताया हुआ जनमानस एक सीमा तक संघर्ष से आगे बढ़ा है। "इसलिए यह धारणा कि मुक्ति की यह प्रक्रिया बिल्कुल ही शांतिपूर्बक पूरी हो जाएगी, यथार्थपरक नहीं है। इसका यह अर्थ भी कतई नहीं है कि जानबूझकर संघर्ष और तनाव की स्थिति बनाई जाए। पर इस प्रक्रिया में संघर्ष और तनाव अवश्य ही निहित हैं।"[121] जिनके वर्गहितों पर आँच आएगी वे दलितों के उत्थान को नहीं सह सकते। आजादी के बाद

हरिजन-सवर्ण-संघर्ष और हरिजन-दहन की ढेरों घटनाएँ सिद्ध करती हैं कि संविधान और सरकार द्वारा निम्न वर्ग के ऊपर उठने की हिमायत के बावजूद उच्च वर्ग इस परिवर्तन के लिए तैयार नहीं है। इसलिए पहल दलितों को ही करनी है। 'अलग-अलग वैतरणी', 'जंगली सुअर', 'धरती धन न अपना' आदि उपन्यासों में यह 'सत्य' प्रखरता से उभरा है।

हालाँकि 'धरती धन न अपना' में अछूतों का संघर्ष अहिंसा की हद से बाहर नहीं गया और उनकी जीत भी नहीं हुई, इसके बावजूद उनकी लड़ाई सामाजिक बदलाव की अनिवार्यता को रेखांकित करती है।[122] दलित बदलाव की आवश्यकता को महसूसें, यह कम महत्त्वपूर्ण बात नहीं है। सदियों से सोई झील का जागना एक ऐतिहासिक घटना से कम न होगा। अन्याय के विरोध में संघर्ष की प्रतिष्ठा 'अलग-अलग वैतरणी' में हुई है। यह संघर्ष व्यक्तिगत न होकर सामूहिक है। हरिजन संगठित होकर सुगनी को सुरजू सिंह के घर बिठाने यानी कि पत्नी का अधिकार दिलाने के लिए जुलूस की शक्ल में चल पड़ते हैं।[123] हालाँकि उनका अभियान सफल नहीं होता, फिर भी उनके गुस्से के भावी परिणामों की चेतावनी देने की दृष्टि से वह असफल नहीं है। जंगली सुअर में भी दलित वर्ग की चेतना का उभार द्रष्टव्य है।[124] 'सोनभद्र की राधा' में उच्च वर्ग के इस मनोविज्ञान को शोषित वर्ग जानता है कि अधिकार माँगने और लेने के पक्ष में वे नहीं होंगे।[125] इसलिए उपन्यास की अंतिम पंक्तियों में संघर्ष का स्पष्ट आह्वान मिलता है—"इस असली सूरज की कसम/तुम्हें मरते दम तक/इस लाल और इंसान सूरज के लिए/संघर्ष करते रहना होगा/ओ प्रिय···मेरे दोस्तो।"[126] 'असगाँव-पसगाँव' में महाजनी सभ्यता के चंगुल में फँसे हरिजनों की मुक्ति चेतना एक छटपटाहट के रूप में व्यक्त हुई है। बहुत सोचने-विचारने के बाद 'संघर्ष' एक मात्र रास्ता दिखाई देता है। लड़कों का नारा—"जो कमाएगा/वह खाएगा" इस समस्या के समाधान की दिशा की ओर इंगित करता है।[127] 'हजार घोड़ों का सवार' में गीधू के नेतृत्व में हरिजनों का प्रदर्शन भी इस संदर्भ में द्रष्टव्य है।

दलित-विद्रोह की सीमा

तमाम संघर्ष के बावजूद दलित वर्ग का संघर्ष अभी जाति-संघर्ष से आगे नहीं बढ़ा है। कुछ मार्क्सवादी विचारक आवेश में आकर हरिजन-सवर्ण संघर्ष को वर्ग संघर्ष मान बैठते हैं।[128] प्रायः देखा गया है कि पिछड़ी और उच्च जाति के भूमिहीन भी इस संघर्ष में अपनी जाति का साथ देते हैं। लेकिन आंचलिक उपन्यासकार इसी पक्ष में दिखाई देते हैं कि जाति-संघर्ष 'वर्गसंघर्ष' का रूप धारण करे। यहाँ वे मराठी के दलित कथाकारों से अलग दिखाई देते हैं। दलित कथाकारों का विद्रोह

'व्यवस्था' या 'शोषणतंत्र' के प्रति उतना नहीं है, जितना उच्च जातियों के प्रति। दया पवार जैसे कथाकार उच्च वर्गों के प्रति इतने कटु और आक्रामक हैं कि वे मल उठाने के कार्य में यानी कि भंगी की नौकरी में सवर्णों के पाँच प्रतिशत आरक्षण की माँग करते हैं।[129] इसके विपरीत आंचलिक कथाकार जातिगत घृणा का अतिक्रमण करते हुए जाति-संघर्ष को वर्गसंघर्ष की शक्ल देने के आकांक्षी हैं। यही कारण है कि वे बार-बार इस तथ्य को सामने लाते हैं कि जातियाँ सिर्फ दो हैं—अमीर, गरीब अर्थात् शोषक-शोषित। यदि 'मैला आँचल' में कहा गया—"जाति क्या है ? जाति दो ही हैं, एक अमीर और दूसरी गरीब।"[130] तो 'जल टूटता हुआ' में भी अनुभव किया गया कि वर्ग केवल दो ही हैं।[131] 'सोनभद्र की राधा' का महंत इसी नतीजे पर पहुँचा है कि असल में दो ही जात होती हैं—अमीर-गरीब।[132] एक सर्वेक्षण के अनुसार पुरानी और नई पीढ़ी के बहुत से लोगों का स्पष्ट विचार है कि आर्थिक असमानता ही व्यक्ति-व्यक्ति के बीच सामाजिक दूरी की खाई को चौड़ा कर रही है।[133] अस्पृश्यता के संदर्भ में उपन्यासकारों का 'विजन' भी इसी ओर संकेत कर रहा है। वे इसे आर्थिक समस्या के रूप में लेते हुए समानता, संघर्ष, त्याग आदि मूल्यों को अपना भरपूर समर्थन देते हैं। ग्रामीण अंचल के संदर्भ में यह उल्लेखनीय है कि छुआछूत आदि को लेकर मूल्यों का संक्रमण युवा मानस के स्तर पर जितना तीव्र है उतना पुरानी पीढ़ी के स्तर पर नहीं। इसीलिए युवा पीढ़ी के औपन्यासिक चरित्र इन विसंगतियों के विरुद्ध पर्याप्त सक्रिय दिखाई देते हैं। 'काली' (धरती धन न अपना), 'कुंजू' (जल टूटता हुआ), 'गीधू' (हजार घोड़ों का सवार), गोबिन (सोनभद्र की राधा), सुवंश-मलारी (परती परिकथा), सागर सुनीत (अग्नि बीज) आदि युवा चरित्र इस संदर्भ में द्रष्टव्य हैं। इनमें भी दलित वर्ग के चरित्रों के मानसिक स्तर पर मूल्यों का संक्रमण अपेक्षाकृत तीव्र और मुखर है। शताब्दियों से सवर्ण हितों के पोषक मूल्यों के विरुद्ध उठ खड़े होना साधारण बात नहीं है।

दलित वर्ग की यह नियति विडंबनापूर्ण है कि उसके कुछ सदस्य शिक्षित और संपन्न होकर न केवल अपने परिकर के लोगों से घृणा करने लगते हैं, बल्कि उनका शोषण भी करते हैं। 'आधा गाँव' में गरीब तबके को नेता परसुराम की खिदमत में उसी तरह जमीन पर बैठना पड़ता है, जैसे कभी जमींदारों के सामने बैठना होता था।[134] 'सोनभद्र की राधा' का बलेसर रैदास हरिजन होते हुए भी हरिजनों से घृणा करता है। चमरौली के लोग उसके सामने खाट या ऊँची जगह नहीं बैठ पाते।[135] इस प्रकार की घृणा के पीछे इन व्यक्तियों का 'डिक्लास' होना तो है ही, अपनी 'हीनताग्रंथि' को ढकने का प्रयास भी एक कारण है। आंचलिक उपन्यासकार अच्छी तरह दिखा पाते हैं कि संपत्ति और अधिकार मिलने पर शोषित वर्ग के ही कुछ व्यक्ति अपने वर्ग के लोगों का शोषण करने लगते हैं। 'हजार

घोड़ों का सवार' में विश्वेश्वर शर्मा ने इस विसंगति को स्पष्ट करते हुए पूँजीवादी विकृतियों के प्रभाव को इसके लिए जिम्मेदार ठहराया है।[136] इसके अतिरिक्त अजीब त्रासदी है कि हरिजनों में आपसी छुआछूत कम नहीं है। चमार भंगी के हाथ का पानी नहीं पीता और भंगी के लिए धोबी अछूत है। चूँकि धोबी रजस्वला नारियों के कपड़े भी धोता है। अतः भंगी उसे नीच और छोटा मानते हैं।[137]

दलित जीवन पर मराठी साहित्य में स्वयं दलित लेखकों द्वारा बहुत लिखा गया है। दया पवार, बाबूराम बागूल, अरुण साधू, राजा ढाले, अर्जुन डाँगले आदि मराठी कथाकारों ने जिस 'दलित' साहित्य की रचना की है, उसमें उत्कट मुक्ति-चेतना मुखर है। उनकी रचनाओं में 'दलित चेतना' से आशय अनिवार्यतः दलितों में 'मुक्ति' की चेतना से है। हर तरह के शोषण से मुक्ति की छटपटाहट और समानाधिकार की समवेत माँग दलित चेतना का प्रमुख पक्ष है।[138] दलितों का लेखन दलितों द्वारा दलितों के लिए है। स्वयं असमानता और जातिभेद के भुक्तभोगी होने के कारण वर्तमान व्यवस्था के प्रति मराठी के दलित लेखक बहुत कटु हैं। वे डॉ. अम्बेडकर के विचारों से प्रभावित हैं और दलितों के लिए कष्टदायी इस व्यवस्था को बदलना चाहते हैं। उनके संबंध में डॉ. चंद्रकांत बांदिवडेकर का यह कथन गौरतलब है–

"प्राणों की बाजी लगाकर लड़नेवाले योद्धा के तेवर में वे लिखते हैं। ऐसी व्यवस्था वे चाहते हैं, जो न्यायोचित विकास के अवसर दे सके, जाति, वर्ण, अर्थ के नाम पर किसी प्रकार की विषमता न रहने दे।"[139]

मराठी कथासाहित्य में असमानता और शोषण आदि अवमूल्यों के प्रति कितना आक्रोश है, इसका संकेत दया पवार के इस प्रस्ताव से मिलता है कि मैला ढोने के काम के लिए ब्राह्मणों का अनिवार्य आरक्षण किया जाए। मराठी दलित-लेखन में अमानवीय मूल्यों से हटकर मानवीय और शुभ मूल्यों की दिशा में संक्रमण काम्य है। हिंदी के आंचलिक उपन्यासों का मूल्यबोध भी दलित-जीवन के संदर्भ में लगभग यही है। लेकिन दोनों में एक अंतर है। चूँकि मराठी लेखक स्वयं दलित वर्ग के हैं, दलित-जीवन की यातनाओं के वे भुक्तभोगी हैं, अतः उनका सोच उग्र और आक्रामक है। उन्होंने यथार्थ के अंगारे को चिमटे से नहीं पकड़ा है, उसे अपनी हथेली पर अनुभव किया है। इसलिए उनके मूल्यबोध में अनुभूत यथार्थ का ताप अपेक्षाकृत अधिक है। वे रूढ़ियों और पुरामूल्यों के प्रति आक्रामक हैं। इनकी तुलना में हिंदी आंचलिक उपन्यासकार प्रायः मध्यवर्ग से आए हैं और मधुकर सिंह जैसे कुछ उपन्यासकारों को छोड़कर अन्य सभी ने दलितों की पीड़ा को दूर से ही देखा और अनुभव किया है। अतः दलित-जीवन के संदर्भ में मूल्यों का तीव्र संक्रमण, उनकी रचनाओं में है अवश्य, लेकिन 'मुक्ति' की ललक और रूढ़ियों के प्रति घृणा उनमें उतनी उत्कट और तीव्र न होकर पर्याप्त संयमित है।

यह आश्चर्यजनक है कि शोषण और उत्पीड़न का विरोध करनेवाले मराठी दलित लेखकों ने मार्क्सवादी विचारधारा से परहेज किया है और प्रायः 'अम्बेडकरवादी' बने रहे हैं। डॉ. अम्बेडकर ने जहाँ दलितों की मुक्ति, शिक्षा और संगठन में निहित मानी है, वहीं धर्म-परिवर्तन को भी वे बहुत कारगर मानते हैं। बौद्ध धर्म अंगीकार करना वस्तुतः करुणा, विश्वमैत्री आदि मूल्यों को स्वीकार करना है। धर्म परिवर्तन को हिंदी उपन्यासकारों ने एकदम खारिज कर दिया है।[140] हिंदी उपन्यासकारों ने प्रायः दलितों की नियति का हल मार्क्सवादी चिंतन के अनुरूप 'वर्ग संघर्ष' के जरिए ढूँढ़ा है। इसके लिए वे 'हिंसा' को भी एक विकल्प के रूप में स्वीकार करते हैं। 'जंगली सुअर' में दलितों का जुलूस, 'सोनामाटी' में दलितों द्वारा घिराव का आयोजन और नागार्जुन के 'वरुण के बेटे' आदि उपन्यासों में जन-प्रतिरोध को अहिंसक नहीं कहा जा सकता है। प्रत्यक्ष अनुभव की कमी को आंचलिक उपन्यासकारों ने अपने सुचिंतित प्रगतिशील चिंतन द्वारा पूरा किया है।

नारी जीवन से जुड़े मूल्यों में परिवर्तन की आहट

आंचलिक उपन्यासों में आए प्रमुख नारी पात्र—'रत्ना' (सागर, लहरें और मनुष्य), 'बदमी' (जल टूटता हुआ), 'परबतिया' (नदी फिर बह चली), 'प्यारी' (कब तक पुकारूँ), 'सनीचर बहू' (जंगली सुअर), 'मलारी' (परती परिकथा), 'मधुरी' (वरुण के बेटे) आदि किसी न किसी मूल्य का प्रतिनिधित्व करती हैं। ये नारियाँ रूढ़ मूल्यों से जूझती हुई सकारात्मक मूल्यों की दिशा में प्रस्थान कर रही हैं। रत्ना अपने पति को नकार देती है। यह नकार पुरुष के निरंकुश एकाधिकार का अस्वीकार करना है। रत्ना आदि सभी नारियाँ श्रमजीवी वर्ग से संबंधित हैं। एक तो श्रमजीवी वर्ग स्वयं रूढ़ियों के मलबे में दबा रहा है, ऊपर से उनकी नारियाँ अपने वर्ग तथा शोषक वर्ग के पुरुषों के द्वारा बराबर उत्पीड़ित होती रही हैं। इस दुहरे दबाव में जी रही नारियों में अपनी अस्मिता के प्रति चेतना का उभार स्वातंत्र्योत्तर परिवर्तनों के मेल में है। नारी-शिक्षा के प्रसार ने नारी चेतना को थोड़ा बहुत बल प्रदान किया है। दलित वर्ग की नारी 'मलारी' शिक्षित होकर सवर्ण सुवंश से विवाह करने का निर्णय करती है।[141] सनीचर बहू का पढ़ा-लिखा होना भूस्वामियों को खटकता है। उसका चमटोली में स्कूल खोलने का निर्णय सवर्ण भूस्वामियों को उनकी 'कुलीनता', 'जातीय श्रेष्ठता', और धन की ऊँचाई पर एक प्रहार सा लगता है।[142] सनीचर बहू हर तरह का अपवाद और अपमान सहकर दलितों में साक्षरता, सम्मान और विद्रोह भाव का प्रसार करती है। न केवल दलितों अपितु अभिजात कहे जानेवाले वर्ग में भी लड़कियों की शिक्षा कुछ समय पहले तक गैरजरूरी मानी जाती थी। शिया मुसलमानों में किसी लड़की का नौकरी करना किसी कयामत से कम नहीं

था, सईदा (आधा गाँव) पढ़कर नौकरी करती है और तमाम अपवाद और लांछन के बावजूद 'स्वावलंबन' और आर्थिक 'मुक्ति' के रास्ते पर चलती है। उसके जमींदार पिता का उससे संवाद खत्म कर देना[143] और पड़ोसियों का अभिभावकों को लड़की की कमाई खाने का ताना देना प्रमाण है कि सईदा का निर्णय उस रूढ़िवादी परिवेश में कितना क्रांतिकारी था। परबतिया का अपने बच्चे को पढ़ाने का निर्णय कम क्रांतिकारी नहीं है। अभिजात वर्ग के व्यक्ति उसके इस निर्णय का विरोध करते हैं क्योंकि उन्हें डर है कि वह पढ़-लिखकर कहीं शोषण-चक्र का विरोध न करने लगे।[144] 'प्यारी' (कब तक पुकारूँ) अपने ढंग से शोषण का विरोध करती है। इन नारी पात्रों के माध्यम से उपन्यासकारों ने ग्रामांचल की नारियों में सुगबुगाती मुक्ति-चेतना को रेखांकित किया है। इस मुक्ति-चेतना के अंतर्गत सामंती और रूढ़िवादी मूल्यों को निरस्त करते हुए संक्रमण 'श्रम', 'सम्मान', 'समानता' आदि मूल्यों की दिशा में हुआ है। इसे उदग्र सामाजिक 'गतिशीलता' का प्रमाण माना जा सकता है। मधुरी (वरुण के बेटे) सिद्ध करती है कि अब नारी जनसंघर्ष में प्रत्यक्ष भाग ले सकती है।

पूरनचंद जोशी के अनुसार—"नए सांस्कृतिक मूल्यों को, जिनमें नारी के प्रति आदर एवं नारी मुक्ति स्वयं सर्वश्रेष्ठ मूल्य है, तब तक नहीं बढ़ाया जा सकता है जब तक परजीविता के प्रोत्साहन देनेवाली आर्थिक व्यवस्था के स्थान पर श्रम, उद्यम, सहयोग और भागीदारी पर आधारित आर्थिक व्यवस्था की स्थापना नहीं होती।"[145] लगभग इसी निष्कर्ष पर आंचलिक उपन्यासकार भी पहुँचे हैं। वे मानते हैं कि हर तरह की मूल्यगत असंगति मौजूदा व्यवस्था के अंतर्विरोधों की देन है। इस व्यवस्था में 'कोइली' (सोनामाटी), 'बदमी' (जल टूटता हुआ), 'बंजारी' (सूरज किरन की छाँव) आदि युवतियों की नियति यही है कि वे सभी भेड़ियों का आहार बनती रहें। वे बनती भी हैं, लेकिन अब इस शोषण को वे भाग्य या ईश्वर की देन मानकर स्वीकार नहीं करती हैं। तीव्र आक्रोश का भाव उनमें खौल रहा है और नए मूल्य-बोध की स्वीकृति का द्योतक है। लेकिन यह विद्रोह भाव अभी कुछ इनीगिनी नारियों के स्तर पर ही उगा है, अधिकतर ग्रामीण नारियाँ—विशेषतः दलित नारियाँ अभी रूढ़ियों और गलत मूल्यों की गुंजलक में छटपटा रही हैं और नास्ति मूल्यों के प्रभाव को व्यंजित करती हैं।

सतीत्व, यौनशुचिता, पतिनिष्ठा आदि नैतिक मूल्यों को लेकर आंचलिक उपन्यासों की नारी का रुख प्रायः परंपरागत है। कोई नारी स्वेच्छा से इनका उल्लंघन नहीं करती। लेकिन कतिपय विशिष्ट संदर्भों में कुछ नारियों को इन लक्ष्मण रेखाओं को लाँघते दिखाया गया है और ऐसे स्थलों पर नई मानसिकता का उभार द्रष्टव्य है। बदमी और कुंजू जानते हैं कि चोरी-चोरी मिलना प्यार को बदनाम करना है लेकिन बिना विवाह के देह-संपर्क उन्हें पाप कतई नहीं लगता।[146] 'मैला आँचल'

में कमली और प्रशांत का विवाह पूर्व संबंध और कमला का विवाहहीन मातृत्व हालाँकि सबके सामने नहीं है, फिर भी कमली कुँआरी माँ बनकर नई मूल्य-मर्यादा का संकेत देती है। उसे महाभारत के मिथकों से बल मिलता है—"माँ रोती क्यों थी ? महाभारत में कुंती, देवयानी, अहल्या, द्रोपदी, कौन ऐसी है जिसको..."[147] इस तरह के नारी चरित्र जहाँ भी यौनशुचिता का अतिक्रमण करते हैं, वहाँ जानबूझकर करते हैं। वे उसके परिणामों से अवगत हैं और प्रायः किसी न किसी सामाजिक रूढ़ि को चुनौती देते हैं। कहीं भी आंचलिक उपन्यासकारों ने यौन-उच्छृंखलता या व्यभिचार को गौरवान्वित नहीं किया है। कमली, बदमी और रत्ना जैसी नारियों में पुराने मूल्यों का अतिक्रमण अमूर्त्त संवेग के स्तर पर नहीं है। यह अहम् या कर्तव्याभिमान के स्तर तक दृढ़ हो चुका है। क्षणिक आवेश में आकर किसी मूल्य को अस्वीकार नहीं किया गया है। ऊपरी तौर पर परंपरागत दृष्टिकोण से ये मूल्य-निर्णय अनुचित और अनैतिक धारणाओं की ओर संक्रमण करते दिखाई देते हैं। लेकिन ऐसा वास्तव में है नहीं। स्थिति विशेष में इनकी प्रासंगिकता है और न तो इन नारियों ने और न उपन्यासकार ने इन्हें 'पाप' या अनैतिक माना है। बल्कि ये मूल्य-निर्णय इस सत्य को उजागर करने में समर्थ हैं कि नारी को वर्जनाओं में बाँधकर नहीं रखा जा सकता। चाहे वह नगर की आधुनिक नारी हो या गाँव की परंपराप्रिय नारी।

सांप्रदायिकता : सकारात्मक मूल्य-दृष्टि

'अलग-अलग वैतरणी', 'आधा गाँव' आदि में सांप्रदायिक मूल्यों को सीधे नकारा गया है। खलील मियाँ, फुन्नन खाँ वगैरह मुसलमान 'पाकिस्तान' को खारिज कर देते हैं। 'पाकिस्तान' को खारिज करने का अर्थ है, दो कौम, दो राष्ट्र के अलगाववादी दृष्टिकोण को नकार देना। अपने पाकिस्तान स्थित पुत्र को जवाब देते हुए खलील मियाँ पाकिस्तान पर लानत भेजते हैं। जिस जमीन में दर्जनों पुश्त गल गए, वह पराई कैसे है। तोहमत लगाकर वतन छोड़ने को वे 'कुफ्र' मानते हैं।[148] हालाँकि उनकी जमीन देवी चौधरी हड़प लेता है, लेकिन वे एक व्यक्ति के चलते समूचे 'वतन' को दोषी नहीं ठहराते। समसुद्दीन (मैला आँचल) फर्जी दावा खारिज होने पर राष्ट्रद्रोही तेवर अख्त्यार करता है, जबकि खलील मियाँ अपनी जमीन चले जाने पर भी नफरत और गुस्से के शिकार नहीं होते। यह अंतर केवल समसुद्दीन और खलील का नहीं, दो परस्पर विरोधी मूल्य-मर्यादाओं का भी है। फुन्नन मियाँ की समझ में भी यह बात नहीं आती कि गंगौली को छोड़कर 'पाकिस्तान' क्यों जाना चाहिए।[149] उधर स्वामियों के लाख भड़काने पर भी आम हिंदू नहीं समझ पाता कि उन्हें मुसलमानों पर क्यों हाथ उठाना चाहिए। उनकी समझ में यह बात आती

थी कि झगड़े की जमीन की फसल काट ली जाए, लेकिन किसी मुसलमान को क्यों कत्ल किया जाए, यह उनकी समझ से बाहर था।

ईसाई सांप्रदायिकता की चर्चा बहुत कम हुई है। 'सूरज किरन की छाँव' में बलात् धर्म परिवर्तन की निंदा की गई है। स्वयं ईसाई डाक्टर इस पक्ष में है कि मरजी से धर्म परिवर्तन हो तभी ठीक है। वह तर्क देता है कि ईशू ने कब कहा था, पर धर्मवालों की सेवा न करो।[150] वस्तुतः जब व्यक्ति भूखा होता है, तब उसे कोई धर्म नहीं दिखाई देता। आदिवासियों के धर्म-परिवर्तन का प्रमुख कारण उनकी गरीबी और भुखमरी थी—"धरम को क्या हम चाटेंगे ? पहले हमारा पेट भरो, दो जून हमें खाने को दो, हाथ भर पहनने को कपड़ा दो, तब धरम की बातें करो।"[151] ग्रेसरी इस सत्य को जानती है कि पैसा न मिले तो कोई भी धर्म-परिवर्तन न करे।[152]

'झूठा सच', 'तमस' वगैरह उपन्यासों में सांप्रदायिकता विरोधी मूल्यों की प्रतिष्ठा के लिए जिन चरित्रों को रचा गया है, उन्हें चीजों को सही परिप्रेक्ष्य में देखने के लिए 'मार्क्सवादी जीवनदृष्टि' से लैस भी किया गया है। आंचलिक उपन्यासों के 'पॉजिटिव' चरित्रों में कोई न तो किसी वामपंथी संगठन का सदस्य है और न वह उस तरह की भाषा बोलता दिखाई देता है। इसके बावजूद उनकी चेतना में यह बात बहुत स्पष्ट है कि रीति-रिवाज, रहन-सहन की विभिन्नता के बावजूद हिंदू-मुसलमान एक साथ रहते आए हैं, एक साथ रह सकते हैं, उनके बीच 'मजहब' के नाम पर संघर्ष का कोई तर्क नहीं है।

अपनी धर्मनिरपेक्ष और मानवीय समझ के बावजूद यदि जनसाधारण साम्प्रदायिक उन्माद का शिकार हो गया तो इसके पीछे सांप्रदायिक शक्तियों द्वारा उनकी भावनाओं को लगातार उभारते रहना था। इस प्रकार व्यवहार में उनके मूल्य-संक्रमण की दिशा अस्ति मूल्य से नास्तिमूल्य की ओर थी। लेकिन आंचलिक उपन्यासों में सांप्रदायिकता की कटु आलोचना करते हुए मानवीय मूल्यों की वकालत की गई है। निश्चय ही वे नकारात्मक दृष्टि को निरस्त करते हुए सकारात्मक सोच की ओर बढ़े हैं। इस संदर्भ में कोई बहुत नया मूल्यबोध नहीं निर्मित हुआ है, लेकिन धर्मशास्त्र और इतिहास का आश्रय लेकर पैदा की जानेवाली घृणा का सशक्त प्रतिरोध करने में यह समर्थ है।

संदर्भ

1. पानी के प्राचीर, पूर्वाभास
2. The traditional value system supports the authority of elders and sancitity of

tradition. —Crisis values, A study in generation gap, p. 5

3. "कंधे पर काँवर रखे हुए, माँ-बाप को इधर-उधर मुर्गों की तरह लटकाकर चलना एक शर्मनाक बात थी। यह मजूदरों का काम था।"—रागदरबारी, पृ. 167
4. वही, पृ. 123
5. "यह अंधा समझता है कि मैं इसे काँवर में बिठाकर ढोता रहूँगा।"—अलग-अलग वैतरणी, पृ. 150
6. "तुम गँवार कहार हो, साहब बेटे की बराबरी करते हो। गाली-वाली बकी तो ठीक नहीं होगा।"—जल टूटता हुआ, पृ. 138
7. "बेटों से बाप में दो अंगुल ज्यादा बुद्धि तो हर हालत में अधिक रहनी ही चाहिए, बौज्यू जो करेंगे, हम लोगों से ज्यादा दूरंदेशी और समझदारी के साथ ही करेंगे।"—हौलदार, पृ. 171
8. रतिनाथ की चाची, पृ. 31
9. "परंतु सद्‌गति तो उनकी तुम्हारे तर्पण ही से होगी। संसार उन्हें खिला सकता है, पिला सकता है, जिला सकता है, पर मरने के बाद उन्हें प्रेत होने से नहीं बचा सकता। वह तुम्हीं कर सकते हो।"—रतिनाथ की चाची, पृ. 95
10. "हम लड़की होय के भी करेजा फारि के मेहनत करीला, बाकी भाई कबौं भरमुँह बात नाहीं करत, हमेसा कोसल और गारी देवल करै ले।"—असगाँव-पसगाँव, पृ. 72
11. रतिनाथ की चाची, पृ. 158
12. लोकऋण, पृ. 33
13. "आज तक भाई साहब ने भी कभी कोई कड़ी बात नहीं कही।...बड़ा भाई मार भी दे तो उसका कुछ भी जवाब न देने की परंपरा आज अचानक भहरा कर गिर गई थी।"—अलग-अलग वैतरणी, पृ. 397
14. बलचनमा, पृ. 47
15. "यह बबुआन की मर्यादा के खिलाफ है कि छोटा भाई बड़े भाई के इंतजाम की नुक्ताचीनी करे।"—अलग-अलग वैतरणी, पृ. 96
16. "लालचन मेरा कोई नहीं।...इसके बाप का ठिकाना नहीं। मेरे बाबूजी के मरने के तीन बरस बाद...", परती परिकथा, पृ. 34
17. मैला आँचल, पृ. 175
18. "कम से कम ऐसी तरकीब करो कि मेरे जीते जी घर में अलग चूल्हा न जले और किसी तरह लस्टमपस्टम में बेड़ा गर्क होने से बच जाए।"—असगाँव-पसगाँव, पृ. 51
19. कभी न छोड़े खेत, पृ. 185
20. वही, पृ. 208
21. जल टूटता हुआ, पृ. 482
22. "जिस दिन तुम चले गए थे, पलटन में भरती होने—दिवान के बौज्यू को खबर

लगी तो दुकान में ताला ठोंककर रिगरूटिंग हौफिस को दौड़े। मगर तुम हाथ नहीं पड़े तो सिर के बालों को हाथों से गुजगुजाते हुए आधीरात को घर लौटे… ।"–हौलदार पृ. 57

23. वही, पृ. 77
24. हौलदार, पृ. 19
25. वही, पृ. 77
26. "कहाँ है रंचमात्र भी इसके भीतर दया माया ? वहाँ तो बस लोभ का अपार कीचड़-कादों जमा है, बारहमासी।"–सोनामाटी, पृ. 11
27. जंगली सुअर, पृ. 62
28. वही, पृ. 63
29. अलग-अलग वैतरणी, पृ. 47
30. वही, पृ. 397
31. राग दरबारी, पृ. 41
32. वही, पृ. 23
33. लोकऋण, पृ. 1
34. वही, पृ. 31
35. बलचनमा, पृ. 94
36. परती परिकथा, पृ. 107
37. वही, पृ. 277
38. अलग-अलग वैतरणी, पृ. 363
39. जिंदगीनामा भाग-1, पृ. 84
40. वही, पृ. 261
41. अलग-अलग वैतरणी, पृ. 150
42. वही, पृ. 319
43. जल टूटता हुआ, पृ. 83
44. वही, पृ. 401
45. वही, पृ. 251
46. सोनामाटी, पृ. 443
47. वही।
48. वही, पृ. 452
49. असगाँव-पसगाँव, पृ. 48
50. "वह औरत ही क्या जिसका मन अपने मर्द के आँखों से ओझल होते ही डोल जाए।"–कभी न छोड़े खेत, पृ. 218-219
51. नदी फिर बह चली, पृ. 410
52. कब तक पुकारूँ
53. आधा गाँव, पृ. 18-19

54. "हम इक्के ठो ब्याह करेंगे। नहीं त करबे न करेंगे।"—आधा गाँव, पृ. 198
55. "मुँह झौंसे के किसी इंग में छूकर भी लाज नहीं है। मुझे अपनी खुरखुरी दाढ़ी और पिचके हुए गाल दिखाने आता है⋯बातें करते भी जी घिनाता है।"—देहाती दुनिया, पृ. 56
56. कथा कहो उर्वशी, पृ. 378
57. माटी के लोग : सोने की दैया, मायानंद मिश्रा, पृ. 12
58. परती परिकथा, पृ. 287
59. माटी के लोग, सोने की दैया, पृ. 130
60. अलग-अलग वैतरणी, पृ. 95
61. लोकऋण, पृ. 142
62. सूरज किरन की छाँव, पृ. 174
63. "हरजाई बड़ी पतिबरता बनी है तो खा अपना पतिबरतापन।" ।—जल टूटता हुआ, पृ. 143
64. अभिज्ञान शाकुंतलम्, पृ. 5-26
65. अमृत और विष, पृ. 496
66. वे दिन, पृ. 204
67. कथा कहो उर्वशी, पृ. 398
68. माटी के लोग : सोने की दैया, पृ. 28
69. नदी फिर बह चली, पृ. 405
70. आधा गाँव, पृ. 103
71. अलग-अलग वैतरणी, पृ. 96
72. जल टूटता हुआ, पृ. 514
73. परती परिकथा, पृ. 389
74. रतिनाथ की चाची, पृ. 26
75. "यह गिरने-गिराने का काम आप लोगों के घरों की बाभनियाँ करती हैं। मुझसे किसी के घर का कुछ छिपा नहीं है।"—जल टूटता हुआ, पृ. 531
76. हौलदार, पृ. 292-293
77. 'बिंदु' (त्रैमासिक), वर्ष 4, अंक-2, सं. नंद चतुर्वेदी, 'हिंदू बनाम हिंदू', पृ. 169
78. 'The hold of religious belief, with its supernatural explanation of caste itself, its doctrine of the elect and the pale 'its attribution of a mystic cleanness and uncleanness, its instillation of reverence and awe, and its over ruling conception of the secred and the profane, is essential to the continuance of the system.'
—Society, R.M. Maciver se charles H. p. 357
79. "जाति बहुत बड़ी चीज है। जातपाँत नहीं माननेवालों की भी जाति होती है। सिर्फ हिंदू कहने से ही पिण्ड नहीं छूट सकता। ब्राह्मण हैं ? कौन ब्राह्मण ! गोत्र क्या है ? मूल कौन है ? शहर में कोई किसी से जाति नहीं पूछता। शहर के लोगों

की जाति का क्या ठिकाना ! लेकिन गाँव में तो बिना जाति के आपका पानी नहीं चल सकता।"—मैला आँचल, पृ. 52

80. परती परिकथा, पृ. 26-27
81. वही।
82. "...दो गाँवों में ठाकुर, दो गाँवों में ब्राह्मण, एक गाँव में कायस्थ तथा एक गाँव में चमार प्रभावी जाति हैं। जमीन आदि भी ग्रामीण प्रभावी जाति के अस्तित्व में प्रभाव रखती हैं। द्वितीय आधार पद और योग्यता तथा तृतीय आधार जाति के सदस्यों की संख्या है।"—'ग्रामीण समाजशास्त्र : साहित्य-परिप्रेक्ष्य में', पृ. 67
83. "गाँव में ठाकुर अभी तक हुकूमत कर रहा है। मैं उस अधिकार की व्यापकता को देखकर सिहर उठता हूँ, क्योंकि वह धर्म की आड़ लेकर इतिहास की शताब्दियों रूपी पसलियों में भाला बनकर धँसा हुआ है। उसको देखकर चमार अभी तक मन में अभाव अनुभव करता है।"—कब तक पुकारूँ, पृ. 40
84. "आए बड़ी इज्जतवाले, चमार और ठाकुर की इज्जत एक हो जाएगी ? हूँह ?"—अलग-अलग वैतरणी, पृ. 249
85. "अपनी खेती हम फुटकपालियों के पास ठहरी नहीं। पराए खेतों में अपने हाड़ों का रस निचोड़ा, तब कहीं जाके हमको चार डाडू जौल मादिरे का नसीब होता है... ।"—हौलदार, शैलेश मटियानी, पृ. 311
86. जाति के अठोत और करम के हीन हैं। आपके चरन की धूर बुहारते पीढ़ियाँ गल गईं।...छोटा-बड़ा। भगवान के द्वार से ही लोग बनकर आते हैं मालिक !—बबूल, पृ. 14
87. "यह बात नहीं है बेटा, छोटे-बड़े भगवान के घर से बनकर आते हैं"—गोदान, पृ. 20
88. राग दरबारी, पृ. 18
89. मैला आँचल, पृ. 28
90. "बाभनों ने तो साफ इनकार कर दिया है। यदि बाभनों के लिए अलग प्रबंध नहीं हुआ तो सरब संघटन में नहीं खाएँगे।"—मैला आँचल, पृ. 29
91. 'कब तक पुकारूँ', पृ. 237
92. अलग-अलग वैतरणी, पृ. 49
93. परती परिकथा, पृ. 145
94. "....आज चारों ओर, हर जाति के लोग गले में जनेऊ डाले फिर रहे हैं।...भूमफोड़ क्षत्री तो कभी नहीं सुना था।"—मैला आँचल, पृ. 16
95. लोहे के पंख, पृ. 275
96. "तीन साल पहले तक जो क्षत्रिय अपने को खास मानसिंह के वंशज बतलाते थे अथवा आल्हा-ऊदल की संतान बताकर दंगाफसाद करते थे—देख लीजिए उन्हें ! उनके लड़के 'शिड्यूल्ड कास्ट' और 'एबॉरिजिनल कम्यूनिटी' की फेहरिश्त में नाम लिखाने के लिए धक्कमधुक्की कर रहे हैं।"—परती परिकथा, पृ. 146

97. वही।
98. वही।
99. बबूल, पृ. 88
100. आधा गाँव, पृ. 329
101. जल टूटता हुआ, पृ. 52
102. "...किसी लकीर को बिना छुए, बिना काटे-पीटे हम उसके नीचे एक उससे बड़ी लकीर खींचकर छोटी कर सकते हैं। तो छोटों को शिक्षा द्वारा अपना स्तर उठाकर बड़ों को बिना छेड़े सहज क्रांति करनी है।"—लोकऋण, पृ. 192-193
103. "ऊँच-नीच का भेद सदा से चला आया है, सदा रहेगा। चार आदमियों के न मानने से क्या आता-जाता है।"—बलचनमा, पृ. 88-89
104. "हमने तुम्हारी बहुत बातें सुन ली हैं, लेकिन हर चीज की हद होती है। हम पत्थर के नहीं हैं, हम भी इंसान हैं।"—धरती धन न अपना
105. "स्थैतिक यथार्थ के प्रावैगिक यथार्थ में बदलाव की सामाजिक-आर्थिक और राजनैतिक प्रक्रिया होती है। हमारे समाज के इस कटे हुए अंग को इससे वंचित रखा गया। सुधारवादी शक्तियाँ इस वर्ग को नया नाम देकर संतुष्ट हो गईं उनका एकमात्र उद्देश्य इनके प्रति छुआछूत को सिर्फ अंकित करना था, इससे अधिक कुछ नहीं।"—आधुनिक हिंदी उपन्यास (संपादक भीष्म साहनी तथा अन्य) राजकमल प्रकाशन, दिल्ली, प्रथम सं. 1980, जगदीश चन्द्र की टिप्पणी, पृ. 342
106. हजार घोड़ों का सवार, पृ. 144
107. रागदरबारी, पृ. 335
108. सोनभद्र की राधा, पृ. 9
109. "और कोई महीना भर पहले चमारों का एक गोल परुसरमवा की लीडरी में पंडिताने के कुएँ पर चढ़ गया और पानी भर लाया।"—आधा गाँव, पृ. 122
110. "हम आपका काम करते हैं, मजूरी लेते हैं। हमें गरज है कि करते हैं। आपको गरज है कि कराते हो। इसका मतलब ई थोड़े हो गया कि हम आपके गुलाम हैं।"—अलग-अलग वैतरणी, पृ. 249
111. जल टूटता हुआ, पृ. 109
112. असगाँव-पसगाँव, शिवकरण सिंह, संजय बुक सेंटर, वाराणसी, प्रथम संस्करण 1979, पृ. 55
113. परती परिकथा, पृ. 306
114. अग्निबीज
115. जल टूटता हुआ, पृ. 532
116. आधा गाँव, पृ. 196
117. मैला आँचल, पृ. 330
118. 'The respondents gave the lowest proportion of liberal responses in the sphere of marraige, the resistance being more to marriage with a Harijan girl than to a low

caste girl.' –The changing concept of caste in India, p. 134

119. 'Between liberty and other social values there is high tension.' –R.T. Harris, Social Ethics, p. 55

120. धर्मयुग, 20 अप्रैल 1980, पृ. 10

121. हजार घोड़ों का सवार, पृ. 371

122. "...यह त्रासदी कहीं गहरे जाकर पाठक की संवेदना को, मनुष्यता के उन्हीं अहम सरोकारों की ओर उत्प्रेरित करती है, आमूल सामाजिक बदलाव की उसी दिशा में सोचने को प्रेरित करती है, जिसके बिना लगता है कि अब कोई निस्तार नहीं है।"–'अलोचना'–51-52, डॉ. शिवकुमार मिश्र, 'प्रेमचंद और परवर्ती कथा परिदृश्य', पृ. 133

123. अलग-अलग वैतरणी, पृ. 305

124. जंगली सुअर, पृ. 119

125. "लोग बाँटने के नाम पर ही बौखला उठते हैं। जब छीनकर लेने की बात उठेगी तब पता नहीं कैसी स्थिति पैदा हो जाएगी।"–सोनभद्र की राधा, पृ. 9

126. सोनभद्र की राधा, पृ. 116

127. असगाँव-पसगाँव, पृ. 145

128. "आज हरिजनों और पिछड़ी जातियों पर जो अत्याचार हो रहा है, वह एक तरह से वर्गसंघर्ष ही है।"–'कथन' मई-जून 1982 में पी.सी.जोशी के विचारों से उद्धृत, पृ. 53

129. श्री वर्षा 15-22 अगस्त, 'दलित किससे कहें, कब तक सहें', पृ. 7

130. मैला आँचल, पृ. 180

131. "हमें तो लगता है कि हमारे इलाके में केवल दो ही वर्ग हैं, एक गरीब का और एक धनी गुंडों का।"–जल टूटता हुआ, पृ. 16

132. सोनभद्र की राधा, पृ. 29

133. "A very large mejority felt that economic inequalities are responsible for increasing social distance between the rich and the poor."–Crisis of values of study in generation gap. K.D. Gangrade, . 238

134. आधा गाँव, पृ. 3

135. सोनभद्र की राधा, पृ. 15

136. "...मुट्ठी भर जो हरिजन शिक्षित हैं, वे अपने से छोटे व अज्ञान के अँधेरे में भटकते हुए लोगों का कभी शोषण करने लग जाएँगे। क्योंकि धीरे-धीरे वे भी पूँजीवादी विकृतियों से ग्रस्त हो जाएँगे।"–हजार घोड़ों का सवार, पृ. 326

137. वही, पृ. 91

138. भाषा, दिसंबर 1989, पृ. 102

139. दस्तावेज, जनवरी 1979, पृ. 86

140. हजार घोड़ों का सवार, पृ. 184

141. परती परिकथा, पृ. 306
142. जंगली सुअर, पृ. 105
143. आधा गाँव, पृ. 311
144. नदी फिर बह चली, पृ. 393
145. आलोचना, जनवरी-मार्च 1986, पृ. 13
146. जल टूटता हुआ, पृ. 276
147. मैला आँचल, पृ. 274-275
148. "काफिर मुझे सता रहे हैं, ऐसा कहना सरासर झूठ होता। बेटे, मुझे लगा कि यह धरती के साथ दगा करना है। झूठी तोहमत लगाकर वतन को छोड़ना सबसे बड़ा कुफ्र है। मैंने बिल्कुल पक्का कर लिया कि कुछ भी हो जाए, मैं करैता छोड़कर नहीं आऊँगा।"—अलग-अलग वैतरणी, पृ. 266
149. "ए भाई बाप-दादा की कबर हियाँ है, चौक इमामबाड़ा हियाँ है, खेती बाड़ी हियाँ है। हम कोनो बुखक हैं कि तोरे पाकिस्तान जिंदाबाद में फँस जाएँ।"
—'आधा गाँव', पृ. 162
150. सूरज किरन की छाँव, पृ. 64-65
151. वही, पृ. 83
152. "यदि ये पैसा देना बंद कर दें तो लोग ईसाइयत से बदल जाएँ। जब आदमी का पेट तड़पता है और जेब खाली रहती है, तब वह धरम नहीं देखता।"—सूरज किरन की छाँव, पृ. 107

चतुर्थ प्रकरण

आंचलिक उपन्यासों में राजनीतिक-आर्थिक मूल्यों का संक्रमण

पिछड़े अंचलों के राजनीतिक-आर्थिक समीकरण स्वतंत्रता के बाद तेजी से बने और बिगड़े हैं। 'तंत्र' और 'यंत्र' दोनों से ग्रामीण जीवन के संपर्क ने बहुत-सी नवीनताएँ पैदा की हैं। हरित क्रांति, श्वेतक्रांति, शिक्षाक्रांति तथा अन्य परिवर्तनों को ग्रामीण मानस सहज ढंग से आत्मसात् न कर सका। इस स्थिति का बयान करते हुए डॉ. विवेकीराय ने लिखा है :

"...अपरिपक्व ग्राम-मस्तिष्क के लिए पंचायत एक संघर्ष है, चकबंदी एक तनाव है, सहकारिता लड़ाई है और वोट पार्टी तथा चुनाव तो जैसे साक्षात् भिड़ाई। यहाँ तक कि कभी-कभी आती हुई बिजली के खंभे, खिंचती सड़क, बँधते बाँध और पुल पुलिया भी गंभीर तनाव बन गए।" [1]

एक सर्वेक्षण में सुरेन्द्रसिंह ने जौनपुर (उ. प्र.) के कुसुम्ही गाँव के आधार पर पाया है कि कृषि नए-नए उपकरणों के प्रयोग से ग्रामीणों की आर्थिक स्थिति सुधरी है। इसके साथ ही उनके रहन-सहन, सोच-विचार में भी फर्क आया है। मालिक-खेतिहर संबंध प्रभावित हुए हैं।[2] इन व्यापक परिवर्तनों के समानांतर मूल्यों के विपर्यय और संक्रमण की प्रक्रिया भी चल रही है। यह देखना पर्याप्त महत्त्वपूर्ण है कि आंचलिक उपन्यासकारों ने आर्थिक-राजनीतिक क्षेत्र में आए देशव्यापी परिवर्तन को किस रूप में देखा और प्रस्तुत किया है।

'श्रम' के मूल्य की प्रतिष्ठा और सामंती शोषण का विरोध

समाजशास्त्रियों के विचार में 'मूल्य' जीवन, मन और समाज के संघर्ष और समूह से पृथक् नहीं होते।[2] मूल्य-संक्रमण के आर्थिक परिपार्श्व को देखते हुए यह स्थापना सर्वथा युक्तियुक्त लगती है। पिछड़े हुए अंचलों में जब उत्पादन के साधनों और भूमिसंबंधों में उल्लेखनीय परिवर्तन हुए, तभी परंपरागत मूल्य कड़ी आजमाइश में पड़ गए। जमींदारी व्यवस्था का अंत और विकसित प्रौद्योगिकी का उपयोग, इन अंचलों को झकझोरनेवाली सर्वप्रमुख घटनाएँ हैं। जमींदारी-उन्मूलन ने जहाँ ह्रासोन्मुख सामंत वर्ग को एक धक्का दिया, वहीं जमींदार और रिआया के संबंधों को नए अर्थ दिए। पहले प्रजा और जमींदार के बीच मेमने और बाघ का रिश्ता होता था।[4] चौधरी और कमीन के मुकाबले गलती हमेशा कमीन की होती थी।[5] छोटा सा भूमिपति भी 'अन्नदाता' का संबोधन पाता था। चूँकि जमींदार नौकरियाँ, खेत वगैरह दे सकता था, इसलिए बहुत से मजूर उसके इशारे पर लड़ने-मरने के लिए तैयार रहते थे।[6] नमक हलाली या स्वामिभक्ति के लिए वे जान पर खेल जाते थे।[7] 'लोहे के पंख' में मँगरू का दादा अपने मलिकार की जमीन के लिए हुई फौजदारी में खेत रहता है।[8] इस स्वामिभक्ति के मूल्य के तौर पर उसके बेटे को बंजर खेत का एक टुकड़ा मिलता है। मँगरू की पीढ़ी तक आते-आते स्वामिभक्ति का मूल्य खंडित हो लेता है। मँगरुआ अपने साहब के दोनों हाथ पकड़ लेता है। वह बिना बात पिटने को तैयार नहीं है।[9]

गाँव में किसानों और मजदूरों का शोषण दो तरह से होता रहा है। एक ओर व्यक्तिगत पूँजीवाले बंधक रखने या सूदखोरी के धंधे में अन्याय और बेईमानी करते हैं और दूसरी ओर भू-स्वामी राज्य का सहारा लेकर जुल्म ढाते हैं।[10] जमींदारी उन्मूलन से धनी भू-स्वामियों को कानून राज्य की सहायता मिलनी बंद हो गई। स्वतंत्रता-प्राप्ति के बाद सरकारी स्तर पर ग्रामीण जीवन में व्याप्त आर्थिक असमानता को दूर करने के लिए जो प्रयास किए गए, उन्होंने ग्रामजीवन की मानसिकता को झिंझोड़ने में कारगर भूमिका निभाई है। जमींदारी उन्मूलन का निर्णय एक क्रांतिकारी कदम था। 'यू.पी. जमींदारी अबोलीशन एण्ड लैण्ड रिफार्म्स एक्ट 1950' तथा 'बिहार लैण्ड रिफार्म्स एक्ट 1950' ने जहाँ भूस्वामियों की चूलें हिला दीं वहीं भूमिहीनों और खेतिहर मजदूरों में आशा का संचार किया। अधिनियमों के माध्यम से भू-सुधार के प्रयास पूरे भारतवर्ष में हुए और इनका प्रभाव मुख्यतः ग्रामंचल पर पड़ा। भूमि और किसानों से संबद्ध अन्य अधिनियमों में 'यू.पी. कान्सोलिडेसन आफ होल्डिंग्स एक्ट 1953', 'यू.पी. विलेज आबादी एक्ट 1947', 'कुमाऊँ एण्ड उत्तराखंड जमींदारी अबोलीशन एण्ड रिफार्म्स एक्ट 1960', 'यू. पी. लैण्ड डेवलेपमेंट टैक्स एक्ट 1972' आदि प्रमुख हैं। इस तरह के अधिनियमों ने

भमि के स्वामित्व, बंधुआ मजदूरी, भूमि के वितरण आदि बहुत से मुद्दों को नया रूप दिया है। कम से कम कानून के स्तर पर शोषण और अत्याचार की समाप्ति की औपचारिक घोषणा ने शोषितों-उत्पीड़ितों को बहुत बल प्रदान किया और शोषण, अन्याय आदि अवमूल्यों के विरुद्ध उठ खड़े होने की प्रेरणा दी।

जब जमींदारों के प्रभाव और आतंक का सूरज तप रहा था, तब भी शोषित-वर्ग में कुछ युवक यह अनुभव कर रहे थे, कि अमीरों का सारा वैभव उनके श्रम की नींव पर खड़ा है। चूँकि अमीरों का खेतों पर अधिकार है अतः वे बिना तिनका तोड़े सुख-भोग करते रहते हैं।[11] 'जिंदगीनामा' में फरमान अली का बोध पुरा मूल्यों का समर्थक है, जबकि मेहर अली का सोच[12] अस्ति मूल्यों की दिशा में गतिशील है। आंचलिक उपन्यासों में यह 'सत्य' विशेष रूप से अंकित है कि स्वतंत्रता मिलने और जमींदारी उन्मूलन के बाद शोषितों का एक बड़ा समूह, जिसमें न केवल युवा हैं, अपितु बड़े-बूढ़े भी हैं, शोषण-विरोधी चेतना से लैस हो गया है। 'अलग-अलग वैतरणी', 'आधा गाँव', 'जल टूटता हुआ' आदि में साफ दिखाई देता है कि अधिकतर ग्रामीणजन जमींदारों की जकड़ से मुक्त हो चले हैं। जमींदारी उन्मूलन के बाद भी कुछ भूस्वामी अपनी निरंकुशता को नहीं छोड़ पाए[13], बावजूद इसके कि राज्य या शासन का सहारा अब नहीं रहा था। लेकिन जनसाधारण ने वास्तविकता को अनुभव करना प्रारंभ कर दिया था। 'स्वामीभक्ति', 'कुलीनता', 'कृतज्ञता' आदि मूल्य बिखरने लगे।[14] कुछ संपन्न भूस्वामियों ने रिआया के बदले तेवर को नहीं पढ़ा तो आखिर में उन्हें टूटना पड़ा। नीची जाति के व्यक्ति का कुर्सी पर बैठ जाना[15] जिनके लिए अपमानजनक था वे ही जूते की दुकान[16] खोलने के लिए बाध्य होते हैं। ऐसे सामंतों द्वारा खयाल किया जाता था कि जमींदारी मजहब की तरह मजबूर है।[17] लेकिन जमींदारी टूट कर रही। जमींदारों के जलसे और प्रस्ताव व्यर्थ साबित हुए। कल तक जो सर्वेसर्वा थे, उनके अपराधों का निर्णय जनता की पंचायत में होने लगा।[18] जो रिआया संस्कारवश या आतंक से जमींदारों को ईश्वर मानती आई, वह अब 'गारी-गार' खाने के लिए तैयार नहीं है। अपने अधिकारों की रक्षा के लिए वह न केवल सचेत है अपितु एकजुट भी, वह अपनी एक-एक आह का बदला लेना चाहती है।[19] कालांतर में भी उसकी विद्रोह-चेतना कुंद नहीं होती। यह आकस्मिक नहीं कि जमींदारी के जमाने की मजदूरी पर खेतिहर मजदूर काम नहीं करना चाहता।[20] बनिहारों-मजूदरों के चेहरों पर बदलाव के चिह्न देखकर भूपतियों के कसे हुए तेवर ढीले होने लगते हैं।[21]

आंचलिक उपन्यासों में बार-बार जोर दिया गया है कि समाज में केवल दो वर्ग हैं—अमीर और गरीब[22] यानी कि शोषक और शोषित। वर्गचेतना का यह उभार जहाँ ईश्वर भाग्य, स्वामीभक्ति, आदि के आगे प्रश्नचिह्न लगाता है, वहीं सत्य, न्याय और अधिकार के लिए जूझ सकने की शक्ति प्रदान करता है। ब्राह्मण, राजपूत,

भूमिहार आदि जातिगत सीमाओं से उबर कर जनसाधारण किसानों और मजूरों के वर्ग को मान्यता देता है। अनपढ़ मेहनतकश की पक्षधरता भी अस्पष्ट नहीं रहती।[23] शोषित जन एकजुट होने की आवश्यकता को तीव्रता के साथ अनुभव करने लगे हैं। शोषितों के समर्थकों की दृष्टि में उस वर्गविहीन समाज की स्थापना काम्य है, जहाँ दासता जैसी चीज बिल्कुल नहीं होगी।[24] गरीबी और जहालत को प्रश्रय देनेवाली व्यवस्था ढह कर रहेगी–"दरार पड़ी दीवार ! यह गिरेगी ! इसे गिरने दो ! यह समाज कब तक टिका रहेगा ?"[25] यह आशा करना मूर्खता है कि भूखे और अतृप्त इंसानों की आत्मा कभी विद्रोह न करेगी।[26] शोषण विरोधी चेतना का व्यक्त रूप 'लोहे के पंख', 'सोनभद्र की राधा', 'बलचनमा', 'बाबा बटेसरनाथ', 'वरुण के बेटे' आदि उपन्यासों में देखा जा सकता है, शोषक वर्ग के प्रति एक तीखी घृणा ने शोषितों को न केवल एकजुट किया है अपितु उन्हें हर तरह की दुरभि संधि का सामना करने की प्रेरणा भी दी है। अब यह सहन नहीं हो सकता कि मजदूर के खून-पसीने पर मिल मालिक ऐश करे।[27] इस वर्ग वैषम्य को दूर करने का एक रास्ता है कि सर्वहारा ईंट का जबाव पत्थर से देना सीखें।[28] 'बलचनमा' में खुलेआम वर्ग-संघर्ष को ही समता, समानता, न्याय आदि मूल्यों की स्थापना का साधन माना गया है–"जमींदार और सरकारी अफसर दुरजोधन ठहरे, उनको जुधिस्ठिल नहीं पस्त कर सकते भैया ! पिटाई पर पिटाई खाना और भेड़-बकरी की तरह पकड़ा कर जेल चले जाना बहादुरी नहीं है। ऐसी सिधाई से पूजा तुम्हारी हो तो जमीन सुई की नोक भर भी नहीं मिलने की, हाँ।"[29] यह बदली हुई रणनीति निश्चय ही अहिंसक संघर्ष से आगे बढ़ी हुई है और बदले हुए संदर्भों में सार्थक है। आदिवासी क्षेत्रों में भी परंपरागत शोषण के प्रति उग्र प्रतिरोध का स्वर उठा है।[30] चाहे साहूकार का कर्जा पटाने के लिए प्रचलित भगेला प्रथा हो या जमीन की अवैध बंदोबस्त[31], शोषित आदिवासी अब अन्याय सहने के लिए तैयार नहीं हैं। उस स्थिति में तो और भी नहीं, जबकि उसे ज्ञात है कि भूमि सुधार संबंधी कानून उनके पक्ष में है।[32] भूमिहीन कृषकों के शोषण के संबंध में अध्येताओं का मत है कि यह तभी रुक सकता है जब शोषक वर्ग का प्रतिनिधित्व करनेवाली राज्य व्यवस्था को तहस-नहस कर दिया जाए।[33] नक्सलवादियों के कार्यक्रम में इस तरह का दुस्साहस सम्मिलित था। लेकिन आंचलिक उपन्यासों में अभी जनतांत्रिक ढाँचे के भीतर बदलाव की आशा धूमिल नहीं हुई है। अतः वहाँ छुटपुट या सामूहिक हिंसा वाले मार्ग का समर्थन नहीं मिलता। लेकिन सामूहिक एवं एकजुट जनसंघर्ष का समर्थन प्रायः प्रत्येक उपन्यासकार ने किया है। 'धरती धन न अपना', 'कब तक पुकारूँ', 'नदी फिर बह चली', 'बलचनमा', 'सोनभद्र की राधा' आदि उपन्यासों में इस जनसंघर्ष को आंशिक या पूर्ण सफलता प्राप्त करते हुए दिखाना इस संदर्भ में उल्लेखनीय है। लेकिन उपन्यासकार जनसंघर्ष के

सिलसिले में राजनीतिक दलों—विशेषतः प्रगतिशील दलों की भूमिका से संतुष्ट नहीं है। सत्ता पक्ष के विधायकों और नेताओं का जन-विरोधी रुख समझ में आता है, लेकिन विपक्षी दलों का समझौतावादी रवैया समझ में नहीं आता। 'रेणु' ने 'मैला आँचल' में जनसंघर्ष को लेकर सोशलिस्ट पार्टी के ढुलमुलपन पर सही व्यंग्य प्रहार किया है। सेक्रेटरी साहब संघर्ष की प्रक्रिया का जो ब्यौरा देते हैं[34], वह निरा किताबी है और उस तरीके से कभी जनसंघर्ष शायद ही छिड़ सके। 'धरती धन न अपना' में काली को कामरेड बिशनदास से ही सहयोग और समर्थन नहीं मिलता।[35] 'लोहे के पंख' में 'इंटक' हड़ताल का विरोध करती है। बाद में सोशलिस्ट नेता भी उदासीन हो जाते हैं। ऐसी स्थिति में यदि मेहनतकश व्यक्ति का विश्वास नेताओं पर से उठ जाता है, तो यह अस्वाभाविक नहीं है।[36] जहाँ संघर्ष की बागडोर शोषितों में से ऊपर उठे जन-नेताओं के हाथ में है, वहाँ संघर्ष सफल होता है, जनविरोधी शक्तियों को झुकना पड़ता है।

ग्रामांचल में शोषितों विशेषतः भूमिहीनों में अपनी स्थिति और श्रम की अवज्ञा को लेकर असंतोष और विद्रोह एक वास्तविकता है। हिंदुस्तान में 5 करोड़ भूमिहीन हैं और इनमें से अधिकतर ग्रामवासी हैं। इन भूमिहीनों में वर्ग-जागरूकता बढ़ रही है। रामबली सिंह ने गाजीपुर जिले के धाखा गाँव के भूमिहीनों के 97 परिवारों के सर्वेक्षण के आधार पर पाया है कि वर्ग-जागरूकता के आधार पर भूमिहीनों की तीन श्रेणियाँ बनाई जा सकती हैं।[37] भूमिपतियों-भूमिहीनों के संघर्ष में भाग लेने के पक्षधरों को अति जागरूक, संघर्ष से सर्वथा अलग रहनेवाले अल्प जागरूक हैं और शोषण विरोधी मानसिकता के बावजूद संघर्ष से विरत रहनेवाले सामान्य जागरूक हैं। जागरूक भूमिहीनों ने केवल प्रत्यक्ष संघर्ष का सहारा नहीं लिया है। अपने पेशों के परित्याग से भी वे वर्ग-संघर्ष को बढ़ावा देते हैं। यह गौरतलब है कि निम्न जातियों के भूमिहीन, पिछड़ी और सवर्ण कही जानेवाली जातियों के भूमिहीनों की तुलना में अधिक जागरूक और सक्रिय है।[38] दलितों में विद्रोह-चेतना का उभार इस संदर्भ में प्रमाण स्वरूप देखा जा सकता है।

'बलचनमा', 'सोना माटी', 'जल टूटता हुआ' आदि उपन्यासों में भूमिहीनों में उगते क्रांति-भाव को नए मूल्योदय के रूप में देखा गया है। ये उपन्यास दर्शाते हैं कि एक ही आर्थिक स्तर के समुदाय में मूल्यों के संक्रमण की गति एक सी नहीं होती। शिक्षा, राजनीतिक समझ आदि कई कारणों से कुछ भूमिहीन अति जागरूक होते हैं और वे सीधे संघर्ष से ही 'मुक्ति', 'समानता', 'समता' आदि मूल्यों की प्रतिष्ठा को संभव मानते हैं। बलचनमा का जुझारू सोच इस संदर्भ में द्रष्टव्य है।[39] 'जगपतिया' (जल टूटता हुआ), 'मँगरू' (लोहे के पंख) 'सुखुआ' (सोनामाटी) आदि किसी भी स्थिति में शोषण को सहने के लिए तैयार नहीं हैं। यह विद्रोह-भाव एक या दो व्यक्तियों का न होकर बहुत से शोषितों-उत्पीड़ितों का सामूहिक

मूल्य-निर्णय है। 'सोनामाटी' में सुखुआ-सिटहला आदि द्वारा विधायक का घिराव[40] इस संदर्भ में द्रष्टव्य है। 'जंगली सुअर' में दलितों का जुलूस और उस पर गोली प्रहार[41] जताता है कि 'न्याय', 'मुक्ति', 'समानता' आदि धारणाएँ दलितों के लिए शब्द या नारा मात्र न होकर वाकई 'जीवन मूल्य' बन चुकी हैं। कई व्यक्तियों का आहत होना सिद्ध करता है कि भूमिहीनों ने मात्र आवेश में आकर विद्रोह नहीं किया है, इसके पीछे कार्य-कारण की स्पष्ट समझ भी है। 'जल टूटता हुआ' में कामरेड जगपति के नेतृत्व में हलवाहे अपनी मजूरी बढ़ाने की माँग करते हैं। उनकी दृढ़ता इस बात से जाहिर है कि उन्होंने कसम खाई है—"जो कोई इस माँग से कम ले, वह अपनी बेटी के साथ शादी करे।"[42] दीनदयाल जैसे शोषक और रामकुमार जैसे छद्म बुद्धिजीवी उनकी मुश्किलों को नहीं समझते हैं, लेकिन मानवीय मूल्यों का पक्षधर सतीश उनकी इस माँग से सहमत है। वह एक ओर मजूरी बढ़ाने का कायल है, दूसरी ओर कथित कुलीनता और धर्म के आडंबर का विरोध करता है। उसका निम्नलिखित कथन छोटे भूस्वामियों के मूल्यबोध में आ रहे परिवर्तन का द्योतक है :

"दो पैसे का जनेव पहनकर सारा धर्म ओढ़ने का दंभ कर रखा है इन लोगों ने। मैं तो कब से चिल्ला रहा हूँ कि धर्म के मिथ्या आडंबर को छोड़ो, अपना काम करना सबसे बड़ा धर्म है, लेकिन कोई सुनता ही नहीं। सारा पाप करेंगे, लेकिन अपना खेत नहीं जातेंगे।"[43]

इस उद्धरण में व्यक्त मानसिकता मजूर विरोधी नहीं है। कथित जातिगत श्रेष्ठता या कुलीनता जैसे अवमूल्यों को खारिज करते हुए दर्शाया गया है कि मँझोले भूस्वामियों के सोच में मूल्यों के संक्रमण की दिशा 'श्रम', 'स्वावलंबन' आदि धनात्मक मूल्यों की ओर होनी चाहिए न कि विलासिता, शोषण आदि अवमूल्यों की ओर। मँझोले दर्जे के भूस्वामियों के टनमना जाने से उत्पन्न समस्याओं और विशेषतः विलासिता में डूबने की ओर संकेत 'मैला आँचल' में स्पष्ट तौर पर है :

"यदि मालिक जवान हो तो तुरंत औन-पौन करने लगता है। हरमुनियाँ, फर्श, शतरंजी, शामियाना, जाजिम, लैट, पंचलैट, पहाड़िया घोड़ा, शम्पनी, टेबुल-कुर्सी, बैंच खरीदकर ढेर लगा देता है। इससे भी जब गरमी कम नहीं होती तब बन्नूक के लैसन के लिए आफिसरों को डॉली देना शुरू करता है...लाल बाग मेला के समय रात-रात भर मुजरा सुनता है और दिनभर आफिसरों के साथ कचहरी में घूमता है। बन्नूक के लैसन के बाद नौटंकी कंपनी खोलता है। उससे भी मगज ठंडा नहीं होता तो कोई खूनी केस होकर समापत्तन।"[44]

यह उद्धरण 'तथ्य चेतना' और 'मूल्य चेतना' को संश्लिष्ट रूप में प्रस्तुत करता है। अर्थ से होनेवाले अनर्थ अय्याशी से शुरू होकर हत्या तक पहुँचते हैं और नैतिक मूल्यों का स्पष्ट तिरस्कार करते हैं। 'परहित', 'सद्भाव', आदि मूल्यों

के लिए वहाँ कोई स्थान नहीं होता। लेकिन हीनतर मूल्यों की दिशा में हुए संक्रमणको उपन्यासकार का समर्थन प्राप्त नहीं है, इस उद्धरण में निहित व्यंग्य से यह तथ्य ध्वनित है।

जमींदारी उन्मूलन के बाद ग्रामांचल में कुछ नए सामंतों का उदय हुआ है। इनमें कुछ तो वे ही टनमना गए भूस्वामी हैं, और कुछ पुराने ही सामंत नए रूप में 'शोषण', 'अन्याय' और 'अत्याचार' को यथावत् बनाए रखने के लिए प्रयत्नशील हैं। सामंत नया हो या पुराना उसकी मानसिकता रूढ़िवादी और जनविरोधी ही है। दूसरों की भूमि और श्रम को हड़पने की हवस ज्यों की त्यों है। 'जंगली सुअर' और 'सोनामाटी' के भू-स्वामियों का लक्ष्य एक है। भाई जी के पिता जी ने मरते समय अपने बेटे से कहा था कि गैर की जमीन हथियाना मेरा सपना था, उसे तुम मरते दम तक पूरा करना।[45] भाईजी ने उस सपने को पूरा करने का भरसक प्रयास किया। यह बात और है कि जमाना बदल जाने के कारण वे जोर-जुल्म के रास्ते[46] को छोड़कर चालाकी और बेईमानी के रास्ते पर अधिक चले। जरूरत पड़ने पर जोर-जुल्म भी काम आया। 'सोना माटी' के हनुमान प्रसाद भी उन नव-सामंतों में से एक हैं, जो येन केन प्रकारेण दूसरों की जमीन-संपत्ति आदि के हरण में प्रवृत्त हैं। हनुमान प्रसाद के ही वर्ग के दीनदयाल ने अपना जो 'दर्शन' प्रस्तुत किया है, वह अवमूल्यों की खान है। उसके अनुसार—"मैं तो सिर्फ मलाई का शौकीन हूँ। ढाई छटाँक रोज मिलनी चाहिए।...कुछ लोगों से कुर्सी सट जाती है, कुछ लोगों से नौकरी चिपक जाती है और मेरी कुण्डली में जमीन है कि अनचाहे जोत में समा जाती है।"[47] उपन्यासकार को आश्चर्य है कि अधिकतर व्यक्ति इसमें कोई अनुचित या गलत नहीं मानते। 'गलत मूल्यों के आगे ऐसा आत्मसमर्पण'[48] उपन्यासकार को छील देता है। जाहिर है, यथार्थ में मूल्यों का संक्रमण उचित और सही के बजाय गलत मूल्यों की दिशा में हुआ है जबकि उपन्यासकार चाहता है कि इसके विपरीत हो। पीड़ितों और शोषित में चेतना और जागृति से वह आश्वस्त होता है। अधिकतर आंचलिक उपन्यासकारों में आश्वस्ति का यह भाव मुखर है।

सरकारी योजनाओं की आंशिक सफलता ने भी भूमिहीनों और पीड़ितों को क्रुद्ध किया है। प्रथम पंचवर्षीय योजना के तीन मुख्य लक्ष्य बताए गए थे—कृषि उत्पादन में वृद्धि, आय का समुचित वितरण कर दरिद्रता को दूर करना, नए कार्य क्षेत्र पैदा कर बेकारी को दूर करना। लेकिन इन उद्देश्यों की सिद्धि आंशिक तौर पर ही हो पाई। हरित क्रांति तो हुई लेकिन शोषण-उत्पीड़न कम नहीं हुआ, बेरोजगारी और बढ़ी, आर्थिक असमानता और बढ़ी। अतः शोषितों ने संघर्ष-संगठित संघर्ष का मार्ग अपनाना उचित समझा। अपनी 'मुक्ति' के लिए 'हिंसा' तक को अनुचित न मानना इस बात का प्रमाण है कि अब श्रमजीवियों ने आखिरी लड़ाई लड़ने का मन बना लिया है और वे सामंती मूल्यों का त्याग कर समाजवादी मूल्यों

को अंगीकार कर चले हैं।

मूल्य संक्रमण : विज्ञान और प्रौद्योगिकी का प्रभाव

यदि सभ्यता की प्रगति को प्रौद्योगिकी की प्रगति के संदर्भ में आँका जाता है तो यह आश्चर्यजनक नहीं है।[49] यांत्रिकी के विकास को लेकर प्रायः यह शंका व्यक्त की जाती है कि यह मूल्यों के लिए घातक है। वस्तुतः जहाँ यांत्रिकी या प्रौद्योगिकी कुछ मूल्यों के लिए संकट पैदा करती है, वहीं मूल्यों के संक्रमण में भी उसकी अहम भूमिका होती है। इसका एक सकारात्मक पक्ष यह है कि सामंतों के एकाधिकार, जमींदारों की निरंकुशता और खेतिहर मजदूरों की दासवृत्ति पर कड़ा प्रहार हुआ। औद्योगिक क्रांति ने सामंतवाद और दासता का एक तरह से समापन कर दिया।[50] भारत जैसे अर्द्धविकसित देश में यांत्रिकी का लाभ जितना नगरों को मिला उतना पिछड़े हुए क्षेत्रों को नहीं। 'लोकऋण' में इस स्थिति पर खेद व्यक्त करते हुए कहा गया–''नगर का बुद्धि या विज्ञानवादी उछलकर चन्द्रमा पर चला गया किंतु गाँव का साधारण किसान कहाँ तक पहुँचा है ? कुछ के हाथ बिजली के स्विच तक पहुँचे जरूर किंतु उस बिजली के प्रकाश में गाँव का अँधेरा भी तो बढ़ गया है। एक अँधेरे से दूसरे नए अँधेरे तक की उसकी यात्रा को कौन सी उपलब्धि कही जाए।''[51] गाँव से एकतरफा निर्यात[52] के कारणों में से एक यह भी है। औद्योगिक क्रांति से अलग-थलग रहने के कारण जूट मिल का साइरन[53], ट्रैक्टर[54], अस्पताल[55], परिवार नियोजन की सामग्री, यातायात के साधन[56] आदि पिछड़े अंचलों के लिए बहुत उल्लेखनीय और नई चीजें हैं। अपने पेशे या व्यवसाय के आधुनिकीकरण या उन्हें वैज्ञानिक रूप देने की कल्पना साकार नहीं हो पाती[57] एक बूँद आई ड्राप के अभाव में सुंदर आँखें हमेशा के लिए ज्योतिहीन हो जाती हैं।[58] जहाँ आवश्यकता है, वहाँ नलकूप का पानी नहीं पहुँचता।[59]

इसके बावजूद जहाँ ट्रैक्टर, पंप, अस्पताल आदि के रूप में विज्ञान का प्रवेश हुआ है, वहाँ 'सोच' के स्तर पर किंचित् परिवर्तन को लक्ष्य किया जा सकता है। परती पड़ी लाखों एकड़ जमीन को कोसी मैया का शाप या अपनी नियति मान लेनेवाली रूढ़ विचारधारा को ट्रैक्टर चलने या मिट्टी का परीक्षण होने जैसी घटनाओं से आघात पहुँचता है। भवेशनाथ और जित्तन के प्रयास यथास्थिति को बदलने की कोशिश में हैं।[60] सिंचाई के लिए अब कथित इंद्र भगवान् या भाग्य के आसरे रहने की आवश्यकता नहीं–''पानी का पम्पू आएगा। इंद्र भगवान की खुशामद की जरूरत नहीं। कमला नदी में पम्पू लगा दिया, मिसिन इसटाट कर दिया और हाथिया सूँड की तरह सब पानी सोख कर खेत पटा देगा।''[61] डाइन मानी जानेवाली विध्वंसक नदी को यंत्रों के सहारे बाँधने की योजना नई मानसिकता से प्रेरित है।[62]

अस्पताल पिछड़े अंचलों की एक बड़ी आवश्यकता है। झाड़-फूँक आदि अंधविश्वास न केवल नास्ति मूल्यों के संवाहक हैं अपितु मानव की प्रगति में बाधक भी। उचित चिकित्सा के अभाव में मरीज की मृत्यु को 'ईश्वर की लीला'[63] या डायन का करिश्मा[64] कहकर स्वीकार लेना उसी भाग्यवादी मनःस्थिति का अंग है, जो मनुष्य को अकर्मण्य बनाती है। नई पीढ़ी इस अवधारणा को खारिज करती हुई स्वावलंबन, कर्म, सहयोग आदि पर बल देती है। चिकित्सा की आधुनिकतम सुविधाएँ नगर में उपलब्ध हैं लेकिन पिछड़े गाँवों को सड़क, मोटर आदि भी उपलब्ध नहीं कि मरीज वहाँ तक पहुँच सकें। इसलिए वैद्य की पुड़िया, पंडिताई, सोखाई आदि पर निर्भर रहना उनकी नियति है। अस्पतालों की जो यूनिटें गाँव में खुली हैं उनमें कभी डाक्टर है तो दवा नहीं है। सभी डाक्टर 'मैला आँचल' के प्रशांत की तरह जानबूझकर जनसेवा के लिए मेरीगंज जैसे पिछड़े अंचलों में नहीं जाते। अधिकतर डाक्टर 'सेवा' के बजाय 'व्यवसाय' और स्वार्थसिद्धि की दृष्टि से इन क्षेत्रों में आए हैं। प्रायः सरकारी दवाएँ[65] बेच दी जाती हैं।[66] प्राइवेट प्रेक्टिस करने वाले डाक्टर भी अर्थलाभ के लिए अंततः शहर या कस्बे चले जाना अच्छा समझते हैं।[67] मानव हित के लिए हुआ हर आविष्कार अंततः पूँजीपतियों के व्यवसाय का साधन बन जाता है। फिर कोई ईमानदार डाक्टर काला आजार जैसे भीषण रोग की ओषधि ढूँढ़कर भी क्या करे।[68] ट्रैक्टर पंप आदि ने जहाँ संपन्न वर्ग की संपन्नता में योग दिया है वहीं बेरोजगारी की समस्या पैदा की है। अपना गाँव छोड़कर मजदूर आदमी मिल में काम करने को विवश हो रहा है।[69] ट्रैक्टर गरीब किसानों के पास जाकर उनकी दशा सुधारने में उल्लेखनीय योग कर सकता था[70] लेकिन उत्पादन के इस महत्त्वपूर्ण साधन पर संपन्न भू-स्वामियों का एकाधिकार है और 'शोषण' के नकारात्मक मूल्य को और प्रश्रय मिल रहा है। सड़क के माध्यम से यातायात के साधनों का प्रवेश पिछड़े अंचलों में होता है, वे नगरों से जुड़ते हैं। लेकिन सड़क जैसी जनउपयोगी माध्यम भी नेताओं की रस्साकशी का शिकार हो जाती है। जहाँ बहुत आवश्यकता है वहाँ भी सड़क नहीं बन पाती।[71] और विकास का रथ वहाँ तक नहीं पहुँच पाता।

कार्ल मार्क्स ने सामाजिक परिवर्तन को एक अनोखी नहीं, वरन् स्वाभाविक घटना कहा है। यह परिवर्तन उत्पादन के साधनों और शक्तियों से बहुत घनिष्ठ संबंध रखते हैं। विज्ञान और प्रौद्योगिकी की सहायता से उत्पादन प्रणाली में बराबर परिवर्तन आया है और सामंतवादी समाज व्यवस्था पूँजीवादी समाज में परिवर्तित होकर समाजवादी व्यवस्था में परिणत हो रही है। हाथ से चलनेवाली चक्की के जमाने में सामंतवादी समाज था और जब भाप से चलनेवाली चक्की आई, तब औद्योगिक पूँजीपति के प्रभुत्ववाली समाज-व्यवस्था निर्मित हुई। इस व्यवस्था में प्रौद्योगिकी स्वार्थ, विलास, शोषण, अनीति आदि नास्ति मूल्यों से जुड़ी रही।

आंचलिक उपन्यासों में दिखाया गया है कि पिछड़े अंचल जिस संक्रमण काल से गुजर रहे हैं, उसमें 'प्रौद्योगिकी' और विज्ञान के आविष्कार पुराने सामंतों या नवधनाढ्यों के एकाधिकार में हैं। आंचलिक उपन्यासकार जनतांत्रिक व्यवस्था का समर्थन इसलिए भी करता है कि उत्पादन के आधुनिक उपकरणों पर वर्गविशेष का एकाधिकार समाप्त हो और उनका लाभ जनसाधारण तक पहुँचे। इसके लिए 'सोनभद्र की राधा', 'वरुण के बेटे', 'धरती धन न अपना', 'मैला आँचल', 'परती परिकथा' आदि में स्थापित आर्थिक-सामाजिक संरचना को बदलने का आग्रह किया गया है। 'रेणु' रामदरश मिश्र, विवेकीराय जैसे कथाकार इस उद्देश्य के लिए 'वर्गच्युति' का उदाहरण भी प्रस्तुत करते हैं, जबकि मधुकर सिंह, नागार्जुन, जगदीशचंद्र आदि संघर्ष-वर्ग संघर्ष में ही व्यवस्था-परिवर्तन और धनात्मक मूल्यों की प्रतिष्ठा का भविष्य देखते हैं।

समानता, अशोषण, स्वतंत्रता आदि प्रजातांत्रिक मूल्यों का समर्थन

आंचलिक उपन्यासों ने बदले हुए परिदृश्य को लिपिबद्ध करते हुए स्पष्ट कर दिया कि शोषक शक्तियों के दिन लद चुके हैं।[72] आजादी के बाद गाँवों में जो नए सामंत पैदा हुए हैं, वे भी जन-असंतोष के रथ को नहीं रोक पा रहे हैं। बल्कि कुछ सामंती तत्त्वों में भी बदलाव आया है। यह बदलाव 'मांसाहार' से 'शाकाहार' की ओर नहीं है। नए युग के नए तेवरों से तहसीलदार (मैला आँचल) और जमींदार (परती परिकथा) सबक लेते हैं और जनसाधारण के हित के लिए सक्रिय दिखाई देते हैं। इनका 'डिक्लास' होना यह सिद्ध करता है कि आर्थिक संबंधों से जुड़े मूल्यों का संक्रमण न केवल सर्वहारा के स्तर पर हुआ है अपितु भूस्वामी भी उससे अछूते न रहे। जहाँ सर्वहारा के स्तर पर संक्रमण की प्रक्रिया तीव्र है, वहाँ संपन्न भूस्वामियों के स्तर पर यह आंशिक और धीमी गति से घटित हो रहा है। तहसीलदार का गरीबों को जमीन लौटा देना[73] एक भावुकतापूर्ण समाधान है, लेकिन सर्वथा अव्यावहारिक भी नहीं है। इसकी तुलना में जित्तन का परिवर्तन अधिक विश्वसनीय लगता है। जित्तन के पिता जमीन के लिए अनेक जालसाजियों से गुजरे लेकिन जित्तन कुछ गरीबों को यूँ ही जमीन दे देता है।[74] अपहरण, शोषण और अनाचार के स्थान पर जित्तन बंधुत्व, सौहार्द, त्याग आदि मूल्यों से संचालित और प्रेरित है। वह स्टेट के समर्थक किंतु जनता के लिए साक्षात् आतंक बकला अहीर, ननकू नट, खत्तर गुलाबछड़ी वाला को स्वयं पुलिस के हवाले कर देता है।[75] धरती के वंध्यापन को तोड़ने के लिए ट्रैक्टर सँभालने वाला जित्तन कहीं से भी शोषक वर्ग का व्यक्ति नहीं लगता। लेकिन सभी भू-स्वामी जित्तन या तहसीलदार नहीं हैं। वे बिना संघर्ष के सूई की नोक भर जमीन देने को प्रस्तुत नहीं। वे बाँटने के नाम

से ही घबराते हैं[76], व्यवहार में लाने पर तो जाने क्या स्थिति हो। इसीलिए नागार्जुन जैसे उपन्यासकार सामंती तत्त्वों की दया का मोहताज न रहकर उस विराट् जनशक्ति में विश्वास प्रकट करते हैं, जिसके आगे कोई भी जनद्रोही तत्त्व नहीं टिक सकता।[77] कुछ उपन्यासकार संघर्षविहीन क्रांति[78] की चर्चा करते हैं, लेकिन वहन तो व्यावहारिक है और न स्थितियों को अच्छी तरह समझने की गवाही देती है। बल्कि एक तरह से यथास्थितिवादी शक्तियों के हक में पड़ती है। इस तरह के स्वर विरल हैं। परिवर्तन के विरोध में पड़नेवाली शक्तियों को प्रायः आंचलिक उपन्यासकारों ने नहीं बख्शा है, भले ही वे प्रगतिशीलता का नकाब लगाए हुए हो। रामकुमार (जल टूटता हुआ), सेक्रेटरी (मैला आँचल), वर्मा (सोनामाटी), डॉक्टर (धरती धन न अपना) इसी प्रकार के छद्म प्रगतिशील व्यक्ति हैं।

वर्ग संघर्ष की धार को कुंठित करनेवाले तत्त्वों में कुछ धार्मिक अवधारणाएँ और पुरातन मान्यताएँ विशेषतः आलोचना का विषय बनी हैं। सामंती और पूँजीवादी शक्तियाँ जनसंघर्ष को कमजोर करने के लिए 'धर्म' को अस्त्र बना लेती हैं। चूँकि हमारे समाज के सैद्धांतिक बाह्य ढाँचे की जड़ें मुख्यतः सामंती अतीत में गड़ी हैं, इसलिए धर्मांधता, जातपाँत, अलौकिक शक्तियों में विश्वास आदि से वर्ग एकता में बाधा पहुँचती है।[79] इसलिए अलगरजिया बाबा जैसे प्रबुद्ध लोग गरीबों को धर्म और ईश्वर के खोखले आतंक से मुक्त करने का आह्वान करते हैं।[80] मजदूरों की हड़ताल के संदर्भ में 'लोहे के पंख' में ईश्वर के अस्तित्व पर लगाया गया प्रश्नचिह्न परंपरागत मूल्यों के विचलन का साक्षी है–"कहाँ है वह भगवान्, जो बैठे बिठाए किसी को खाना दे देता है···दस हजार हड़ताली मजदूरों के लिए राम कहाँ अंतर्धान हो गए थे ?"[81] प्रायः उपन्यासकारों ने 'धर्म' को अलौकिकता, पाखंड और शोषण से अलग करके ही स्वीकार्य माना है। धर्म यदि कुछ लोगों के स्वार्थसाधन का उपकरण है[82], धर्म के नाम पर अमानवीय शोषण का क्रम चलता रहता है तो वह मानव-विरोधी है। ऐसे धर्म का त्याग बेहतर है–"जो धर्म हमारी खुशी को मिटाता हो, हमारा खून पीता हो, हमें कुत्ते से बदतर जिंदगी जीने के लिए बाध्य करता हो उस धर्म में रहने से क्या फायदा ?"[83] भगवान् के न्याय का भी कोई विश्वास नहीं।[84] प्रगतिकामी और प्रतिगामी शक्तियों के संघर्ष के दौरान भी धर्म और धर्म के प्रतिनिधियों की भूमिका दूषित और धार्मिक होती है। प्रगतिशील नीतियों के विरुद्ध 'परती परिकथा' में पुजारी, परमादेव के स्वप्न को प्रचारित करता है।[85] इस तरह के जनविरोधी चरित्रों का चित्रण करके उपन्यासकारों ने जहाँ ईश्वर जैसे 'चरम मूल्य' में अपनी अनास्था व्यक्त की है, वहीं जनसाधारण की बढ़ती हुई समझदारी को भी रेखांकित किया है कि वह नास्ति मूल्यों की अप्रासंगिकता से अवगत हो रहा है। बढ़ते हुए वर्ग वैषम्य को देखकर कट्टर आस्तिक भी संशयग्रस्त हो चला है।[86] असली है भूख। पहले पेट है, फिर धर्म।[87] भूख

धर्म के शिकार लोगों का नया धर्म बनाना चाहिए–"...वह धर्म होगा--मनुष्यता, गरीबी...उस धर्म को माननेवाला आदमी जातियों में नहीं बँट सकता।...उस धर्म के विरुद्ध एक और धर्म होगा--अमीरी।"[88] वर्ग विषमता के पीछे कुछ निहित स्वार्थों की साजिश को जनसाधारण पढ़ रहा है और यह उसकी समझ में आ गया है कि रंगभेद, वर्गभेद आदि के लिए ईश्वर का इस्तेमाल किया जाता है।[89] सामंती अधिकार को सदा धर्म का संरक्षण प्राप्त रहा है।[90]

गांधीवादी मूल्यों के प्रति संदेहात्मक दृष्टि

राजनीतिक आजादी स्वस्थ मूल्यों की समूची व्यवस्था के रूप में जानी जाती है। इसके अंतर्गत न्याय, राष्ट्रीयता, सेवा, एकता, समता आदि अनेक मूल्य समाहित हैं। जनमानस में आजादी की जो संकल्पना थी, उसके तहत यह विश्वास निर्मूल न था कि आजादी मिलते ही न केवल भ्रष्टाचार, दमन और शोषण से मुक्ति मिलेगी अपितु न्याय, ईमानदारी और सहयोग आदि को प्रश्रय मिलेगा। 'ब्रह्मपुत्र' के अंधे सूरदास का विचार था कि फिरंगी के राज्य में न्याय कहीं नहीं है।[91] स्वतंत्रता के बाद भी न्याय ढूँढ़े से नहीं मिलता।[92] जनसाधारण अवाक् था कि आत्मबलिदान, राष्ट्रीयता और अन्याय के विरुद्ध संघर्ष की जिन मूल्य-मर्यादाओं के सहारे स्वाधीनता का संग्राम लड़ा गया था, वे आजादी के बाद अप्रासंगिक ठहरा दी गईं और उनकी खुली अवज्ञा होने लगी। रेणु ने दिखाया है कि किस तरह कथित जनसेवक जनसेवा के नाम पर अपने स्वार्थों की पूर्ति के लिए उत्सुक हो उठा।[93] स्वयं गांधीवादियों ने गांधी की अहिंसा को विनोबा के अनाथालय में भेज दिया।[94] सुराज एक क्रांति के रूप में आया लेकिन जनसाधारण के लिए बेमानी रहा–"करान्ती (क्रांति) एक बार हुई। सुराज हुआ। पर जमाने की शक्ल नहीं बदली और दिन पर दिन बिगड़ गई।"[95] सरकार या प्रजातंत्र उनके लिए है जो समर्थ हैं। गरीब के लिए भगवान् तक पहुँचना आसान है, लेकिन न्यायालय या सरकार तक उसकी पहुँच नहीं हो सकती।[96] वास्तविक आजादी उन्हें मिली जो जनसेवक की खाल में शोषक और स्वार्थी हैं।[97] स्वार्थ जिनका चरम मूल्य है, अवसरवाद मूल प्रवृत्ति। अवसरवादी नेताओं ने समय रहते ही टोपियाँ बदल लीं। जिन्होंने वास्तव में आजादी की लड़ाई में सक्रिय भाग लिया, वे पीछे धकेल दिए गए। जमींदारों ने कांग्रेस की अगुवाई हथिया ली।[98] स्वाधीनता संग्राम के स्वयंसेवकों के साथ दुर्व्यवहार करनेवाले तत्त्व[99] सत्तारूढ़ दल के कर्ताधर्ता बन गए।[100] सर्वोदय, अहिंसा, जनसेवा, सत्याग्रह आदि को स्वयं गांधीवादियों ने खारिज कर दिया। कथन और आचरण की असंगति स्पष्ट दिखाई देने लगी। गांधी से जुड़े संस्थानों में मांसाहार और मदिरा सेवन खुलेआम होने लगा। आपत्ति करने पर बहुत ढिठाई

से अपने आचरण को संगत बताने के उदाहरण कम नहीं मिलते।[101] गांधीजी के देहावसान के बाद कांग्रेसी नेताओं में इस बात की होड़ लगती है कि गांधीजी की भस्म कौन लाएगा। इस होड़ के मूल में श्रद्धाभाव न होकर सार्वजनिक छबि निखारने का स्वार्थ सक्रिय है।[102]

ऐसा नहीं कि मूल्यों की गिरावट केवल सत्तारूढ़ दल में आई। अन्य राजनीतिक दल भी 'चुनाव' और 'कुर्सी' की राजनीति में मानवीय और जनधर्मी मूल्यों का उल्लंघन करते दिखाई देते हैं। सोशलिस्ट पार्टी के सदस्य भी चुपचाप चंदा वसूल कर हजम कर जाते हैं।[103] कथित वामपंथी भी 'नीति' की अवहेलना कर राजनीति करने में संलग्न दिखाई देते हैं।[104] कामरेड मकबूल जैसे लोग लाभदायक योजनाओं का विरोध करते हैं क्योंकि जनमत अभी उन्हें स्वीकार नहीं कर पा रहा है।[105] समूची राजनीति अनीति या उखाड़-पछाड़ पर केंद्रित हो चली है।[106] आंचलिक उपन्यासों में राजनीतिक दलों की गिरावट को जहाँ व्यंग्य के साथ प्रस्तुत किया गया है, वहीं पिछड़े अंचलों के जनसाधारण पर उसके दुष्प्रभाव को बहुत चिंता के साथ देखा गया है। "कुटिल राजनीति के प्रवेश ने ग्रामीणों के बीच नए ढंग का वैमनस्य रोपा, हिंसा-द्वेष को बढ़ावा दिया और आत्मीयता, सहयोग, परोपकार आदि मूल्यों को गंभीर क्षति पहुँचाई। इस तरह पहली नजर में यही लगता है कि गाँवों में राजनीति का प्रवेश महाअशुभकर सिद्ध हुआ।"[107] लेकिन यह कहना अनुचित होगा कि राजनीति के संपर्क के अभाव में ग्रामीण जीवन अधिक सार्थक और स्वस्थ होता। राजनीति समकालीन जीवन की महत्त्वपूर्ण सचाई है और इससे निरपेक्ष रहने का अर्थ समकालीन यथार्थ के एक बहुत बड़े आयाम को अनदेखा करना है।

राजनीतिक मूल्य संक्रमण को स्पष्ट तौर पर दर्शाने के लिए उपन्यासकारों ने सही और गलत मूल्यों के दो परस्पर विरोधी 'मॉडल' रचे हैं। महीपसिंह (जल टूटता हुआ), वैद्यजी (रागदरबारी), परसराम (आधा गाँव), सुखदेव (अलग-अलग वैतरणी), छोटन बाबू (जुलूस), लुत्तो (परती परिकथा), सागरमल, दुलारचंद कापरा (मैला आँचल), रामकुमार (जल टूटता हुआ), बड़ोदकर (लोहे के पंख), फूलबाबू (बलचनमा), जनार्दन राय (नदी फिर बह चली) आदि चरित्र सुविधाजीवी, स्वार्थी और जनविरोधी नेतृत्व का प्रतिनिधित्व करते हैं। इनमें जनसेवा का चोला पहने हुए भूतपूर्व सामंत धनी भू-स्वामी और पूँजीपति तो हैं ही, जनसाधारण से उभरे परसराम, रामकुमार, सुखदेव आदि व्यक्ति भी हैं, जिनकी गतिविधियाँ अंततः जनता के हितों के विरोध में पड़ती हैं। ये चरित्र स्पष्ट करते हैं कि आजादी के बाद राजनीतिक मूल्यों का संक्रमण उच्चतर मूल्यों से हीनतर मूल्यों की दिशा में हुआ है। सुविधाजीवी नेताओं ने व्यक्तिगत इच्छाओं अभिरुचियों को महत्त्व देते हुए सामाजिक आवश्यकता और नैतिकता की खुली अवहेलना की है। त्याग, जनसेवा,

संघर्ष, ईमानदारी आदि उनके लिए प्रासंगिक नहीं रह गए। संक्रमण का यह दृश्यालेख वर्तमान यथार्थ के मेल में है।[108] लेकिन सत्य, ईमानदारी और जनहित के लिए संघर्षरत नेता भी मिल जाते हैं, भले ही उनकी संख्या कम है। अतः उपन्यासकारों की संक्रमण की उस सही दिशा की ओर भी संकेत किया है जो भविष्य में उच्चतर लक्ष्यों की ओर होगी। इसी उद्देश्य के लिए कुछ जनधर्मी और जुझारू जनसेवियों के बिंब को चमकाया गया है। इनके अपने निश्चित जीवन मूल्य हैं और कार्य करने का उद्देश्य सुस्पष्ट है। वे हर तरह की अनीति और 'भ्रष्टाचार' के विरुद्ध अलख जगाते देखे जा सकते हैं।

वामनदास (मैला आँचल), रंगलाल गुरु (परती परिकथा), देवकांत, अतुल (ब्रह्मपुत्र), गीधू (हजार घोड़ों का सवार), जैकिसुन (बाबा बटेसरनाथ), मंगल (नदी फिर बह चली), सतीश (जल टूटता हुआ), मोहन माँझी (वरुण के बेटे) आदि वास्तविक अर्थों में जनप्रतिनिधि हैं और सत्य, न्याय, राष्ट्रहित आदि मूल्यों के लिए संघर्ष करते हुए प्रायः आहत होते हैं। भारतमाता को अपनी माँ से अधिक महत्त्व देनेवाले[109], अंतिम क्षण तक आदर्शच्युत न होनेवाले[110] और सामंती-पूँजीपति गँठजोड़ के विरुद्ध जनसमूह की चेतना को जाग्रत करनेवाले इन नेताओं का वर्ग निश्चय ही स्वार्थी, पदलोलुप और भाई भतीजावाद को प्रश्रय देनेवाले नेताओं से अलग अपनी निजी पहचान रखता है।[111] इन्हें छुरा भोंककर बेहयाई से मुस्कुराने वाली राजनीति नहीं आती।[112] साधन और साध्य की पवित्रता का बोध अभी उन्हें है और वे राजनीति को आदर्श से अलहदा करके नहीं देख पाते।[113] चूँकि उन्हें विरासत में सच और न्याय की पक्षधरता का पाठ मिला है[114], इसलिए वे इन आदर्शों से नहीं डिग पाते।

व्यवस्था-परिवर्तन और क्रांति के प्रति बढ़ती आस्था

बहुत से नागरिकों को मौजूदा प्रजातांत्रिक व्यवस्था की प्रासंगिकता संदेहास्पद लगती है, जिस पर कल के देशद्रोहियों और बहुरूपिये जनसेवकों का आधिपत्य है।[115] युवा नेतृत्व यथास्थिति में परिवर्तन के लिए वास्तविक संघर्ष का हामी है। वास्तविक संघर्ष का अर्थ है कि जनसाधारण की सामाजिक-आर्थिक व्यवस्था विकसित हो। आज जनता भाषण नहीं, अपने सवालों के सच्चे और जिंदा चित्र चाहती है।[116] शोषितों की पहली और अंतिम दिलचस्पी सम्मान से पेट भरने में है।[117] इस उद्देश्य के लिए आवश्यक है कि नई व्यवस्था गढ़ी जाए।[118] नेताओं का यह वर्ग अभी अल्पमत में से है। इनकी सृष्टि के पीछे उपन्यासकारों का स्पष्ट संकेत है कि राजनीतिक मूल्यों के संक्रमण की सही दिशा यही है। कहना न होगा कि यह दिशा नास्तिमूल्यों से अस्तिमूल्यों की ओर प्रयाण की है। 'बाबा बटेसरनाथ', 'बलचनमा',

'लोहे के पंख', 'नदी फिर बह चली', 'हजार घोड़ों का सवार' आदि उपन्यासों से स्पष्ट है कि धीरे-धीरे जनसाधारण भी सही गलत राजनीति का अंतर पहचानने लगा है और उसका मूक या मुखर समर्थन उसके लिए संघर्षरत नेतृत्व को प्राप्त है। लेकिन समग्रतः जनमानस एक दुविधा या संशय या मूल्यमूढ़ता की मनःस्थिति से गुजर रहा है। सत्ता पक्ष की पदलोलुपता, अवसरवाद और विरोध पक्ष की ढुलमुल नीति ने जनसाधारण को 'चुनाव' 'जनतंत्र' 'संसद' आदि के प्रति उदासीन बनाया है। राजनीतिक हो-हल्ले में यह पता नहीं चलता कि सफेद क्या है, स्याह क्या है।[119] वोट कोई छप्पन टके की चीज तो है नहीं, जो चाहे ले जाए।[120] 'मत' और 'मतदान' से आम मतदाता की यह अरुचि[121] कुरूप यथार्थ को देखकर जन्मी है। पक्ष या विपक्ष में होने के फैसले तात्कालिक दबावों के फलस्वरूप किए जाते हैं। यही कारण है कि भूतपूर्व जमींदारों का समर्थन वामपंथी नेता पाण्डेयजी को प्राप्त होता है।[122] बहुत से राजनीतिक दलों की उपस्थिति ने जनसाधारण को भ्रमित किया है। 'मैला आँचल' में कांग्रेस, सोशलिस्ट, साम्यवादी आदि कई दलों की होड़ में जनसाधारण के मतिभ्रम को रेखांकित किया गया है। इस मतिभ्रम के बावजूद जनसाधारण अपने वर्गशत्रु या वर्गमित्र की पहचान करने लग गया है। उसे यह पता है कि उसके हितों की रक्षा कौन सी पार्टी कर सकती है। अनपढ़ और राजनीतिक समझ से शून्य श्रमजीवी को भी समाजवादी विचारधारा के दल आकर्षित करते हैं।[123]

जनतांत्रिक व्यवस्था के अंतर्विरोधों की चर्चा करते हुए आंचलिक उपन्यासकारों ने 'चुनाव', 'मतदान' आदि के नाम पर होनेवाली भद्दगियों को नंगा किया है। 'सोनामाटी' में डैन जार्जकस के कथन ''वी सीक क्रियेटिव वैंडेटिज्म''–हम लोगों को कुछ रचनात्मक गुंडई करनी चाहिए[124], का हवाला दिया गया है। भारतीय साहित्य में यह गुंडई घटित हुई या नहीं, यह शोध का विषय है। लेकिन 'राजनीति' में गुंडई खुले रूप से होती रही है। 'सोनामाटी' में ही 'चुनाव' के मौके पर अपनाए गए–साम-दाम दंड-भेद आदि का विस्तृत वर्णन यह दर्शाने के लिए हुआ है कि इस 'गुंडई' ने जनतांत्रिक मूल्यों को किस तरह कुचलकर रख दिया है। मगनचोला के चुनाव के समय संदेहास्पद वोटरों को डरा धमका कर घर से नहीं निकलने दिया जाता। बहुतों को कंबल और नोट के सहारे खरीद लिया जाता है। इस स्थिति पर रामरूप का यह कथन द्रष्टव्य है–''समूचे राजनीतिक सिद्धांत जैसे कूड़े के ढेर हैं, जिनके ऊपर निर्वाचन की बरसात में कठफुले जैसी कुर्सियाँ उगती हैं और लूट पड़ जाती है।''[125] यह सब सिद्धांतहीन राजनीति के दबाववश होता है, जिसका एकमात्र लक्ष्य है–कुर्सी। सिद्धांतहीन राजनीति एक ओर आत्मीयता, सद्भाव आदि मूल्यों को नष्ट करती है, दूसरी ओर मानवीयता की बलि चढ़ा दी जाती है।[126] स्वार्थ, दलबदल, परपीड़न आदि अवमूल्यों को खुला प्रोत्साहन मिलता है। राजनीतिक

गुंडई की चर्चा 'जल टूटता हुआ' में भी है। रामकुमार स्कूल और गाँव की समस्याओं के समाधान हेतु राजनीति का प्रयोग कर रहा है–"...स्कूल हो चाहे गाँव, चाहे देश, सभी जगह गुंडई भर गई है। गुंडे राज्य करते हैं। या तो इनकी गुंडई खत्म करने के लिए सामूहिक प्रयास किया जाए या इनसे मिलकर अपनी रक्षा की जाए। वह देख रहा है देश में जो गुंडई बढ़ी है, बड़े से लेकर छोटे पैमाने तक उसका प्रतिरोध करने की शक्ति किसी में नहीं दीख रही है। गुंडई सामूहिक है और प्रतिरोध अलग-अलग।"[127] इस उद्धरण में राजनीतिक मूल्यों के देशव्यापी संक्रमण को रेखांकित किया गया है। एक बातचीत में विवेकीराय ने बताया है कि दिल्ली की जो राजनीति है, ठीक वही राजनीति गाँव में प्रतिबिंबित हो जाती है।[128] देश की राजनीति में साधुता, सेवा, त्याग आदि मूल्यों का तिरस्कार कर अनुशासनहीनता, अवसरवाद, उद्दंडता आदि को ही 'मूल्य' समझने का जो दुष्चक्र चल रहा है, उसकी यथार्थ झाँकी आंचलिक उपन्यासों में है। लेकिन सभी उपन्यासकारों ने 'राजनीतिक गुंडई' से जुड़े अवमूल्यों से अपनी गहरी असहमति व्यक्त की है। 'जल टूटता हुआ' में रामकुमार को क्षोभ है कि सतीश उसकी 'राजनीति' में सहयोग नहीं करता। यह असहयोग केवल सतीश का नहीं उसके स्रष्टा रचनाकार का भी है। सतीश सनकी समझे जाने की हद तक जाकर भी 'आदर्श' की रक्षा करता है[129], 'सिद्धांतहीन राजनीति' का समर्थन नहीं करता। जाहिर है, वास्तविकता के स्तर पर राजनीतिक मूल्य जनविरोधी और स्वार्थी होने का प्रमाण दे रहे हैं। आंचलिक उपन्यासकार इस अवमूल्यन से संतुष्ट नहीं हैं और वे स्वस्थ, मानवीय एवं जनधर्मी मूल्यों की ओर राजनीतिक संक्रमण के पक्ष में हैं। वे 'चुनाव', 'संसद' आदि की पवित्रता बनाए रखने के कायल हैं अतः कुछ उपन्यासों में यह दर्शाया गया है कि अवमूल्यों से लैस राजनीतिज्ञ पराजित होते हैं तथा जमीन से जुड़े और जनहित के लिए समर्पित राजनीतिज्ञ अंततः जीत जाते हैं। 'नदी फिर बह चली' में मंगल बाबू के हाथों जनार्दन राय की पराजय[130] इस संदर्भ में द्रष्टव्य है। इसी चुनाव के संदर्भ में उपन्यासकार ने 'राजनीति' में 'जेनुइन' व्यक्तियों को सुनियोजित ढंग से पीछे ढकेलने के षड्यंत्र की चर्चा की है–"क्या यह सच नहीं है कि अपनी ख्याति पर आँच न आने देने के लिए ही बड़े-बड़े नेताओं ने सरदार भगतसिंह, चंद्रशेखर आजाद वगैरह को 'रांग बॉक्स' में डाल दिया।"[131] यानी कि 'अयोग्य' को प्रश्रय और योग्य की टाँग घसीटने की प्रवृत्ति पुरानी है। यह नहीं कहा जा सकता कि यह स्वातंत्र्योत्तर विकृति है। सेवा, त्याग, संघर्ष आदि स्वतः मूल्यों के आज कुर्सी-प्राप्ति के साधन मूल्य बन जाने की त्रासदी से आंचलिक उपन्यासकार सबसे चित्रित हैं।

आंचलिक उपन्यासकारों ने जनतांत्रिक व्यवस्था के अंतर्विरोधों को रेखांकित करते हुए भी उसे एकदम अस्वीकृत नहीं किया है। लेकिन 'बैलेट' की सहायता

से अहिंसक तरीके से परिवर्तन के प्रति वे आश्वस्त नहीं लगते। ब्रिटिश साम्राज्यवाद से जूझते समय केवल अहिंसा का मार्ग अपर्याप्त लगा था।[132] आज भी किसी बड़े परिवर्तन के लिए अहिंसा पर्याप्त नहीं लगती। प्रबुद्ध ग्रामीण सोचने लगा है कि क्या छुटपुट हत्याओंवाला सशस्त्र क्रांति का मार्ग ही हमारा मुक्तिमार्ग होगा।[133] गांधीवादी मूल्यों से यथास्थिति को ही बल मिलने लगा है अतः नपुंसकीय अहिंसा के त्याग की अपील[134] बेमानी नहीं लगती। उपन्यासों में जनविरोधी शक्तियों की अमानवीयता और निरंकुशता को रेखांकित करते हुए संकेत किया गया है कि लोकतंत्र बुर्जुआ लोकतंत्र से अधिनायकवाद की ओर संक्रमण का खतरा बढ़ रहा है। अधिनायकवाद और फासीवाद से जूझने के लिए जनता को हिंसा का सहारा लेना पड़ सकता है। पिछड़े अंचलों में हिंसा या खूनी संघर्ष का उद्घोष अपरिचित नहीं रहा—"...बदलते इतिहास के बीच दूसरे-दूसरे गाँवों में कितना-कितना क्या-क्या नहीं बदल गया ? यह दिन भी देखना पड़ा कि दलितोन्मेष खूनी क्रांति का उद्घोष बन घहराने लगा है। सुदूर चीन से चल कामरेड माओ निचाट ग्रामांचल में पहुँचने लगा है।"[135] बलचनमा ने इस सत्य को बहुत पहले अनुभव कर लिया था कि सिधाई से साधारण अधिकार नहीं मिल सकते।[136] अब सर्वहारा अपने खून को आखिरी बूँद तक अपने अधिकारों के लिए जूझने के हित कटिबद्ध है।[137]

संदर्भ

1. आम रास्ता नहीं है, पृ. 31
2. सामाजिकी, खंड-1, 1980, पृ. 86
3. "Values are not transcendent, not isolated from the struggle and concourse of life mind and society." —Dynamics of Morals, p. 220
4. अलग-अलग वैतरणी, पृ. 47
5. धरती धन न अपना
6. जल टूटता हुआ, पृ. 378
7. अलग-अलग वैतरणी, पृ. 221
8. "मेरे रहते भी कोई मालिक के खेत में छेब लगा दे तो यह जिनगी अकारथ है।"—लोहे के पंख, पृ. 21
9. लोहे के पंख, पृ. 264
10. विनिमय की शर्तें और वर्ग संबंध, पृ. 21
11. "घोड़े पर चढ़ इधर-उधर खेतों पर नजर मारी, मशीरी की और हर फसल के दाने अपने कोठों में भर लिए। पसीना बहाया सो काम्मियों ने"—जिंदगीनामा, पहला भाग, पृ. 80

12. वही
13. "जमींदारी प्रथा खतम हुई, लेकिन तहसीलदार जमीन से बेदखल कर रहा है।"—मैला आँचल, पृ. 197
14. "अब कभी दशहरे के मौके पर असामियों की भीड़ जुहार करने नहीं आती···न तो अब छावनी के लड़कों को देखकर कोई सत्तर साल का बूढ़ा झुककर सलाम करता··· ।"—अलग-अलग वैतरणी, पृ. 32
15. आधा गाँव, पृ. 279
16. वही, पृ. 341
17. "परसुराम की बातें सुनकर वे खुश होते, पर उनके दिलों में बैठा हुआ सदियों का डर उन्हें तोड़ देता। जमींदारी मजहब की तरह मजबूत थी। शख्सियत उसके चंगुल में थी।"—आधा गाँव, पृ. 306
18. "ये सारे दरिद्र जिनसे मैं जूतों से बात करता था, पद पुरान के लिए पंचायत में इकट्ठे हुए हैं।"—जल टूटता हुआ, पृ. 515
19. "···आज उनकी सारी जमींदारी शान समझने को तैयार हूँ, अपनी एक-एक आह का बदला लेने को खड़ा हूँ, माई का दूध पिए हों तो आ जाएँ।"—जल टूटता हुआ, पृ. 379
20. असगाँव-पसगाँव, पृ. 55
21. लोकऋण, पृ. 153
22. मैला आँचल, पृ. 180, जल टूटता हुआ पृ. 16, सोनभद्र की राधा, पृ. 29
23. "हम लोग गरीब किसान-मजूर दल के हैं, हम लोगों में अगर कोई गलती करेगा, तो भी मैं उसी का साथ दूँगी··· ।"—नदी फिर बह चली, पृ. 406
24. "···उस संगठन द्वारा सारा सर्वहारा वर्ग अपनी शक्ति से उस राज्य की पुनःस्थापना करेगा जहाँ कोई वर्ग नहीं होगा। जहाँ निजी संपत्ति भी नहीं होगी। जहाँ तमाम लोग मिल-जुलकर काम करेंगे और सारे सुखों व आनंदों का मिलकर उपभोग करेंगे। जहाँ दासता नहीं रहेगी।"—हजार घोड़ों का सवार, पृ. 149
25. मैला आँचल, पृ. 187
26. वही, पृ. 185
27. "खून पानी एक करें हम—मजूर लोग और मौज उड़ाए मिल मालिक।"—आधा गाँव, पृ. 294-295
28. हजार घोड़ों का सवार, पृ. 160
29. बलचनमा, पृ. 185
30. जंगल के फूल, राजपाल एण्ड संस, संस्करण 1976, पृ. 85
31. "संथाल लोग अच्छी तरह जानते हैं, कोई साथ देनेवाला नहीं।···अरे तीर तो है। यही सबसे बड़ा साथी है।"—मैला आँचल, पृ. 201
32. "···तुम लोग ही जमीन के असल मालिक हो। कानून है, जिसने तीन साल तक जमीन को जोता-बोया है, जमीन उसी की होगी।"—मैला आँचल, पृ. 201

33. विनिमय की शर्तें और वर्ग संबंध, पृ. 22
34. "कामरेड, अभी संघर्ष मत छेड़ो। सबसे पहले अभी-अभी किसी एक इलाके में, एक एरिया लेकर इसको इसपारमिन करेंगे"सो भी संघर्ष से एक महीना पहले दरखास्त देना होगा लोगों से, फिर इनकुआएरी फिर एजकूटी मिटिंग, तब जाकर राय निकलेगी कि संघर्ष करना चाहिए कि नहीं।"—मैला आँचल, पृ. 200
35. धरती धन न अपना, पृ. 297
36. "मुझे तो ऐसा लगता है कि देश के नेताओं ने तरह-तरह के सिद्धांतों की रट लगा-लगाकर मजदूर किसानों के दिमागी कंधे पर लोहे के पंख बाँध दिए हैं।"—लोहे के पंख, पृ. 404
37. सामाजिकी, खंड-1, 1980, पृ. 74
38. वही, पृ. 77
39. बलचनमा, पृ. 185
40. सोनामाटी, पृ. 431
41. "फिर कभी वे टस से मस नहीं हुए थे। वे तो संकल्प लेकर गए थे कि जब तक न्याय नहीं मिलेगा—गोली खाकर मर जाएँगे, मगर वापस नहीं आएँगे।"—जंगली सुअर, पृ. 100-101
42. जल टूटता हुआ, पृ. 414
43. वही, पृ. 416
44. मैला आँचल, पृ. 234-235
45. "बीच में गैर की जमीन मिल जाए और उसे तुमने हड़प नहीं लिया तो तुम्हें असल बूँद का पैदा नहीं समझूँगा। मेरे माथे पर हाथ रखकर कसम खाओ कि तुम मेरा सपना मरते दम तक पूरा करोगे।"—जंगली सुअर, पृ. 63
46. जंगली सुअर, पृ. 63
47. सोनामाटी, पृ. 80
48. वही।
49. 'Not surprisingly, the march of civilization has frequently been measured by technological advance in terms of materials from stone to bronze, from bronze to iron from iron to steel, in terms of energy, from human muscle power to animals, to wind and water, to steam and oil, to rockets and nuclear power; in terms of machines from hand tools to powered tools to mass production lines to computer controlled factories.'—The American review spring 1979 Technology and human values, Melvin Kranzleerg, p. 22
50. Ibid, p. 23
51. लोकऋण, पृ. 166
52. अलग-अलग वैतरणी, पृ. 674
53. मैला आँचल, पृ. 320

54. परती परिकथा
55. मैला आँचल, पृ. 11
56. आधा गाँव, पृ. 279
57. "गढ़ पोखर का जीर्णोद्धार होगा आगे चलकर और तब मलाही गोढ़ियारी के ग्रामांचल मछली पालन व्यवसाय का आधुनिकतम केंद्र हो जाएँगे।...इकतल्ला सैनिटोरियम बनेगा।"–वरुण के बेटे, पृ. 34
58. मैला आँचल, पृ. 101
59. लोकऋण, पृ. 174
60. परती परिकथा, पृ. 129
61. मैला आँचल, पृ. 320
62. अर्द्धनग्न जनता का विशाल दल। पर्वत तोड़ो हइयो। पत्थर तोड़ो हइयो। हम कोसी को साधेंगे...खून पसीना एक कर बिखरी ताकत जोड़कर। पर्वत पत्थर तोड़कर। इस डायन को साधेंगे।"–परती परिकथा, पृ. 528
63. "ईश्वर की लीला भी कितनी विचित्र है बेटा, कभी कुछ करता है कभी कुछ, किसी को किसी तरह मारता है, किसी को किसी तरह। हम लोग तो उसके हाथ की कठपुतली हैं।"–जल टूटता हुआ, पृ. 371
64. मैला आँचल, पृ. 263
65. जल टूटता हुआ, पृ. 371
66. राग दरबारी, पृ. 340
67. अलग-अलग वैतरणी, पृ. 633
68. "क्या होगा मानव कल्याण करके ?...आखिर पाँच आने का एक एम्पुल पचास रुपये तक बिकेगा। यहाँ तक उसकी पहुँच नहीं होगी।"–मैला आँचल, पृ. 223
69. वही, पृ. 320
70. "मैं कहता हूँ, क्यों नहीं हम दस किसान भाई पर एक वैसी मशीन दिलवा देते ? भोंज पर खेत जोतने और बैलों के लिए पैसे जुटाने की तबाही से तो हम लोग बच जाते।"–नदी फिर बह चली, पृ. 357
71. सोनामाटी, पृ. 275
72. "तू जिस युग में पैदा हुआ है, वह राजाओं-जमींदारों और सेठों-साहूकारों का युग नहीं, बल्कि तेरे जैसे आम नौजवानों का जमाना है...।"–बाबा बटेसरनाथ, पृ. 52
73. "अरे, यह जमीन तो उन्हीं किसानों की है, नीलाम की हुई, जब्त की हुई, उन्हें वापस दे रहा हूँ।"–मैला आँचल, पृ. 331
74. परती परिकथा, पृ. 107
75. वही, पृ. 277
76. "लोग बाँटने के नाम पर ही बौखला उठते हैं। जब छीन कर लेने की बात उठेगी तब पता नहीं कैसी स्थिति पैदा हो जाएगी।"–सोनभद्र की राधा, पृ. 9
77. बलचनमा, पृ. 168

78. "...किसी लकीर को बिना छुए, बिना काटे पीटे हम उसके नीचे एक उससे बड़ी लकीर खींचकर छोटी कर सकते हैं। तो छोटों को शिक्षा का स्तर उठाकर बड़ों को बिना छेड़े सहज क्रांति करनी है।"—लोकऋण, पृ. 192-193
79. साहित्य और राजनीति (सं. कुँवरपाल सिंह), मार्क्सवादी बुद्धिजीवियों की भूमिका—बी. टी. रणदिवे, भाषा प्रकाशन, प्रथम संस्करण 1981, पृ. 16
80. "तुम सभी गरीबों को ईश्वर और धर्म के खोखले आतंक से मुक्त करो। उन्हें कहो कि सत्य, बुद्धि, प्रेम और समता ही ईश्वर है।"—हजार घोड़ों का सवार, पृ. 159
81. लोहे के पंख, पृ. 385
82. "जब धर्म केवल कुछ लोगों की बपौती बन जाए, चंद तिजोरियों में सिमट कर रह जाए तो वह हमारे काम का नहीं रह जाता।"—असगाँव-पसगाँव, पृ. 3
83. हजार घोड़ों का सवार, पृ. 184
84. कब तक पुकारूँ, पृ. 149
85. परती परिकथा, पृ. 114
86. "बाकी ई है सोचे की बात। हम्माद सभे का हक मारे है, तब्बो मजे में हैं। अल्लाह मियाँ होते त हम्माद की कमान अइसे ना बढ़ सकती रही।"—आधा गाँव, पृ. 268
87. सूरज किरन की छाँव, पृ. 109
88. हजार घोड़ों का सवार, पृ. 147
89. लाल पसीना, पृ. 300
90. कब तक पुकारूँ, पृ. 39
91. ब्रह्मपुत्र : देवेन्द्र सत्यार्थी, पृ. 417
92. "अंधेर मचा हुआ है। न रिश्वत समाप्त हुई है न सिफारिशों का जोर कम हुआ है। दीया जलाकर ढूँढ़ देखो न्याय नाम की चीज नहीं मिलती"—ब्रह्मपुत्र, देवेन्द्र सत्यार्थी, पृ. 446
93. "सब मेले-मंतरी होना चाहते हैं बालदेव। देस का काम, गरीबों का काम चाहे मजूरों का काम जो भी करते हैं, एक ही लोभ से।"—मैला आँचल, पृ. 310
94. बाबा बटेसरनाथ, पृ. 140
95. बबूल, विवेकीराय, पृ. 155
96. वही, पृ. 54
97. "आजादी ! छिः आजादी मिली है हमारे उग्रमोहन बाबू को, कुलानंददास को...कांग्रेस के टिकट पर जो भी चुने गए हैं। उन्हें मिली है आजादी।"—बाबा बटेसरनाथ, पृ. 127
98. "बड़े-बड़े जुल्मी जमींदार अब अपने को कहीं न पाकर कांग्रेस में शामिल हो रहे हैं। बहुत जोर आजमाइश की कांग्रेस से संघर्ष करने की, कानून को तोड़ने की; किंतु हार मानकर कांग्रेस में लौट रहे हैं और कांग्रेस उन्हें सम्मान दे रही है।"—जल टूटता हुआ, पृ. 15
99. मैला आँचल, पृ. 136

100. राग दरबारी, पृ. 41

101. "अरे सब चलता है यार ! इस दफ्तर में कौन गांधीवाद का इम्तहान लेने आ रहा है। दफ्तर से बाहर जब प्लेटफार्म या किसी सभा के पंडाल पर ऐसी भूल करूँ और तुम टोको तो कुछ ईमान भी दूँगा।"—लोहे के पंख, पृ. 197

102. मैला आँचल

103. परती परिकथा, पृ. 75

104. "नीति नहीं, राजनीति तो हुई। राजनीति में यह सब कुछ क्षमा है, जायज है। आप लोग राजनीति और आदर्श को एक करके मत देखिए।"—जल टूटता हुआ, पृ. 296

105. "कामरेड विश्वकर्मा, बहुमत जिस बात के विपक्ष में हो उसका समर्थन करके हम अपने पाँव में कुल्हाड़ी क्यों मारें।"—परती परिकथा, पृ. 475

106. "दुश्मन को जैसे भी हो चित करना चाहिए। यह न चित कर पाएँगे तो खुद चित हो जाएँगे।"—रागदरबारी, पृ. 190

107. विवेकीराय, 'स्वातंत्र्योत्तर हिंदी कथा साहित्य और ग्रामजीवन', पृ. 85

108. आचार्य नरेन्द्रदेव ने कांग्रेसियों की कुर्सी लिप्सा पर लिखा है :
'A mad race for power, office and many has taken the place of selfless service.' Sunday 27 Jan.80. 'A Martist who understood in Indian situation Brahmanand, p. 2

109. "...मरने से पहले भारतमाता की हथकड़ी और बेड़ी जितनी भी ढीली कर सकूँ, उतना ही अच्छा है।"—ब्रह्मपुत्र, पृ. 77

110. मैला आँचल, पृ. 318

111. बाबा बटेसरनाथ, नदी फिर बह चली, पृ. 395

112. जल टूटता हुआ, पृ. 389

113. वही, पृ. 296

114. "...सच बोलना ही सबसे बड़ा धरम है। भलाई ही सही उपकार है। आदमी को न तो अन्याय चाहिए और न अन्याय सहना चाहिए। दोनों ही पाप हैं।"—हजार घोड़ों का सवार, पृ. 71

115. नदी फिर बह चली, पृ. 338

116. वही, पृ. 339

117. "...इन शोषित लोगों को जागरण की भारी भरकम बातों में अधिक दिलचस्पी नहीं है...उनकी अभी पहली और अंतिम दिलचस्पी है कि वे सम्मान से पेट कैसे भरें ?"—हजार घोड़ों का सवार, पृ. 306

118. वही।

119. अलग-अलग वैतरणी, पृ. 116

120. राग दरबारी, पृ. 258

121. "यह चुनाव है कि वोट की डकैती है ? शोरशराबा हड़बड़ी हल्ला कर लोगों का उल्लू सीधा करने का यह कैसा प्रजातंत्र है ?"—लोकऋण, पृ. 186

122. "बाकी अगर हम लोगों के आदमी हवालात में जाने लगे तो हम पांडे जी के साथ होने के सिवाय कर ही क्या सकते हैं ?"—आधा गाँव, पृ. 354
123. बलचनमा, पृ. 182
124. सोनामाटी, पृ. 430
125. वही, पृ. 313
126. वही, पृ. 296
127. जल टूटता हुआ, पृ. 405
128. विवेकीराय से वेदप्रकाश अमिताभ की बातचीत
129. जल टूटता हुआ, पृ. 406
130. नदी फिर बह चली, पृ. 399
131. वही, पृ. 398
132. "न अकेली अहिंसा आजादी दिला सकती है, न केवल हिंसा ही।"—ब्रह्मपुत्र, पृ. 418
133. बाबा बटेसरनाथ, पृ. 147
134. "हृदय गरीब और शोषित लोगों का तो बदला जा सकता है पर पाषाण व निरंकुश लोगों का नहीं···इसलिए अहिंसा, असहयोग और सत्याग्रहों के साथ-साथ नपुंसकीय अहिंसा का त्याग भी जरूरी है।"—हजार घोड़ों का सवार, पृ. 158
135. सोनामाटी, पृ. 209
136. "जमींदार और सरकार। अफसर दुरजोधन ठहरे, उनको जुधिष्ठिल नहीं पस्त कर सकते भैया। पिटाई पर पिटाई खाना···ऐसी सिधाई से पूजा तुम्हारी हो तो जमीन सूई की नोक भर नहीं मिलने की···।"—बलचनमा, पृ. 185
137. गंगा मैया, पृ. 121

पंचम प्रकरण

आंचलिक उपन्यासों में मूल्य-संक्रमण : सांस्कृतिक परिदृश्य

मैकाइवर आदि समाजशास्त्रियों ने सभ्यता और संस्कृति के अंतर को रेखांकित करते हुए सभ्यता का संबंध उपयोगिता के क्षेत्र से और संस्कृति का संबंध मौलिक मूल्यों से माना है। डॉ. देवराज ने व्यक्ति के संदर्भ में संस्कृति को मूल्य-चेतना के साथ-साथ तथ्य-चेतना भी कहा है—"किसी भी व्यक्ति की संस्कृति वह मूल्य-चेतना है, जिसका निर्माण उसके संपूर्ण बोध के आलोक में होता है। सांस्कृतिक चेतना जितनी मूल्य-चेतना है, उतनी ही तथ्य-चेतना भी है।"[1] नंदकिशोर आचार्य ने सांस्कृतिक प्रक्रिया को 'सनातन मूल्यों के अर्जन की प्रक्रिया' के रूप में देखा है—"किसी भी संस्कृति की प्रकृति, स्वरूप और गति का निर्धारण वे आदर्श या मूल्य करते हैं जिनकी सिद्धि में ही कोई समाज या व्यक्ति अपने अस्तित्व की सार्थकता का बोध कराता है। संस्कृति को इसीलिए मूल्य-दृष्टि कहा जाता है क्योंकि उन सनातन मूल्यों के अर्जन की प्रक्रिया ही सांस्कृतिक प्रक्रिया है।"[2] लेकिन सनातन मूल्यों से आशय वर्गविशेष अर्थात् अभिजात वर्ग के मूल्यों से नहीं है। समाजशास्त्रियों ने बलपूर्वक कहा है कि उच्चतर सांस्कृतिक मूल्यों पर अभिजात वर्ग का आधिपत्य नहीं होना चाहिए।[3] निश्चय ही लोकसंस्कृति के मूल्य वास्तविक और सनातन सांस्कृतिक मूल्य हैं।

लेकिन सांस्कृतिक मूल्यों को सीमित नहीं माना जाना चाहिए। राधाकमल मुखर्जी ने मूल्यों के जो तीन आयाम जैविक, सामाजिक और आध्यात्मिक माने हैं[4] वे सब सांस्कृतिक मूल्यों में समाहित हो जाते हैं। संस्कृति में एक ओर स्वास्थ्य, सुरक्षा आदि जैविक मूल्यों की व्याप्ति है, दूसरी ओर न्याय, समानता आदि

सामाजिक मूल्य इसके अंग हैं और 'सत्य' 'पवित्रता' आदि अमूर्त और आध्यात्मिक कही जानेवाली धारणाएँ संस्कृति के अंतर्गत आती हैं। धर्म, इतिहास, दर्शन आदि ज्ञान-क्षेत्रों की सभी श्रेष्ठ उपपत्तियाँ 'संस्कृति' में समाहित होती हैं।

डॉ. ह.क. कडवे के अनुसार—"आंचलिक उपन्यासों का उद्देश्य अंचल विशेष के जन-जीवन की संस्कृति का अर्थात् लोक-संस्कृति का चित्रण ही है।"[5] रेणु[6], नागार्जुन[7] से लेकर विवेकीराय तक आंचलिक उपन्यासकार अभिजातवर्गीय संस्कारों और मूल्यों से विद्रूप भाव रखते हुए लोक-संस्कृति और लोकजीवन से रस-ग्रहण और विचार-ग्रहण का प्रमाण देते हैं। लोकजीवन से गहरे जुड़ाव के फलस्वरूप जहाँ एक ओर इन उपन्यासों में धर्म, पाप-पुण्य आदि की रूढ़ और स्थिर मान्यताओं के पुनःपरीक्षण का भाव प्रबल है, दूसरी ओर श्रम, समानता, सद्भाव आदि मानवीय मूल्यों को महत्त्व देने का प्रयास हुआ है। इनमें सांस्कृतिक पर्वों और उत्सवों तथा लोकगीतों-लोककथाओं का विस्तृत उल्लेख केवल 'तथ्य-निरूपण' के आग्रहवश नहीं हुआ है। ये लोकमानस में धँसे हुए मूल्यों का परिचय देने के साथ आज के संदर्भ में इनके विचलन और परिवर्तन को भी रेखांकित करते हैं। डॉ. शशिभूषण सिंहल का यह कथन महत्त्वपूर्ण है कि आंचलिक उपन्यास मुख्य रूप से लोकसंस्कृति को प्रस्तुत करते हैं।[8]

धर्म, पाप-पुण्य आदि मान्यताओं का पुनःपरीक्षण

लोकजीवन पर धर्म की पकड़ आज 'कम्प्यूटर' के युग में भी मजबूत है। धर्म की यह पकड़ दो रूपों में द्रष्टव्य है। एक ओर बाह्याचार पाखंड आदि से युक्त धर्म का स्वरूप है, जो मुख्यतः अभिजातवर्ग और बुर्जुआ वर्ग की तथाकथित संस्कृति का अंग है। दूसरी ओर धर्म का वह स्वरूप है, जो जन-साधारण के 'अभ्युदय' और 'निःश्रेयस' में अपनी मौन भूमिका निभाता रहा है। आंचलिक उपन्यासों में आचरणभ्रष्टता और अनैतिकता से जुड़े तथाकथित धर्म को एकदम अस्वीकार कर दिया है। 'मैला आँचल' में मठ और उससे संबद्ध अनैतिकता का वर्णन, विस्तार से हुआ है[9] और यह सादृश्य है। रेणु दिखाना चाहते हैं कि सदाचार, ईश्वरोपासना और परोपकार आदि के केंद्र माने जानेवाले मठों का वास्तविक रूप क्या है ? नए महंत द्वारा रामपियारी को सार्वजनिक रूप में रखैल के रूप में मान्यता पतन की चरम सीमा है। डॉ. इंदुप्रकाश पांडेय ने मठ और महंत से जुड़े भ्रष्टाचार के इस बयान को यथार्थ की दृष्टि से कमजोर माना है।[10] वस्तुतः ये प्रसंग वास्तविक हैं और सांस्कृतिक मूल्यों के हीनतर दिशा में संक्रमण की गवाही देते हैं। ये बताते हैं कि 'परमार्थ' का स्थान शुद्ध स्वार्थ ने ले लिया है और महंत आदि परलोक सुधारने के बजाय इसी लोक के सारे सुख भोग लेने के लिए कृत-संकल्प हैं। धर्म

का एक सकारात्मक पक्ष यह रहा है कि वहाँ भक्ति या उपासना के स्तर पर 'समानता' की बात कही गई है। 'जात-पाँत' पूछे नहीं कोई/हरि को भजै सो हरि का होई' यह मध्यकालीन भावबोध आज संकीर्णता-ग्रस्त हो चुका है। बड़े-छोटे का भेद संपूर्ण तीक्ष्णता के साथ हमारे सामाजिक जीवन का नासूर बन गया है। धार्मिक संस्थाएँ और धर्म-पुरुष इस भेद का विरोध करना दूर, इसे प्रश्रय और प्रोत्साहन देती देखी जाती हैं, ऐसी स्थिति में दलितों का यह सोचना कि धर्म-परिवर्तन से वे हीनता-मुक्त हो सकते हैं, अमनोवैज्ञानिक नहीं है। 'हजार घोड़ों का सवार' का चैतू इस संबंध में यूँ ही उग्र नहीं है–"जो धर्म हमारी खुशी को मिटाता हो, हमारा खून पीता हो, हमें कुत्ते से बदतर जिंदगी जीने के लिए बाध्य करता हो, उस धर्म में रहने से क्या फायदा।"[11] दलितों में यह नया बोध किसी नई मूल्य-व्यवस्था के प्रभाव या टकराहट से नहीं जन्मा है। यह उनके अपने आत्मालोचन से प्राप्त हुआ है। यह आवेगबहुल निर्णय न होकर स्थितियों के मूल्यांकन के बाद सोच-समझकर एक नए क्रांतिकारी विचार तक पहुँचने का प्रयास है। सोरोकिन ने जिस 'उदग्र गतिशीलता' की चर्चा की है, वह यहाँ द्रष्टव्य है। दलितों के विचार में ममता और समानता की प्राप्ति एक दूसरी सामाजिक व्यवस्था का अंग बन जाने पर ही संभव है। अन्य आंचलिक उपन्यासों में भी धर्म के नाम पर भेदभाव और धर्म के उच्चादर्शों के तुच्छ स्वार्थों में परिणत हो जाने का हादसा वर्णित है। मोहर्रम के करुणार्द्र वातावरण में भी हुसैन अली मियाँ को यह बोध बना हुआ है कि कोई सय्यदजादा किसी मीरासी का बाजू नहीं बन सकता। वे नज्जन मीरासी को सोजखानी की चौकी से गरेबान पकड़कर नीचे उतार देते हैं।[12] स्पष्ट है कि चैतू आदि दलित (हजार घोड़ों का सवार) जिस दूसरे सामाजिक परिवेश में अपनी मुक्ति देखते हैं, वहाँ भी छोटे-बड़े का भेद वैसा ही है। धर्म और ईश्वर का खोखला आतंक सब जगह है। इसीलिए अलगरजिया बाबा का आह्वान है–"तुम सभी गरीबों को ईश्वर और धर्म के खोखले आतंक से मुक्त करो।"[13] यह आह्वान वास्तविक धर्म के लक्षणों–क्षमा, सत्य, प्रेम, पवित्रता आदि की पुनःस्थापना का आह्वान है।

आंचलिक उपन्यासों में कई स्थलों पर दिखाया गया है कि धार्मिक बाह्याचारों से पीड़ितों-शोषितों की यातना में वृद्धि हुई है और उनके मन में यह धारणा बलवती हुई है कि भगवान् केवल अमीरों का है।[14] 'लोहे के पंख' में ईश्वर के अस्तित्व पर ही संदेह व्यक्त हुआ है।[15] जब गरीब सब कुछ लुटाकर इस नतीजे पर पहुँचता है कि ईश्वर नहीं है, पैसा ही ईश्वर है[16], तो यह संस्कारों की गूँज न होकर उसके घावों की चीख जान पड़ती है। ईश्वर के अस्तित्व पर संदेह का अर्थ चरम मूल्य में संदेह करना है।

दुराचार और नकारात्मक मूल्यों से दूर रखने के लिए भारतीय संस्कृति में

अनेक वर्जनाएँ और निषेध दैनिक आचरण के अंग बनाए गए हैं। पुनर्जन्म और कर्मनाद आदि धारणाएँ अनैतिकता और कदाचार के प्रति मनोवैज्ञानिक और नैतिक भय की सृष्टि करते हैं। "पाप का फल अवश्य मिलता है"[17] यह धारणा जनमानस में बैठे प्राकृतिक न्याय में विश्वास को व्यक्त करती है। यह विश्वास न्याय, ईमानदारी, परोपकार, प्रेमभाव आदि धनात्मक मूल्यों का पोषक भी है। आंचलिक उपन्यासों में यह लोकविश्वास प्रायः उपन्यासकारों की जीवन-दृष्टि का हिस्सा बनकर आया है। मार्टिन दंपति का भयानक अंत दिखाकर रेणु पाप के भयानक फल में अपना विश्वास जताते हैं।[18] 'कथा कहो उर्वशी' में जिस तरह धौली की मानसिकता सहज और अनायास स्फूर्त है, वही स्थिति ग्रामीण अंचल के सभी निवासियों की होती है—"···बुरे को दुराचरण का फल मिलकर रहता है। इस बात ने जाने सर्वप्रथम किस युग में धौली के मन में घर कर लिया।"[19] मन में घर कर बैठी यह धारणा एक तरह का मूल्य-निर्णय है और यह कभी सीधे और कभी किंवदंतियों और लोक-कथाओं के व्याज से व्यक्त होता रहता है। 'मैला आँचल' में कमला मैया के माहात्म्य से संबद्ध कहानी में गृहपति की नीयत खराब होने और इसके फलस्वरूप उसका वंश-नाश भी प्रकारांतर से पापी को फल मिलने की सूचना देता है। 'कब तक पुकारूँ' में अन्यायी रुस्तम खाँ और उसके अन्याय की शिकार प्यारी दोनों रोग ग्रस्त होने पर एक ही नतीजे पर पहुँचते हैं कि यह यंत्रणा उनके पाप का फल है। रुस्तम खाँ का विचार है—"मैंने जो कुछ किया है, वह सब मेरी नापाक जिंदगी की लंबी-काली फेहरिश्त है।"[20] प्यारी का सोचना है—"थोड़ा सा पाप किया था प्यारी ने कि वह इसके संग आके रही थी, सो भगवान् ने उसका भी संग ही दंड दे दिया।"[21] 'सोनामाटी' के खुबवा का विश्वास है कि अन्याय नहीं फलेगा।[22] महंत सेवादास का अंधा होना (मैला आँचल), दीनदयाल का दयनीय स्थिति को प्राप्त होना (जल टूटता हुआ), निरोती बामन की दुर्गति (कब तक पुकारूँ), शोषकों की पराजय (वरुण के बेटे) आदि प्रसंग भी सत्यापित करते हैं कि पाप का फल मिलना अनिवार्य है। जब भी सामाजिक न्याय की आशा नहीं होती, दलित और उत्पीड़ित व्यक्ति ईश्वरीय न्याय का मुँह जोहने लगता है। गोमती (कगार की आग) गजार देवता के थान पर अक्षत फेंक कर मनौती मानती है—जो अन्याय करे उसका नास कर नास।

लोकोत्तर सत्ता (चरम मूल्य) में संदेह

लेकिन उपन्यासकारों ने हर स्थिति में ईश्वरीय न्याय या पाप-पुण्य के फल में विश्वास व्यक्त नहीं किया है। उनके बहुत से चरित्र यह देखकर स्तब्ध हो जाते हैं कि पापी आनंद करते हैं, उनका बालबाँका नहीं होता तथा निरीह पुण्यात्मा कष्ट

पर कष्ट सहता जाता है। ऐसी स्थिति में ईश्वरीय न्याय में उसका विश्वास हिल जाता है। 'कब तक पुकारूँ' में ठाकुरों और पुलिस के अत्याचार से चमारों का मुहल्ला वीरान हो जाता है। भगत जैसे पुरातनपंथी इसे पापों का परिणाम मानते हैं—"...क्योंकि हम रोज पाप करते हैं। भगवान् जिला-जिलाकर दंड देता है।"[23] लेकिन सुखराम को ऐसा नहीं लगता। वह जाति और डंडे के बल पर गरीबों की खाल खींचनेवाले बड़े लोगों को ही पापी मानता है। वह कहता है कि इन पापियों को दंड दिलवाने का प्रयास करूँगा—"यह दुनिया तो ऐसी ही रहेगी, पर पापी को दंड भरना ही होगा।"[24] इसी प्रकार 'हजार घोड़ों का सवार' में चेतू कमेड़ी प्रसंग में पाप-पुण्य का सवाल उठाया गया है। मेघू इन दोनों के आचरण को 'अनाचार', 'महापाप' और समाज पर 'कलंक' मानता है।[25] लेकिन लेखक उनके 'प्रणय' को अनैतिक या पाप नहीं मानता। वह उनके पलायन को 'स्वस्थ जीवन जीने' के निमित्त मानता है।[26] इन उदाहरणों से स्पष्ट है कि जनसाधारण पर परंपरागत मान्यताओं की पकड़ को दर्शाते हुए उपन्यासकारों का मत है कि जहाँ ये मान्यताएँ 'लोकहित' या 'व्यक्तिहित' से संबद्ध हैं, वहाँ तो इनका कुछ महत्त्व है। जहाँ ये शोषक वर्ग का हथियार बनती हैं, वहाँ इन पर पुनर्विचार अपेक्षित है। ऐसी स्थितियों में धर्म, पाप-पुण्य आदि मर्यादाएँ अमूर्त संवेग बनकर रह गई हैं, उनकी हैसियत 'नैतिक प्राप्तिमान' की नहीं है। अतः कहा जा सकता है कि कुछ प्रसंगों में ईश्वर और धर्म से जुड़े मूल्य या तो अप्रासंगिक रह गए हैं या वे 'साध्यमूल्य' के स्थान पर 'साधन मूल्य' मात्र रह गए हैं। लोकोत्तर सत्ता पर जनसाधारण का विश्वास टूट रहा है। इस टूटन को उपन्यासकार का पूरा समर्थन मिला है। 'भूख' अब नया धर्म है और इस धर्म में जातियों का विभाजन नहीं होगा—"...वह धर्म होगा—मनुष्यता, गरीबी...उस धर्म को माननेवाला आदमी जातियों में नहीं बँट सकता।...उस धर्म के विरुद्ध एक और धर्म होगा—अमीरी।"[27]

कुछ समाजशास्त्रियों के विचार में सांस्कृतिक मूल्यों के निर्धारण में अभिजात वर्गीय रुचियों और स्वार्थों का आधिपत्य नहीं होना चाहिए। वर्गीय स्वार्थ के लिए मानवीय मूल्यों पर वर्ग विशेष का दबाव अनुचित है। आंचलिक उपन्यासकारों का सोच उससे बहुत मिलता हुआ है वे लोकसंस्कृति और उससे संबद्ध मूल्यों के कायल इसलिए भी हैं कि उन पर सामंती या पूँजीवादी अभिरुचि का दबाव कम है।

धार्मिक सहिष्णुता और सद्भाव

भारतीय संस्कृति की 'विचारमुद्रा' 'सहिष्णुता' और 'सद्भाव' को महत्त्व देते हुए 'कट्टरता' या 'घृणा' को अस्वीकारने की रही है। धर्म, संप्रदाय आदि के नाम पर किसी भी मानवता विरोधी कृत्य को भारतीय मनीषियों ने समर्थन नहीं दिया है।

आंचलिक उपन्यासों की वैचारिकता भी कमोबेश यही है। धर्म के नाम पर हिंसा और लूटपाट की भर्त्सना 'जल टूटता हुआ', 'आधा गाँव' आदि उपन्यासों में द्रष्टव्य है। कुछ समय पूर्व गाँव की संस्कृति में त्यौहार और उत्सव भिन्न संप्रदाय के लोगों को निकट लाने और भाई चारे के निमित्त थे। 'आधा गाँव' में मुहर्रम केवल मुसलमानों का पर्व नहीं है। मुहर्रम के ताजियों के साथ अहीरों का लट्ठबंद गिरोह चलता था जो उलतियाँ गिराकर रास्ता बनाया करता था। एक विधवा ब्राह्मणी की उलती को बिना गिराए बड़ा ताजिया आगे बढ़ जाता है तो वह आनेवाली मुसीबत के भय से काँप उठती है—"...जरूर कोई मुसीबत आनेवाली है नहीं तो भला ऐसा हो सकता था कि बड़ा ताजिया उसकी उलती गिराए बिना चला जाता।"[28] हिंदू के लिए इमाम साहब पूज्य थे तो मुसलमान के लिए बाबा का मठ भी कम सम्माननीय न था। लेकिन कुछ ही दशकों में यह असांप्रदायिक 'आस्तिकता' का भाव नेपथ्य में चला गया और सबके अपने-अपने भगवान् या खुदा कट्टरतापूर्वक निश्चित हो गए। धर्म और धार्मिक पर्व मेलजोल के बजाय द्वेष और हिंसा के आलंबन बन गए।

'सांप्रदायिकता' की मनोवृत्ति मानवीय मूल्यों में धर्मनिरपेक्षता आदि के विरोध में पड़ती है। सांप्रदायिक शक्तियाँ अपने निहित स्वार्थों के लिए जनसाधारण के आपसी सद्भाव, मेलजोल, मानवीयता आदि को दाँव पर लगा देती हैं। 'मैला आँचल' के 'मेरीगंज' में एक भी मुसलमान नहीं है। लेकिन काली टोपीवाले संयोजक जी कथित म्लेच्छ संस्कृति के विरोध का वातावरण तैयार करने में लगे हैं।[29] हिंदू सांप्रदायिकता का नारा है कि आर्यावर्त्त में केवल शुद्ध हिंदू या आर्य ही रह सकते हैं।[30] मुस्लिम सांप्रदायिकता हिंदुओं की 'सिन्सिआरिटी' को मशकूक मानती है।[31] दोनों जनसाधारण को बेबुनियाद बातों से डराती हैं। हिंदू सांप्रदायिकता के पास सबसे बड़ा उदाहरण औरंगजेब का है, जिसने बहुत से मंदिरों को ढहा दिया था। 'आधा गाँव' का छिकुरिया इस सब पर विश्वास नहीं कर पाता क्योंकि गंगोली में तो मुसलमान जमींदार न केवल दशहरे का चंदा देते थे, बल्कि मठ के बाबा को भी कुछ बीघों की माफी दे रखी थी। वह मास्टर साहब की बात नहीं मानता। रहा औरंगजेब, वह जरूर कोई बदमाश होगा।[32] 'छिकुरिया' उस समूचे जनसाधारण का प्रतिनिधि है, जो धर्म, संप्रदाय की दीवारों को नहीं जानता, लेकिन कुछ पढ़े-लिखे लोग कोंच-कोंचकर उन्हें एक-दूसरे से नफरत करने के लिए तैयार करते हैं। व्यक्तियों के माध्यम से यह दो तरह के मूल्यों का जबर्दस्त संघर्ष है। एक ओर संयोजक जी हरगौरी (मैला आँचल), मास्टर साहब, फारुक आदि (आधा गाँव), समसुद्दीन (परती परिकथा), महीप सिंह, सैयद साहब (जल टूटता हुआ) आदि प्रतिक्रियावादी व्यक्ति हैं, दूसरी ओर धर्मनिरपेक्षता, राष्ट्रभक्ति, आपसी आत्मीयता आदि मूल्यों के संवाहक छिकुरिया, फुन्नन मियाँ (आधा गाँव), खलील (अलग-अलग

वैतरणी), मन्ने (सत्ती मैया का चौरा) आदि चरित्र हैं, जो आदमी-आदमी को लड़ानेवाले हर षड्यंत्र के विरुद्ध हैं। 'सत्ती मैया का चौरा' में लेखक ने साफ तौर पर लिखा है कि यह लड़ाई हिंदू-मुसलमानों की न होकर कुछ राजनीतिक संगठनों की राजनीति का कुफल है।[33]

यह आकस्मिक नहीं कि आमने-सामने खड़ी दोनों सांप्रदायिकताओं का 'सोच' कई बिंदुओं पर मिलता-जुलता है। दोनों ही कल्पित हादसों से जनसाधारण में आतंक पैदा करती हैं और अतीतजीवी हैं। यदि हिंदू सांप्रदायिकता उन मंदिरों की ईंटें गिनने में समय बिता रही है[34] जिन्हें औरंगजेब ने धराशायी किया था और मुस्लिम सांप्रदायिकता 'इस्लाम खतरे में है' की भावना उभार कर मुसलमानों को उत्तेजित करती रही है। वह यह नहीं भूलना चाहती कि मुसलमान खालिद बिन वलीद और मुहम्मद बिन कासिम की औलाद है।[35] दोनों तरह की सांप्रदायिकता अपने विरोधी संप्रदाय के सदस्यों की तुलना में अपने संप्रदाय के उन लोगों को खतरनाक मानती है जो पारस्परिक सौहार्द में विश्वास रखते हैं। यदि हरगौरी यवनों का पक्ष लेनेवाले हिंदुओं से क्षुब्ध है[36] तो मुस्लिम लीगी नौजवान हाजी गफूर जैसे मुसलमानों से क्रुद्ध होते हैं। एक समय मौलाना अब्दुल कलाम आजाद जैसे राष्ट्रवादी मुसलमानों को क्या कुछ नहीं सुनना पड़ता था। 'तमस' (भीष्म साहनी) में भी मुस्लिम सांप्रदायिकता के इस पहलू को मौलादाद के माध्यम से प्रस्तुत किया गया है।[37] दोनों प्रकार की सांप्रदायिकता का नेतृत्व प्रायः अभिजात वर्ग के हाथ में है, जो स्वयं नहीं लड़ता, अपने वर्गहितों के लिए साधारण जनता को लड़ाता रहता है। इस सत्य को 'जल टूटता हुआ' का सुग्गन मास्टर समझता है। महीपसिंह और सैयद साहब धर्म के नाम पर लोगों को लड़ा देते हैं—"कितने लोग धर्म के नाम पर मरे किंतु धर्म के रक्षक बाबू साहब और सैय्यद साहब धर्म की रखवाली में घर में ही पड़े रहे ···धर्मात्मा बने हुए। उन्हें न चोट आई, न उनके परिवारों का कोई आहत हुआ और धर्म की रक्षा हो गई।"[38] स्वार्थ ऐसे व्यक्तियों के लिए चरम मूल्य है। स्वार्थ के लिए ऐसे व्यक्ति पास पड़ोस, राष्ट्र, सच्चाई, ईमानदारी आदि को तिलांजलि देने से नहीं हिचकते। 'परती परिकथा' का समसुद्दीन फर्जी दावा खारिज होने पर अल्पसंख्यकों के शोषण की दुहाई देने लगता है[39] लुत्तो जैसे कांग्रेसी 'पॉलिटिक्स' के नाम पर इस हथकंडे का समर्थन करते हैं।[40] कतिपय समझदार मुसलमान भी परिस्थितिवश सांप्रदायिक विचारों से लैस हो जाते हैं।[41]

सांप्रदायिक उन्माद ने जहाँ देश का बँटवारा कराया, वहीं असीम धन और जनहानि के लिए वह जिम्मेदार रहा। थोड़ी देर के लिए सांप्रदायिकता-विरोधी शक्तियाँ असहाय दिखाई दीं, लेकिन वे समाप्त नहीं हुईं। दोनों संप्रदायों में कुछ लोग निश्चय ही समझदार थे।

आंचलिक उपन्यासों में जहाँ धर्म लोक संस्कृति का अंग है, वहाँ उसकी

भूमिका 'अफीम' या 'पोटेशियम साइनाइड' जैसी नहीं है। आस्तिकता सहित अनेक लोकविश्वास किसी को आहत नहीं करते बल्कि दुखदग्ध जनसाधारण को जब तब संबल और आश्रय देते हैं। हालाँकि यह संबल एक मनोवैज्ञानिक प्रतिरक्षा से अधिक नहीं है, फिर भी इसमें न तो मूल्यों और उच्चादर्शों की गिरावट दिखाई देती है और न इस प्रकार का धर्म 'अमानवीयकरण' की ओर बढ़ानेवाला है। जब धर्म का निर्धारण कुछ व्यक्तियों विशेषतः अभिजात और संपन्न वर्ग के स्वार्थों के अनुरूप होने लगता है तो वह अमानवीयता और खूनखराबे का पर्याय बन जाता है। जबकि लोकजीवन में कई स्तरों पर हिंदू मुस्लिम का भेद नहीं है। पूर्वी उत्तर-प्रदेश में हिंदू घरों में रज्जे बाबा और पाँचों पीर का पूजन बताता है कि धार्मिक सहिष्णुता कोई नई अवधारणा नहीं है।[42] 'सूरज किरण की छाँव' में नेहरू जी के साक्ष्य से धर्म सद्भाव और धर्मनिरपेक्षता का समर्थन किया गया है।[43]

डॉ. विश्वंभरनाथ उपाध्याय के अनुसार "...असली भारतीय संस्कृति मनुष्य की स्वच्छंदता की साधना में है। यह आजादी समाज, व्यक्ति आदि प्रत्येक स्तर पर होगी और स्तर और व्यक्ति एक नहीं अनेक हैं। वहाँ स्वच्छंदता में अराजकता न होकर, दूसरों की स्वच्छंदताओं का आदर भी उक्त धारणा में स्वीकृत होगा।"[44] भारतीय संस्कृति में 'धार्मिक सहिष्णुता' इसी आजादी का परिचय देती है। दूसरों के धार्मिक विश्वासों को खारिज करना और खूनखराबे पर उतर आना उक्त सहिष्णुता का खुला उल्लंघन है और एक नकारात्मक मूल्य का आभास देता है। आंचलिक उपन्यासों में धार्मिक कट्टरता और दुराग्रह का विरोध इसी नकारात्मकता का विरोध करते हुए 'सहिष्णुता' को सकारात्मक मूल्य के तौर पर व्याख्यायित किया गया है। यहाँ उपन्यासकारों का मूल्यबोध 'वास्तविकता' की प्रतिक्रिया है सहज और प्रगतिशील प्रतिक्रिया। वास्तविक जगत् में मूल्यों का संक्रमण उच्चादर्शों से नीचता और टुच्चेपन की दिशा में हुआ है। इस अवमूल्यन को देखकर आधुनिक मनुष्य का 'समग्र परंपरागत सांस्कृतिक प्रवाह'[45] के प्रति संशयग्रस्त होना स्वाभाविक है। लेकिन आंचलिक उपन्यासों में इस तरह का संशय प्रायः नहीं है। उपन्यासकारों का निर्भ्रांत मत है कि धर्म के क्षेत्र में समानता, सहिष्णुता, सद्भाव आदि मूल्यों की ओर प्रयाण श्रेयस्कर है। जिस मिश्रित संस्कृति (कम्पोजिट कल्चर) की चर्चा स्वातंत्र्योत्तर भारत में बहुत हुई है, उसका एक पक्ष—सर्व धर्म सद्भाव, इन उपन्यासों में खास तौर पर रेखांकित हुआ है।

मानवीय स्वतंत्रता और मानवीय हित का आह्वान

आंचलिक उपन्यासों में कथित संस्कृति की आड़ में शोषण, ऊँच-नीच, स्वार्थ आदि नास्ति मूल्यों को गौरवान्वित करने का प्रयास नहीं हुआ है। 'मानवहित' का भाव

यहाँ सर्वाधिक स्पष्ट और प्रबल है। कुछ उपन्यासों में यह कम महत्त्वपूर्ण नहीं कि अभावग्रस्त मजदूर अपने स्वार्थ को मजदूर भाइयों के लिए गद्दारी का पर्याय समझता है।[46] आर्थिक दृष्टि से बहुत कमजोर तबका भी दूसरों का पेट काटने के षड्यंत्र में सम्मिलित नहीं होता।[47] 'बाबा बटेसरनाथ' में दृढ़तापूर्वक कहा गया कि परोपकार के लिए जीना ही जीना है।[48] परमार्थ में जो विघ्न डालते हैं, वे वास्तविक अर्थ में मनुष्य नहीं हैं–"मानुस जन्म पाकर हम परमारथ के बदले सोआरथ देखें तो इससे बढ़कर क्या पाप हो सकता है ? परमारथ में जो 'विघिन' डालते हैं वे मानुस नहीं।"[49] इन पंक्तियों में 'परहित सरिस धर्म नहीं भाई' की नैतिक गूँज के साथ-साथ मानव-मानव के बीच किसी प्रकार के अमानवीयकरण का स्पष्ट निषेध भी है। गरीबी और गुलामी में जीता हुआ व्यक्ति भी इंसान बना रहता है–"हुकूमत और दौलत उसकी असलियत उससे छीन लेती हैं और वह असलियत है इंसानियत।"[50] पहला काम है जानवर बन गए आदमी को इंसान बनाना।[51] इन सभी उदाहरणों से इन उपन्यासों के मानवीय बोध की पुष्टि होती है और 'साबार ऊपर मानुष सत्य' का समर्थन होता है।

अधिकतर आंचलिक उपन्यासों में मेहनतकश वर्ग मानव विरोधी धार्मिक बेड़ियों और कथित आध्यात्मिक मूल्यों से उबरने की कोशिश में है। अपनी स्थितियों की वायवीय या आध्यात्मिक व्याख्या से उसका समाधान नहीं होता। लेकिन अधिसंख्यक जनसमुदाय 'धर्म' के आततायी और अमानवीय रूप से अवगत होते हुए भी ईश्वर के अस्तित्व में अपने विश्वास को नहीं छोड़ पाया है। एक अजीब-सी द्वंद्वात्मक स्थिति है। बोध के स्तर पर लोग भाग्य, नियति, आस्तिकता की अर्थहीनता का अनुभव कर रहे हैं लेकिन संस्कारवश या भावना के स्तर पर उन्हें सर्वथा अस्वीकार नहीं कर पाते। संभवतः इसीलिए ईश्वर का एकांत निषेध या धर्म की निरर्थकता का प्रतिपादन आंचलिक उपन्यासों में बहुत दृढ़ता के साथ नहीं हो सका है। बल्कि कुछ कृतियों में धर्मस्थानों के पुजारियों को वर्गसंघर्ष के सहायक या मानवीयता के संरक्षक तत्त्वों के रूप में सम्मान दिया गया है। 'अलगरजिया बाबा' (हजार घोड़ों का सवार), पुजारी जी (जंगली सुअर), महंत (सोनभद्र की राधा) आदि चरित्र इस संदर्भ में देखे जा सकते हैं। इनकी बदली हुई भूमिका को पुजारी (परती परिकथा), महंत (मैला आँचल) आदि के कृत्यों की तुलना में देखने पर साफ लगता है, मूल्यों के संक्रमण की दिशा व्यक्तिवादी और समाजविरोधी मूल्यों से मानवतावादी और नैतिक मूल्यों की ओर है।

मानवीय स्वतंत्रता और लोक हित का सीधा संबंध नैतिक मूल्यों से है। भारतीय मनीषा ने शौच, संयम, वैराग्य, सत्य और अहिंसा–इन पाँच नैतिक मूल्यों को सर्वोच्च माना है।[52] ये मूल्य 'व्यक्ति' के बृहत्तर सरोकारों से जुड़ने के सूचक हैं। मार्क्सवाद का सूत्रवाक्य इस संदर्भ में द्रष्टव्य है–"मानवीय स्वतंत्रता ही समस्त

नैतिक मूल्यों की बुनियाद है; मानवीय कल्याण ही सर्वोच्च शुभ है।"[53] कई उपन्यासों में इस सर्वोच्च 'शुभ' को मान्यता दी गई है और कई हीनतर मूल्यों का पर्यवसान 'मानवीय कल्याण' में हुआ है। मैला आँचल में तहसीलदार साहब का हृदय परिवर्तन चौंकानेवाला है लेकिन वह मूल्य-संक्रमण की दृष्टि से आकस्मिक नहीं है। बदलते युग की आहट सुनकर और आंतरिक दबाववश सामंती मनोवृत्ति के तहसीलदार और जित्तन आदि एक स्वस्थ और मानवीय दिशा की ओर मुड़ जाते हैं। तहसीलदार को मालूम है लोग उसे पागल समझेंगे क्योंकि हड़पी हुई जमीन लौटा देना अनहोनी है–"ठीक है पागल क्यों नहीं समझोगे···जमीन।···धरती। एक इंच जमीन के लिए हायकोठ तक मुकदमा लड़ते हैं लोग। और मैं सौ बीघे जमीन दे रहा हूँ···।"[54] उनके इस निर्णय से मुर्दा चेहरों पर लौटती लाली दिखाकर रेणु 'शोषण' के अवमूल्य को समाप्त करने की एक दिशा सुझाते हैं। जित्तन भी सामंत वर्ग के अवमूल्यों–शोषण, अपहरण आदि के स्थान पर 'त्याग', 'बंधुत्व' आदि मूल्यों को व्यवहार में लाता है और बहुत से गरीबों को यूँ ही जमीन दे देता है।[55] संभव है, इस तरह का हृदय-परिवर्तन 'सर्वोदय' की विचारधारा के प्रभाव से हुआ हो। लेकिन 'लोकऋण', 'सोनामाटी' आदि उपन्यासों से स्पष्ट है कि हृदय परिवर्तन का यह दौर क्षणिक और सीमित रहा होगा। नव-सामंत वर्ग केवल 'स्वार्थ' और 'शोषण' के संदर्भ में सोचता और करता है; 'मानवीय कल्याण' की चिंता उन्हें दूर-दूर तक नहीं है। रेणु के अतिरिक्त संभवतः किसी अन्य आंचलिक उपन्यासकार को सामंतों की मानवीय सदाशयता पर विश्वास नहीं है। अपनी स्वतंत्रता और हित-कामना का भाव अब जनसाधारण को 'उपहार' में नहीं मिलता। वह उसके अपने भीतर से उग रहा है। पिछड़े अंचलों के शोषित जन और शिक्षित युवा अब 'अत्याचार', 'आतंक' और 'शोषण' को सहन करने के लिए तैयार नहीं हैं। 'अलग-अलग वैतरणी' में सरूप भगत का यह कहना कि हम आपके गुलाम नहीं हैं[56], शोषितों में अपने अधिकारों की चेतना का प्रमाण है। इसी तरह विपिन के अत्याचार विरोध पर खलील मियाँ की टिप्पणी संभावनासूचक है :

"यह एक नई किस्म की आँधी है बब्बन बेटा ! जिसमें गर्द नहीं, गर्मी होती है। इसकी आँच में तमाम पुख्ता दीवालें गल जाती हैं, जो इंसाफ के रास्ते में रुकावट बनकर खड़ी होती है।"[57]

मानवीय मूल्यों के संक्रमण के एक छोर पर बद्रीबाबू (राग दरबारी) हैं, जो 'इंसानियत' को मनुष्य की कमजोरी मानते हैं, दूसरा सिरा विपिन (अलग-अलग वैतरणी) है, जो मानव-विरोधी मूल्यों के विरोध में सक्रिय है। दोनों तरह के संक्रमण को दर्शाते हुए उपन्यासकारों ने अवमूल्य से मानवीय कल्याण से जुड़े मूल्यों–न्याय, समता आदि की दिशा में हुए संक्रमण को अपना समर्थन दिया है।[58]

लोक सांस्कृतिक तत्त्व एवं मानवीय मूल्य

अधिकतर आंचलिक उपन्यासों में लोक सांस्कृतिक तत्त्वों का समावेश इस समझ के साथ हुआ है कि लोक संस्कृति लोकजीवन के यथार्थ का ही नाम है।[59] प्रायः उन्हीं संदर्भों को महत्त्व दिया गया है, जो लोकजीवन को संघर्ष में शक्ति देते हैं, सामूहिकता देते हैं।[60] जिन उपन्यासों में उपन्यासकार की दृष्टि रोमानी और यायावरी है, वहाँ अवश्य ये तत्त्व उपन्यासकार की बहुज्ञता के साक्षी मात्र हैं। 'ब्रह्मपुत्र' के संबंध में कहा गया है कि लोकसाहित्य के प्रति विशेष अनुराग होने से सत्यार्थी अपने आंचलिक समाज का यथार्थ-चित्रण नहीं कर सके हैं।[61] बहुत से उपन्यासों में ये तत्त्व 'कथ्य' में संश्लिष्ट एवं अन्तर्भुक्त हैं। इस संबंध में डॉ. रामदरश मिश्र ने लिखा है—"ग्रामजीवन के गहरे सरोकारों से विच्छिन्न करके जो लोग ग्रामजीवन की प्रकृति, मौसमों, पर्वों, गीतों आदि की योजना करते हैं, वे केवल आंचलिक रंगत प्रदान करते हैं। मैंने अपने उपन्यासों में ग्रामजीवन के गहरे राजनीतिक-सामाजिक-आर्थिक प्रश्नों के साथ इन्हें जोड़कर लोकसंस्कृति की पहचान करनी चाही है।"[62] न केवल 'जल टूटता हुआ' अपितु 'मैला आँचल', 'जंगल के फूल', 'सोना माटी', 'आधा गाँव', 'अलग-अलग वैतरणी', 'असगाँव-पसगाँव' आदि अनेक आंचलिक उपन्यासों में 'आंचलिक रंगत' को साध्य नहीं माना गया है। इन सभी उपन्यासों में 'लोक-तत्त्व' व्यापक विचार मंथन मूल्य-संकट और सांस्कृतिक संक्रमण को व्यक्त करने का माध्यम बनकर अन्तर्भुक्त हैं।

ग्राम-संस्कृति मुख्यतः कृषि-संस्कृति है और इसे ही भारतीय संस्कृति का पर्याय मानना असंगत नहीं है।[63] इस दृष्टि से देखने पर यह असंगत नहीं लगता कि अधिकतर लोकोत्सव, पर्व, लोकगीत एवं लोककथाएँ 'कृषि' से कहीं न कहीं जुड़ी हुई हैं। 'परती परिकथा' में 'सुन्नारि नैका' और 'दंता राकस' की कथा को 'रेणु' ने बंजर-धरती को उपजाऊ बनाने के प्रयासों से जोड़कर उसका एक नया भाष्य प्रस्तुत किया है। दंता राक्षस, आधुनिक वैज्ञानिक संयंत्र है और 'सुन्नारि नैका' और कुछ नहीं आधुनिक विकास-योजना है।[64] यह व्याख्या 'अंधविश्वास' के 'तर्क' में और मानवेतर शक्ति के विश्वास के मानवीय 'श्रम' में आस्था में संक्रमित होने की गवाही देती है। लोककथा और उसकी आधुनिक व्याख्या दोनों में एक चीज समान है। वह है प्रयोजनीयता। यह प्रयोजन 'पानी' अर्थात् जीवन से सीधे संबद्ध है। आंचलिक उपन्यासकारों ने लोक-पर्वों, लोकगीतों आदि में प्रयोजनीयता को बराबर रेखांकित किया है। प्रयोजनीयता ही मूल्यों का निर्धारण करती है और मूल्य प्रयोजन तथा संस्कृति में अटूट संबंध होता है।[65] 'नदी फिर बह चली' में आई एक 'लोककथा'[66] को नए ढंग से व्याख्यायित नहीं किया गया है, लेकिन आत्मतुष्टि या स्वार्थ के हीन या नास्तिमूल्य की अवमानना का प्रयोजन

उसमें स्पष्ट है। इस तरह की लोककथाएँ दर्शाती हैं कि कतिपय सकारात्मक मूल्यों की स्थिति यथावत् है और यदि संक्रमण हुआ भी है तो वह इतना धीमा है कि परिवर्तन स्पष्ट तौर पर नहीं दिखाई देता।

'ब्रह्मपुत्र' में दबूर पूजा के त्यौहार का वर्णन, 'जल टूटता हुआ' में दशहरे के मेले का संदर्भ, 'मैला आँचल' में जाट-जट्टिन लोकनृत्य, 'अलग-अलग वैतरणी' में देवी के मेले की चर्चा और 'सोनामाटी' में विभिन्न लोकाचारों और 'झिरहिरी' का प्रकरण, जहाँ कृषि संस्कृति से सीधे संबद्ध हैं, वहीं वे लोकमानस में विद्यमान मूल्यों से परिचय कराने के साथ-साथ 'तब' और 'अब' की तुलनात्मक स्थिति को भी रेखांकित करते हैं। मीरी बस्ती में दबूर पूजा के पीछे धारणा यह है कि यदि इंद्र की दो बार पूजा न की गई तो इतनी वर्षा होगी कि त्राहि-त्राहि मच जाएगी। दबूर-नृत्य में गाए जानेवाले लोकगीतों में न केवल अच्छी कृषि के लिए प्रार्थना है अपितु प्रेम, मित्रता, सद्भाव आदि मूल्यों की प्रतिष्ठा की चेतना भी है। इंद्र देवता को संबोधित लोकगीतों में कहा गया है—"....धरती धानवती हो। स्त्रियाँ पुत्रवती हों। गाँव में सुख शांति रहे। धान-धान से मिले। आदमी-आदमी से मिले। कोई किसी से शत्रुता न करे। कोई किसी से ईर्ष्या न करे।"[67] 'जल टूटता हुआ' में दशहरे के दिन बच्चे नीलकंठ से सीता तक संदेश ले जाने का गीत गाते हैं।—"नीलकंठ निलबारी बारी/सीता से कहिह भेंट अँकवारी/हमार नाँव किसन मुरारी।"[68] इस गीत की व्याख्या करते हुए उपन्यासकार ने लिखा है—"सीता कैद है, रावण के यहाँ, आज ही मुक्त होगी। सीता धरती की बेटी है, धरती की बेटी कैद है, धरती के शोषक के यहाँ। धरती के बेटे बेचैन हैं, अपनी बहन से मिलने के लिए, उन्हें मालूम है कि राम आज उद्धार करेंगे सीता का। भेंट अँकवार कह देना सीता से ओ भाई नीलकंठ ! तुम्हीं कह सकते थे, परिंदे हो और शिव के प्रतिरूप हो।"[69] इस व्याख्या में कई महत्त्वपूर्ण संकेत छिपे हुए हैं। ग्रामवासियों के लिए परंपरागत दशहरा एक तरह से शोषण मुक्ति का पर्व है। धरती पुत्री सीता तो शोषक के पंजे से मुक्त हो गई थी लेकिन धरती पुत्री की बहुत सी धरती आज भी शोषकों के चंगुल में है। स्थिति के इस विपर्यय के बावजूद लोकजीवन में 'शोषण' सरीखे नास्ति मूल्य को खारिज करने तथा समानता-समता स्थापित होने का आशावाद सबल है। वास्तविक स्थिति शोषण की भयावहता को दिखाते हुए जन-मन में संचित शोषण-मुक्ति की आकांक्षा को व्यक्त करना नकारात्मक मूल्यों की ओर से सकारात्मक और मानवीय मूल्यों की ओर प्रयाण करना है। गाँव और शहर में 'नीलकंठ' की दो भिन्न-भिन्न स्थितियाँ दो भिन्न मूल्य-मर्यादाओं की सूचक हैं—"किंतु यह नीलकंठ शहरों में बंद कर लिया गया है। बहेलिया उसे पिंजड़े में बंद करके दर-दर घुमाता है और धर्मप्राण नगर जन दर्शन करते हैं, अपने पाप-ताप का शमन करते हैं...बहेलिए का नीलकंठ दो पैसे में धर्म बाँटता फिर रहा है।"[70]

'आस्था' की 'व्यावसायिकता' और दिखावे में यह परिणति उच्चादर्शों के हीनतर दिशा में संक्रमण की द्योतक है।

'लोकऋण', और 'सोनामाटी' में उपन्यासकार इस सत्य की ओर संकेत करता है कि औद्योगिक विकास और वैज्ञानिक प्रगति ने लोकजीवन की लय को बिगाड़ दिया है। फलतः, युद्ध मानव-संस्कृति के दर्शन अब आदिवासियों में ही किए जा सकते हैं।[71] कृष्णा अग्निहोत्री कृत 'नीलोफर' भी इस दृष्टि से द्रष्टव्य है। आंचलिक उपन्यासों में लोकपर्वों और उत्सवों के संदर्भ में पर्यावरण असंतुलन और प्रदूषण की चर्चा भी हुई है। प्रदूषण के फलस्वरूप नदी, तालाब आदि सूख चले हैं और उनके साथ ही पर्वों का उल्लास समाप्तप्राय है। कुछ व्यक्तियों की स्वार्थी मनोवृत्ति ने भी गाँव के सांस्कृतिक उल्लास को नष्ट किया है। 'लोकऋण' में तालाब पर कब्जे और बनगंगी महादेव की उपेक्षा का परिणाम यह होता है कि खिचड़ी अमावस्या के पर्व पर बक्सर जानेवाला दल अब गाँव में नहीं आता।[72] 'सोनामाटी' में बरसात के दिनों के आयोजन 'झिरहिरी' का विशद वर्णन है, 'झिरहिरी' के मंच पर शत्रु भी एक साथ बैठते और गाते हैं। 'झिरहिरी' का अर्थ है, थोड़ी देर के लिए ही सही आत्मीयता, आपसीपन और रागात्मकता की अभिव्यक्ति। लेकिन उपन्यासकार ने यह दिखाया है कि आज के अभावग्रस्त परिवेश में 'झिरहिरी' भी औपचारिकता मात्र बनकर रह जाती है–"झिरहिरी तो जोर लगाकर ला दिया पर वह पहलेवाला उल्लास कहाँ से लाएँ।"[73] इसके बावजूद 'झिरहिरी' जैसे उत्सव इस बात के प्रमाण हैं कि कुछ स्वस्थ और सही मूल्यों के प्रति निष्ठा कमोबेश बची हुई है। 'सोनामाटी' में लोकाचारों का विस्तार से वर्णन हुआ है और इसके माध्यम से हमारी सांस्कृतिक मान्यताओं की पहचान हो सकी है। कमली के विवाह के प्रारंभ में 'मानर पूजा' अर्थात् चमारिन की डुग्गी की पूजा वस्तुतः 'श्रम' की पूजा और सम्मान का प्रमाण है। इसी तरह विवाह के आयोजन में नाई, सेनुहरवा आदि की उपस्थिति[74] जताती है कि तमाम वर्णभेद और जाति-भेद के मध्य 'सहयोग', 'सद्भाव' आदि मूल्य गौरवान्वित होते रहे हैं। रामरूप को विवाह और उससे संबद्ध नेग आदि सांस्कृतिक शोषण व्यापार के अंग नहीं लगते। शोषण व्यापार में नाई, पंसारी, चमारिन आदि का क्या काम ? बल्कि उपन्यासकार का विचार है–"भला ये मांगलिक मौके न होते तो इस युग में हम अपनी सामाजिक पहचान शायद एकदम भूल जाते।"[75] सचमुच इन पर्वों और लोकाचारों के माध्यम से हमारे सामाजिक-सांस्कृतिक मूल्यों की पहचान होती रहती है और व्यक्तिगत क्षुद्रताओं और तुच्छताओं को उभरने का अवसर नहीं मिलता। आंचलिक उपन्यासों में लोकपर्वों, लोक-साहित्य आदि का समावेश उपन्यासकारों की बहुज्ञता या लोकजीवन से उनके निकट संपर्क का गवाह मात्र नहीं है, यह उनके लोकोन्मुखी मानवीय दृष्टिकोण की अभिव्यक्ति का सफल माध्यम भी है। 'अलग-अलग वैतरणी' में

उपन्यासकार का यह निष्कर्ष लोकजीवन में प्रचलित मिथकों और आख्यानों से छनकर आया है–"जब शिवृत्व तिरस्कृत होता है, व्यक्ति के हक छीने जाते हैं, सत्य और न्याय अवहेलित होते हैं, तब जन-जन के आँसुओं की धारा वैतरणी में बदल जाती है। नरक की नदी बन जाती है।"[76] शिव के आँसुओं से वैतरणी का बनना लोक-प्रचलित सत्य है।

आंचलिक उपन्यासों में लोकजीवन में अपसंस्कृति के प्रसार और क्षमा, त्याग, सहयोग, धैर्य, सद्भाव आदि मूल्यों के संकटग्रस्त होने को चिंता के साथ देखा गया है। औद्योगीकरण और मशीनीकरण ने लोक पर्वों को नष्ट और पुराने मूल्यों को आहत किया है लेकिन इसका एक दुष्प्रभाव यह हुआ है कि मनुष्य की प्रवृत्तियों और आवेगों पर से मूल्यों का नियंत्रण हट गया है। लोक पर्वों और त्यौहारों के कम होते जाने से इन आवेगों के उदात्तीकरण की प्रक्रिया भी अवरुद्ध हुई है। इन सबने नास्ति मूल्यों को पनपने का अवसर दिया है। पूरनचंद्र जोशी के अनुसार–"मनुष्य और मनुष्य-समाज मूल्यों या संस्कृति के बिना पशु और पशु समाज के कितना निकट है, इस तथ्य का ऐसे संकटकाल में ही निकटता से अनुभव होता है।"[77] 'मैला आँचल' में तहसीलदार साहब निरंतर नगर के संपर्क में हैं, कृषि संबंधी नई प्रौद्योगिकी–ट्रैक्टर पंप आदि से परिचित हैं, उसके इस्तेमाल के नाते लोगों में चर्चा के केंद्र बनते हैं। "तहसीलदार साहब इस बार टक्टर खरीद रहे हैं···आदमी की क्या जरूरत ? पानी का पंपू आवेगा। इंदर भगवान की खुशामद की जरूरत नहीं।···जब इंदर भगवान को ही नून-नेब चटा रहे हैं तहसीलदार साहेब, तो आदमी उनके हुजूर में क्या है ?"[78] तहसीलदार का उत्पादन के साधनों पर एकाधिकार उसे धूर्तता, अत्याचार, बेईमानी आदि अवमूल्यों या नास्ति मूल्यों से युक्त कर देता है। 'सोनामाटी' के हनुमानप्रसाद का स्वच्छंद आचरण भी नास्ति मूल्यों के उभार का द्योतक है। ये गैर मूल्य उनकी संतान में और प्रखर हो गए हैं कि क्योंकि वह राजनीतिक कुटिलता और शहरी मानसिकता के संपर्क में अपेक्षाकृत अधिक रहा है। ऐसे व्यक्ति को यदि विवाह संबंधी लोकाचार 'बदतमीजियाँ' लगते हैं तो यह अस्वाभाविक नहीं है–"ह्वाट ए शेम ! मैं एसेम्बेली में कोश्चन उठाऊँगा। यह सब बदतमीजियाँ गाँवों में बंद होनी चाहिए। यह कैसा जंगली कल्चर है ?"[79]

लोक संस्कृति के तत्त्वों को 'जंगली कल्चर' कहना उस मूल्य-संक्रमण का परिचायक है, जिसके तहत मानवीय उल्लास, निष्कपटता, वर्जनाविहीनता की परिणति एक कृत्रिम गंभीरता और सभ्यता में होती गई है। यह कथित सभ्यता हर तरह के अनाचार को अपने में छिपाए हुए है और उसे मुक्त लोक संस्कृति के कुछ तत्त्व अश्लील और भदेस लगते हैं। आंचलिक उपन्यासकारों ने स्पष्ट किया है कि लोक-संस्कृति 'जंगली कल्चर' न होकर वस्तुतः जंगलियों को सुसंस्कृत और

मानवीय बनाने का कार्य करती रही है। 'जंगल के फूल', 'लोकऋण', 'मैला आँचल' और 'नीलोफर' में आए आदिवासी कथित सभ्यों की तुलना में अधिक सुसंस्कृत और मानवीय गुणों से संपन्न हैं।

लोकगीतों, लोककथाओं और लोकनाट्यों में दमित-उत्पीड़ित जनसमुदाय का हृदय खोलकर रख दिया जाता रहा है। यही कारण है कि घोर अभाव और शोषण के मध्य ये लोकतत्त्व इन जनसमुदाय को बहुत राहत पहुँचाते रहे हैं। आंचलिक उपन्यासकारों ने लोकगीत आदि का उपयोग जहाँ अंचल को उसकी समग्र सांस्कृतिक धरोहर के साथ उभारने में किया है, वहीं जनसमुदाय को विरासत में प्राप्त मूल्यों का बोध कराने में भी इनकी भूमिका महत्त्वपूर्ण है। अधिकतर वे ही लोकगीत उल्लिखित हैं, जिनमें अन्याय, शोषण और असमानता की भयावहता को दर्शाते हुए 'मुक्ति' की छटपटाहट व्यंजित है। 'मैला आँचल' में बिकटा ने पटवारी, चौकीदार आदि के हाथों जनसाधारण के उत्पीड़न को बहुत हल्के-फुल्के ढंग से कह दिया है :

थारी बेंच पटवारी के दे लियै
लोटा बेंच चौकीदारी
....
कहे कबीर सुनो भाई साधो
सब दिन करी बेगारी।[80]

जिंदगी भर बेगार करनेवाले, अपढ़ गँवार और अर्द्धनग्न और टूटी झोंपड़ीवाले लोग यदि विद्यापति के गीतों और लोकगीतों में जिंदगी का 'मधुरस'[81] पाते हैं तो यह आकस्मिक नहीं है। जब अन्याय और अधर्म का प्रतिकार करने में लोग असमर्थ रहते हैं तो ये लोकगीत 'विरेचन' का कार्य करते हैं। 'जल टूटता हुआ' में लोकगीत का उपयोग लोगों में 'न्याय', 'धर्म' के समर्थन का भाव जगाने के लिए किया गया है। कुंजू बीच बाजार में गाता है :

कि अइहो लोगवा
रोवे ले जिनगिया
जुलुमवा की छइयाँ कि अइहो लोगवा
काँपे ले नियाउ
और धरमवा की गइया कि अइहो लोगवा !
पान खा के, छुरिया छिपा के बेइमनवाँ
हँसेला कसइया कि अइहो लोगवा।[82]

इस गीत में आए 'कसाई' और 'गाय' के बिंब द्वारा शोषक वर्ग की क्रूरता को उभार कर नकारात्मक मूल्यों के वचस् को रेखांकित किया गया है। लेकिन वेदना के साथ ही सही, इन अवमूल्यों के प्रति विद्रोह का भाव भी उपर्युक्त लोकगीत

में है। स्पष्ट है कि लोकसंस्कृति में शोषक शक्तियों के सामने निरीह समर्पण नहीं है। सतीश ने इस गीत का उपयोग पंचायत के चुनाव में मानवीय मूल्यों की पक्षधरता हेतु किया है। उसी के शब्दों में–''कुंजू ने अपने संगीत के जादू से जो कुछ कहा है, वह कटु यथार्थ है...इसलिए आप लोग सोच समझकर वोट दें, पंच चुनें...।''[83] यह कथन तथ्य चेतना के विपरीत न्याय, समानता आदि मूल्यों की ओर जनभावना के संक्रमण की आवश्यकता पर बल देता है। 'बलचनमा' में किसानों की सभा में जो गीत गाया जाता है, वह भी संभवतः लोकगीत ही है। इस गीत का उपयोग ग्रामीणों में शोषण-विरोधी चेतना जाग्रत करने के लिए किया गया। नागार्जुन ने इसके माध्यम से दर्शाया है कि अब शोषकों के 'अन्याय' और 'बेईमानी' को अस्वीकारते हुए खेतिहर मजदूर न्याय, समता, स्वतंत्रता आदि महत्तर मूल्यों के लिए संघर्षरत है :

करजा करि के खेती कैलू, मरि गेलइ सब धान
रे, फिकरिया मारलक जान !
बैल बेचि रजवा के दूलूँ, छोड़ए नहिं बइमान
जमींदार के जुलुम रोकड, चेत भाई किसान [84]

कई अन्य आंचलिक उपन्यासों में भी भाग्यवाद, गुलामी, कायरता आदि को झटककर 'श्रम', 'पुरुषार्थ' और 'साहस' से भरपूर जिंदगी बिताने का आह्वान है।[85] ऐसे स्थलों पर उपन्यासकार स्पष्ट कर देना चाहते हैं कि धर्म, संस्कृति आदि के नाम पर मनुष्य-मनुष्य में भेद और एक वर्ग विशेष द्वारा जनसाधारण का शोषण भयावह असंगति है। अब श्रमजीवी इस असंगति का अर्थ समझने लगा है। इस तरह मूल्यों के संक्रमण की दिशा सकारात्मक और महत्तर मूल्यों की ओर मुड़ी है। 'मुक्ति' स्वतःमूल्य है और श्रम, ईमानदारी, एकजुटता सद्भाव आदि साधनमूल्यों को शोषित-उत्पीड़ित वर्ग ने अपने व्यवहार में उतार लिया है। कुछ उपन्यासकारों का विचार है कि सामाजिक कोण से उठे अलगाव को सांस्कृतिक कोण पाट देता है।[86] होली आदि लोकपर्वों और विवाह से संबंधित लोकाचारों में यह शक्ति है कि थोड़ी देर के लिए जाति-भेद-वर्गभेद की दीवारें गायब लगती हैं। लड़की की विदा जैसे करुण अवसरों पर शोषकों की क्रूरता भी कुछ देर के लिए निस्तब्ध दिखाई देती है। लेकिन यह बदलाव अस्थाई है।

आंचलिक उपन्यासकारों ने लोकगीतों के माध्यम से केवल वर्ग-संघर्ष को ही संकेतित नहीं किया है। लोकजीवन की विवशता, रागात्मकता और बेचैनी के अन्य कई संदर्भ भी इनमें उभरे हैं और वे किसी न किसी कमाए हुए जीवन सत्य को प्रतिबिंबित करते हैं। पूर्वी उत्तर प्रदेश में रोजगार का अभाव और उसके फलस्वरूप युवकों का कलकत्ता आदि महानगरों में नौकरी करते हुए दयनीय जीवन बिताना एक आम बात है। अभावग्रस्त जीवन के बावजूद लोक नारी अपने पति को परदेश

नहीं जाने देना चाहती, उसके सामीप्य के लिए वह कैसा भी मूल्य चुकाने को तैयार है :

सेर भरि गोहुँवा बरसि पीसि खइबौं
पियऊ जाये न देबों हो…
तोहका पुरुबी बनिजिया, पियऊ जाये ने देबों हो।[87]

इन पंक्तियों में 'प्रेम' को सर्वोच्च मूल्य का दर्जा मिला है, लेकिन वास्तविकता इतनी कुरूप है कि अंततः 'रोटी' सर्वोच्च मूल्य बन जाती है। एक मजबूरी सारे कोमल भावों पर छा जाती है।[88] यह लोकगीत मार्मिक उद्‌गार मात्र न होकर हमारी उस जनतांत्रिक व्यवस्था पर कठोर टिप्पणी भी है, जो 'समता', 'समानता' की दुहाई देने के बावजूद बेकारी और बेरोजगारी का कोई समाधान नहीं कर पाई। आम तौर पर कहा जाता है कि समाज-व्यवस्था में समाज की विभिन्न इकाइयों में सक्रिय संबद्धता होनी चाहिए। "लेकिन जिस देश का आम आदमी गरीबी, भुखमरी और बेरोजगारी से त्रस्त हो, वहाँ विभिन्न संस्थाओं द्वारा मान्य उद्देश्यों के अनुसार कार्य करना अथवा किसी प्रकार की सक्रिय-संबद्धता का होना शायद दूर की कौड़ी खोजना ही होगा।"[89] 'सोनामाटी' आदि उपन्यासों में आए लोकगीतों का निहितार्थ भी बहु-आयामी और दूरगामी है। उपन्यासकार ने भुवनेश्वर के विवाह के समय गाए गए गीत के माध्यम से लोकजीवन में मान्य 'कौमार्य' और 'यौनशुचिता' सरीखी मूल्य-मर्यादाओं को गौरवान्वित किया है–"बनवा में फूले ले बेइलिया/त देखत सोहावन…इन जंगली बेइलि पर माली हाथ बढ़ाता है। बेइलि टोकती है, अभी नहीं…दुलहा हाथ बढ़ा रहा है, अब मैं ब्याह करूँगा।…नहीं धैर्य धारण करो। अभी ठीक समय नहीं आया। अभी तो मैं अपने बाबा की हूँ।"[90] आगे चलकर उपन्यासकार ने भुवनेश्वर-कांता-संबंध की चर्चा की है जिसका आधार यह धारणा है कि हम मैरेज जैसी सड़ी-गली चीज के चक्कर में नहीं पड़ेंगे।[91] यह आज का यथार्थ है। लोकगीत में व्यक्त मूल्यबोध से इस यथार्थबोध की तुलना करने से स्पष्ट हो जाएगा कि उच्च मूल्यों का संक्रमण अनैतिक और अनुचित समझी जानेवाली नई धारणाओं की दिशा में हो रहा है। लेकिन उपन्यासकार का अपना समर्थन 'लोकगीत' में व्यक्त सांस्कृतिक मर्यादा को प्राप्त है। 'नदी फिर बह चली' में प्रयुक्त लोकगीत में व्यंग्यात्मक लहजे में आज की वधू के 'शौकीन' हो जाने की चर्चा है। धूम्रपान की शौकीन ग्रामवधू अपने कपड़ों में आग लगा लेती है :

बबुनी बीड़ी पियत जात रहली डोली में
आग लगवनीं चोली में ना।[92]

युवतियों के 'धूम्रपान' के प्रति लोकजीवन में तिरस्कार का भाव और आज की नारियों गें अवमूल्यों के प्रसार को इस गीत में पढ़ा जा सकता है। नारी जीवन से जुड़े हादसों को बयान करनेवाले कई लोकगीत इन उपन्यासों में आए हैं और

नारी संबंधी सामाजिक मान्यताओं की गवाही देते हैं। गरीब किसान की लड़की वृद्ध विवाह और बहु विवाह आदि कुरीतियों की शिकार प्रायः होती है। 'पराधीनता' और पुरुष के निरंकुश एकाधिकार को स्वीकारना नारी-जीवन का कटु सत्य है। एक लोकगीत में वृद्ध से ब्याही गई युवती रो रही है और उपन्यासकार नारी तथा पुरुष के लिए अलग-अलग प्रतिमानों की उपस्थिति पर चोट कर रहा है। 'जंगली सुअर' में आया यह लोकगीत कुछ रूढ़ बद्ध अवमूल्यों की मजबूती को दर्शाता है[93] :

अइसन देखवल दुख
सपना भइल सुख
सोनवा में उलल सोहगवा, ए बाबू जी
बुढ़ऊ से सादी भइल
घर पर हर चलवल हो बाबूजी
अबहूँ से कर चेत
देखिके पुरान सेत
डोला काढ़ि मोला मोलइह मत बाबूजी

कैथरिन हैंसन ने रेणु की आंचलिकता का विश्लेषण करते हुए लिखा है कि पाठक उनके उपन्यास पढ़कर वयस्क गांभीर्य को त्याग कर भाव-समृद्ध लोकगीतों के सहारे अपनी बाल्यावस्था में जाने को विवश होता है।[94] बाल्यावस्था में जाने का अर्थ यदि अतीतजीविता है तो यह कथन कुछ ही अंशों में सत्य है। वस्तुतः न केवल 'रेणु' अपितु अधिकतर आंचलिक उपन्यासों में एक 'वयस्क गांभीर्य' बराबर बना हुआ है, चाहे लोकगीत, लोककथा आदि का संदर्भ ही क्यों न हो। यह गांभीर्य मुख्यतः अपने युग के अवलोकन से जुड़ा है। डॉ. सुवास कुमार ने रेणु के संबंध में जो लिखा है[95], वह कमोबेश सभी उपन्यासकारों पर लागू होता है। यह अवश्य है कि नागार्जुन, भैरवप्रसाद गुप्त आदि कुछ उपन्यासकारों की दृष्टि बद्ध और निश्चित है, इसके बावजूद यह तय है कि लोक तत्त्वों के माध्यम से नवीन परिस्थितियों का साक्षात्कार उनके उपन्यासों में यथास्थान हुआ है। इस साक्षात्कार में मूल्यों का संक्रमण एक विशिष्ट पक्ष है। यहाँ एक तथ्य और गौरतलब है कि लोक तत्त्वों की ओर उपन्यासकारों का रुझान आधुनिकता का निषेध नहीं है और ग्रामांचल की पृष्ठभूमि लेने के बावजूद वहाँ नगरीय चेतना का एकांत निषेध नहीं है। इन उपन्यासों में नगर या तो परोक्ष रूप में उपस्थित है या 'कंट्रास्ट' के रूप में। जहाँ 'कंट्रास्ट' के रूप में कोई व्यक्ति या संदर्भ है वहाँ वह मूल्य-विपर्यय या मूल्य-संकट का सूचक है और उससे हीनतर स्थितियों की ओर मूल्य-संक्रमण की प्रतीति होती है।

'मूल्य' को ऐसा प्रेषणीय 'सांस्कृतिक पैटर्न' माना गया है, जिसको अनुभव,

निर्णय और विचार प्रतिकर्म—गर्भित करते हैं।[96] आंचलिक उपन्यासों में व्यक्त सांस्कृतिक मूल्यों की पड़ताल से ज्ञात होता है कि आंचलिक उपन्यासकारों ने इन मूल्यों का अनुभव और निर्णय तो किया है, लेकिन नए मूल्यों के सृजन के प्रमाण नहीं मिलते। प्रायः पाप-पुण्य, धर्म-अधर्म, न्याय-अन्याय, लोकहित-स्वार्थ, मुक्ति-पराधीनता आदि के द्वंद्व को दर्शाते हुए आंचलिक उपन्यासकारों ने अपना समर्थन 'मुक्ति', 'लोक कल्याण', 'मानवीय स्वतंत्रता', 'न्याय' आदि को दिया है। इसीलिए वे 'धर्म' और 'पुण्य' को नए ढंग से पारिभाषित करते दिखाई देते हैं। लोकजीवन में स्वार्थपरता और अनैतिकता के प्रसार ने मूल्य-संकट को जन्म दिया है लेकिन इन उपन्यासकारों ने लोक सांस्कृतिक तत्त्वों के माध्यम से सकारात्मक और मानव-हित में सहयोगी मूल्यों की दिशा में संक्रमण को काम्य ठहराया है। यहाँ उनकी मूल्य-चेतना, तथ्यचेतना से किंचित् पृथक् है। 'विदापत' नामक लोकनृत्य में लोकगीतों की कड़ियों के माध्यम से मैला आँचल में श्रमजीवियों का शोषण-विरोध ध्वनित है।[97]

यह गौरतलब है कि आंचलिक उपन्यासों में लोक सांस्कृतिक तत्त्वों की उपस्थिति उत्तरोत्तर कम होती गई है।[98] 'सोनामाटी' अवश्य इसका अपवाद है। 'मैला आँचल' में 'जाट-जट्टिन', 'मछमरी', 'सतुआनी' आदि अनेक पर्वों की चर्चा है, लेकिन परवर्ती उपन्यासों—'हजार घोड़ों का सवार', 'धरती धन न अपना' आदि की संरचना में पर्वों, लोकगीतों और लोककथाओं का योगदान महत्त्वपूर्ण नहीं है। लोकसांस्कृतिक तत्त्वों की कमी भी सांस्कृतिक मूल्य-संक्रमण के इसी पक्ष की ओर इंगित करती है कि सहयोग, मित्रता, सद्भाव आदि मूल्यों की जगह 'स्वार्थ' 'अकेलापन' आदि अवमूल्यों ने ले ली है। आंचलिक उपन्यासकारों का इस स्थिति से क्षुब्ध और असंतुष्ट होना स्वाभाविक है। लोकजीवन में पर्वों और त्यौहारों के कम होते जाने का एक कारण आर्थिक अभाव है। 'आधा गाँव' में ताजिए के संदर्भ में जिस स्थिति का वर्णन[99] किया गया है, वह आर्थिक कारणों से उत्पन्न हुई है। विवेकीराय ने अपने एक साक्षात्कार में कहा है कि आर्थिक मूल्यों ने सांस्कृतिक मूल्यों को पीट दिया है।[100] विपिन देवनाथ (अलग-अलग वैतरणी), रंगनाथ (राग दरबारी), मन्ने (सत्ती मैया का चौरा) आदि का गाँवों से शहरों की ओर पलायन भी सांस्कृतिक मूल्यों की पराजय का प्रतीक है। लेकिन मूल्य-चेतना के स्तर पर अधिकतर उपन्यासकार सांस्कृतिक मूल्यों की पुनःस्थापना का समर्थन करते हैं।

संदर्भ

1. संस्कृति का दार्शनिक विवेचन, पृ. 175
2. संक्रांति और सनातनता, छगन मोहता, पृ. 9 से
3. The Social structure of values, p. 6
4. समाजवादी विचारधारा : काम्टे से मुखर्जी तक, पृ. 351
5. हिंदी उपन्यासों में आंचलिकता की प्रवृत्ति, पृ. 289
6. आलोचना, अक्टूबर-दिसंबर, 1988, पृ. 63
7. आलोचना, उपन्यास विशेषांक, पृ. 209
8. हिंदी उपन्यास की प्रवृत्तियाँ, पृ. 121
9. मैला आँचल, पृ. 27
10. हिंदी के आंचलिक उपन्यासों में जीवन सत्य, पृ. 154
11. हजार घोड़ों का सवार, पृ. 184
12. आधा गाँव, पृ. 68
13. हजार घोड़ों का सवार, पृ. 159
14. असगाँव-पसगाँव, पृ. 3
15. लोहे के पंख, पृ. 385
16. सोनामाटी, पृ. 254
17. आलोचना, अक्टूबर-दिसंबर, 1988, पृ. 62
18. कथा कहो उर्वशी, पृ. 99
19. मैला आँचल, पृ. 15
20. कब तक पुकारूँ, पृ. 136
21. वही।
22. सोनामाटी, पृ. 225
23. कब तक पुकारूँ, पृ. 345
24. वही, पृ. 346
25. हजार घोड़ों का सवार, पृ. 49
26. वही, पृ. 50
27. वही, पृ. 147
28. आधा गाँव, पृ. 75
29. "यवनों ने हमारे आर्यावर्त्त की संस्कृति, धर्म, कला-कौशल को नष्ट कर दिया है। अभी हिंदू संतान म्लेच्छ संस्कृति की पुजारी हो गई है।"–मैला आँचल, पृ. 126
30. वही।
31. आधा गाँव, पृ. 163
32. वही, पृ. 182
33. सत्ती मैया का चौरा, पृ. 654

34. "उन्हें तो उन मंदिरों की ईंटें गिननी थीं, जिन्हें उनके खयाल में मुसलमानों ने तबाह किया था और उन्हें तो इसका हिसाब लगाना था कि मुगलों और पठानों ने हिन्दुस्तानी तहजीब के बदन पर कितने दाग लगाए हैं।"—आधा गाँव, पृ. 182
35. आधा गाँव, पृ. 254
36. "संजोजक जी ! यवनों पर मुझे क्रोध नहीं आता। यवनों का पक्ष लेने वाले हिंदुओं की तो गरदन उड़ा देने को जी करता है।"—मैला आँचल, पृ. 126-127
37. "मुसलमान का दुश्मन हिंदू नहीं है, मुसलमान का दुश्मन वह मुसलमान है, जो दुम हिलाता हिंदुओं के पीछे-पीछे जाता है, उनके टुकड़ों पर पलता है।"—तमस, पृ. 90
38. जल टूटता हुआ, पृ. 24
39. "सभी मुसलमानों के दस्तखत और अँगूठे की टीप लेकर कलक्टर साहब के पास जाएँगे। साफ कहेंगे, यदि हिन्दुस्तान में न रहने देना है तो साफ-साफ जवाब दे दीजिए, हम लोग पाकिस्तान चले जाएँगे।"—परती परिकथा, पृ. 218
40. "यह तो पौलटीस है। जरूर दीजिए दरखास्त। साफ-साफ कहिए कलेक्टर साहेब से। आपने ठीक ही सोचा है। कहिए कि हम लोग पाकिस्तान भागने के लिए मजबूर हैं। जरूर फतेह होगा, आपका।"—परती परिकथा, पृ. 218-219
41. कालाजल, पृ. 301
42. सोनामाटी, पृ. 385
43. सूरज किरन की छाँव, पृ. 148
44. जलते उबलते प्रश्न, पृ. 217
45. आधुनिकता, साहित्य के संदर्भ में, गंगाप्रसाद विमल, पृ. 119
46. "मैं सोचता था कि मेरा यह अकेले का फायदा मेरे सारे मजदूर भाइयों के लिए बहुत भारी गद्दारी साबित होगा।"—लोहे के पंख, पृ. 333
47. "···नहीं सरकार, दूसरों का पेट काटकर हमको मत दीजिए हाँ अपने खेतों में से देना चाहते हैं तब तो···।"—बलचनमा, पृ. 185-186
48. "जीने के लिए जीना, जीना नहीं है, परोपकार के लिए जीना ही जीना है। अगर मेरी मृत्यु जनसाधारण के लिए लाभप्रद हो तो नहीं चाहिए, मुझको यह जीवन।"—बाबा बटेसरनाथ, पृ. 17
49. मैला आँचल, पृ. 30-31
50. कब तक पुकारूँ, पृ. 569
51. मैला आँचल, पृ. 182
52. सौंदर्य मूल्य और मूल्यांकन, पृ. 54
53. वही, पृ. 56
54. मैला आँचल, पृ. 331
55. परती परिकथा, पृ. 107
56. अलग-अलग वैतरणी, पृ. 249
57. वही, पृ. 363

58. राग दरबारी, पृ. 107
59. हिंदी के आंचलिक उपन्यासों की शिल्पविधि, पृ. 59
60. रामदरश मिश्र के साथ वेदप्रकाश अमिताभ की बातचीत।
61. हिंदी के आंचलिक उपन्यासों में जीवन-सत्य, पृ. 40
62. वेदप्रकाश अमिताभ के साथ बातचीत।
63. स्वातंत्र्योत्तर हिंदी कथा-साहित्य और ग्रामजीवन, विवेकीराय, पृ. 235
64. हिंदी उपन्यास : उत्तरशती की उपलब्धियाँ, पृ. 7
65. रचना और आलोचना की द्वंद्वात्मकता, पृ. 39
66. नदी फिर बह चली, पृ. 128-129
67. ब्रह्मपुत्र, पृ. 174
68. जल टूटता हुआ, पृ. 119
69. वही, पृ. 120
70. वही।
71. लोकऋण, पृ. 176
72. वही, पृ. 6
73. सोनामाटी, पृ. 452
74. वही, पृ. 137
75. वही, पृ. 138
76. अलग-अलग वैतरणी, 'तटचर्चा'।
77. आलोचना, जनवरी-मार्च 1986, पृ. 8
78. मैला आँचल, पृ. 320
79. सोनामाटी, पृ. 337
80. मैला आँचल, पृ. 88
81. वही, पृ. 89
82. जल टूटता हुआ, पृ. 299
83. वही, पृ. 300-301
84. बलचनमा, पृ. 170
85. कहो ना जि नगिया रे, कायर इदिमिया के
    सबके बरोबर अधिकार
    करम के झखनी मत अब झखीहऽ
    अपना बल प आसरा रखीहऽ—जंगली सुअर, पृ. 53
86. सोनामाटी, पृ. 208
87. जल टूटता हुआ, पृ. 103
88. वही।
89. हिंदी कहानी : सामाजिक संदर्भ, डॉ. अश्वघोष, पृ. 39
90. सोनामाटी, पृ. 347

91. वही, पृ. 349
92. नदी फिर बह चली, पृ. 341
93. जंगली सुअर, पृ. 59
94. आलोचना, अक्टूबर-दिसंबर 1988, पृ. 52
95. "अपने अंचल की लोककथा, लोकभाषा, लोककला में रच-बस कर उनका कलाकार व्यक्तित्व तैयार हुआ है अतः वे अपने कथाक्षेत्र के जनमानस के संस्कार और स्वभाव से संपूर्णतः परिचित हैं, लेकिन उनकी दृष्टि बद्ध नहीं है। दृष्टि का खुलापन उन्हें नवीन परिस्थितियों के साक्षात्कार निषेध और स्वीकार के लिए तैयार रखता है।" —आलोचना, अक्टूबर-दिसंबर 1988, पृ. 63
96. सौंदर्य मूल्य और मूल्यांकन, पृ. 34
97. समीक्षा, जनवरी-मार्च 1989, डॉ. गोपाल का आलेख, पृ. 10
98. समकालीन हिंदी उपन्यास, पृ. 96
99. आधा गाँव, पृ. 308
100. वेदप्रकाश शर्मा के साथ बातचीत।

उपसंहार

लघुता की ओर दृष्टिपात, सांस्कृतिक पुनरुद्धार और लोकतंत्र की जड़ों की तलाश की सम्मिलित विचारोत्तेजना ने आंचलिक उपन्यास को जन्म दिया है। जनपदीय आंदोलन, प्रगतिशील लेखन, कल्लोल आंदोलन आदि की प्रेरणा से भी हिंदी कथाकार जनतांत्रिक आकांक्षाओं और कुरूप वास्तविकताओं के द्वंद्व को ग्रामांचल के संदर्भ में देखने और आँकने की ओर उन्मुख हुआ। अधिकतर आंचलिक उपन्यास उन कथाकारों द्वारा लिखे गए हैं, जिनके पास न केवल पिछड़े अंचलों के जीवन का प्रत्यक्ष अनुभव है अपितु संपूर्ण वास्तविकता को देखने-परखने के लिए वांछित सुस्पष्ट और सुस्थिर जीवन-दृष्टि भी है अतः यह आकस्मिक नहीं है कि जीवनमूल्यों के व्यापक संक्रमण को व्यक्त करते हुए आंचलिक उपन्यासकारों की केंद्रीय चिंता मानव-हित और जन-कल्याण से बराबर संबद्ध रही है।

'मूल्य' को समाजशास्त्रियों, दार्शनिकों, अर्थशास्त्रियों आदि ने अपने-अपने ढंग से पारिभाषित किया है। इन परिभाषाओं का निचोड़ यही है कि मूल्य जीवन के वे कमाए हुए सत्य हैं, जिनके लिए व्यक्ति या समुदाय जीवित रहता है और जिसके लिए वह दुख सहने, कोई भी कीमत चुकाने यहाँ तक कि मृत्यु को भी स्वीकार करने के लिए सन्नद्ध होता है। 'मूल्य' स्वेच्छा से जीवन-पद्धति का अंग बनाई गई वे अवधारणाएँ हैं, जो एक ओर मनुष्य को नैतिक बल प्रदान करती हैं, दूसरी ओर अशुभ और अमानवीयता से बचकर स्वस्थ मानवीय आचरण की प्रेरणा भी देती हैं। कतिपय मूल्य विरासत में मिलते हैं और कुछ अपनी आवश्यकता और युग की माँग के अनुरूप अर्जित किए जाते हैं। मूल्यानुभव में व्यक्ति या समुदाय की अभिरुचि, संस्कार, आवश्यकता और उपयोगिता आदि की महत्त्वपूर्ण भूमिका होती है। मूल्यों का वर्गीकरण कई तरह से किया गया है। उपयोगिता के आधार पर दो वर्ग—साध्यात्मक और साधनात्मक किए गए हैं। जो मूल्य जीवन के लक्ष्य

होते हैं, वे साध्य या स्वतः मूल्य कहे गए और जो उस लक्ष्य के साधन हैं, वे साधनमूल्य हैं। किन्हीं विशेष परिस्थिति में साधनमूल्य 'साध्य' भी बन जाते हैं। शुभ या श्रेयस् को ध्यान में रखकर 'अस्तिमूल्य' और नास्तिमूल्य जैसे वर्ग भी बनाए गए हैं। यद्यपि मूल्य-निर्णय प्रायः सामाजिक होता है, फिर भी 'व्यक्तिगत' मूल्यों का अपना महत्त्व और अस्तित्व है।

अनेक विचारकों के साक्ष्य से कहा जा सकता है कि प्रभावशाली आवेशगुच्छ, नई वैज्ञानिक धारणाएँ, समाज व्यवस्था में परिवर्तन आदि बहुत से कारक मूल्य-संकट, और मूल्य-विघटन की स्थितियों को जन्म देते हैं। बदले हुए संदर्भों में मूल्यों के अर्थ भी बदल जाने के प्रमाण मिलते हैं। वैज्ञानिक दृष्टिकोण और प्रौद्योगिकी के विकास ने निश्चय ही नई मूल्य-व्यवस्था को जन्म दिया है और कतिपय पुरा मूल्य कड़ी आजमाइश में पड़ गए हैं। मूल्य-संकट और मूल्य-विघटन आदि मूल्य-संक्रमण की ही गवाही देते हैं। विचारकों ने मूल्य-संक्रमण की दो प्रमुख स्थितियों की चर्चा की है। जब कोई 'उच्च' और प्रासंगिक समझा जानेवाला मूल्य स्थानच्युत होता है या कोई 'हीन' मानी जानेवाली अवधारणा 'मूल्य' के रूप में मान्य होती है या साधन-मूल्य और साध्यमूल्य अपनी जगह बदल लेते हैं तब मूल्य-संक्रमण की एक गतिशील स्थिति सामने आती है। मूल्य-संक्रमण की इस स्थिति में 'विकल्पहीनता' का संकट पैदा नहीं होता। लेकिन एक अन्य स्थिति यह होती है कि पुराने मूल्य अप्रासंगिक करार दे दिए जाते हैं लेकिन उनका स्थान न लेने के लिए कोई स्पष्ट 'मूल्य' नहीं उभर पाता। असमंजस की यह स्थिति अधिक विषम होती है। इस स्थिति में कभी-कभी विवेक के अभाव में व्यक्तिगत मूल्य-निर्णयों को भी 'मूल्य' की सी गरिमा दे दी जाती है। मूल्य-संक्रमण प्रौद्योगिकी के विकास औद्योगीकरण-मशीनीकरण, क्रांतिकारी विचारधाराओं के प्रसार आदि का परिणाम तो है ही, एक समुदाय या संस्कृति के सदस्यों के दूसरे समुदाय या संस्कृति के सदस्यों के संपर्क और द्वंद्व से भी इसे बल मिलता है। मूल्य-संक्रमण के पाँच स्तर या पाँच चरण माने जा सकते हैं–(1) आधुनिकता के दबाव से पुरामूल्यों की अप्रासंगिकता का बोध (2) नए-पुराने विचारों का संघर्ष और असमंजस की स्थिति (3) पुरामूल्यों के पुनर्मूल्यांकन की आवश्यकता (4) अस्ति मूल्य, साध्यमूल्य, उच्चतर मूल्यों का नास्तिमूल्य, साधनमूल्य और हीनतर मूल्यों की दिशा में संक्रमण। कई बार इसका उल्टा भी होता है। (5) कतिपय नए मूल्यों की प्रतिष्ठा। लेकिन यह स्मरणीय है कि विचार और धारणा के स्तर पर होनेवाला हर परिवर्तन मूल्य-संक्रमण का द्योतक नहीं है, मूल्य-संक्रमण गंभीर और दीर्घ विचार-मंथन से संबद्ध है। कभी यह 'विचार मंथन' एक ही स्तर के मूल्यों के एक समूह से दूसरे समूह में स्थानांतरण के लिए पृष्ठभूमि बनाता है और कभी एक सामाजिक स्तर से दूसरे सामाजिक स्तर पर मूल्यों के स्थानांतरण को प्रेरित करता है। मूल्य-संक्रमण

व्यक्ति और समूह के विचार और व्यवहार में व्यापक परिवर्तन का सूचक होने के साथ-साथ परंपरा के पुनर्नवीकरण और आर्थिक-सामाजिक ढाँचे में आए बदलाव का मुखर प्रमाण भी है।

चूँकि आंचलिक उपन्यासों में स्वातंत्र्योत्तर ग्रामीण परिवेश में हुए व्यापक परिवर्तनों—राजनीतिक चेतना के उभार, कृषि-क्रांति, बढ़ती आर्थिक असमानता, घोर जाति भेद के समानांतर संस्कृति, परिवार और व्यक्ति के स्तर पर वैचारिक विचलन को विस्तार से अंकित किया गया है, अतः यह आकस्मिक नहीं है कि मूल्य-विघटन, मूल्य-संकट और मूल्य-हीनता के विभिन्न आयाम आंचलिक उपन्यासों के युगबोध और वैचारिकता में अनिवार्यतः संश्लिष्ट हो गए हैं। एक पिछड़े अंचल के माध्यम से अपने युग के मूल्य संक्रमण को रेखांकित करना आंचलिक उपन्यासों का मुख्य प्रतिपाद्य माना जा सकता है।

संदर्भ चाहे व्यक्तिगत मूल्यों का हो या सामाजिक मूल्यों का, सर्वत्र आंचलिक उपन्यासकारों का दृष्टिकोण प्रगतिशील है।

व्यक्तिगत मूल्यों के संक्रमण को रेखांकित करते हुए भी आंचलिक उपन्यासकारों ने प्रायः प्रगतिशील चिंतन का सहारा लिया है। 'बलचनमा', 'गंगा मैया', 'कब तक पुकारूँ, 'धरती धन न अपना' आदि में मार्क्सवाद की गूँज बहुत स्पष्ट है, जबकि 'मैला आँचल', 'परती परिकथा', 'नदी फिर बह चली' आदि उपन्यासों में समाजवादी चिंतन का प्रभाव मुखर है। 'ब्रह्मपुत्र', 'सागर लहरें और मनुष्य', 'सूरज किरन की छाँव', 'हजार घोड़ों का सवार' आदि कृतियों में मानवतावादी दृष्टिकोण है। स्पष्ट है कि आंचलिक उपन्यासकारों ने व्यक्तिगत मूल्यों के संक्रमण को चित्रित करते समय उन्हीं जीवनदृष्टियों का आश्रय लिया है, जो समाज-सापेक्ष और मानवतावादी हैं, परिवर्तन में जिनका विश्वास पर्याप्त पुष्ट है। उनकी मूल्य-दृष्टि पर उनके जीवन-संघर्ष का प्रभाव पर्याप्त है।

व्यक्तिगत मूल्यों में 'प्रणय' के संक्रमण पक्ष पर आंचलिक उपन्यासों में सर्वाधिक ध्यान दिया गया है। अधिकतर कृतियों में 'प्रणय' को पावनता उत्सर्ग और पारस्परिक आत्मीयता से जोड़ते हुए न केवल विचार अपितु अनुभव और व्यवहार के स्तर पर भी पर्याप्त मूल्यवान ठहराया गया है। प्रायः चरित्र हीनतर स्थितियों का अतिक्रमण करते हैं और उच्चतर स्थिति की ओर बढ़ते हैं। भोग पक्ष वर्जित नहीं है। लेकिन उस भोग में अय्याशी या विलासिता का भाव न होकर एक-दूसरे को समझने, पाने और एक-दूसरे के व्यक्तित्व का अनिवार्य अंग बन जाने की मनःस्थिति प्रधान है। इस क्रम में पातिव्रत, कौमार्य, विवाह आदि मर्यादाओं का उल्लंघन भी होता है। लेकिन आंचलिक उपन्यासों में 'प्रेम' न तो सेक्स तक सीमित हुआ है और न 'प्लेटोनिक लव' की मुद्रा धारण करता दिखाई देता है। यह एकदम परंपरा विरोधी न होते हुए भी रूढ़ियों और यौन वर्जनाओं का विरोध

करता है। प्रेम को कहीं भी समाज-निरपेक्ष रूप में नहीं दिखाया गया है। प्रायः 'प्रेम' को 'श्रेय' से संबद्ध किया गया है। चाहे आदिवासियों का प्रेम हो (जंगल के फूल) या करनटों (कब तक पुकारूँ) का या शिक्षित-सभ्य कहे जानेवाले व्यक्तियों (मैला आँचल, अलग-अलग वैतरणी, ब्रह्मपुत्र) का या किसानों-मजदूरों (वरुण के बेटे, बलचनमा, नदी फिर बह चली, धरती धन न अपना) का प्रेम हो, कहीं भी प्रेम विकृति नहीं बनता। प्रायः प्रेम कोरी भावुकता से उबर कर एक बौद्धिक समझदार निर्णय के रूप में व्यक्त हुआ है। उपन्यासकारों ने प्रायः समाज में प्रेम के अवमूल्यन की चर्चा की है, लेकिन उनका अपना बोध इस यथार्थ के मेल में नहीं है। वे प्रेम को पर्याप्त मूल्यवान मानते हैं। प्रायः दो मॉडलों को आमने-सामने रखकर—'प्रेम' की एकांतिकता और निजी अनुभवशीलता से सार्वजनिक सक्रियता, कर्तव्यनिष्ठा, उत्तरदायित्वपूर्ण निष्ठा की ओर संक्रमित होता दिखाते हैं। 'परती परिकथा', 'आधा गाँव' और 'अलग-अलग वैतरणी' में दो पीढ़ियों के मॉडल आमने-सामने हैं और स्पष्ट करते हैं कि प्रणय का संक्रमण यौन-अतृप्ति प्रगाढ़ प्रेम जनित उन्माद और आभिजात्यपूर्ण (प्लेटोनिक) मुद्रा से रूढ़ नैतिकता को चुनौती देनेवाले युवा दुस्साहस की दिशा में हुआ है।

उपन्यासकारों ने 'सेक्स' को जैवीय आवश्यकता मानते हुए भी कहीं यौन उच्छृंखलता को अपना समर्थन नहीं दिया है। नकारात्मक मूल्यों के संवाहक चरित्र 'सेक्स' को महत्त्वपूर्ण मानते हैं, लेकिन नरनारी संबंधों में यौनविच्युति को किसी मूल्य पर स्वीकार न करनेवाले पात्रों के सामने वे बहुत तुच्छ और निम्न सिद्ध होते हैं। यह बात बहुत बल देकर कही गई है कि जहाँ 'संभोग' केवल 'सेक्स' की भूख है, वहाँ व्यभिचार है। यौन तुष्टि एक अराजक आचरण नहीं है, इसे एकनिष्ठता, नैतिक जिम्मेदारी और गंभीर लगाव से संबद्ध होना चाहिए। सेक्स से जुड़े मूल्य-विपर्यय या मूल्यबोध का आंचलिक उपन्यासकार समर्थन नहीं करते।

जहाँ 'प्रणय' के साथ निष्ठा, लगाव और नैतिक उत्तरदायित्व घुले-मिले हैं, वहाँ विवाह की औपचारिकता को उपन्यासकार अनिवार्य नहीं मानते। सुलक-महुआ, कुंजू-बदमी, फुन्नन-कुलसूम, जित्तन-ताजमनी आदि युग्म इस धारणा को झुठलाते हैं कि विवाह के बंधन में बँधकर ही प्रणय की सार्थकता हो सकती है।

आंचलिक उपन्यासों में व्यक्ति स्वातंत्र्य का संक्रमण 'सामूहिक मुक्ति' की दिशा में हुआ है। कोरे व्यक्ति-स्वातंत्र्य या चरम स्वातंत्र्य की अवधारणा का समर्थन प्रायः उपन्यासकारों ने नहीं किया है। व्यक्ति की स्वतंत्रता का बोध कहीं वर्ग की स्वतंत्रता के प्रश्न में बदल गया है तो कहीं मानव मात्र की मुक्ति का पर्याय बन गया है। मार्क्स और ऐंगिल्स की राय में मानव के अग्रगामी विकास में व्यक्तित्व का 'स्वातंत्र्य' आवश्यक है, लेकिन वह व्यक्तियों के सार्वत्रिक विकास से संबंधित है। आंचलिक उपन्यासकार की विचारधारा बहुत कुछ इससे मिलती-जुलती है। वे

व्यक्ति के विकास या स्वातंत्र्य का अंधा विरोध नहीं करते। लेकिन सामाजिक प्रतिमानों के विरुद्ध व्यक्ति के वरण की स्वतंत्रता को वही समर्थन मिला है, जहाँ सामाजिक प्रतिमान रूढ़ियों की शक्ल में व्यक्ति और समाज की प्रगति में आड़े आते हैं। कुछ उपन्यासकारों ने 'व्यक्ति-स्वातंत्र्य' को 'नारी-स्वातंत्र्य' के सदंर्भ में देखा है और इस निष्कर्ष पर पहुँचे हैं कि जिन वर्गों और जातियों में नारी घर की चार दीवारी के बाहर 'श्रम' से जुड़ी हुई है, वहाँ उसे अधिक स्वतंत्रता प्राप्त है। उच्च वर्ग की नारियाँ नाममात्र के लिए स्वतंत्र हैं। इस तरह नारी-स्वातंत्र्य का प्रयाण दासता, विवशता आदि हीनतर स्थितियों से आत्म निर्भरता, स्वाभिमान, सहयोग आदि उच्चतर स्थितियों की ओर होते दिखाया गया है।

यद्यपि आंचलिक उपन्यासों में कुछ चरित्र आज के माहौल में खुद को अकेला और अजनबी पाते हैं फिर भी आंचलिक उपन्यासकार अकेलापन, आत्मनिर्वासन आदि अनुभवों को 'मूल्य' नहीं मानते। ये तथ्य हैं, लेकिन इनके प्रति कर्ता की प्रतिक्रिया ने किसी मूल्य-भावना को जन्म नहीं दिया है। हाँ, इनसे कतिपय मूल्यों के प्रति उपन्यासकारों की चिंता अवश्य व्यक्त हुई है। जहाँ तक व्यक्तिगत नैतिकता-सत्य पालन, ईमानदारी आदि का प्रश्न है, आंचलिक उपन्यासों में इन्हें मानव-व्यवहार और मानसिकता के लिए अनिवार्य ठहराया गया है। 'स्वार्थ' के व्यापक प्रसार को रेखांकित करते हुए उसके स्थान पर 'परहित' को प्रतिष्ठित करने के लिए सचेष्ट चरित्रों की सृष्टि की गई है। यहाँ संक्रमण नकारात्मक पक्ष से धनात्मक पक्ष की ओर है। यही स्थिति यौन नैतिकता को लेकर है। आंचलिक उपन्यासों के मूल्य बोध का एक महत्त्वपूर्ण पक्ष यह है कि व्यक्तिगत मूल्यों को प्रायः साधन मूल्यों का दर्जा दिया गया है, उन्हें साध्य या सर्वोच्च मूल्यों के रूप में स्थापित करने का आग्रह नहीं मिलता। इसी तरह उन्होंने व्यक्तिगत मूल्यों को 'व्यक्तिवादी' बनने से बचाया है। समाज-संबद्धता का भाव आंचलिक उपन्यासों में बराबर मौजूद है।

आंचलिक उपन्यासों में पारिवारिक मूल्य-मर्यादाओं के संक्रमण से गुजरते हुए पाया गया है कि संयुक्त परिवार का विघटन वस्तुतः पारंपरिक मूल्य-व्यवस्था का विघटन है। अर्थाभाव, नई रोशनी, पीढ़ियों का द्वंद्व आदि अनेक कारणों से बड़ों के अधिकार, परंपरा की पवित्रता, पातिव्रत आदि अवधारणाएँ कठोर आजमाइश में पड़ गईं। पारिवारिक मूल्य-संकट की चर्चा करने के बावजूद रेणु, शिवप्रसाद सिंह, राही मासूम रजा, रामदरश मिश्र, विवेकीराय आदि बहुत से उपन्यासकार बंधुत्व, श्रद्धा, सम्मान, गुरुभक्ति पारिवारिक सहयोग मूल्यों के विघटन से प्रसन्न नहीं लगते। वे इन मूल्यों को 'पॉजिटिव' मानते हुए किन्हीं विशेष परिस्थितियों में ही इनके उल्लंघन के पक्ष में हैं। उपन्यासकारों की सहानुभूति किसी पीढ़ी के प्रति न होकर कतिपय सकारात्मक मूल्यों के साथ है यदि कहीं रूढ़ियों के विरुद्ध कोई साहसपूर्ण

और सार्थक कदम उठाता है तो इसका उपन्यासकारों ने विरोध नहीं किया है। कुलीनता और कुलमर्यादा जैसे मूल्य उन्हें प्रासंगिक नहीं लगते।

विवाह से संबद्ध पातिव्रत, सतीत्व और एकनिष्ठा आदि मूल्यों के प्रति आंचलिक उपन्यासकार का रवैया प्रायः समर्थन का रहा है। कुछ विशेष स्थितियों में पति के परमेश्वरत्व को नकारा गया है। इस नकार के पीछे 'पति' की अपात्रता उत्तरदायी है। यौन बुभुक्षा के लिए परपुरुषगामी नारियाँ आंचलिक उपन्यासों में विरल हैं। जो हैं, उन्हें उपन्यासकारों की सहानुभूति नहीं मिली है। जहाँ पति की निरंकुशता और नीचता सीमा पार कर गई है, वहाँ किसी अन्य पुरुष से रागात्मक लगाव को स्वीकृति दी गई है। इस तरह आंचलिक उपन्यासों में 'मनुस्मृति' की यह व्यवस्था आँख मींचकर स्वीकार नहीं की गई है कि पति का पत्नी पर पूरा अधिकार होता है। परंपरा से यह विचलन न केवल प्रासंगिक है, अपितु हीनतर मूल्यों से उच्चतर मूल्यों की ओर प्रयाण का द्योतक भी। नर-नारी की यौन शुचिता आंचलिक उपन्यासों में प्रायः मान्य है। वर्जित यौन संबंधों को नैतिक मूल्यों का विरोधी ठहराया गया है। नगरीय-महानगरीय जीवन के उपन्यासों में वर्णित और अपसामान्य यौन संबंधों को जिस तरह गौरवान्वित किया गया है उसका आंचलिक उपन्यासों में अभाव है। लेकिन यौन-नैतिकता से जुड़े मूल्य भी साधन मूल्य ही हैं, उन्हें साध्य मूल्य के रूप में नहीं रखा गया है।

सामाजिक मूल्यों के संक्रमण को रेखांकित करते समय आंचलिक उपन्यासकारों ने एक ओर वस्तुस्थिति को दर्शाया है, दूसरी ओर उसका अतिक्रमण करते हुए स्वस्थ प्रगतिशील मूल्यों को जबर्दस्त समर्थन दिया है। आंचलिक उपन्यासों में जाति से जुड़े परंपरागत मूल्यों का संक्रमण त्रि-आयामीय है। एक ओर 'स्वार्थ' के आगे जातिगत मर्यादाएँ विचलित हो रही हैं यानी कि नास्ति मूल्यों का संक्रमण नास्ति मूल्यों में ही हो रहा है। दूसरी ओर प्रबुद्ध जनसमूह वर्ण-जाति से जुड़े मूल्यों पर प्रश्नचिह्न लगा रहा है। अस्पृश्य कही जानेवाली जातियों और दलित जनों में अपने 'हीनत्व' की तीखी प्रतिक्रिया हो रही है और वे जाति व्यवस्था को खारिज कर रहे हैं। उपन्यासकारों ने दूसरी और तीसरी स्थिति का स्वागत किया है। वे हीनतर मूल्यों के उच्चतर मूल्यों की ओर संक्रमित होने के पक्षधर हैं। मानवीय संबद्धता के मूल्यों को वे बौद्धिक और हार्दिक स्तर पर भरपूर समर्थन देते हैं। दलितों के शोषण और उत्पीड़न से सर्वथा असहमत होते हुए उनके संघर्ष और अधिकारों की माँग का समर्थन किया गया है। इस तरह जनतांत्रिक मूल्यों—सहयोग, समता, स्वतंत्रता, समानता आदि को पूरी तरह मान्यता मिली है। कुछ उपन्यासकार जातिगत-वर्णगत समानता के लिए सामूहिक रूप से आर्थिक समता पर बहुत बल देते हैं। इस संदर्भ में उन्होंने मार्क्सवाद, समाजवाद, मानववाद आदि विचारधाराओं से पर्याप्त प्रेरणा ली है। 'जंगली सुअर', 'सोनभद्र की राधा', 'हजार घोड़ों का सवार'

आदि से यह बोध बहुत तीखेपन के साथ व्यक्त हुआ है कि आवश्यकता पड़ने पर दलित वर्ग सशस्त्र संघर्ष पर भी उतर सकता है। अब उसने भाग्यवाद, पुनर्जन्म, कुलीनता आदि अवधारणाओं को झटक कर दूर फेंक दिया है। लेकिन इस संदर्भ में उसका मूल्यबोध मराठी दलित लेखन की तुलना में कहीं संयमित है।

सांप्रदायिकता को बढ़ावा देनेवाले नास्ति मूल्यों में आंचलिक उपन्यासों का विश्वास कतई नहीं है। इनकी तुलना में धर्म निरपेक्षता, राष्ट्रभक्ति, पारस्परिक सौहार्द आदि मूल्यों को उभारा गया है। इस तरह उपन्यासकार नकारात्मक दृष्टि को निरस्त करते हुए सकारात्मक सोच की ओर बढ़े हैं नारी संबंधी मूल्यों में यदा-कदा शुभ न समझी जानेवाली धारणाओं की ओर संक्रमण दर्शाया गया है, लेकिन यह अपरिहार्य स्थिति में ही हुआ है और नई मूल्य-मर्यादा के उदय का सूचक है।

जमींदारी उन्मूलन और सामंतों के दबदबे की समाप्ति को आंचलिक उपन्यासकारों ने शोषण, अन्याय और उत्पीड़न की समाप्ति के तौर पर लिया है। इन उपन्यासों में बार-बार यह कहा जाना कि समाज में वर्ग केवल दो हैं—अमीर और गरीब, इस बात का सूचक है कि वर्गचेतना के उभार को महत्त्व दिया गया है। इस संदर्भ में मूल्य-संक्रमण, शोषण, अन्याय आदि नास्ति एवं अमानवीय मूल्यों को निरस्त करते हुए न्याय, समानता, समजीविता आदि स्वस्थ एवं सकारात्मक मूल्यों की दिशा में हुआ है। 'बलचनमा', 'हजार घोड़ों का सवार' आदि कई उपन्यासों में वर्गसंघर्ष के माध्यम से ही न्याय आदि मूल्यों की स्थापना संभव बताई गई है। हालाँकि उपन्यासकार इस सत्य से अवगत हैं कि पुराने सामंतों की जगह नए सामंतों ने ले ली है, अत्याचार और उत्पीड़न कम नहीं हुआ है, फिर भी अभी वे जनतांत्रिक ढाँचे के भीतर ही बदलाव का स्वप्न देखते हैं। अब शोषितजन संगठित हैं, अन्याय सहने को तैयार नहीं हैं, इसके बावजूद अभी नक्सलियों की तरह वर्ग शत्रु के वध की सार्थकता और प्रासंगिकता इन उपन्यासों में नहीं दिखाई गई है। 'मैला आँचल', 'धरती धन न अपना', 'सोना माटी', 'जल टूटता हुआ' में जनसंघर्ष की सीमाओं और अंतर्विरोधों पर भी अँगुली रखी गई है। अधिकतर उपन्यासों में यह सत्य व्यंजित है कि मजूरों-किसानों के स्तर पर संक्रमण की प्रक्रिया तीव्र है, लेकिन भूस्वामियों और नव-सामंतों के स्तर पर युग-सत्य को स्वीकारने और मानवीय मूल्यों की ओर प्रयाण की गति धीमी है। समता और समानता आदि मूल्यों को गौरवान्वित करते हुए आंचलिक उपन्यासकारों ने यथास्थितिवादी शक्तियों और परिवर्तन-विरोधी तत्त्वों का खुला विरोध किया है। धर्म से अनुशासित भाग्य, पाप-पुण्य, पुनर्जन्म आदि कई अवधारणाओं का आश्रय लेकर वर्गसंघर्ष की धार कुंद करने का प्रयास होता रहा है। आंचलिक उपन्यासों में इस प्रयास को आर्थिक-विषमता बढ़ानेवाला माना गया है। 'आधा गाँव', 'कब तक पुकारूँ', 'लाल

पसीना' आदि उपन्यासों में इन अवधारणाओं को प्रायः अप्रासंगिक करार दिया गया है।

आंचलिक उपन्यासों में इस यथार्थ का उद्‌घाटन गंभीरता से हुआ है कि गाँवों में प्रौद्योगिकी के प्रवेश ने मूल्यों के विचलन और विघटन में योग दिया है। कृषि और उत्पादन के अन्य क्षेत्रों में ट्रैक्टर, मशीन, ट्यूबवेल, यातायात के साधनों के सहयोग से न केवल उत्पादन बढ़ा है अपितु आर्थिक-विषमता की खाई और चौड़ी हुई है। इसका एक कारण तो यही है कि उत्पादन के इन साधनों पर कुछ ही लोगों ने एकाधिकार कर लिया है यंत्रों के आगमन ने अंधविश्वास और जड़ता पर प्रहार किया है। अस्पताल और डॉक्टर के आगमन ने जनसमुदाय को कूपमंडूकता और कुस्वास्थ्य से मुक्त किया है। सड़कों और यातायात के साधनों ने जहाँ कुछ सुविधाएँ पैदा की हैं, वहीं इनके माध्यम से नगर जीवन की कृत्रिमता, निस्संगता और कथित अनैतिकता गाँवों में जा घुसी है। इससे वहाँ पहले से चले आ रहे आपसी सौहार्द को पर्याप्त क्षति पहुँची है। आंचलिक उपन्यासों में पिछड़े अंचलों में नई प्रौद्योगिकी की आवश्यकता को अनुभव करते हुए यह अपेक्षा की गई है कि यह शोषक वर्ग के एकाधिकार से मुक्त होकर 'लोकहित' के लिए प्रयुक्त होगी।

चूँकि कई आंचलिक उपन्यासों में स्वतंत्रता पूर्व का संदर्भ भी है, अतः गांधीवादी मूल्यों—अहिंसा, बलिदान, राष्ट्रीयता, सबके प्रति प्रेमभाव आदि की चर्चा स्वाभाविक है। कई उपन्यासों में दिखाया गया है कि वर्तमान राजनीतिक परिप्रेक्ष्य में अहिंसा राष्ट्रीयता, प्रेम, त्याग, सेवा आदि मूल्य काम के नहीं रहे। यह धारणा गांधीवादी कहे जानेवाले नेताओं और राजपुरुषों के आचरण को देखकर बनती है। न केवल सत्ताधीश अपितु सभी राजनीतिक दलों में स्वार्थ पदलोलुपता और 'अवसरवाद' मूल्य के रूप में स्थापित हो गए। नैतिक मूल्यों का खुला अस्वीकार देखने में आया। इस तरह यथार्थ जगत् में उच्च राजनीतिक मूल्यों का प्रयाण हीनतर मूल्यों की दिशा में हुआ है। लेकिन 'वामनदास' (मैला आँचल), 'देवकांत' (ब्रह्मपुत्र), 'सतीश' (जल टूटता हुआ), 'गीधू' (हजार घोड़ों का सवार) आदि कई सकारात्मक चरित्रों की रचना कर उपन्यासकारों ने सत्यनिष्ठा, जनसेवा, न्याय आदि मूल्यों में अपनी आस्था व्यक्त की है। ये चरित्र झंझावात में निष्कंप दीपशिखा की तरह जनधर्मी और मानवीय मूल्यों का प्रकाश बिखेर रहे हैं।

राजनीतिक सुविधावाद, भ्रष्टता और घोर स्वार्थपरता का वर्णन करते हुए 'नदी फिर बह चली', 'बाबा बटेसरनाथ', 'हजार घोड़ों का सवार', 'लोकऋण' आदि कई उपन्यासों में जनतांत्रिक व्यवस्था को अपर्याप्त और अक्षम माना गया है। यह गौर तलब है कि समता, समानता आदि जनतांत्रिक मूल्यों का विरोध नहीं किया गया है। लेकिन इनकी प्राप्ति के लिए इस व्यवस्था में परिवर्तन की माँग की गई है। यद्यपि आंचलिक उपन्यासों में 'बैलेट' के स्थान पर 'बुलेट' से समस्याओं के

समाधान में विश्वास व्यक्त नहीं किया गया है, फिर भी नपुंसकीय अहिंसा और कृत्रिम हृदय-परिवर्तन आदि के प्रति उपन्यासकार कतई आश्वस्त नहीं हैं। भैरवप्रसाद गुप्त, नागार्जुन, हिमांशु श्रीवास्तव आदि उपन्यासकारों ने 'समाजवादी व्यवस्था' को विकल्प के रूप में संकेतित किया है। लेकिन 'जल टूटता हुआ', 'सोनामाटी', 'धरती धन न अपना', 'अलग-अलग वैतरणी', रागदरबारी आदि उपन्यासों में लेखकों को असमंजस में देखा जा सकता है। इन उपन्यासों में 'विकल्प' खुला हुआ है। लेकिन यह निश्चित है कि वे आर्थिक-राजनीतिक मूल्यों के 'जनहित', 'जनसेवा', 'अशोषण', 'आर्थिक समानता' आदि की दिशा में अग्रसर होने के पक्षधर हैं। अधिकतर उपन्यासकार संक्रमण के इस पक्ष से चिंतित हैं कि सेवा, त्याग, परहित आदि जो मूल्य कभी राजनीति में स्वतः मूल्य के रूप में स्वीकृत थे, वे आज 'सत्ता' या 'स्वार्थ' की प्राप्ति के लिए साधन मूल्य बन गए हैं।

आंचलिक उपन्यासों में सांस्कृतिक मूल्यों के संकट और गिरावट को चिंता की दृष्टि से देखा गया है। यह पाया गया है कि मौजूदा परिवेश में न केवल स्वास्थ्य और सुरक्षा जैसे जैविक मूल्य संकट में पड़ गए हैं अपितु न्याय, समानता, सत्य, पवित्रता आदि सामाजिक नैतिक मूल्यों के अस्तित्व के लिए भी खतरा बढ़ गया है। नगरीकरण और मशीनीकरण के दबाव ने पिछड़े हुए अंचलों में रहनेवालों को विरासत में प्राप्त मूल्यों को कई स्तरों पर विचलित किया है। इस विचलन के फलस्वरूप कहीं धर्म, अधर्म, पाप, पुण्य आदि की रूढ़ अवधारणाओं पर आघात पहुँचा है और कहीं-कहीं चरम मूल्य—ईश्वर की सत्ता में संदेह की स्थिति पैदा हो गई है। इसके बावजूद कृषि-संस्कृति में निहित 'सर्वजनहित' का भाव खंडित नहीं हुआ है, सांस्कृतिक संक्रमण के इन सभी पक्षों को आंचलिक उपन्यासों में रेखांकित किया गया है।

लोकजीवन पर 'धर्म' की गहरी पकड़ का उल्लेख करते हुए पाया गया है कि दलित वर्ग में धर्म और ईश्वर के खोखले आतंक से मुक्ति की चेतना बल पकड़ रही है। प्राकृतिक न्याय में विश्वास अभी बना हुआ है, इस तथ्य की पुष्टि 'कथा कहो उर्वशी', 'मैला आँचल', 'कब तक पुकारू' आदि कृतियों में है। लेकिन जहाँ जनसाधारण को लगता है कि धर्म, पाप-पुण्य आदि अवधारणाएँ वर्ग विशेष का हथियार बनकर सामाजिक न्याय के मार्ग में बाधक हैं, वहाँ इन अवधारणाओं की स्थिति, 'अमूर्त संवेग' की है। वे 'नैतिक प्रतिमान' की तरह जनसाधारण के व्यवहार को अनुशासित नहीं करते हैं। 'आधा गाँव', 'जल टूटता हुआ', 'अलग-अलग वैतरणी', आदि उपन्यासों में धार्मिक सहिष्णुता और सद्भाव को जिस तरह गौरवान्वित किया गया है, उससे पता चलता है कि समाज में मूल्य-संक्रमण की दिशा 'वैमनस्य' आदि अवमूल्यों की ओर है, लेकिन उपन्यासकार सहिष्णुता और सद्भाव के कायल हैं। इस संदर्भ में उपन्यासकारों की मूल्य-पक्षधरता

'वास्तविकता' की सहज और प्रगतिशील प्रतिक्रिया है। नेहरू युग में जिस 'मिश्रित संस्कृति' की चर्चा हुई थी, उसके एक पक्ष सर्वधर्म सद्‌भाव को आंचलिक उपन्यासों में पूरा समर्थन मिला है।

आंचलिक उपन्यासों में मानवीय स्वतंत्रता और मानव-हित को 'साध्य मूल्य' के रूप में स्वीकारा गया है। सत्य, बंधुत्व, सहयोग आदि मूल्य इस साध्य मूल्य के साधन मूल्य हैं। धर्म, ईश्वर आदि से संबद्ध मूल्य कुछ उपन्यासों में 'साधन मूल्य' के रूप में ही स्वीकृत हैं। 'हजार घोड़ों का सवार', 'सोनभद्र की राधा', 'जंगली सुअर' आदि उपन्यासों में महंतों और पुजारियों को सामाजिक न्याय और समानता के लिए संघर्ष करते या सहायता देते देखा जा सकता है। 'परती परिकथा' और 'मैला आँचल' के पुजारी और महंत का आचरण एक घृणित वास्तविकता है। अधिकतर उपन्यासों में इस वास्तविकता का अतिक्रमण करते हुए व्यक्तिवादी और समाजविरोधी मूल्यों को त्यागकर मानवतावादी और प्रगतिशील मूल्यों की दिशा में संक्रमण का समर्थन किया गया है।

कुछ आंचलिक उपन्यासों में लोकसंस्कृति के तत्त्वों—लोककथाओं, लोकगीतों, लोकपर्वों आदि के माध्यम से सांस्कृतिक मूल्यों की पहचान की गई है। 'सुन्नरि नैका और 'दंता राकस' (परती परिकथा), 'शिव के आँसुओं से वैतरणी का निर्माण' (अलग-अलग वैतरणी), 'नीलकंठ के माध्यम से सीता को संदेश' (जल टूटता हुआ), 'विवाह संबंधी लोकाचार' (सोनामाटी) आदि के समावेश से एक साथ कई उद्देश्यों की सिद्धि हुई है। ये सभी लोक सांस्कृतिक तत्त्व सिद्ध करते हैं कि लोकसंस्कृति मुख्यतः कृषि-संस्कृति है। इस संस्कृति का शुद्ध रूप केवल आदिवासियों के जीवन में द्रष्टव्य है। इनसे यह भी ज्ञात होता है कि 'मानवीय कल्याण' से संबंधित सकारात्मक मूल्यों को जो सम्मान लोकजीवन में पहले प्राप्त था, वह आज भी यथावत् है। इन उपन्यासों में लोकसांस्कृतिक तत्त्वों का समावेश केवल 'आंचलिक रंगत' प्रदान करने या उपन्यासकार की बहुज्ञता और अनुभव-संपदा के प्रदर्शन के निमित्त नहीं हुआ है। ये लोकजीवन के गहरे सरोकार और न्याय, सद्‌भाव, सहयोग आदि मूल्यों से सीधे संबद्ध हैं। अपसंस्कृति के प्रसार से क्षमा, त्याग, सहयोग, परहित आदि मूल्यों के संकट ग्रस्त होने को इन उपन्यासों में चिंतापूर्वक अभिव्यक्त किया गया है। वे यह भी दर्शाते हैं कि लोकपर्वों और उत्सवों का रंग फीका हो जाने से लोकजीवन का रंग फीका हो गया है और आवेगों के उदात्तीकरण के अवसर कम रह गए हैं। फलतः अवमूल्यों का प्रादुर्भाव अस्वाभाविक नहीं है। आंचलिक उपन्यासकारों के सांस्कृतिक बोध में 'तथ्य चेतना' और 'मूल्य चेतना' का पार्थक्य स्पष्ट है। तथ्य यह है कि लोकजीवन में संक्रमण हीनतर और नकारात्मक मूल्यों की दिशा में हो रहा है जबकि उपन्यासकार इस संबंध में निर्भ्रांत हैं कि उच्च, नैतिक और मानव-हितकारी मूल्यों की दिशा में संक्रमण वांछनीय है।

न केवल सांस्कृतिक परिदृश्य अपितु सभी क्षेत्रों में वास्तविकता का बोध या तथ्य चेतना का रूप यही है कि श्रद्धा, सम्मान, स्वास्थ्य, बंधुत्व, सतीत्व यौन शुचिता, न्याय, सत्य, ईमानदारी, सेवा, परोपकार आदि शुभ, उच्च और मानव-हितकारी माने जानेवाले मूल्यों का संक्रमण हीनतर मान्यताओं और अवमूल्यों की दिशा में हुआ है और गंभीर 'मूल्य-संकट' उत्पन्न हुआ है। अवज्ञा, शत्रुता, यौन स्वच्छंदता, बेईमानी, अन्याय, शोषण, स्वार्थ आदि नकारात्मक मूल्यों के उभार और वर्चस् ने समूचे परिवेश को अस्त-व्यस्त किया है और अनेक असंगतियों को जन्म दिया है। प्रत्येक आंचलिक उपन्यास में कुछ सकारात्मक चरित्र इन असंगतियों से टकराते हैं और प्रकारांतर से उपन्यासकारों की मानवीय मूल्यों में आस्था को व्यक्त करते हैं। स्पष्ट है कि आंचलिक उपन्यासों में न तो केवल 'मूल्य-संकट' और 'मूल्य-विघटन' को दर्शाने में रचना-कर्म की इतिश्री मानी गई है, न कहीं 'मूल्य-हीनता' जैसी निरपेक्ष स्थिति की कल्पना की गई है। मूल्य-संकट और विघटन की भयावहता को रेखांकित करने के साथ सकारात्मक और स्वस्थ मूल्यों को 'विकल्प' रूप में प्रस्तुत करना आंचलिक उपन्यासों के मूल्य-बोध का उल्लेखनीय पक्ष है। यह मूल्य-बोध 'रोमानी' या 'वायवीय' कतई नहीं है। यह सीधे 'माटी' से संबद्ध है। लेकिन 'माटी' से जुड़ने का अर्थ अंचल-विशेष के फूल-पत्ती, नदी-झरने, लोकगीत-लोककथा आदि का चित्रण वर्णन न होकर मानव और उसके जीवन के नियामक मानवीय मूल्यों को गौरवान्वित करना और मानवीय संवेदना का प्रसार करना है। मुक्ति, जड़ता, अन्याय, शोषण और अंधविश्वास से 'मानव-मुक्ति', आंचलिक उपन्यासों में व्यक्त सर्वप्रमुख मूल्य है। इसे 'स्वतःमूल्य' के रूप में प्रतिष्ठित किया गया है। पातिव्रत, सतीत्व, अहिंसा आदि कई मूल्यों को स्थिति विशेष में नकार कर आंचलिक उपन्यासकारों ने स्पष्ट किया है कि वे मान्यताओं के पुनर्नवीकरण और पुनर्मूल्यांकन के पक्ष में भी हैं। मानव-मुक्ति को अपना प्रतिपाद्य मानने और समता, समानता, सत्य, न्याय और सद्‌भाव आदि मूल्यों को महत्त्व देने के फलस्वरूप आंचलिक उपन्यासों का मूल्य-बोध स्पष्टतः प्रेमचंद की कथा-परंपरा और हिंदी उपन्यास की मुख्य धारा के प्रगतिशील सोच के मेल में है।

□□□